PERSPECTIVES ON AMERICAN MUSIC, 1900–1950

ESSAYS IN AMERICAN MUSIC
VOLUME 3
GARLAND REFERENCE LIBRARY OF THE HUMANITIES
VOLUME 2107

ESSAYS IN AMERICAN MUSIC
JAMES R. HEINTZE AND MICHAEL SAFFLE, *Series Editors*

PERSPECTIVES ON AMERICAN MUSIC, 1900–1950

edited by
MICHAEL SAFFLE

GARLAND PUBLISHING, INC.
A MEMBER OF THE TAYLOR & FRANCIS GROUP
NEW YORK & LONDON
2000

Published in 2000 by
Garland Publishing, Inc.
A member of the Taylor & Francis Group
29 West 35th Street
New York, NY 10001

10 9 8 7 6 5 4 3 2 1

Library of Congress Cataloging-in-Publication Data

Perspectives on American music, 1900–1950 / edited by Michael Saffle.
    p. cm. — (Essays in American music ; v. 3) (Garland reference library of the
humanities ; v. 2107)
    Includes bibliographical references and index.
    Contents: Boston's "French Connection" at the turn of the twentieth century /
Ellen Knight — Ticklers' secrets : ragtime performance practices, 1900–1920, a
bibliographic essay / Karen Rege — Mapping the blues genes : technological,
economic, and social strands, a spectral analysis / Raymond D. Dessy — Some
American firms and their contributions to the development of the reproducing piano /
Kent Holliday — Dances, frolics, and orchestra wars : the territory bands and ballrooms of Kansas City, Missouri, 1925–1935 / Marc Rice — Thomas A. Dorsey and
the development and diffusion of traditional Black gospel piano / Timothy M. Kalil
— Western swing : working-class Southwestern jazz of the 1930s and 1940s / Jean
A. Boyd — The art of noise : John Cage, Lou Harrison, and the West Coast Percussion Ensemble / Leta Miller — Melville Smith : organist, educator, early music
pioneer, and American composer / Mark DeVoto — Toscanini and the NBC Symphony Orchestra : high, middle, and low culture, 1937–1954 / Donald C. Meyer —
Cinema music of distinction : Virgil Thomson, Aaron Copland, and Gail Kubik /
Alfred W. Cochran — The new Tin Pan Alley : 1940s Hollywood looks at American
popular songwriters / John C. Tibbets.
    ISBN 0-8153-2145-7 (alk. paper)
    1. Music—United States—20th century—History and criticism. I. Saffle, Michael
Benton, 1946– . II. Series: Essays in American music ; vol. 4. III. Series:
Garland reference library of the humanities ; vol. 2107.
ML200.5.P478   1999
780'.973'0904—dc21   99-35937
                                            CIP

Cover: Program from a percussion concert at Mills College, 18 July 1940,
featuring Lou Harrison, John Cage, and William Russell.

Printed on acid-free, 250-year-life paper
Manufactured in the United States of America

Contents

Series Editors' Foreword

Essays in American Music celebrates the rich and varied heritage of this country's music by bringing together articles written by distinguished scholars about significant and unique events, persons, places, and compositions. It continues a tradition in the historiography of American music that dates to the mid-1800s when the first calls went out requesting that information about American music be collected so that a history of the music of this country could be written.

> We have been for some time engaged in collecting materials for a series of papers upon this subject, which are intended to embrace a General History of Music in this country, from the settlement of Plymouth to the present time. Doubtless there are many who can render us important assistance in this undertaking, by forwarding all the information they may possess, which has any bearing upon the matter in question. We should be happy to receive from our friends throughout the country, any particulars relating to music they may be able to furnish—either statistical or anecdotal—which will aid us in carrying out our plan.
>
> *Musical Review,* 23 May 1838, 35.

The historiography of American Music has advanced considerably since those first attempts to codify this country's musical heritage, although the importance of individual efforts in gathering and reporting that information remains the same. Today readers may choose from a vast body of literature on American music, including several excellent histories and surveys, numerous critical studies and facsimile editions, monographs on individual musicians, topical studies, and reference works (including bibliographies, indexes, encyclopedias, and dictionaries) as well as articles in journals devoted specifically to American music. Yet the content of the topics addressed in the essays contained in this series offers evidence for the fact that there is still much to discover about this country's musical past. The purpose of this series is to provide a sampling of areas of research currently under pursuit and, nearing the onset of the twenty-first century, to provide a stimulus for future research into American music. The volumes in the series progress chronologically. Volume One covers the period prior to 1865. Volume Two focuses on the periods 1861–1918. Volume Three covers the first half of the twentieth century. Finally, Volume Four covers the years from 1950 to the present. All the contributors to the series are recognized authorities in their respective areas of investigation and represent prominent organizations devoted to the study of American music, including for example, the College Music Society, the Sonneck Society for American Music, the Hymn Society in the United States and Canada, and others. Within the space allotted to them, all contributors have provided essays on topics of their choice and were encouraged to apply their own critical points of view.

Michael Saffle
James R. Heintze

Introduction

Perspectives on American Music, 1900–1950 reflects the range and depth of our nation's musical activities and idioms during the first half of the twentieth century. During those fifty years the United States became not merely the world's foremost military and industrial power, but her foremost source of musical entertainment as well. Nevertheless, the rise and triumph of jazz, swing, blues, and other popular genres were not our only musical accomplishments during a half-century that encompassed two world wars, the Great Depression, and the birth of the Atomic Age. The art music of Charles Ives, John Cage, Aaron Copland, and a host of other figures also made the United States an important and influential force wherever the "cultivated" traditions of European "classical" music were admired. Finally, American contributions to music technology and dissemination—to radio and television broadcasting, to film, and to the invention, improvement, and manufacture of musical instruments of all kinds—brought our nation's composers and performers before enormous numbers of people, both in the United States and abroad.

The essays comprising the present volume are arranged by subject in roughly chronological order. A few essays refer to individuals and events associated with the 1880s, 1890s, 1950s, and early 1960s as well as with the years 1900–1950.

Ellen Knight examines Boston's musical life in and around the year 1900, especially insofar as that city's growing enthusiasm for French music and musicians was concerned. Dr. Knight concentrates her attention particularly on the activities and reputation of Charles Marie Loeffler

(1861–1935), one of America's leading composers of art-music before and during as well as after World War I.

Karen Rege tackles an exciting and much-discussed aspect of early twentieth-century American popular music: the performance of ragtime. Drawing upon such turn-of-the-century pedagogical publications as *Ben Harney's Ragtime Instructor* (1897) and Scott Joplin's *School of Ragtime* (1908), as well as upon 78-r.p.m. recordings dating from the 1920s, Professor Rege explains how and why piano rags ought to be played in particular ways.

Prominent scientist and amateur musician Raymond D. Dessy evaluates the impact of technological, economic, and social influences on the birth and dissemination of the blues between approximately 1904 and the 1930s. Professor Dessy's observations encompass topics ranging from the origin of the term "blues" to the emergence of radio and phonograph recordings as the "colliding technologies" of the 1920s, and the opinions of *Billboard* magazine and other periodicals on the emergence and acceptance of blues throughout American society.

Kent Holliday documents America's contributions to the design and use of reproducing pianos (also known as player pianos), contributions that began in 1913 and extended until the early 1930s. Professor Holliday's survey ranges from design innovations introduced by firms such as Duo Art, Ampico, and Welte-Mignon, to the quality of surviving reproducing-piano rolls made by some of this century's foremost keyboard performers.

Kansas City, Missouri—in the opinion of many performers and scholars, the birthplace of "real" jazz—is the focus of Marc Rice's discussion of African American jazz orchestras in and around that city during the 1920s and 1930s. Among the ensembles Professor Rice discusses are those led by Duke Ellington, Fletcher Henderson, and Bennie Moten.

Timothy M. Kalil surveys gospel piano music in general and the 1930s career of Thomas A. Dorsey (1899–1993), the acknowledged early master of that idiom.

Western swing is the subject of Jean Boyd's essay, which concentrates on the multicultural influences that resulted in the rise and dissemination of "working-class southwestern jazz" during the 1930s and 1940s. Professor Boyd also traces the careers of "cowboy" entertainers, among them the Musical Brownies and Bob Wills and his Texas Playboys.

Leta Miller examines the avant-garde musical activities of John Cage and Lou Harrison, two of America's leading art-composers, in and around the San Francisco Bay Area and especially during the years 1938–1942. Included in Professor Miller's examination are accounts of groundbreaking concerts at Mills College in Oakland, of performances of works by Henry Cowell, and of the origins of Harrison's own *Simfony #13*.

Mark DeVoto summarizes and interprets the life and career of American composer, teacher, and influential organist and Baroque performance-practice pioneer Melville Smith (1898–1962). Professor DeVoto also brings into focus the attitudes and activities of many of Smith's colleagues and friends, including individuals such as Aaron Copland, Walter Holtkamp, and Robert Russell Bennett.

Don Meyer reassesses one of the most controversial aspects of art-music performance in modern America: the spectacularly successful career of Italian-born Arturo Toscanini (1867–1957) during his tenure as conductor of the NBC Symphony Orchestra. In discussing the Toscanini "reception" and "cult" of the 1930s, 1940s, and early 1950s, Professor Meyer also reexamines Joseph Horowitz's notorious assessment of these same phenomena.

Alfred W. Cochran explains how and why art-composers like Virgil Thomson, Copland, and Gail Kubik strove during the 1940s to establish themselves as Hollywood film composers. Professor Cochran also evaluates some of their most successful film scores, including the music Copland composed for movies such as *Our Town, The Red Pony,* and *Of Mice and Men.*

Finally, John C. Tibbetts discusses Hollywood's musical "biopics": feature films (most of them made during the 1940s and early 1950s) about the lives and loves of composers and performers great and not so great. Movies ranging in scope and quality from *Yankee Doodle Dandy*—about popular songwriter George M. Cohan—to *Till the Clouds Roll By*—about songwriter and Broadway "star" Jerome Kern—are among the special subjects of Professor Tibbetts's investigations.

I would like to express my sincere appreciation to James Heintze of The American University, Washington, D.C., for his suggestions and patience. I also would like to thank each and every contributor to this volume; their researches have enriched our understanding of American musical and cultural history. Finally, I would like to thank the staff of Garland Publishing—and especially Soo Mee Kwon, an editor of intelligence, enthusiasm, and determination—for their encouragement and assistance.

Michael Saffle

PERSPECTIVES ON AMERICAN MUSIC, 1900–1950

CHAPTER 1

Boston's "French Connection" at the Turn of the Twentieth Century

ELLEN KNIGHT

Composer Arthur Shepherd once described musical Boston as "an outpost of German music culture,"[1] a just observation looking back upon the late nineteenth century. German dominance in the repertory of American concert stages prior to the twentieth century is well known. That German dominance extended to original compositions of American composers, many of whom were trained in Germany or by those who had been, also has long been recognized. Furthermore, that national hostilities during World War I allowed the music of France (and other countries) a greater entrée into American concerts at the time of the war also is well known, as is the emergence of Paris as a fashionable spot for composers to study after the war.

During the late 1910s, however, French music did not arrive in Boston as a complete stranger. Between 1880 and 1915 musical exchanges did pass between Boston and Paris, and before the war some musical figures in Boston had already ardently espoused the cause of French music, a cause they continued to champion during and after World War I.

In 1906 Edward Burlingame Hill wrote to *Le Mercure musical* that "Boston is certainly the most informed American city about modern French music."[2] Whatever the relationships between the music of France and other American cities (which lie outside the scope of this essay), Boston did have a distinct rapport with Paris through a circle of French and American musical figures in the city. Francophiles in Boston not only sought to introduce the music and musicians of France to America but also to inform the French about musical activities in America. Their views and reports doubtless influenced French perception of music not only in Boston but also in America in general.

Most of this activity occurred after 1880 when concert music in Boston came into full bloom simultaneously as instrumental music flourished in France. Before this time French music was not altogether unknown. Thomas Ryan, who arrived in Boston in 1845, remarked in regard to ballet music that during his early years in Boston "the best composers of the period" were "mostly French."[3] Yet most music in Boston was not associated with the opera or ballet, as Boston did not have a resident opera company until the twentieth century. In the realms of orchestral, chamber, and recital repertory, French music was rare.

As Boston developed its concert life throughout the nineteenth century and especially after 1865, German musicians and conductors, who came to the United States in large numbers after the revolutions of 1848, took the lead. For example, Germans Carl Zerrahn and Bernard Listemann led orchestras in the city prior to the founding of the Boston Symphony Orchestra (BSO). The BSO itself was conducted by a series of Germans, who were in charge of so many German and German-trained musicians in that organization that they could conduct rehearsals in the German language. In chamber music, again, it was Germans such as Wulf Fries and Franz Kneisel who formed the premier ensembles and set standards for local musicians.

Not surprisingly, German musicians favored German composers and established the German sound and style as the core of the then-current concert repertory. This preference for German music extended into teaching studios and even into university education. The leading instructors and local composers of the nineteenth century in New England—John Knowles Paine and George Whitefield Chadwick, among others—were educated in Germany and passed on German traditions, helping to establish Boston, as Shepherd said, as a colony of German culture.[4]

As for the music of France, an unsigned article published in 1890 in the *Boston Home Journal* and titled "Boston's Musical Bigotry" complained about the dearth of performances of French music. This writer wanted to hear Delibes, Massenet, Bizet, or "the many interesting works of others of the modern French school":

> They are not deemed worthy, however, of a place upon the Symphony
> programs or the dignity of evening dress; when they are played it is at a
> "Young People's Popular" where they are performed almost with an

apology and treated with frock-coated indifference. . . . We grope about in German mists, which have blown in upon us and settled at our own whistling; and we daily accustom ourselves to the thick, damp fog and say it is purer and healthier than clear air and a blue sky.[5]

When French music began to be imported, it encountered some resistance. The music was not simply by French composers; it was by modern French composers who, following the Franco-Prussian War, were deliberately searching for a distinct national identity, an *ars gallica*. They gave instrumental music new attention, producing a new repertory and a new style.

Boston traditionalists, by and large, were not interested in such innovation, distinct from the tradition with which they were familiar and upon which they had modeled their ideas of musical excellence. With the immigration of French musicians and francophiles, however, the serious introduction of French music began. Although French composition never supplanted the German repertory, within twenty years some others who wrote about French music performance, such as Hill and critic Philip Hale, were able to comment on Boston's familiarity with French composers, in particular the modern French school.

The beginning of this change can surely be traced to the most active and influential champion of French music in Boston during the last two decades of the nineteenth century, Charles Martin Loeffler (1861–1935). Loeffler was assistant concertmaster of the BSO from 1882 to 1903, a chamber musician and recitalist, and a composer of music that his American colleagues deemed to be of the French School.

While most immigrant orchestral musicians were, like Loeffler, German by birth, most were not, like him, trained in France and enamored of all the French arts. While studying violin and composition in Paris and playing with Jules Étienne Pasdeloup's orchestra, Loeffler had been completely overcome by Parisian modes. His francophilia lasted throughout his lifetime. After he settled in Boston, Loeffler revisited France (and other European capitals) and lived in Paris during the winter of 1904–1905. Each year he developed enthusiasms for even newer French music. He became acquainted with several French composers, including Vincent d'Indy, Edouard Lalo, and Gabriel Fauré, with conductors, and with performers. These French acquaintances often looked to Loeffler as a liaison and unofficial representative in America.

Loeffler's first efforts to promote French music in Boston consisted primarily in performing it himself. He premiered works with the BSO such as Benjamin Godard's *Concerto romantique,* Lalo's *Fantasie norvégienne* and *Symphonie espagnole,* and Camille Saint-Saëns's first Violin Concerto. One critic wrote "we have to thank [Mr. Loeffler] for almost all the chances we get nowadays of hearing French music."[6] Loeffler's efforts extended to influencing others, such as BSO conductors and the Kneisel Quartette, to select French compositions for performance. After returning from Paris in 1905, for example, he persuaded the BSO to perform Ernest Chausson's Symphony, Op. 10. He also induced Schirmer's to publish some French music, including works by Fauré.

Not all welcomed this new music. Conservatives John Sullivan Dwight and Otto Dresel, who had exerted profound influence over musical society's tastes during the nineteenth century stood solidly behind the traditional repertory. Clara Rogers reported that Otto Dresel's response to the news that Loeffler would play at her soirée was a weary, hopeless "He—will—play something by Lalo!"[7]

Opportunities for hearing French music increased as more French musicians, especially Georges Longy (1868–1930), arrived in the city. Longy, who quickly became Loeffler's great good friend, was a conductor as well as an oboist and composer. A native of Abbeville, France, he was a student at the Paris Conservatoire and a member of the Lamoureux and Colonne orchestras. From 1898 until 1925, when he returned to France, Longy was principal oboist with the BSO.

After arriving in Boston, Longy soon set about conducting an orchestra and a chamber ensemble similar to La Société de Musique de Chambre pour Instruments à Vent, which he had reestablished in France in 1895. With his ensembles he introduced yet more French composers to Boston audiences. With the Longy Club, active from 1900 to 1917, for example, Longy performed compositions by Emile Bernard, André Caplet, Leland Cossart, Fauré, Edouard Flament, Charles Gounod, Théodore Gouvy, Reynaldo Hahn, Jean Huré, d'Indy, Charles Lefebvre, Alberic Magnard, Edmond Malherbe, André Maquarre, Léon Moreau, Jules Moquet, A. Perilhou, Gabriel Pierné, Paul Florimond Quef, and Paul de Wailly.

From 1899 to 1911 Longy conducted the Orchestral Club of Boston. Under the direction of Listemann and Chadwick, the group played principally the works of familiar German composers. For example, in one 1891 concert, the Club performed compositions by Mendelssohn, Schubert, Bruch, Raff, and Spohr. At Longy's first concert, however, they played works by Gounod, Jules Massenet, Saint-Saëns, Emile Pessard, and Théodore Dubois.

Over the years, while not fashioning exclusively French programs, Longy selected primarily French compositions for this ensemble. The orchestra also premiered a number of works in America. Some composers whose works he chose to perform also were taken up by other conductors and are now familiar names, including Hector Berlioz, Georges Bizet, Claude Debussy, Léo Delibes, Emmanuel Chabrier, d'Indy, Paul Dukas, Lalo, Maurice Ravel, Erik Satie, and Charles-Marie Widor. The names of other composers, however, may be as unfamiliar now as when first placed on Longy's programs. These included L. A. Bourgault-Ducoudray, Caplet, Camille Chevillard, Georges Hüe, Silvio Lazzari (a naturalized Frenchman), Lefebvre, Guillaume Lekeu, Léon Moreau, Emile Pessard, Gabriel Pierné, E. Tavan, Julien Tiersot, and Henri Woollett.

Longy conducted other ensembles, including the MacDowell Club and the Boston Musical Association. The latter was formed, according to a statement in its program book, "for the purpose of stimulating the development of young musicians and composers of talent by giving them frequent opportunities of appearing under favorable auspices before the public." At each concert a new work by an American composer was performed "and if the work has an unusual success there will be opportunity for its performance by the Société Nationale de Musique de Paris."[8]

The programs for concerts presented by the Association were more varied than those of the Orchestral Society, mixing works by American, French, Spanish, British, and Russian composers. Still, French compositions were prominant. During the Association's first season, in addition to choosing works by Debussy, Fauré, Chausson, and Saint-Saëns, Longy led the group in the first American performances of Ravel's *Trois Poèmes de Mallarmé,* Salzedo's *3 Poems by Sara Yarrow,* and Louis Thirion's String Quartet, Op. 10. In the second season the Association gave either the Boston or American premiere of Charles Bordes' *Rapsodie Basque,* Alfred Bruneau's *Penthésilée,* Maurice Delage's *Quatre poèmes Hindous,* Ravel's *Alborada del Gracioso,* and Florent Schmitt's *Chant de Guerre.* Thirion's Quartet was performed at the second Musical Association Concert by a guest ensemble that itself had the distinction of performing and premiering French works, not surprisingly since the ensemble was formed by Loeffler. This was the American String Quartette.[9]

Although Loeffler himself performed less and less in public after his retirement from the BSO in 1903, in 1908 he founded a quartet made up of his women students. This ensemble continued his custom of including

French works among those of the standard repertory. When the chamber group first debuted, in 1909, one of their attractions was the Debussy Quartet. In New York in 1918, when the group played both the Debussy violin sonata—still considered new by the *New York Times*—and the Franck Quintet (another of Loeffler's favorites), it won acclaim for both works.[10]

Like their founder, the quartet premiered French compositions in America. In February 1917, it participated in a special concert of Jean Huré's music, prepared by Longy, at Jordan Hall. With pianist Renée Longy, it presented the American premiere of Huré's piano quintet. Gertrude Marshall, first violinist of the quartet, and Longy also performed Huré's Sonatine for violin and piano (winner of the "Prix des Quarante-Cinq"). In January 1920 the same ensemble premiered the Thirion Quartet. In April of the following year, at a Harvard Musical Association concert, on a program with music by Ippolitov-Ivanov and Fauré, the ensemble played the Quartet in B minor of Paul Roussel, a composer of whom little is known except that he disappeared at Verdun in June 1916. This composition (left unfinished with only two movements completed) had just been published the year previously, evidently through Loeffler's influence, by the Boston Music Company.

Longy also included on programs of the Orchestral Club and the Longy Club compositions by his friend Loeffler (as well as his own works). As a composer, as well as a performer, Loeffler espoused the French style, again taking the lead in this regard in the city—as well as in the country.

During the 1880s and 1890s, before Longy's arrival, Loeffler each year gave Bostonians a taste for French music through his own compositions. Although his compositional style was eclectic and originally quite strongly influenced by Slavic music, it developed along French Impressionistic or Symbolist lines. His music gave Bostonians (and many other Americans) their introduction to the style later associated with Debussy and Ravel.[11]

Many listeners—to judge by critical response—did not comprehend and resisted what they termed Loeffler's "decadent" style. After his cello concerto was performed in New York in 1895, for example, a critic for the *New York Times* objected that Loeffler's work had

> no form . . . [and] no thematic development. It is an impressionistic picture in tones. It is splendidly scored, and it has warmth, body, élan, spirit. But it is inchoate. It is not without fascination, but it is the fasci-

nation of a disembodied spirit. Mr. Loeffler has no business to introduce Maeterlinkism into music.[12]

In time, however, Loeffler found sympathetic listeners and even allies in his cause. Critic Lawrence Gilman waxed quite rhapsodic in his appreciation:

He [Loeffler] is a seeker after the realities of shadowy and dim illusions, a painter of grays and greens and subtle golds. . . . Loeffler is, primarily, a creator of atmosphere, a weaver of evanescent and slender arabesques. His music has the subdued and elusive beauty of antique tapestries.[13]

Among fellow composers in Boston, Loeffler did not immediately find kindred spirits. Arthur Foote and D. G. Mason, for example, were not impressed with their colleague's music. Even Edward MacDowell, who was one of the first American-born composers and performers to study in Paris, was not in sympathy with Loeffler's French education. Just as Loeffler had left Germany in 1877 to study in France, so MacDowell (resident in Paris from 1876–1878) had left France to move on to Germany. Whereas Loeffler was enchanted with everything French, MacDowell—as his great admirer and biographer Lawrence Gilman commented—had no "appreciable affinity with the prismatic subtleties of the younger French school" and took his inspiration from the Germans.[14] Although MacDowell lived contemporaneously with Loeffler in Boston from 1888 to 1896, there was apparently no association between them, except that Loeffler as a member of the BSO would have performed some of MacDowell's works.

Some Bostonian composers, though not espousing the same mode, did enjoy Loeffler's style. One such was Arthur Whiting. A few other New England composers left America to study in Paris and returned as converts. Prominent among these latter figures was Edward Burlingame Hill (1872–1960), a native of Cambridge, Massachusetts, a graduate of Harvard, and, in 1898, a student of Widor. Hill was one of the few composers within Loeffler's circle of friends who came under his, and France's, influence and himself adopted the Impressionistic style.

Hill also promoted the music of France through his work as an educator. In 1910, two years after he commenced teaching at Harvard University, he began a course on French composers. He delivered lectures on the subject at the Lowell Institute in Boston in 1920 and under the auspices of the Universities of Strasbourg and Lyon in the summer autumn of 1921. These lectures became the basis for his 1924 book *Modern French Music*.[15] From the time of Loeffler's arrival in Boston in 1882 through Longy's arrival in 1898 and onward, and with the efforts of educators like Hill and performers such as the Kneisel and American Quartets, Bostonians had opportunities to hear the music of France and learn about it. In 1905 Loeffler wrote to the readers of *Le Mercure musical:* "It is agreeable to report that interest in French music is more lively in America than perhaps in any other country out of France." The occasion for his writing this was the appearance of d'Indy as guest conductor with the BSO, which Loeffler himself had negotiated. He wrote that several of d'Indy's works were well known and had been well performed in this country and claimed that "the musical world here is firmly convinced of the importance of his visit."

Loeffler then proceeded to list recent and upcoming performances of French music, including the chamber music concerts conducted by Longy that saw the American premieres of the *Nocturne* of Fauré, the *Quintette* by Caplet, a *Scherzo* by Lefebvre, *Variations symphoniques* by Lacroix, and the Nonette by Malherbe. Music by Fauré and d'Indy, Loeffler reported, would be played by the Hess Quartet, and quartets by Ravel, d'Indy, and Chausson by the "incomparable Kneisel Quartette." D'Indy himself performed with the Kneisel Quartette for their concert on 24 December 1905 in New York. Loeffler also reported that "Mme Hopekirk, the distinguished pianist," performed at her first recital *Poème des Montagnes* by d'Indy, *Barcarolle* by Debussy, as well as *Clair de lune, l'Isle joyeuse,* and *Masques.* Loeffler also noted the first performance in New York, during the last season, of Debussy's *Prélude à l'après-midi d'un faune.* "In a word," Loeffler concluded, "the cause of French music is upheld well in our country."[16]

After d'Indy conducted the BSO in December 1905, critic Philip Hale (Loeffler's friend) reported that d'Indy found a number of music lovers in Boston interested in the modern French school. In contrast to the complaint of musical bigotry in 1890, Hale, who began writing music criticism for the Boston papers in 1889, wrote that Boston had always been curious to hear the voice of foreign composers, and he claimed that the German population was not so large nor their spirit so narrow as to succeed in germanizing musical taste. In recent years (Hale wrote), Loeffler, Franz Kneisel, B. J. Lang, local singers and pianists, Longy, Paur, and "above all" Wilhelm Gericke had introduced compositions of the modern school to Bostonians. Hale claimed that, of all the works conducted by d'Indy—including works by Fauré, Dukas, and d'Indy himself—the only one unknown to the symphony audience was an excerpt from Franck's *Psyche*.[17]

Did the French have a corresponding interest in the music of America beyond the opportunities that the country might hold for their own music? What did the French know of American music? That performances of American music did occur in France is known, though they were doubtless rare. If, in its own country, American music struggled to be heard and labored against a prejudice that it was second-rate and derivative, it may be concluded that it was so also abroad. Various reports bear this out.

At the Exposition of 1889, for example, American music—specifically works by Foote, MacDowell, Chadwick, Dudley Buck, Henry Huss, Paine, Arthur Bird, Margaret Lang, and Frank Van der Stucken (who also conducted)—was performed. After the concert, presented on 12 July at the Trocadéro, Julien Tiersot reported that

> [this] young [American] school is not yet distinguished by characterizing tendencies nor temperament. By preference it takes its inspiration from the neo-classic German school: Mendelssohn, Brahms, Raff, appear to be its preferred models. . . . also certain but superficial influence of Wagner in some harmonic arrangements and tonal combinations. . . . At times also it makes one think of the music of our best known French masters, Massenet, Gounod, even Ambroise Thomas. But in place of originality, the workmanship is serious, correct, solid, and always practical.

Tiersot also commented that the school seemed active, already having a large number of representatives.[18]

When Loeffler was in Europe, he was able to arrange performances of some of his works, through his own influence. Paris apparently did not have a figure like Loeffler or Hill championing American music.

Thirty-five years later Loeffler himself had occasion to comment on the indifference of Europeans, including his beloved Parisians, to American music. He wrote to Elizabeth Sprague Coolidge during postwar years that

> my experience has taught me, that composers of this country are not treated fairly in the old countries of Europe. . . . The various Mutual

Admiration Societies of England, Germany, and the other countries of
the Continent—mostly Internationalistic in appearance, but chauvinis-
tic in reality, are to a man, against everything coming from this country, except our—dollars! Carpenter had no luck in Paris, nor did
Eichheim, if I may judge from the French Press notices. For the most
part, American Music is presented—if at all—insufficiently rehearsed
and in the end insufficiently played. Those of use who ever sent any
compositions to the committees of the various Salzburg, Zurich,
Prague International festivals, invariably found, that their packages
had never been opened even.[19]

Whether they heard or valued American music, the French received
news of music and musical happenings in America. That the reports from
their foreign correspondents came principally from Boston was due—
again—to Loeffler and his friends. After he spent the winter of
1904–1905 in Paris, for example, Loeffler's Parisian acquaintances
turned to him for information about America. Some of this information
was confined to personal inquiries, for example about the prospects of
concert tours or about having music published or performed in America.
In addition, Loeffler gave France news of music in America. For two
years, after which he was succeeded by Arthur Farwell, he was a correspondent to the French periodical *Le Mercure musical,* edited by Jean
Marnold, whom Loeffler had met in Paris.

In his initial report for this periodical, entitled "La musique en
Amérique," Loeffler reported on performances of French music in
Boston (quoted above). In particular, he reported on d'Indy's guest appearance with the BSO and his American tour.[20] In this and other reports,
he established a tradition of including the repertory of the BSO, excluding any other but a one-time mention of the New York Philharmonic
when performances of d'Indy's music were involved. Loeffler thereby
may have conveyed to the French the impression that Boston was the
musical center of the nation.

Loeffler did little to inform the French about American composition.
During his second year as correspondent, a comment on Frederick Converse's opera *The Pipe of Desire* was Loeffler's only contribution about
an American composer. The editor of *Le Mercure musical* appended to
one of his reports a review of Loeffler's *La Villanelle du Diable,* written
by Louis Elson. But Loeffler's main effort was not to report on American
but rather French composition.

In 1906 two contributions by E. B. Hill were published in *Le Mer-*

cure musical. One was a reprint of an article on the piano music of Debussy from *The Musician* that had appeared in Boston in August 1906. The second was "An American Opinion on the Music of Ravel." It was in this second essay that Hill stated that Boston was the most informed American city about French music. He continued, however, "while we have heard, at intervals too widely spaced, several major works for orchestra by Franck, d'Indy, Chausson, and Debussy, other important compositions by them and by different French composers are never produced for us." He had heard (Hill wrote) music by César Franck, d'Indy, Debussy, Chausson, and Lekeu; however, the names Déodat de Sévérac, Isaac Albeniz, and Dukas—except *The Sorcerer's Apprentice*—were, in fact, unknown to connoisseurs. In any event, Hill deemed French music significant. "French music today is evolving towards a free and unfettered harmonic system, favorable to a new and lively poetic suggestion. On account, the young French school is well advanced over any contemporary school."[21]

In 1907 Arthur Farwell took over as American correspondent for the journal when it became the *Bulletin français de la société internationel de musique.* Farwell, who had studied briefly with Alexandre Guilmant in Paris, shared with Loeffler an interest in contemporary composition, though he was more dedicated to the cause of the American rather than the French composer, as was reflected in his reports.

Farwell continued to report on the programs of the BSO and on the Kneisel Quartette. He reported on French music only to the extent that he included a review by Hale of a performance of Ravel's quartet and reported the visit of Saint-Saëns. About the latter, Farwell wrote:

> The charm of his person joined with the prestige of his art assured him of public favor. His talent as a pianist was a revelation for many listeners, despite his reputation as a virtuoso, were accustomed for a long time to see him only as a composer. . . . His glory rests on a solid foundation of which he has a right to be proud.[22]

But Farwell soon began to use his reports to champion not French but American music. Furthermore, he turned his attention away from Boston to the West. First, Farwell claimed that the environment of the West was more open to French music than Boston was:

> The music of the West is full of promise for the future, but at this moment it finds itself in a curious state of fermentation, and it is impossi-

ble to predict what will emerge. It is an interesting fact: it is west of the Mississippi that modern French music finds many more lovers than on the opposite bank. That does not precisely indicate a keener taste in the home of the inhabitant of the Far West, but rather a more impartial state of spirit. It is not that the classics are imposed on him but rather more that the moderns do not frighten him. He will savor Debussy there entirely at his ease where more than one musician of the East will be shocked.[23]

In short, Farwell found less tradition and prejudice in the West than elsewhere. Although his report continued to mention concerts in Boston—specifically, those presented by the Kneisel Quartette and the Longy Club—he chose to comment specifically on one figure working in the West: Arthur Shepherd, the conductor of the symphony orchestra in Utah. Born in the west, Shepherd had come east to study at the New England Conservatory. He was a great admirer and became a friend of Loeffler's.

In a subsequent report written for *Le Mercure musical* and published in 1907, Farwell went on to observe that the musical center of America seemed to be shifting from Boston to Chicago. He wrote that recently a Boston gentleman (unidentified) made a sensation in Chicago by, in a talk, proclaiming the latter city to be the center of American culture. If so, Farwell said, Europeans who are interested in American art will be obliged to move the center of artistic gravity toward the West. Farwell claimed that this confirmed his own previous opinion. "It was hoped," he wrote, "that the menacing commercial decline of Boston would be at least compensated by an artistic renaissance, but we know now that this hope is vain."[24] He, therefore, reported on the Chicago orchestra as well as the Boston orchestra. Not surprisingly, in his next communication Farwell chose to write about another westerner, Frederick Ayres of Colorado Springs.

Yet Farwell returned, in his next contribution, to reporting on music in the East, writing on the repertory of the BSO and on its new conductor Karl Muck and commenting on a performance of Converse's *Job* at Worcester. A major portion of this last report was an essay on national art in America and universality in art. The critics, Farwell wrote, are indifferent and disdainful toward composers of their own country. Society, he maintained, does not have an idea that music other than European music exists. He concluded that fashion held more sway than value.[25] His closing remarks were about his own Wa-Wan Society, dedicated to American composers.

Farwell reported once more in 1907, this time primarily on the use of Indian music in contemporary composition and on universality in music. He stated that in Europe four countries—France, Germany, England, and Russia—were interested in the issue of using Indian melodies in art music. Farwell expressed his own support for the idea of using elements from native music, born from the Indian spirit, because "the truth and beauty of the mythology, philosophy, and psychology of the Indian life are universal and the moment is opportune to revivify art at its source."[26] Printed after Farwell's essay were comments by Louis Laloy on Farwell's Wa-Wan Press.

In 1908 Farwell's last submission to *Le Mercure musical* appeared in print. After some comments on performances, he embarked on another nationalistic essay, reporting that

> the author of these lines has been blamed of being guilty, through the intermediary of *Le Mercure musical,* of performing in Paris (impudence without name) "missionary work" for American composers. This action would be culpable if it concerned embarking for this far voyage composers drawn from the province and feeble imitators of the masters: such is not the case. What is remarkable is that they are at the same time capable of holding back the invading wave of musical Europe in America and to make one appreciate their independent, progressive creative effort.[27]

Paris, Farwell said, should understand the American War for Independence and the long succession of artistic wars, and Paris should

> appreciate uniquely individual expression, the march towards progress, however humble and remote its origin. I believe that Parisian interest for a work of personal talent would never be diminished (whatever Americans think) because the author had the misfortune to be born in Goshen, Indiana, or Evanston, Illinois. France knows too well how to appreciate the value of the national effort for the development of the musical art.

Americans, he wrote, are slow to recognize personal native expression. "It will come, in its time, with a slow but regular step. But, while waiting, and for always, there remains Paris!"[28]

However, Farwell felt Parisians ought to feel, in fact their interest fell far short of his own. Space devoted to news from America subsequently

began to shrink severely in *Le Mercure musical*. In 1909 no American report appeared in its pages. In 1910 there appeared only a short report on
music in Boston. In 1911 Georges Barrère reported on tours made by
American orchestras, particularly a nationwide tour by Damrosch, and
Louis Elson reported the highlights of the season in Boston. There the
record ends. By this time *Le Mercure musical* had consolidated with *La
Revue musicale* and gave up its link with Boston.

The idea of having an American correspondent was not taken up by
other French journals. The first six volumes of *Revue d'histoire et de critique musicales* (which commenced publication in 1901) made no mention of American music. The seventh volume (published in January
1907) contained an article entitled "La musique et la magie des primitifs
chez les Américains" by L. Lejeal, while the eighth volume (published in
1908) contained an article on American music by "S." on the subject of
works by Farwell, Loomis, Carlos Troyer, and Louis Campbell-Tipton. A
later journal, *Revue de musicologie,* at first ignored music in America altogether when it commenced publication in 1922.

The connection between Paris and Boston was not broken, however.
With the advent of World War I, when musical Boston turned against the
music and musicians of Germany, Bostonians looked to France for conductors, musicians, and music. Several Bostonians helped raise funds for
France and her musicians through benefit concerts. Some French musicians found positions in America, brought more knowledge of French
music, and helped more French compositions find their way onto more
programs. Again Loeffler and Longy were active, managing benefits and
recommending musicians on their behalf. Loeffler performed such service for French musicians that he was elected a chevalier of the Légion
d'Honneur in July 1919.

Whatever opportunities musical Bostonians had to embrace Parisian
musical modes before the war, it was still primarily the sentiment of the
war years that turned the city's attention so widely to France. Even so,
some were never won by French music or musicians. Mason, for example, who had been born in Brookline and educated at Harvard, never took
to it. To Mason, Loeffler's music was "a mass of decay"[29] and music in
France no better. Mason went to Paris in 1913 and studied with d'Indy,
for whom he had some admiration, but on the whole was not impressed:

> The maddening thing about the Parisian mode at that period was its ar-
> tificiality, its narrow cliquism, its self-conscious complacence and in-
> tolerance, its itch for personal publicity and indifference to any larger

beauty. There were of course sincere musicians there—d'Indy, Dukas, Fauré, Florent Schmitt, and within their narrow limits even Debussy and Ravel—but those who made the most noise and succeeded in hypnotizing the world of fashion, after all indifferent to beauty, were the arrivistes, the poseurs, the snobs and the bluffers.[30]

Mason also wrote to Hill:

> Debussy and Ravel and all their lesser fellows sometimes interest, often amuse, but never move me. . . . The French have precious little interest in music one way or the other. They are immeasurably less musical, I believe, that we are, certainly less so than the Germans. As a result music is an artificial product here, and suffers from the anaemia of snobs.[31]

No matter how Loeffler and Longy's contemporaries in Boston reacted to French music, a new generation of composers was influenced favorably. Walter Piston, for example, was exposed to the French repertory while attending rehearsals of the New England Conservatory Orchestra[32] and while playing in the Boston Musical Association under Longy.

The younger generation may never have known Loeffler or played under Longy or studied with Hill, but French music had become a part of the concert music scene in Boston around them. It was in the air, exerting an influence, helping create a more international scope to music appreciation, and preparing the way for the postwar lure of Paris as an center for young musicians.

NOTES

[1]Arthur Shepherd " 'Papa' Goetchius in Retrospect," *The Musical Quarterly* 30 (July 1944):308.

[2]E. B. Hill, "Une opinion Américaine sur Maurice Ravel," *Le Mercure musical* 2 (1906):307.

[3]Thomas Ryan, *Recollections of an Old Musician* (New York: E. P. Dutton & Company, 1899):17.

[4]For a more detailed discussion of the German domination of Bostonian music, see Ellen Knight, *Charles Martin Loeffler* (Urbana: University of Illinois Press, 1993); and Nicholas E. Tawa, "Why American Art Music First Arrived in New England," *Music and American Culture, 1861–1918,* ed. Michael Saffle [Essays in American Music, 2] (New York: Garland, 1997):141–165.

[5]*Boston Home Journal,* reprinted in the *Musical Record* (December 1890):7
[6]*Boston Evening Transcript* (14 November 1887):1.

[7]Clara Rogers, *The Story of Two Lives* (Norwood, MA: Plimpton Press, 1932):83–84.

[8]Whether this opportunity was realized is yet to be discovered.

[9]For a history of this quartet see Ellen Knight, "The American String Quartette: Loeffler's Feminine Flonzaleys," *The Sonneck Society Bulletin* 18/3 (Fall 1992):98–101.

[10]*New York Times* (18 January 1918). Favorable press notices from five New York papers were printed in an American String Quartette flyer.

[11]It is important to note that Loeffler's symbolist style developed simultaneously with that of Debussy, whose music Loeffler did not know until the twentieth century.

[12]*New York Times* (8 February 1895). Further reviews and discussion of Loeffler's style can be found in Knight, *Charles Martin Loeffler,* passim.

[13][Lawrence Gilman], "Some Remarkable Songs," *Harpers Weekly* 48 (16 January 1904):109.

[14]Gilman, *Edward MacDowell* (New York: John Lane Company, 1908):101.

[15]Edward Burlingame Hill, *Modern French Music* (Boston: Houghton Mifflin Company, 1924).

[16]Charles Martin Loeffler, "La Musique en Amérique," *Le Mercure musical* 1 (1905):638–639, translated from the French. All translations in this essay are by the present author.

[17]This review was reprinted, in French, in *Le Mercure musical* 2 (1906):222–227, as part of Loeffler's report as an American correspondent.

[18]*Musiques pittoresques: Promenades musicales à l'exposition de 1889* (Paris: Librarie Fischbacher, 1889):55.

[19]Quoted from a letter addressed by Loeffler to Elizabeth Sprague Coolidge, 30 December 1925, and owned by the Loeffler Collection, Library of Congress.

[20]Loeffler "La musique en Amérique," *Le Mercure musical* 1 (1905): 638–639.

[21]Hill, "Une Opinion Américaine sur Maurice Ravel," *Le Mercure musical* 2 (1906):307–308.

[22]*Le Mercure musical* 3 (1907):102.

[23]Ibid.:431.

[24]Ibid.:774.

[25]Ibid.:1,206.

[26]Ibid.:1,041.

[27]*Le Mercure musical* 4 (1908):829.

[28]Ibid.:830.

[29]Daniel Gregory Mason, *Music in My Time* (New York: The Macmillian Company, 1938; reprint Westport, CT: Greenwood Press, 1970):78.

[30]Mason, *Music in My Time:*254.

[31]Mason, *Music in My Time:*255.

[32]According to Victor Yellin's biography of George Chadwick, Piston credited Chadwick with introducing him to works of the modern French orchestral school at rehearsals of the conservatory orchestra. See Yellin, *Chadwick: Yankee Composer* (Washington, D.C.: Smithsonian Institution Press, 1990):82.

CHAPTER 2

Ticklers' Secrets
Ragtime Performance Practices, 1900–1920—A Bibliographic Essay

KAREN REGE

Contemporary ragtime pianists understand the difficulty of recreating historical performances because the source material is so diverse and sparse. Finding sources that lend clues to the technical aspects of tempo, bass lines, phrasing, dynamics, and improvisation is a genuinely difficult task, and, perhaps for this reason, scholars of ragtime have neglected to write confidently about performance practices. The purpose of this bibliographic essay is to examine a variety of sources of information available about performance practices in both literary and nonliterary forms. Part I describes these various resources, while Part II looks at how these resources may be used to answer specific questions about the performance practices of piano ragtime. This essay will consider piano ragtime during approximately the first two decades of the twentieth century, excluding ragtime songs using piano accompaniment, novelty piano, and stride piano. It does include, however, piano renditions of ragtime songs, "ragged" versions of preexisting unsyncopated music, and original dance music.

The origin and the definition of "ragtime" are the subjects of two scholarly debates reaching beyond the scope of this paper. During the heyday of ragtime, the primary medium of performance was not the piano, but the voice, yet comparatively little research has been done on vocal ragtime.[1] Perhaps scholars have chosen to concentrate on piano ragtime because of the easy accessibility to an abundance of surviving player piano rolls and a plenitude of sheet music. Ragtime revivals in the 1940s and early 1970s were in part due to the publication of numerous articles on ragtime that appeared in jazz magazines in the 1940s, the publication of *Scott Joplin's Complete Piano Works* edited by Vera Brodsky Lawrence in 1973, the recordings of Joplin's music by Joshua Rifkin in 1974, and the soundtrack to the film *The Sting* from 1974 featuring Scott Joplin's "The Entertainer." These same resources, period and contemporary, print and nonprint, not only document the history of ragtime composition, but the performance practices of the players as well.

LITERARY RESOURCES

Most of the histories and sources of general information are a result of the ragtime revival of the early 1970s. In 1978, scholar John Hasse published "The Study Of Ragtime: A Review and A Preview," one of the first attempts to survey the major bibliographic research in the field.[2] Hasse briefly examined general history sources from the turn of the century through 1978 and offered a comparative critique. Using a chart, he compares the amount of documentation, the number of illustrations, and the size of the bibliographies and discographies in eight of the general sources.

Ragtime scholar Edward Berlin has subsequently published a more recent indication of where the field is going and what questions need to be answered. *Reflections and Research on Ragtime* contains a brief summary of the research already accomplished in the areas of biography, analysis, performance practices, the use of ragtime in theater, regional studies, and includes a list of questions still unanswered.[3]

Many of the general histories cited in Hasse and Berlin offer information useful to the study of performance practices of ragtime. A brief survey of these sources will give the reader an idea of where to begin gathering information.

Although a revival of interest in ragtime began in the 1940s with several articles appearing in small jazz magazines such as *Jazz Journal* and *Record Changer,* the first full-length book on ragtime did not appear until 1950.[4] *They All Played Ragtime* by Rudi Blesh and Harriet Janis was an effort to record not only the history but also the social aspects of primarily piano ragtime. Although the work was intended for the lay person and thus lacks documentation necessary for scholarly research, it does, however, contain many valuable interviews with ragtime figures. Blesh and Janis introduce some important concepts that became the foundation for later ragtime research. Hasse summarizes these concepts as "(1) ragtime bears a relationship to folk music, (2) the Midwest, especially Missouri, was the cradle of ragtime, (3) blacks had a central role in originating ragtime music (4) ragtime took many forms but the most significant was that of a piano music, (5) a 'classic [piano] ragtime' of great merit existed whose "big three" composers were Scott Joplin, James Scott, and Joseph Lamb, (6) Tin Pan Alley songwriters turned out cheap imitations of genuine ragtime which both eclipsed and degraded the high-class rags, and good ragtime deserves to be performed, heard, and appreciated once again."[5]

Chronologically, the next major history to appear was *The Art of Ragtime,* a collaborative effort by professors William Schafer and Johannes Riedel.[6] They assert that piano ragtime pieces were often the solo versions of many folk songs "in the air" at the time; a brief discussion of performance practices, including tempo and improvisation versus strict reading also is presented.

An excellent survey of the piano ragtime repertoire entitled *Rags and Ragtime: A Musical History,* was co-authored by two of the leading sheet music, piano roll, and record collectors, David A. Jasen and Trebor Jay Tichenor.[7] The book not only functions as a bibliography, discography, and rollography, but it contains the first biographical material of some of the lesser-known performers/composers. The authors' major contribution is their attempt to categorize piano ragtime composition into "Early Ragtime, 1897–1905," "The Joplin Tradition," "Popular Ragtime, 1906–1912," "Advanced Ragtime, 1913–1917," "Novelty Ragtime 1918–1928," "Stride Ragtime," and "The Ragtime Revival, 1941–1978."

Edward Berlin's *Ragtime: A Musical and Cultural History* is divided into three main sections: a survey and discussion of the perception of ragtime as it was viewed by its contemporary critics, an analysis of the changing stylistic traits of piano ragtime, and the changing perception of ragtime by current ragtime scholars.

John Hasse's full-length book on ragtime entitled *Ragtime: Its History, Composition, and Music* is a collection of essays on various topics concerning ragtime.[8] For example, there is an article on ragtime piano rolls, a reprint of several interviews with James P. Johnson, an abridged version of S. Brunson Campbell's autobiography, an article on Jelly Roll Morton, the role of women in ragtime, banjo music, band music, and an article on the correlation between ragtime and country music, to name a few. Perhaps the best tools of the book are the appendices that contain extensive discographies, list of compositions, a list of compositions by women, a list of period and contemporary method books, and an extensive systematically arranged bibliography.

More recently published books have been primarily biographies, with the exception of Ross Laird's 1995 discography entitled, *Tantalizing Tingles.*[9] A bio-bibliography of James Scott was authored by Scott DeVeaux and William Kenney in 1993. At least four biographies of Scott Joplin appeared between 1990 and 1997, the most notable of which is Edward Berlin's.[10] Berlin's thorough sleuthing uncovered numerous new facts about Joplin, including some about his performances.

Little information concerning ragtime piano performance can be found in the most prominent music periodicals of the time such as *Etude, The Musical Courier,* or *Musical America,* since many writers thought ragtime was a fad and largely ignored it. Most articles on ragtime that did appear were concerned with the issue of morality in ragtime.[11] Information about performances can occasionally be found, however, in newspaper accounts and obscure popular music magazines. The earliest popular music periodical with major coverage of ragtime is *Cadenza.* Beginning in 1894, this magazine, subtitled "For Banjo, Guitar, and Mandolin," was published in Boston by Walter Jacobs, but sometime between 1913 and 1915 the subtitle was changed to "A Magazine for the Musical Home and the Professional Pianist." While most of the articles in the earlier issues are concerned with the stringed instruments, many of the later issues contain articles about ragtime piano playing in schools, club engagements of local pianists, tips on vaudeville and orchestra pit playing, and sheet music reviews. From March 1915 to October 1916, Edward Winn published a monthly column in *Cadenza* entitled "Ragtime Piano Playing: A Practical Course of Instruction for Pianists" that contained a great amount of information on performance practice.[12]

The "Czar of Ragtime," Axel Christensen, a White pianist noted for his ragtime instruction schools, began publishing his own magazine from Chicago in December 1914 entitled *Christensen's Ragtime Review: A Monthly Magazine for Amateur and Professional Pianists.* It is dedicated solely to ragtime and each issue contains three to four pieces of sheet music. Most articles were written by Christensen and promote either ragtime or the Christensen schools of piano ragtime. Fictional articles on such topics as the use of ragtime as an anesthetic in place of cocaine at the dentist's office are frequently found alongside of question-and-answer sections offering enlightening information on the technical aspects of performance.

As mentioned above, several magazines from the 1940s and 1950s contain articles written during the first ragtime revival. Interviews with pianists such as Brun Campbell and James P. Johnson appear in *Jazz Review, Jazz Monthly, Jazz Journal* (which later became the current *Jazz*

Journal International), Record Changer, and *Jazz Report* (the latter two being record collector's magazines). Beginning in the 1960s, several social clubs dedicated to ragtime were formed, two of which published a monthly newsletter. The Ragtime Society of Toronto still publishes *Ragtimer* and the Maple Leaf Club of Los Angeles still publishes *Rag Times. Mississippi Rag,* a more recent publication, continues to publish well-researched articles on the history of ragtime. These more recent publications often serve as an outlet for the most recent research on ragtime, and provide many reprints of articles that appeared in earlier magazines from the 1940s and 1950s.

Another written source of performance practice information is ragtime instruction manuals. The earliest manual appears to be *Ben Harney's Ragtime Instructor* dated 1897, which was designed to teach the amateur pianist to "rag" preexisting melodies. It is comprised of a series of first lines from popular tunes in chorale form with an alternate "rag" rendition following each entry.

In 1903 in Chicago, Axel Christensen founded the Axel Christensen School of Ragtime, which by the mid-1910s had become a nationally renowned business with over fifty franchises. In the following year, Christensen published the first of six editions of *Christensen's Rag-Time Instructor.* This method attempted to teach the beginner how to play simple ragtime by using one of three rhythmic figurations to fit over one to four different chords, depending upon the harmonic rhythm of the piece. This method was by far the most popular of the day.

To scholars, the best-known instruction manual is Scott Joplin's *School of Ragtime: Six Exercises for Piano* published in 1908. These exercises were meant to teach the student to play ragtime by dissecting the rhythmic values of the syncopated figurations. Each exercise is preceded by a short written explanation.

Edwin R. Winn established a chain of ragtime schools to compete with Christensen, and he published *How to Play Ragtime (Uneven Rhythm),* the compilation of his series of articles that appeared in *Cadenza* magazine. This method began by teaching the pupil to play "straight bass," (octave/chord or oom-pah bass) with correct harmonies and to play the melody in octaves in the right hand, as opposed to concentrating on the rhythmic figures in the right hand as did the other instruction manuals. As the method progresses, variations of both the bass and melody are presented.

These and other instruction manuals were primarily aimed at the novice ragtime player who could read music. They served a twofold purpose. First, the instruction manuals deciphered the music theory used in ragtime, thereby making the often difficult to play pieces more accessible, and in turn, creating a wider market for sheet music. Second, the music theory in these manuals teach the student how to apply the technique of "ragging" a piece to other familiar tunes, and offer a foundation needed by players who wished to deviate from or dispense with the score.

NONLITERARY RESOURCES

The most information about performance can be gleaned from the three types of nonliterary resources: sheet music, player piano rolls, and 78 r.p.m. records. Each of these sources has its own limitations, however, and all three types of resources should therefore be examined in order to receive a complete picture of the performance practices of ragtime. One of the most productive ways to study performance is by gathering together the original manuscript, the sheet music, the player piano roll, and the recording of the same piece by the same performer.[13]

The greatest limitation of the sheet music is its subjection to editing. It is often difficult to determine if the tempo, phrasing, articulation, and dynamic markings were intended by the composer or added by the editor. Some publishers, such as H. A. French of Nashville, rarely added any marks to the score; others edited on a regular basis. Later rags, especially those from the East Coast, were often published in simplified versions to make them more marketable. For example, the 1914 edition of "The Junk Man Rag" composed by C. Luckyeth Roberts and published by Joseph W. Stern, bears the word "Simplified" under the title. In an interview with Rudi Blesh, Axel Christensen said "If such pieces [rags] were published as it was played by . . . ragtime composers and musicians, not one pianist in a thousand could play them."[14]

Player piano rolls also were subject to editing, whether the perforations were cut by hand or the music was "hand played" on a piano with a mechanism attached to mark the perforations on the paper. Notes were often added, especially in the bass, to create a fuller, more orchestral sound. Each piano roll company had its own style of editing to enhance its marketability. For example, it was common practice for the Connorized company that produced the hand-played rolls by Scott Joplin to recut the roll so that some notes would be slightly arpeggiated to create a lilting effect.[15] The majority of the ragtime player piano rolls cannot recreate the dynamics or the phrasing and articulation of the original performance.[16]

While the 78 r.p.m. recordings produced the single most accurate representation of performance, early recording techniques had some limitations. The performer had three minutes to perform, and may have had to leave out repeats of strains marked in the music, or cut short any improvisation. Many recordings were made using acoustical recording devices, and because the piano recorded poorly, few dynamics could be used. In surveying the records that have been rediscovered thus far, most of the performers who recorded were classically trained White pianists, therefore rendering a partially inaccurate representation of the types of pianists performing ragtime.[17]

RESOURCES AND PERFORMANCE PRACTICES

In piano ragtime, the central questions concerning performance are similar to those concerning the performance of any other style of music. We are interested in who was playing the music, what they were playing, when they were playing, where they were playing, why they were playing, and most importantly, how they were playing it. While the majority of these questions have been approached in general histories, the question of how ragtime was played, that is, the technical performance practices of the music, will be addressed in the remainder of this essay.

In attempting to perform piano ragtime in an historically accurate style, the performer must contend with the following questions: What type of articulation was used? Were dynamics used? What tempos were used? Were other bass notes and rhythms added besides the regular oom-pah bass? And was the music played directly from the sheet music as written, or was it improvised?

Tempo

The most often cited sources describing tempos used in period piano ragtime are the tapes of New Orleans pianist, Jelly Roll Morton, made by Alan Lomax in 1938 at the Library of Congress. On one recording, Jelly Roll first demonstrates how the "Maple Leaf Rag" was played in St. Louis around 1908, and then he performs the piece at a much slower tempo according to how he says he played it in 1915. Jelly Roll's memory has proven fallible in past anecdotes, however, although it has been documented that he did visit St. Louis. Therefore, it is difficult to determine much from his "Joplin-style rendition," and his own later style of piano playing contains more elements of early jazz such as right-hand improvisation, melodic bass lines, and Hispanic rhythms than commonly found in traditional ragtime.

Besides Jelly Roll Morton, other performers and scholars have discussed tempo. Although they never heard Joplin's playing first hand, Blesh and Janis describe it as "a supple, legato, singing style of moderate tempo, thoroughly musical and suited to his rags."[18] Since there are no accompanying citations, this assertion was probably derived from a description by an undocumented source, or Blesh and Janis may have speculated about Joplin's playing based on the tempo indications on his printed rags. Ed Berlin suggests that by 1901, Joplin possibly lacked the necessary finger control due to early symptoms of dementia paralytic caused by syphilis.[19]

The ragtime instruction manuals offer some help. In his own, Joplin marks each exercise slow *march tempo (count two)* and remarks, "We wish to say here, that the 'Joplin ragtime' is destroyed by careless or imperfect rendering, and very often good players lose the effect entirely, by playing too fast." In this comment, Joplin was perhaps making reference to pianists who played so fast that they made mistakes or blurred the intricate inner voices.

"All ragtime should be played in regular two-step time (not too fast)" was the advice of Axel Christensen in his ragtime instruction manual.[20] Each of the pieces in the instruction manual are marked *moderato*. Likewise, Ben Harney marks the compositions in his manual *tempo moderato,* although neither one discusses what this tempo indication actually means.[21]

The few available descriptions of tempos by period pianists contradict the notion that ragtime was played at a medium tempo. The clearest surviving example is from S. Brunson Campbell (1884–1952), Scott Joplin's only White student and reportedly an excellent pianist who could read as well as improvise. In his autobiography, he points out that "Some played march time, fast time, slow time and some played ragtime blues style."[22] Based on Campbell's observations and the results of the following study, one can conclude that ragtime was played at a variety of tempos, depending on the piece, the performer, and the audience.

Besides what published accounts, instruction manuals, and histories tell us, much can be yielded from a systematic study of the tempo markings in published sheet music. While one must remember that some tempo marks were added by editors and should not be considered as a definitive source, others do reflect the wishes of the composer. A survey of approximately 135 rags on sheet music yielded some interesting results.[23] The majority of the Joplin rags were labeled *Tempo di Marcia, Slow March Time,* or *Not (Too) Fast.* In addition, nine rags published between 1907 and 1909 carry the following notice: "Note: Do not play this piece fast. It is never right to play 'Ragtime' fast. The Composer."

Despite this note, four of those pieces have rather fast metronome markings. One of the printings of "Fig Leaf Rag," published by John Stark in 1908, is marked ♩ = 100. "Sugar Cane" and "Pine Apple Rag," both published in 1908 by Seminary Music of New York, are marked *slow march tempo.* "Eugenia," published in 1905 by Will Rossiter of Chicago, is marked *slow march tempo* (i.e., ♩ = 72).[24]

Four of Joplin's pieces have faster tempo markings. "Stoptime" published in 1910 by Joseph Stern of New York is labeled "fast or slow." "Scott Joplin's New Rag" published in 1912 by Joseph Stern is marked *Allegro moderato* (i.e., ♩ =112–132 on the metronome). "Magnetic Rag," published in 1914 by Scott Joplin Music of New York, is marked *Allegretto ma non troppo,* but it is in $\frac{4}{4}$ meter rather than the traditional $\frac{2}{4}$ meter.

Rags composed by pianists other than Joplin bear some more ambiguous tempo markings. "The 'Bolo' Rag" by Albert Gumble published in 1913 is labeled *Tempo di Rago* followed by the words "slowly but surely." "St. Louis Tickle" by Barney and Seymore (1904) bears the marking *Tempo Niggerino* and is subtitled "Two-step." The early "march and two-step" entitled "The Smoky Topaz" by Grace Bolen (1901) is indicated *Tempo di Cakewalk.* Perhaps the clearest marking is on Harry Jentes' 1916 piece entitled "Bantam Step," which is marked "Fox Trot" and (♩ = 88) and "One Step" (♩ = 126). The relationship between ragtime tempos and dance will be discussed later in this chapter.

Player piano rolls are not of much value in determining tempos. Once upon the tracker bar, the music can be played at any desired speed depending on how fast one pedals the paper across the tracker bar and the speed at which one sets the roll to turn. There are suggested speeds at the beginning of each roll, but they are placed there by editors and do not necessarily reflect common tempos.

The most accurate source of information on tempo is the recordings despite various playback speeds of early equipment and the fact that only White musicians, many of whom were formally trained, were allowed to record before the 1920s. Thus, the performance practices of many of the African American musicians who may have been working professionally on the vaudeville/concert circuit or in brothels, are excluded. Several of the most noted performers of the day were captured on disc, however.

Although Charles H. Booth recorded "Creole Belles" for the Victor Talking Machine Company in 1901, we know of few piano rags recorded before Mike Bernard's 1912–1913 recordings for Columbia records.[25] Mike Bernard, self-proclaimed as "The Ragtime King," was noted for his phenomenal technique developed from classical training, which helped him to win many cutting contests. Perhaps Bernard's virtuosic technique explains the fast tempo at which he performed on records. Tempos often change with each new strain, especially in medleys such as "Battle of San Juan," "Medley of Ted Snyder's Hits," and "Medley of Irving Berlin Songs."[26] For example, the tempos in "Medley of Ted Snyder's Hits" range from the metronome markings ♩ = 116–132 and at one point even reach ♩ = 152. At times he speeds up in the middle of the strain, even in dance tunes such as "Everybody's Two-Step" and "Tango Bonita," whose second strain starts ca. ♩ = 108 and ends up at ♩ = 116. This is quite different from Scott Joplin's perception of ragtime.[27]

Tempo still remains one of the most highly debated issues among modern performers. In an article reprinted in John Hasse's book, Roland Nadeau discusses tempo using the markings in Joplin's music as examples. He writes:

> Its tempo should range from a moderato to an easy allegro. Whether a rag is graceful or raucous, the player discovers its tempo by a combination of musical intuition and an analysis of its structure. In general, the more subtle and sophisticated the interaction of rhythmic, melodic, textual, and harmonic factors is, the more conservative the tempo must be. No matter what the tempo, the beat is almost always rigorously steady.[28]

Nadeau is not the only one with the idea that musical content dictates tempo. At a panel discussion on performances practices at the Scott Joplin Ragtime Festival in Sedalia, Missouri, in 1989, noted ragtime pianist Max Morath discussed the implications of Joplin's tempo marks. While many of the pieces are indicated "March Time" (commonly considered 120 beats per minute), this tempo is much too fast for many of the rags with more intricate textures. Morath and other members of the panel, including Yvonne Cloutier, John Arpin, and David Jasen, agreed that tempo often depends on personal style and how the piece lies under the hands. [29]

ARTICULATION AND PHRASING

In the above quote, Blesh and Janis describe Joplin's playing as "a supple, legato, singing style." Was this true of all ragtime performers? Schafer and Riedel maintain that "ragtime must be at once fluid rhythmically and clear, and percussive in accent. . . . Most scores show clearly how phrases should be accented, and playing and listening to ragtime will help make the idiomatic or conventional rhythmic phrasing clear."[30] In 1914, however, Axel Christensen wrote "Real ragtime must be played with a firm, strong, legato touch and the time must be absolutely even and correct."[31] Although both speak of rhythmic fluidity, they offer somewhat contradictory ideas of articulation: Schafer and Riedel speak of percussive accents and Christensen says it is to be played legato.

I would like to propose that articulation depends on several factors: the type of piece, the person who is playing the piece, and the audience. A piece from the Joplin or "classic ragtime" school with numerous inner voices will naturally be played more legato than an early folk rag piece. A musically educated pianist may be more likely to interpret the marks on the page as written and may have a wider range of articulations technically available to them than the musically illiterate player. And the intent of the performance must be taken into consideration. Highly accented, percussive, swinging pieces would probably have appealed more to cutting contest audiences in local bar rooms than would supple legato playing. For example, although Joplin was considered musical in his playing, Berlin notes that in the Chestnut Valley, "the scene of hot piano playing, of seething cutting contests. . . . Joplin could not compete. Among the St. Louis pianists, few had anything favorable to say."[32]

The most detailed period description of articulation described the accentuation of off-beats. No authorship is given for this article in 1913 issue of *Cadenza* magazine, which states,

> It was stated above that the two beats, or half section of the measure, should be accented equally, but this must be modified in an instance like the one following. In this example, the fifth note [pulse] in the measure, if the rule were followed, would have as strong an accent as the first note, but here *it is not struck at all*. This means that the fourth note, which ordinarily would have no accent whatever, must now be given a double accent, as it is doing duty for two notes.[33]

The idea the author is trying to convey here is that the accent that would normally occur on beat three is anticipated on the second half of beat two, causing the syncopation and the accent.

Joplin leaves us a clear example of how to play legato over syncopation. The fourth exercise in the Joplin *School of Ragtime* (Figure 2.1) contains slurs in the melody above which is written: "Slurs indicate a legato movement." Since Joplin published the exercises himself, and no other exercises contain markings, one might assume that Joplin placed slur marks where he wanted them and unmarked music was not necessarily played legato. As in the case of tempo, Joplin is clear about how he wants his music to be played. For example, he marked "Fig Leaf Rag" legato in the fourth strain.

Articulation in the sheet music is a complicated subject. No one can be absolutely sure whether the articulation was placed there by the composer, editor (that is, if the sheet music was given to him in manuscript form), or by the transcriber (in the case of people such as blind Charles Hunter from Nashville who would have had to have someone transcribe his performance).[34]

Each publisher was trying to get the public to buy his music and may have added articulation or simplified the music in a certain manner to create a company "trademark." For example, "A Tennessee Jubilee" by Thomas Broady, published by H. A. French in 1899 in Nashville, has no articulation markings save for three staccato notes in the right hand as a lead into the repeat of a melody and the accent mark on the last note of each strain; according to scholar David Joyner, French did not heavily edit the music.[35] Compare this piece to Mike Bernard's "The Stinging Bee," published by Will Rossiter of Chicago in 1908, which has accents written over off-beats and tied notes, as well as staccato runs in the right hand.

When compared with the manuscript, Harry Thomas' 1917 recording of "A Classical Spasm" offers some interesting insights into articula-

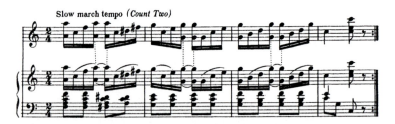

Figure 2.1. Exercise No. 4 from Scott Joplin, *The School of Ragtime*

tion.[36] Thomas, a Canadian composer who was apparently self-taught but possessed excellent technique and knowledge of classical music, played basically what was on the page.[37] The composition is divided into two parts, the first of which is based on "Polish Dance" by Scharwenka, and the second based on a Minuetto by Paderewski. Phrasing is not marked in the manuscript. For the most part, he used four-bar phrases common to a sixteen-bar strain. The melody to "A Classical Spasm" was written, however, in a manner that caused the phrasing to overlap (see, for example, measures 4–5 in the second strain).

The manuscript contains few articulation markings. There are several accented notes in the bass in the pick-up to the second and third strains of the "Polish Dance" that he played as written, and there are some staccato notes in the last written section of the trio that he does play, but not sharply. Accents not found in the manuscript can be heard in the recording on the off-beats and tied notes. For example, in the first two measures of the first strain of the Polish Dance, he plays the accents

Figure 2.2. Bass-line rhythm from Harry Thomas, *Classical Spasm* (Polish dance section).

And he plays the accents in the first two measures of the Minuetto as

Figure 2.3. Bass-line rhythm from Harry Thomas, *Classical Spasm* (Minuetto section).

For the most part, anything that is pianistic—runs, arpeggios, and so forth is played legato. Anything else usually has tied syncopation and the tied notes are accented. The octaves in the bass are usually punched and the chords are played more softly, to create the effect of a string bass playing on beats one and three.

Mike Bernard's recording of "Tantalizing Tingles" reveals some similar articulation patterns to those of Harry Thomas. Figure 2.4 shows the first three bars of the second strain in the sheet music. Notice the accents. On the Columbia recording, however, he performs it as shown in

Figure 2.4. From Mike Bernard, *Tantalizing Tingles,* 2nd strain (from the score).

Figure 2.5. Notice the similarities in the rhythm and accents of the bass line (Figure 2.6) and the Minuetto example of Thomas's shown previously. These examples illustrate how common it was to deviate from the score, either printed or manuscript, in actual performance, at least for the professional performer.

Figure 2.5. From Mike Bernard, *Tantalizing Tingles,* 2nd strain (from the recording).

Figure 2.6. Bass-line rhythm from Mike Bernard, *Tantalizing Tingles,* 2nd strain (recording).

DYNAMICS

In 1915, Axel Christensen gave the advice, "Learn to shade your tones from loud to soft as the requirements of the piece and your interpretation of it may require."[38] In an interview with Tom Davin, pianist James P. Johnson said,

When playing a heavy stomp, I'd soften it right down—then, I'd make
abrupt changes like I heard Beethoven do in a sonata. Some people
thought it was cheap, but it was effective and dramatic. . . . Another
time, I'd use pianissimo effects in the groove and let the dancer's feet
be heard scraping the floor.[39]

Here are the voices of two period pianists telling us that ragtime performance did include the use of dynamics. While one would expect the bar-
room/brothel professional piano players to play loudly only in order to
be heard above the noise, at a cutting contest or any sort of performance
where there was a seated audience, surely dynamics were used as part of
the dazzling effect. When interviewed by John Hasse, contemporary ragtime pianist and scholar Max Morath addressed this problem faced by
early performers.[40] That is, the use of dynamics depended upon the environment in which the music was performed. Morath explains that on the
concert stage, he adheres more closely to the written music and uses
many dynamic changes, but in a night club, he plays "more loudly, more
percussively, and faster."[41]

Instruction manuals tell us little about the use of dynamics. Edward
Winn's book has no dynamic marks. Ben Harney's instructor contains
the piece, "Plantation Echoes" by Theodore H. Northrup, which is
marked with a number of dynamics, mostly *mf* and crescendos to *f*.
Axel Christensen's arrangement of "Simple Confessions," which appeared in his instruction book, has the markings *f* *crescendo* to *ff*.
Joplin wrote no dynamics in his *School of Ragtime,* but did use them frequently in his sheet music.

In the sheet music, the same problem occurs as with articulation; it
is impossible to determine which markings belong to the composer, and
which are editorial. Some pieces contain a wide variety of dynamics. For
example, "Mandy's Broadway Stroll" by Thomas Broady, published in
1898 by H. A. French of Nashville who did not heavily edit the music,
contains the dynamic markings of *ff*, *f*, *mf*, *p*, *pp*, as well as several
crescendos and decrescendos in the same piece. Others, such as "A Tennessee Jubilee" by the same composer, published by the same publisher
only one year later, contain no dynamic marks whatsoever.

By looking at self-published and manuscript pieces, we can get a
better idea of how much dynamics were used. Take, for example, Joplin's
"Magnetic Rag," which he published himself in 1914, and the manuscript of Harry Thomas's "A Classical Spasm." Joplin's piece contains a
number of dynamic markings, although they are only *f*, *mf*, or *crescendo*.

Harry Thomas's manuscript has quite a number of dynamics, including *ff*, *f*, *crescendo,* and *decrescendo,* as well as *f* e *crescendo* [*sic*] and *mf*=*f* (meaning, play the repeat louder). The self-published sheet music and manuscripts are the best source of information about dynamics, as the piano rolls and early recording are unable to offer help. The majority of the piano rolls are not reproducing and cannot recreate the dynamics of an original performance. Written instructions on the roll tell the pedaler when to add the soft pedal, but these again are editorial comments and are not a reflection of the original performance. The piano was not well suited to early recording techniques. Thus, in early recording sessions, the piano was played loudly in order for it to properly record, foregoing the use of dynamics.

IMPROVISATION

Perhaps the most controversial subject in the performance of ragtime is the notion of improvisation versus score performance. The general public of the early 1900s that bought the sheet music at the local five-and-ten-cent store must surely have learned the music by reading the notes off the page and performed the score as written. Composers who were not phenomenal performers were reported also to have played their music as written. For example, Joe Jordan recalls never hearing Joplin "play any rags other than his own, and he played them almost exactly like the sheet music."[42]

Most of the professional pianists who were playing in brothels, barrooms, or cutting contests, however, either could not or did not read rags from the sheet music. In fact, Eubie Blake could not conceive of even his own music appearing in print. According to Blake biographer Al Rose, "In common with most of his Eastern colleagues, he [Eubie Blake] considered most of what he composed a mere point of departure for his personal improvisations. The music on the paper wasn't designed to be played literally; in fact it would change in each rendition."[43]

The subject of ragtime and improvisation was formally discussed in published form in two articles appearing in the *Journal of Jazz Studies* in 1976 and 1977. In his article, "The Transition from Ragtime to Improvised Piano Style," independent scholar Eli Newberger attempts to show that although a separate style, ragtime was the forerunner to the improvised style known as jazz piano, which blossomed in the late 1910s.[44] He based his argument on transcriptions of six different recordings of the "Maple Leaf Rag": Scott Joplin's player piano roll, and recordings by Brun Campbell, Eubie Blake, Jelly Roll Morton, James P. Johnson, and Willie "the Lion"

Smith. Viewing Joplin's roll as the authoritative source, Newberger compares "meter, tempo, and rhythm" (i.e., swing eighths) of the other recordings with Joplin's. However, the recordings he used are dated beyond the time period he was discussing. That is, the recordings Newberger compared were made after 1920 and the performances of this traditional rag may have been influenced by early jazz and its improvisation.[45]

For this reason and because of Newberger's assumption that all ragtime was written music, Edward Berlin offered a different opinion.[46] He proposed that "true ragtime is an improvised music; notated, published ragtime is but a simplified and pale reflection of the authentic style that, for lack of recordings, has been lost to posterity."[47] Berlin acknowledged that Joplin, Turpin, and others may not have improvised and intended their compositions to be played as written, suggesting that Joplin's warning against "imperfect rendering" of his compositions in Exercise 6 of his *School of Ragtime* and Artie Matthews "Don't Fake" indication on "Pastime Rag No. 1" proves that performers improvised. Berlin also notes several firsthand descriptions of pyrotechnics by James Weldon Johnson, James P. Johnson, and Tom Fletcher that do not appear in the sheet music, concluding that we should "consider jazz as a continuation of an already flourishing art of improvised ragtime."[48]

Unfortunately, Berlin does not discuss what can be learned from comparing player piano rolls and early recordings to manuscripts and or sheet music, nor does he examine ragtime instruction books in depth. The goal of the majority of the instruction manuals was to teach the student to "rag" or improvise in a ragtime style upon a preexisting melody.

To what extent *was* the music improvised? Do a few embellishments qualify as improvisation? Should the melody be retained at all times or is it possible to depart totally from it as in later jazz piano styles? Must only the melody be improvised upon or may the bass also be improvised upon as well?

While it is not possible to delve into each question due to the length of this chapter, a short example of what can be learned about improvisation from the sources of information existing can be provided by examining the subject of left-hand deviations from the steady oom-pah movement commonly found in piano ragtime. Let's examine the literary resources first. Eubie Blake described the playing of pianist William Turk (1866–1911) as this:

> He could play the ragtime stride bass, but it bothered him because his stomach got in the way of his arm so he used a walking bass instead. I can remember when I was thirteen—this was in 1896—how Turk

would play one note with his right hand and at the same time, four with his left. We called it "16"—they call it "boogie-woogie" now.[49]

Some resources note left-hand harmonies and chord voicings. Louis Chauvin was said to have performed ninths, tenths, and thirteenths in his left hand ahead of his time, and in his conversations with Tom Davin, James P. Johnson mentions a departure from the standard harmonies of the ragtime bass:

> New York developed the orchestral piano—full, round, big, wide spread chords and tenths—a heavy bass moving against the right hand. The other guys from the South and West at that time played in smaller dimensions—like thirds played in unison [octaves?]. . . . In rags, that full accompaniment was played as early as 1910. Even Scott Joplin had octaves and chords but he didn't attempt any big hand stretches.[50]

James P. Johnson went on to describe his own playing as having left-hand improvisations. "I played rags very accurately and brilliantly—running chromatic octaves and glissandos up and down with both hands."

Axel Christensen also remarked about left-hand improvisation. In answering a question about stage performance posed by a reader of the *Christensen Ragtime Review,* he responded "For an encore play another well-known melody, first in straight rag, then in arpeggio rag, playing the melody in the bass with ragtime variations and runs for the right hand."[51]

As mentioned above, the ragtime instruction books may provide a clue to improvisation. Both the Christensen and the Winn methods aimed to teach the amateur pianist to improvise a ragtime version of a preexisting melody. Besides teaching the reader how to "rag" the melody, the Winn method, originally copyrighted in 1915, teaches the "Passing Bass," where octaves are used to "connect any two chords." Winn writes, "Good taste and judgment must be relied upon in deciding when to introduce Passing Bass. It is most effective when used in contrary motion to the melody or where the melody part is stationary or moves slowly."[52] Winn goes on to present variations of the passing bass, including the "Novelty Passing Bass," which uses octaves in eighth notes (sometimes chromatic) to connect chord tones, a "Rolling Tenth Bass," and a "Syncopated Bass." He advises the reader to "aim to produce variety," but notes, "Acquire facility in playing a composition in 'straight' time and with the 'Winn' [oom-pah] Bass before attempting to employ the modern embellishments and various forms of bass."[53]

PIANISTS AND RAGTIME

There appeared to be three types of pianists playing ragtime:

1. The first group, the professional performers, can be divided into two subgroups. First, there were the itinerant pianists, both Black and White, working the club circuit and in sporting houses many of whom were probably musically illiterate. They performed professionally for the purpose of dancing, for parlor entertainment in sporting houses, and occasionally engaged in "cutting contests" to determine the best performer.[54] Second, there were also a number of concert or vaudeville performers. Many of these, like Mike Bernard, were highly trained pianists who possessed good reading capabilities and virtuosic technique.

2. There was the "Joplin school," a group of composer/performers (including Joplin himself, James Scott, and Joseph Lamb) who read and composed music of a fairly high standard, a style termed by editor John Stark as "classical ragtime." These men were not necessarily professional performers; rather they earned their income by publishing their compositions and teaching.

3. The consumers of the sheet music comprised the third group of ragtime pianists. They were most often young middle-class White men and women who performed this music in their parlor for their friends and their own enjoyment. Since the later two groups probably adhered strictly to the written music for phrasing, dynamics, tempo, and articulation, it is more desirable to explore the performance practices of the first group.

Another aspect of ragtime music that may offer clues to performance practices is the relationship between ragtime and dancing (both social and stage dancing). While some historians such as Jasen and Tichenor contend that the syncopation made ragtime too difficult to dance to, period accounts prove that it was in fact used for dancing. While often dance music was provided by orchestras and dance bands, many of the smaller clubs, brothels, and restaurants could not afford to employ an orchestra nightly. We know from several written sources that the music was provided by solo pianists. In *They All Played Ragtime,* Joplin's colleague Arthur Marshall, describes playing for dances in Sedalia, Missouri, as follows:

> Joplin and I and many others played for numerous dances at the parks,
> all piano only. We played the rags of note and they did dances to the

ragtime. They would do a buck and wing, a regular ragtime, and then
make up six or seven different steps just like the eccentric dancing that
came later.[55]

J. Rosamond Johnson describes the playing of Scott Joplin and similar
musicians: "As restless as a rolling stone, the dance-hall musicians
reeled and rocked from one end of the keyboard to the other, inserting
new idioms as the dancers rolled along."[56]

Several period articles describe the types of steps performed to this
music. An April 1914 *New York Times* article summarized a meeting of
dancing instructors from New York City who were trying to standardize
the steps to several of the fad dances such as the Maxixe, Tango, Lame
Duck, and Hesitation Waltz. One of the noted speakers at that meeting
was Arthur Farwell, whose main topic was "The Psychology of Ragtime," but who also discussed the "technical construction" of ragtime
with the aid of musical examples.[57]

In answering another question posed by a reader of *Christensen's
Ragtime Review,* Axel Christensen describes the dance rhythms as follows:

> There is no particular difference in the rhythm of a one-step and that of
> a two-step, except that the one-step is played a great deal faster as in
> dancing a one-step the dancer only two steps are taken in each measure
> while in the two-step, three steps are taken in each measure [*sic*]. Both
> are written in two-four time. The real tango is a slow six-eight move-
> ment, although the word has been used a great deal in reference to the
> one-step and many people call the one-step the tango. The Fox Trot is
> written in four-four time, the musical rhythm being very similar to the
> old Schottisches.[58]

Quotations like the one above leave several clues to performance practices. First, it confirms that much of the music was meant for dancing
rather than listening. It reveals that many of the dances were inter-
changeable and that many steps did not necessarily require specific musical beats. It also tells us that the same piece could be played fast or
slow.

In general, period books and instruction manuals on social dancing
made little note of the music. There were several exceptions, however. In
their 1914 instruction manual *Modern Dancing,* Irene and Vernon Castle
may have inadvertently left a clue to the change of tempos with the

change of dance styles. "Then came the rag, the rag with its syncopated tempo and its subtle phrasing, to which the world turkey-trotted. Now we have the slower and more artistic music of the moment."[59]

In 1980, Samuel Floyd and Marsha Reisser published an article in *Black Perspectives in Music* in which they attempted to trace the history of social dance music written by Black American composers from the early nineteenth century to ragtime. In this analytical study, they surveyed the forms, characteristic rhythms, and "multimetrics" of sheet music from the pre-Civil War era to the middle of the ragtime period. They concluded that there was an "unbroken line of development from the music of early black composers of social dance music to the beginnings of notated ragtime." Their discussion, however, rests solely upon the printed music and makes no mention of the correlation between the actual dance steps and the music. Oddly, they completely ignored the ragtime waltzes, which perhaps would have been the clearest example of music to prove their hypothesis, since ragtime waltzes survive as a specific ragtime form while the quadrilles and polkas do not.

In his dissertation, Edward Berlin notes many similarities between ragtime and Caribbean dance music, although he maintains that they were distinctly separate styles. Contrary to Floyd and Reisser, he believes that ragtime was not a derivative of social dance music, but rather grew out of the march. "It is true that all of these dances [cotillions, quadrilles, Scottisches, and polkas] share with the rag a common sectional format, an additive structure joining complete musical units. But as these dances do not, in this respect, add to the rag anything that was not obtained from the more direct source of the march, any indebtedness must be regarded as slight.[60]

While the discussion of whether or not ragtime was derived from social dance music or the march continues, there can be no doubt that ragtime eventually became social dance music. This can be determined not only from several literary sources as listed above among others, but it can be determined from the music itself.

The first clue is the use of subtitles such as "Fox Trot," "One-Step," "Two-Step," "Tango," and "Waltz." Another indication is the more specific markings such as the one mentioned above in conjunction with tempo. "Bantam Step" by Harry Jentes lists two different tempo markings for the same piece, according to which dance was to be performed.

Another indication is the specific markings for dancers in the printed sheet music. In Scott Joplin's 1906 "Rag-Time Dance," uncharacteristic breaks are written in the music. Breaks also occur in George Gould's "Whoa! Nellie!"(1915) where the word *stop* is written in. On the last *stop,* there is a footnote that reads "stopping here leaves dancers without music—very effective." Dance historian Elizabeth Kendall has suggested that, "At crescendos and stoptimes, they [Irene and Vernon Castles] always had showier tricks."[61]

Knowing the music was danced to and that it was at times improvised, what restrictions did the dancing place on the performance practices of ragtime? Tempo is one, meter another, and even perhaps the number of repeats and amount of melodic variation.[62] Tempo was dictated by the level of intricacy of the dance steps, that is, a one-step was faster than a two-step because there were fewer steps involved. Certain dance steps such as the fox-trot had specific meters associated with it. If the dance floor was crowded, the musicians probably repeated the song a number of times to keep the floor filled. And although the dancers probably wished to hear the melody at least the first time through, repeats meant improvisation.

After reviewing what information all the various resources have to offer, what *were* the performance practices of piano ragtime? The answer is it depends on the type of music that was being played and who was playing it. The professional pianist performing in barrooms and brothels were less likely to read the sheet music, especially if the music was being danced to. As mentioned above, tempos may have varied, but they were always danceable. Articulation and dynamics may have been less important to these pianists working in noisy rooms, but the music had to groove. And improvisation must have been the norm, especially to keep the dancers moving.

The stage performer, whether in concert or in vaudeville, played music that was more flashy technically. Many of these performers were trained pianists whose fingers moved through breakneck tempos, showy tricks, and a variety of dynamics and articulations. They probably improvised as well, especially over familiar folk and western classical melodies. These performers also were the early recording artists and perhaps the inspiration of thousands of players.

As ragtime gained popularity, young people wanted to play it. Those who were musically literate bought the sheet music and probably only played it in the comfort of their own parlor. They performed the pieces as written, adhering to tempo, articulation, and dynamics, and it is doubtful that they improvised much. Sheet music publishers edited the music to make it more saleable by adding in tempo, dynamic, articulation, and phrase marks. Many of the pieces were difficult to play, however, and therefore simplified versions appeared and instruction manuals and schools sprang up. With the consumers of sheet music in mind, Tin Pan Alley cranked out hundreds of ragtime tunes containing styles and performance practice notations that were rather different from what was being played by the professional musicians.

While this chapter has attempted to determine what information is revealed about performance practices by studying historical accounts of ragtime in books and articles, player piano rolls, recordings, and sheet music, the answers are not all there. Any modern ragtime performer can easily debate tempo, dynamics, phrasing, articulation, and the use of improvisation. Much of performance is naturally dominated by personal style. But styles develop out of patterns in history. Only by examining all available resources can we begin to determine what ragtime, through all its variants, must have sounded like.

NOTES

[1]See Ann Charters (compiler), *The Ragtime Songbook* (New York: Oak Publications, 1965); and Edward Berlin, "Ragtime Songs," *Ragtime: Its History, Composers, and Music,* ed. John Hasse (New York: Schirmer Books, 1985):70–78.

[2]Hasse, "The Study of Ragtime: A Review and A Preview," *Discourse in Ethnomusicology,* ed. Caroline Card (Bloomington, IN: University Ethnomusicology Publications Group, 1978):161–190.

[3]Berlin, *Reflections and Research on Ragtime*, ISAM Monograph No. 24 (Brooklyn: Institute for Studies in American Music, 1987).

[4]See, for example, Roy Carew, "New Orleans Recollections," *Record Changer* (February 1943):28–29, reprint *Record Changer* (July 1947):9.

[5]Hasse, "The Study of Ragtime":166.

[6]William Schafer and Johannes Riedel, *The Art of Ragtime* (New York: Da Capo Press, 1973).

[7]David A. Jasen and Trebor Jay Tichenor, *Rags and Ragtime: A Musical History* (New York: Seabury Press, 1978).

[8]*Ragtime: Its History, Composers, and Music,* ed. John Hasse (New York: Schirmer Books, 1985).

[9]Ross Laird, *Tantalizing Tingles: A Discography of Early Ragtime, Jazz, and Novelty Syncopated Piano Recordings, 1889–1934* (Westport, CT: Greenwood Press, 1995).

[10]Berlin, *King of Ragtime: Scott Joplin and His Era* (New York: Oxford University Press, 1994).

[11]For an excellent discussion of the types of arguments for and against ragtime, see Part Two of *Piano Ragtime* in Berlin, *Ragtime: A Musical and Cultural History* (Berkeley and Los Angeles: University of California Press, 1980).

[12]A discussion of this series follows in the section on period instruction manuals.

[13]In an attempt to do this, I have collected a copy of the manuscript, a recording of the piano roll, and a copy of the 78 r.p.m. recording of the Canadian pianist Harry Thomas's "A Classical Spasm." The manuscript is marked as being received by the United States Copyright Office in 1917, the same year that the record was made, while the piano roll was dated 1919. This piece, in its various media, will be used in Part Two of this chapter for a technical discussion of performance practices.

[14]Rudi Blesh and Harriet Janis, *They All Played Ragtime* (New York: Alfred A. Knopf, 1950):138.

[15]Michael Montgomery, personal communication, Southfield, MI, 1 August 1989. Mr. Montgomery is a collector of sheet music, player piano rolls, and selected 78 r.p.m. records. He has most notably produced the recordings of Scott Joplin's and others' player piano rolls. For further information, see the liner notes to Biograph BLP 1006Q, *Scott Joplin 1916, The Only Known Solos Played By The King Of Ragtime And Others.*

[16]Those rolls that can recreate dynamics, phrasing, and articulation are called "reproducing" rolls. The majority of these rolls were created for western European classical music.

[17]Several secondary resources have been published to help gain access to ragtime on early recording, namely discographies and rollographies such as David Jasen, *Recorded Ragtime, 1897–1958* (Hamden: Archon Books, 1973), and Ross Laird's *Tantalizing Tingles: A Discography of Early Ragtime, Jazz, and Novelty Syncopated Piano Recordings, 1889–1934* (Westport, CT: Greenwood Press, 1995).

Jasen's book is formatted in two parts: Part One lists the songs alphabetically, and Part Two is a list of composers. There is no performer index and there is no indication to the type of instrumentation used, which makes it difficult when searching for solely piano ragtime. The book is still useful, however, if one is searching for a matrix number or a recording date.

Rollographies also can be useful sources of information to determine who performed ragtime, what the most popular pieces were, and to help trace the history of a particular tune. Rollographies are listed in the back of Blesh and Hasse.

[18]Blesh and Janis, *They All Played Ragtime:* 65.

[19]Berlin, *King of Ragtime,* 103–104.

[20]Axel Christensen, *Christensen's Rag-Time Instruction Book for Piano* (Chicago: A. W. Christensen, 1915):25.

[21]Ben Harney, *Ben Harney's Rag Time Instructor* (Chicago: Sol Bloom, 1897).

[22]S. Brunson Campbell, "The Ragtime Kid: An Autobiography," *Jazz Report* 6/1 (1967):7–12.

[23]For this study, I surveyed all of the Joplin rags (thirty-six) found in *The Collected Works of Scott Joplin,* ed. Vera Brodsky Lawrence (New York: New York Public Library, 1971); as well as other examples from the "Joplin School," "folk rags," "popular rags," and "advanced rags" reprinted in Trebor Jay Tichenor (compiler), *Ragtime Rarities Complete Original Music For 63 Piano Rags* (New York: Dover Publications, 1975); David A. Jasen (compiler), *Ragtime Gems: Original Sheet Music of 25 Ragtime Classics* (New York: Dover Publications, 1986); as well as various rags contained in the Montgomery Collection, University of Michigan, School of Music Library.

[24]Schafer and Riedel suggested that John Stark placed the metronome marking of one hundred beats to the minute [$\quarternote = 100$] on the compositions. See Schafer and Riedel, *The Art of Ragtime:* 144.

[25]Jasen, *Recorded Ragtime:* 9.

[26]Columbia recordings A1266, A1313, A1386, A1266, and A1590 respectively.

[27]The later style of novelty ragtime of the late teens and early 1920s was noted for its fast tempos.

[28]Roland Nadeau, "The Grace and Beauty of Classic Rags," in Hasse, *Ragtime: Its History, Composition, and Music.* Reprinted from *Music Educators' Journal* 59 (April 1973):57–64.

[29]Max Morath, David Jasen, Yvonne Cloutier, Edward Berlin, and John Arpin. Panel discussion. Scott Joplin Ragtime Festival, Sedalia, MO, 2 June 1989.

[30]Schafer and Riedel, *The Art of Ragtime,* 147–148. Many scores have no articulation or phrasing marks. I would also like to suggest that some pieces contain articulation marks added by editors of the sheet music.

[31]Axel Christensen, "The Popularity of Ragtime," *Christensen's Ragtime Review* No. 1 (December 1914):2.

[32]Berlin, *King of Ragtime:*103.

[33]"Some Hints on Playing Ragtime," *Cadenza* 20/6 (November 1913):11.

[34]A study of pieces we know were transcribed by others might give some important clues to performance practices. We know that Scott Joplin transcribed pieces for his friends who could not read music like Louis Chauvin.

[35]David Joyner, *Southern Ragtime and Its Transition to Published Blues* (Ph.D. dissertation, Memphis State University, 1986).

[36]Victor recording 18229B.

[37]According to Norman Creighton, Harry Thomas was born Reginald Thomas Broughton in 1890 in Bristol, England. He arrived in Canada in 1909

where he remained until his death in 1941. He was most noted for his accompaniments to silent films, his duets with Willie Eckstein, and later his work with his piano, saxophone, and xylophone trio. He made a number of recordings for Victor records beginning in 1916, although not all have been rediscovered. We do not know how much of his music survives, as bio-bibliographical work on him is only beginning. From the sources we do have, his compositions are virtuosic in the manner of classical composition; they are not full of the stock passages characteristic of "novelty piano."

[38] Axel Christensen, "Tone and Touch For Ragtime," *Ragtime Review* 1/7 (July 1915):5.

[39]Tom Davin, "Conversations With James P. Johnson," *Jazz Review* 2 (June 1959):14–17; 2 (July 1959):10–13; 2 (August 1959):13–15; 2 (September 1959):26–27; 3 (March 1960):10–13. Reprinted in abridged form in Hasse, *Ragtime: Its History, Composers, and Music:*166–177.

[40]Max Morath's view represents both scholarly opinion and practical knowledge as a performer. Morath has thoroughly researched much of the material he presented in his 1960s television show on ragtime and the material he presented in his recent stage show "Living a Ragtime Life."

[41]Hasse, *Ragtime: Its History, Composers, and Music:*191.

[42]Dick Zimmerman, "Joe Jordan and Scott Joplin," *Rag Times* $\frac{2}{4}$ (November 1968):5. St. Louis pianist Charles Thompson tells of Tom Turpin playing the music as written in Trebor Tichenor, " 'The Real Thing': As recalled by Charles Thompson," *Ragtime Review* 2 (April 1963):5.

[43]Al Rose, *Eubie Blake* (New York: Schirmer, 1979):41.

[44]Eli Newberger, "The Transition From Ragtime to Improvised Piano Style," *Journal of Jazz Studies* 3 (Spring 1976):3–18.

[45]Brun Campbell's recording dates from the 1940s, Morton's recording was made in 1938, Blake's c. 1958, James P. Johnson's in 1946, and Willie "the Lion" Smith's in 1957.

[46]Berlin, "Ragtime and Improvised Piano: Another View," *Journal of Jazz Studies* 4/2 (Spring–Summer 1977):4–10.

[47]Berlin, "Ragtime and Improvised Piano":6.

[48]Berlin, "Ragtime and Improvised Piano":9.

[49]Blesh and Janis, *They All Played Ragtime:*141.

[50]For information on Louis Chauvin, see Dick Zimmerman, "A Visit With Joe Jordan," *Rag Times* 2/3 (29 September 1968):6. Trebor Jay Tichenor, " 'The Real Thing': As Recalled by Charles Thompson," *Ragtime Review* 2 (April 1963):5 [reprinted in *Rag Times* 5/4 (November 1971):3]; and Tom Davin, "Conversations with James P. Johnson," Part 1:17.

[51]Axel Christensen, "Questions and Answers," *Christensen's Ragtime Review* 1/1 (December 1914):3.

[52]Edward R. Winn, *How to Play Ragtime (Uneven Rhythm)* (New York: Edward R. Winn, 1915):14.

[53]Winn, *How to Play Ragtime:*2.

[54]An excellent description of an East Coast sporting house or "hookshop" and the music played there can be found in Al Rose, *Eubie Blake* (New York: Schirmer Books, 1979):19–22.

[55]Blesh and Janis, *They All Played Ragtime:*28–29.

[56]Sterling A. Brown. "Negro Producers of Ragtime," in Patterson, Lindsay. *The Negro in Music and Art,* International Library of Negro Life and History, Vol. 16. (New York: Publishers Co., 1967):49.

[57]Dance Puzzle Stirs Teachers to Action," *New York Times* (20 April 1914):9.

[58]Axel Christensen, "Questions and Answers," *Christensen's Ragtime Review* 1/15 (May 1915):18.

[59]Irene and Vernon Castle, *Modern Dancing* (New York: Harper and Brothers Publishers, 1914):161.

[60]Berlin, *Piano Ragtime: A Musical and Cultural Study* (Ph.D. dissertation, City University of New York, 1976):210.

[61]Elizabeth Kendall, *Where She Danced* (New York: Alfred A. Knopf, 1979):97.

[62]Here is where the dance steps need to be explored. If the early dances were similar to contradances, repeats must have been played in order to get the dancers back to their original starting points.

APPENDIX: A BIBLIOGRAPHY OF RAGTIME MATERIALS

Books and Articles

Berlin, Edward A. *The King of Ragtime: Scott Joplin and His Era.* New York: Oxford University Press, 1994.

———. *Piano Ragtime: A Musical and Cultural Study.* Ph.D. dissertation. New York: City University of New York, 1976.

———. *Ragtime: A Musical and Cultural History.* Berkeley and Los Angeles: University of California Press, 1980.

———. "Ragtime and Improvised Piano; Another View," *Journal of Jazz Studies* 4/2 (Spring/Summer 1977):4–10.

———. *Reflections and Research on Ragtime.* ISAM Monograph No. 24. Brooklyn: Institute for Studies in American Music, 1987.

Blesh, Rudi, and Harriet Janis. *They All Played Ragtime: The True Story of an American Music.* New York: Alfred A. Knopf, 1950. 4th ed. Oak Press, 1971.

Brown, Sterling A. "Negro Producers of Ragtime," in Patterson, Lindsay, *The Negro in Music and Art,* International Library of Negro Life and History, Vol. 16. New York: Publishers Co., 1967:49.

Campbell, S. Brunson. "From Rags to Ragtime; a Eulogy," *Jazz Report* 5/5 (1967):5–6.

———. "The Ragtime Kid," *Jazz Report* 6/1 (1967): 7–12. Abridged reprint in Hasse, John, *Ragtime: Its History, Composers, and Music*. New York: Schirmer Books, 1985:146–153.

Carew, Roy. "Those Days Are Not Gone Forever," *Playback* 2 (July 1949):6.

———. "New Orleans Recollections," *Record Changer* (February 1943):28–29. Reprint in *Record Changer* (July 1947):9.

Castle, Irene and Vernon. *Modern Dancing*. New York: Harper and Bros. Publishers, 1914.

Charters, Ann R. Danberg. "Negro Folk Elements in Classic Ragtime." *Ethnomusicology* 5/3 (September 1961):174–83.

Charters, Ann (comp.). *The Ragtime Songbook*. New York: Oak Publications, 1965.

Christensen, Axel. *Christensen's Rag-Time Instruction Book for Piano*. Chicago: Axel Christensen, 1909.

———. "Questions and Answers," *Christensen's Ragtime Review* 1/15 (May 1915):18.

———. "The Popularity of Ragtime," *Christensen's Ragtime Review* No. 1 (December 1914):2.

———. "Tone and Touch For Ragtime," *Ragtime Review* 1/7 (July 1915):5.

Creighton, Norman. "Whatever Happened to Harry Thomas?", *The Atlantic Advocate* (September 1963):33–40.

"Dance Puzzle Stirs Teachers to Action," *New York Times* (20 April 1914):9.

Davin, T. "Conversations With James P. Johnson," *Jazz Review* 2 (June 1959): 14–17; 2 (July 1959):10–13; 2 (August 1959):13–15; 2 (September 1959):26–27; 3 (March/April 1960):10–13. Reprinted in Hasse, John, *Ragtime: Its History, Composers, and Music*. New York: Schirmer Books, 1985.

Deveaux, Scott and William Kenney. *The Music of James Scott*. Washington, D.C.: Smithsonian Institution Press, 1993.

Floyd, Samuel A. and M. J. Reisser. "Social Dance Music of Black Composers in the Nineteenth-Century and the Emergence of Classic Ragtime," *The Black Perspective in Music* 8 (1980):161–193.

Gammond, Peter. *Scott Joplin and the Ragtime Era*. London: Angus and Robertson, 1975.

Goodrich, A. J. "Syncopated Rhythm vs. Ragtime," *Musician* 6 (November 1901):336.

Harney, Benjamin. *Ben Harney's Ragtime Instructor*. New York: M. Witmark and Sons; Chicago: Sol Bloom, 1897.

Hasse, John Edward. *Ragtime: Its History, Composition, and Music.* New York: Schirmer Books, 1985.

———. "The Study of Ragtime; a Review and a Preview," in *Discourse in Ethnomusicology,* ed. Caroline Card. Bloomington: Indiana University Ethnomusicology Publications Group, 1978:161–190.

Heermans, Jerry. "Mike Bernard: The Ragtime King," *Rag Times* (November 1972):6–8.

Jasen, David A. and Trebor Jay Tichenor. *Rags and Ragtime: A Musical History.* New York: Seabury Press, 1978.

———. "Ragtime Explained," *Storyville* 37 (October–November 1971):4–7.

Jasen, David A. (comp.). *Ragtime Gems: Original Sheet Music for 25 Ragtime Classics.* New York: Dover Publications, Inc., 1986.

Johnson, James Rosamond. "Why They Call American Music Ragtime," reprinted in *The Black Perspective in Music* 4/2 (July 1976).

Johnson, James Weldon. *The Autobiography of an Ex-Colored Man.* Boston: Sherman, French, and Co., 1912.

Joyner, David. *Southern Ragtime and Its Transition to the Published Blues.* Ph.D. dissertation, Tennessee, Memphis State University, 1986.

Kendall, Elizabeth. *Where She Danced.* New York: Alfred A. Knopf, 1979.

Klaphake, Lillian Rose. *Improved Rapid System of Ragtime Piano Playing.* Cincinnati: Cincinnati School of Popular Music, 1910.

Lawrence, Vera Brodsky, ed. *The Collected Works of Scott Joplin.* New York: New York Public Library, 1971.

Mitchell, Bill. "Maple Leaf Rag on Records," *Rag Times* 1 (September 1967).

Moderwell, Hiram K. "American Ragtime," *New Republic* 4 (16 October 1915):284–286.

Montgomery, Michael. "A Visit With Joe Lamb," *Jazz Report* (December 1957).

Morath, Max. "First There Was Ragtime," *Jazz Report* 2 (January 1962):8–9.

———. *Guide to Ragtime.* New York: Hollis Music, 1964.

———. "Ragtime-Folk Music of the City," *Music Journal* 22 (November 1964):29–30, 64–65.

Nadeau, Roland. "The Grace and Beauty of Classic Rags," in J. E. Hasse, *Ragtime: Its History, Composition, and Music.* Reprinted from *Music Educators' Journal* 59 (April 1973):57–64.

Newberger, Eli H. "The Transition from Ragtime to Improvised Piano Style," *Journal of Jazz Studies* 3/2 (Spring 1976):3–18.

"Origin of Rag-Time," *Brainard's Musical World* 1 (Autumn 1896):6.

"Origin of Rag-Time," *Metronome* 17 (August 1901):7.

"Origin of Rag-Time," *The New York Times* (23 March 1924): Part 9, 2.

Perry, Edward Baxter. "Ragging Good Music," *Etude* 36 (June 1918):372.

"Rag-Time," *Musician* 5 (March 1900):83.

"Ragtime," *Outlook* 104 (24 May 1913):137.

"Ragtime as a Source of National Music," *Musical America* 17 (15 February 1913):37.

"Ragtime Music (Invented in St. Louis) Is Dead," *St. Louis Post-Dispatch* (22 October 1901):1.

"Ragtime Piano Era in St. Louis Recalled in Jazz Course Here: Charley Thompson Tells Class of Competing With Other Top Pianists of That Time," *St. Louis Post-Dispatch* (1 March 1956).

Rose, Al. *Eubie Blake*. New York: Schirmer, 1979.

"St. Louis Just a Ragtime City," *St. Louis Post-Dispatch* (22 October 1901):1.

Schafer, William J. and Johannes Riedel. *The Art of Ragtime*. New York: Da Capo Press, 1973. Reprinted 1977.

Simms, B. D. and Ernest Borneman. "Ragtime History and Analysis." *Record Changer* 4 (October 1945):8.

Smith, Willie "The Lion," *Music on My Mind: The Memoirs of an American Pianist*. George Hoefer, ed. Garden City, New York: Doubleday, 1964.

"Some Hints on Playing Ragtime," *Cadenza* 20/6 (November 1913):11.

Stearns. Marshall and Jean. *Jazz Dance*. New York: MacMillan, 1968.

"Ted Snyder Talks About the Old Days," *Metronome Orchestral Monthly* (1923). Reprint *Rag Times* 10 (September 1976):4–5.

Thompson, Kay C. "Early Cake Walks: The Roots of Ragtime., *Jazz Journal* (1952).

———. "Reminiscing in Ragtime: An Interview with Brun Campbell." *Jazz Journal* 3 (April 1950):4–5.

Tichenor, Trebor Jay. " 'The Real Thing' as Recalled by Charles Thompson," *Ragtime Review* 2 (April 1963):5–6. Reprinted in *Rag Times* 5 (November 1971):3–4.

———. "Ragtime in St. Louis," *Black Music Research Bulletin* 10/2 (Fall 1988):3–5.

———. *Ragtime Rarities: Complete Original Music for 63 Piano Rags*. New York: Dover Publications, Inc., 1975.

Tick, Judith. "Ragtime and the Music of Charles Ives," *Current Musicology* 18 (1974):105–113.

"To Jazz or to Rag," *Literary Digest* 73 (6 May 1922):37.

VanGilder, Marvin. "He Remembers James Scott," *Rag Times* 12 (September 1978):1.

Waldo, Terry. *This is Ragtime*. New York: Hawthorne Books, 1976.

Winn, Edward R. "Ragtime Piano Playing," *Cadenza* 21–23 (March 1915–October 1916).

————. *How to Play Ragtime (Uneven Rhythm)*. Edward R. Winn, 1915. Reprinted New York: Jerry Vogel Music Co.

Zimmerman, Dick. "Joe Jordan and Scott Joplin," *Rag Times* 2 (November 1968):5.

————. "A Visit With Joe Jordan," *Rag Times* 2 (September 1968):6.

————. "The Original Maple Leaf Club," *Rag Times* 8 (May 1974):3.

Discographies and Bibliographies

Blesh, Rudi, and Harriet Janis. *They All Played Ragtime: The True Story of an American Music*. New York: Alfred A. Knopf, 1950. Reprint, 4th ed. Oak Press, 1971.

Carey, David. "A Listing of Ragtime Recordings," *Jazz Journal* 3 (February 1950).

Jasen, David A. *Recorded Ragtime, 1897–1958*. Hamden: Archon Books, 1973.

Jasen, David A., and Trebor Jay Tichenor. *Rags and Ragtime: A Musical History*. New York: Seabury Press, 1978.

Laird, Ross. *Tantalizing Tingles: A Discography of Early Ragtime, Jazz, and Novelty Syncopated Piano Recordings, 1889–1934*. Westport, CT: Greenwood Press, 1995.

McCarthy, Albert J. "Early Piano Jazz and Ragtime Played on Piano Rolls," *Jazz Monthly* 185 (July 1970).

Rogers, Charles Payne. "Discography of Ragtime Recordings," *Jazz Forum* 4 (April 1947).

Rust, Brian A. L. *Complete Entertainment Discography from the Mid-1890's–1942*. New Rochelle, NY: Arlington House Publishers, 1983.

————. "Ragtime on Records," *Storyville* 27 (February/March 1970):110–113.

Schafer, William J. and Johannes Riedel. *The Art of Ragtime*. New York: Da Capo Press, 1973. Reprint, 1977.

Walker, Edward Samuel. "Ragtime and Jazz on Cylinders," *Jazz Monthly* (December 1970).

————. "Piano Rolls on the Phonograph," *Jazz Report* 1/5–6 (1968–1969).

CHAPTER 3

Mapping the Blues Genes
Technological, Economic, and Social Strands—A Spectral Analysis

RAYMOND E. DESSY

The dead tan odor of oxidizing paper crawled down my throat; disintegrating, crackling yellow fragments filled my fingerprints; and fading bleached colors stained my eyes. The collection of music scores, so lovingly husbanded, was slowly vanishing in the heat and humidity of the Garden District of New Orleans. It will not survive the end of the century in which it all began. A vibrant, virile music coupled with an earthy poetry born of soul and sorrow would vanish, to live only as vibrations in the air from the thousands of recordings that listeners collected, rerecorded, anthologized, discographized, and eulogized. But this music has a potency that has left a trail around the globe, and even floods the World Wide Web with homepages of praise, adoration, and fanaticism. The blues! Listen to what one African-American writes:

> It is the blues
> crawling over evening for a feast.
> Nobody hears my dungeon screams
>   as loneliness tap-dances inside my skull.
> The windmill of moans churns
>   and the long gulf of pain stretches in veins. . . .
> It is the blues / lowdown in evil.
> Sending their spikes through teeth and spines.
> The upset stomach of dreams / dizzy and longing for rest. . . .
> It is the blues. The long road / crooked with yesterday's steps
>   and zigzagging with tomorrow's trails.
> The wandering journey through blistered feet. It is the blues.
> —Sterling Plumpp (1985)[1]

This brief tour of early blues starts with the obligatory "guessistory" of the origins, passes through a somewhat irreverent analysis of its maturation, and ends with a more detailed reprise. The route is marked with appropriate signs.[2] The road explores the synchronicity among various blues forms, technology, the marketplace, politics, and society that made the music.

BIG ROAD BLUES

The blues are a century old, and a century young. They are a crop that grew well in the fertile Mississippi Delta from seeds that were brought from Africa, nurtured by the sweat and sadness of an uprooted people who sang, stomped, and strummed on the only instruments allowed. Like the Didjeridu, they are a much more complex medium than a first glance conveys. Even the name has an enigmatic aspect. Examine the *Oxford English Dictionary* for usages:

Is the root within the mysterious plasma of a flame as some have suggested:

> The Lights burne blew! It is now dead midnight. (Shakespeare, *Richard III*, V.iii.180)

> Ribands black and candles blue; For him that was of men most true. (Beaumont and Fletcher, *The Knight of the Burning Pestle,* 1611)

> That most wise and solid suggestion, that when the candles burn blue the Devil is in the room. (Defoe, *History of the Devil,* 1739)

Or does it lie in some mysterious festering of the soul:

> Great panic exists here, and even the knowing ones . . . look very pale and blue. (Disraeli, in a letter to his sister, 1886)

> We encounter . . . the miserable Dr. Blandling in what is called . . . a blue funk. (*Saturday Review* [23 November 1861])

> I'm not a bit blue over the prospect. (*Harper's Magazine* [March 1883])

Whatever the source, by the beginning of this century "blues" was a term in common use by African-Americans:

> Standin' at de winder, Feelin' kind o' glum,
> Listenin' to de raindrops, Play de kettle drum,
> Lookin' crost de medders, Swimmin' lak a sea;
> Lawd 'a' mussy on us, What's de good o' me?
>
> Mandy, bring my banjo, Bring de chillen in,
> Come in f'om de kitchen, I feel sick ez sin.
> Call in Uncle Isaac, Call Aunt Hannah, too,
> Tain't no use in talkin', Chile, I's sholy blue.
> —Paul Dunbar (1872–1906)[3]

The word, even the written word, seemed a natural paint for the songs that grew in the Delta, and created a family that eventually "covered the Earth."

But why try to capture on paper something that, by its very nature, does not fit on staves or pages? The aural media of records and CDs might seem a better home. It is not simply because it is there; it is because we need to have it here—to have the music and lyrics before our eyes so one can create customized variations. The blues are a quintessential personal experience. The song is never the same thing twice. It flickers in the shadow of our emotions, and flames when exposed to our fears.

THE PLACE

Drained and cleared just before the Civil War, the Mississippi Delta, a flat, black expanse of alluvium stretching from Memphis to Vicksburg, and bounded on the west by the Mississippi River and on the East by the Yazoo, is now split by Highway 61. The country, Delta, or folk blues that grew here migrated along the highways and rails to become the city or urban blues. It spread to Chicago, Texas and West Coast blues. It infused jazz, and its genes are found in rhythm-and-blues and country music. Our mapping will be limited to the early years, the first thirty years of this century. It will focus not on the people, whose memories have been enlarged to legends, but on the simple words and music that need no idolatry.

THE HISTORY

The Senegambia slave coast in Africa was dry, and had no great forests. Instead of the great wooden drums found further south, there was a wealth of stringed instruments, ranging from one-stringed gourd fiddles to two- to four-stringed guitarlike lutes. Because of close contact with the Berber and Arab cultures to the North there was a vocal tradition of solo singing and long melodic lines unusual in African music. Group singing was polyphonic and polyrhythmic. The harmony was not the resolving harmony of European music, but parallel melodies sung at intervals of a third, or a fourth and fifth, from each other. The latter two diodic harmonies did not mix with the former.[4]

Further south, in the Congo-Angola region, where Bantu and pygmy influence was felt, the choral music was among the most highly developed in Africa. Even in call/response singing the leader and chorus often overlapped. Solos, duets, and trios emerge from a dense choral background. Some vocal music included whooping (jumping an octave) and falsetto.

The music in general was participative, where anyone could join in response; or involved hocketing, where a multitude of one- or two-note parts blended in a complex polyphony. But paramount was the vocality of the music. The Yoruba and Akan people speak a pitch-tone language, like Chinese, in which a syllable's meaning depends upon pitch profile. In Chinese "ma" can mean "mother-in-law," "horse," and several other things. In the African pitch-tone languages, a dropping frequency often conveys deep emotion. In the African music flutes, drummers, xylophones, and partially vocalized dialogue entwined in figurative or literal speech patterns. Instrumentalists, especially flutists, sang or hummed while blowing to give voicelike character to their music. Voice masking, originating in ceremonial face masks, led to the incorporation of bizarre chest growls, and false bass notes. The rhythmic quality of "swing," not in the jazz sense, but of "a forward-propelling directionality," was prominent. All these are found in the blues.

> Woke up this mornin', with a sound in my head,
> Woke up to new sounds, rattlin' round in my head,
> Singing of things, things that were long, long dead.

THE BLENDING

All that merged and blended as the Africans were forcefully migrated to the American South. The musical strain was rehybridized with southern White religious songs, British folk music, and plantation orchestral themes. This, in turn, was reshaped by the need of spirituals to encourage the soul, worksongs to relieve drudgery, field shouts to communicate or relieve loneliness in the vast acreage, ring shouts for emotional Christian worship, jump-ups (short, unrelated lines over chorded accompaniment), narrative ballads, and a pervasive rhythmic percussion of hand, feet, and body. Not being hampered by keyboard instruments, the vocal tradition used intonations determined by natural vocal harmonic resonances.[5]

> Easy Rider, what's your music done?
> See See Rider, where's your music from?
> If I don't catch you, I'll have lost my fun.

THE EMERGENCE

By the end of the nineteenth century, an oral and aural tradition of narrative phrases and inexpensive, simple stringed musical accompaniment provided a pool from which talented performers could improvise music for themselves, and for others. The original country blues usually have as common features a twelve-measure AAB structure, bent or flattened blue notes, a shuffling triplet rhythm, a half-speaking vocal quality, a pervasive syncopation, and a special modality. The blues mode will not work without syncopation, and the twelve-measure scheme will not work without the blues mode. Among the framework of the mode are the flatted blue notes—a microtonal affair of a quarter tone or even a semitone as they must be on keyboard instruments. They may involve a glide either upward or downward, a slur between notes a semitone apart so that there are two blue notes, or even a microtonal shake. This, and the inherent vocalization of the melody line, make the genre a natural for the recorder, which can both play music and speak. The decreasing frequency of blue note use is the third, seventh, fifth (and the sixth). Any selection of the blue notes can be found mixed up with ordinary major intervals. They provide a kind of melodic instability, analogous to harmonic dissonance, which can be resolved.[6]

> That theory stuff's OK, a'hangin' on your wall,
> Oh Yeh, Theory's OK, a'hangin' on your bare wall,
> But theory's no good at all, when you get that Blue's call.

Why an awkward interval like the minor third comes so naturally to the human voice, and to the blues, is an interesting question. But it has precedent, such as in Gregorian Chant and schoolyard songs. The origin may lie in the filtering of musical notes by the basic formant frequencies of the vocal tract. Men, women, and children are a minor or a major third apart, respectively, in this regard. Some musicologists divide the blues melodic mode or scale into two tetrachords. In such models, the flatted seventh in the second tetrachord mirrors the flatted third in the first. Others examine tribal quartal and quintal harmonies, and note that fusion of two diodic forms produces a scale that contains all the blues notes. We'll let you decide, as others theorize, whether the origin of blue notes involved pentatonic African scales that didn't "fit" diatonic western scales. This speculation suggests that slaves, attempting to resolve the misfit, bent some notes out of shape to fuse the two. Whatever happened, worked.

> What my seat can't stand, Mama, my mind won't bear,
> What my mind don't stand, Mama, my ear won't hear,
> I like the blues, Mama, it's the theory I fear.

The center of gravity of the blues lies toward the beginning, in contrast to much Western music where it lies toward the end. The dropping frequency of the blue notes may reflect the tendency in pitch-tone languages in Africa to drop for conveyance of emotion. The blues mode is a ladder of thirds that often goes a third above the dominant, or a third below the tonic. Sometimes it does both in the same tune. In folk music, the contrast between relative major and minor is so slight that the modes almost fuse into one. There are some blues tunes that are entirely in the major, and others where every third is minor, and an infinite number of combinations in between. Both Cecil Sharp, the song-catcher of the Appalachians and England, and his contemporary, Percy Granger, commented on the "single loosely knit modal folk-song scale" of folk music from Great Britain and their exports to the southeastern United States. The blues is a unique American fusion about whose origins there is much confusion.

> It takes a long handled shovel, to dig a six foot hole,
> It takes a long handled hammer, to break a great big stone,
> It takes a long-winded theory to satisfy my soul.

THE RHYTHM

The African cross-rhythm influence on blues rhythm is often blatant, sometimes subtle. In the blues the distinction between simple and compound time breaks down, with duplets and triplets freely interspersed. Think about the hemiola of courant and galliard dances. It became concretized in the triple time of the waltz and minuet. But its relationships to complex African drum rhythms (1,2 / 1,2 / 1,2 / 1,2,3 / 1,2,3) is obvious. In the blues, the distinction is not so much between simple and compound, but between simple and [compound + simple]. It is uncommon for a common-time beat in the blues to go on without being disrupted by some irregular rhythm. Particularly at the end of phrases, four/four patterns will be broken by two/four or three/four patterns.

Syncopation methods may involve (1) a Scotch snap, creating an accent where it would not normally be found; (2) a note replaced with a rest; or (3) a premature accented note. These techniques are not exclusive to the blues, and may be found in British folk dance music, American banjo tunes, and Celtic music. The mixing and hybridization that took place in the planting fields as African slaves and immigrant indentured servants from the British Isles worked together can't be ignored. Just don't be afraid to lean (delay) your notes to get the rhythm you want, when you want it.

> I'm a long-line skinner, from places out West,
> I'm a long-line skinner, waitin' for a rest,
> Lookin' for the teacher, that'll teach me best.

MELODY AND ACCOMPANIMENT

The interaction between the singing and instrument, or in their alternation, is characteristic of the blues. The bluesman is not accompanied by the instrument; he sings with it. Therefore the metrical precision, the accuracy of the notes, and the melody as a whole are less important than the emotion of the synergy. Let yourself go in that relationship. Bend (flatten) the notes where you wish, lean (delay) them where you want, and let the harmony follow. This is in keeping with the blues' general independence of melody and accompaniment.

To many theorists, the "traditional" twelve measure blues instrumental bass accompaniment pattern of

I–IV–I–V–I

seems to resurrect memories of the Gregory Walker

I–IV–I–V : I–IV–I–V–I

pattern (ca. 1530), rather than the usual

I–IV–V–I

pattern of the European classics. The Walker pattern was probably kept alive by semiprofessional musicians who found audiences liked the potential to-and-fro pattern, and by the mid-1800s it was undergoing a revival. Many historians tie together Gregory Walker/blues pairs such as "Darling Nellie Gray"/"Railroad Bill," "Before I'd Be a Slave"/"Hattie Bell," and "Beckie Dead"/"Troubled in Mind." Others tie the basic harmony to the diodys in parallel fourths and fifths referred to earlier. But as the blues matured, increasingly complex chordal sequences appeared.

One is not dealing with classical harmonic progressions. Although African and European architectures fused in the blues, it's dangerous to analyze too deeply. Some authors have even examined the possibility of attempted incorporation of the Neapolitan or German augmented sixths into traditional blues! The concept of a double tonic suggests an actual modulation to a new key, and does give some idea of the abrupt nature of the changes often found. But van der Merwe prefers the term "shifting levels," because it is so vague and noncommittal. A shift of level is a more basic and primal matrix. Renaissance dance music used the technique, and it faded before the pressures of the Baroque. In the twentieth century, blues reinvented it for its own reasons (cf. boogie-woogie bass). As the song lyrics say, "Why they changed it I can't say, / Maybe they liked it better that way" (from "Istambul" by Kennedy and Simon). It's probably best to leave the theorists at this point, with their arguments of who was most adept to adopt or adapt, and just live and grow with the blues.

THE WORDS

A blues stanza consists of a rhymed couplet, each line divided by a caesura (strong pause) and end-stopped. The vocal part of the blues phrase (the call) generally ends before the phrase itself is completed. Inspirations for an improvised section (the response) may be drawn from the preceding melody, or involve entirely new material. Samuel Charters, the famous blues researcher, always implied the question, "Is poetry necessarily the work of a single mind?"[7] If so, the blues fail the criterion. But, if you accept folk artists who blend traditional phrases in new ways, listen to the moods and messages of these verses:

> When a woman gets the blues, she wrings her hands and cries,
> I say, when a women is blue, she pulls her hair and cries,
> But when a man gets the blues, he grabs a train and rides.[8]

You can lead a horse to water, can't make 'em drink,
Send your kids to school, but can't make 'em think,
Dig a pit for someone else, 2 to 1 you'll trip in it yourself.
(sung by Brownie McGhee, "Life is a Gamble")

The water keeps risin', families sinkin' down,
Fifty men and children, come to sink and drown,
I couldn't see nobody home, and was no one to be foun'.
(Charley Patton, 1927 Mississippi Flood,
"High Water Everywhere")

Early one mornin', just about half past three,
You done something, that's really worryin' me,
Come on Baby, take a little walk with me,
Back to the same old place, where we long to be.
(Robert Lockwood, "Take a Little Walk With Me")

Just listen to this song I'm singin brother, you know its true,
If you're black and got to work for a living, here's what people will say,
Now if you're white, you're all right, And if you're brown, stick around;
But if you're black, oh brother, Get back, get back, get back.
(Big Bill Broonzy, "Black, Brown, and White Blues")

Sleepy John Estes said: "The blues is a feeling. You got something happen to you, and then you can sing it off. It's a feeling that comes to you when there's anything you want to do and can't. And when you can sing it off in a song, that gives you a thrill."[9]

THIS HOUSE ON FIRE

The blues fire has been burning for a century, and its smoke permeates the air of American music. But the fog of time obscures our vision of the first two decades of the blues. Myth and reality mingle, history is continuously rewritten. From where does the excellent blues book, *This House on Fire,* derive its name? Is it from John Donne, which led to William Styron's book title *Set This House on Fire,* referring to the body? Does it come from Edward Taylor's poem?

An anvill Sparke, rose higher,
And in thy Temple falling,
Almost set this house on fire.[10]

Does it come from Bacon's comment, "It is the nature of extreme self-lovers, as they will set a house on fire, and it were but to roast their eggs"? Or, is it really from "Southern Blues" by Ma Rainey?

> House catch on fire, and ain't no water 'round,
> Throw your trunk out the window, buildin' burn on down.[11]

That's the gamut of the blues. It is easy to create a maze of truth in any desired image.

My first whiff of the psychogenic and addictive charm of the blues began in the musty rooms of the William Ransom Hogan Archives at Tulane University, where I held the sheet music for the Furber-Braham "Limehouse Blues," a titular blues published in 1922. This curious mixture of jazz, Dixie, and blues has since become a staple with John Coltrane, Stan Kenton's *Festschrift* Mellophonium Orchestra, and Bobby Byrne:

> Like a long, long sigh, Never go away;
> Queer sob sound, Sad, mad blues.

Our passion for sound, and sound recordings, tends to focus attention on a blues' life that begins with the first "race" recording in 1920 of "Crazy Blues," sung by Mamie Smith, and composed by Perry Bradford. Ralph Peer of Okeh records coined that term to include blues, gospel, jazz, and ragtime. Bessie Smith recorded "Down Hearted Blues" for Columbia in 1923, and Ma Rainey made her first cut that year of "Bo-Weavil Blues."[12] But the blues had obviously already painted the docklands of London, and Gershwin's *Rhapsody in Blue* was just a year away. The blues was poised to jump from the Mississippi Delta farmlands to the foyer of Carnegie Hall, where W. C. Handy and the Jubilee Singers played in 1928. What had seemingly so suddenly created such a matured and varied collection?

Some perspective: Scott Joplin wrote "Maple Leaf Rag" in 1899. America's popular music from 1900–1920, and its sheet music, was heavily populated by Black composers. The first jazz recording was made in 1917. Louis Armstrong, and the Hot Five, recorded for Okeh in 1925 with trumpet, clarinet, sax, trombone, and banjo! A lot of music and memories fed this blues fire. Copies of old Black newspapers advertising and reporting the blues were already beginning to yellow with age in 1923.

DEEP BLUES

Most views of the blues are a phantasmagoria of illusions painted with modern pastels: bone-weary, dusty, bib-overall clad performers with row crops for a background, sequin-gowned songstresses in a broken-down bar; a raunchy tune in a juke joint. It is, of course, a vibrant art form that is reborn every generation in new minds. Today's record and CD listeners, often focusing on the anguished or blatantly suggestive lyrics, don't think about the psychological distance between the performers and their original *live* audiences, a distance that might have made the lyrics close to humorous, and certainly the rhythm right for stompin'.

Our retrospective image, reflected from the spinning black disk, is usually of a blues canvas of realism that was bicolored; first with a ground color of lost loves, lost hopes, lost futures, and then with accentuating speckles and blobs of raunchy lyrics. Does it paint a perfect portrait of a people and an era before civil rights and equal opportunity, a Hogarthian image of the ills an insensitive society had created?

The race records' frat-house double entendres of squeezed lemons, broken yo-yos, black snakes, mountains, valleys, or jelly-rolls, may seem somewhat sophomoric by today's standards, but they caught someone's ear. The records appeared with Decca, Columbia, Paramount, and Victor labels, as well as those of Vocalion, Okeh, Bluebird, and Black Swan. Sometimes the titles were segregated into a different catalogue, sometimes they were at "the back of the bus," sometimes they were mixed with spirituals, sermons, and novelties. What was the origin of the themes, their distribution, and impact four generations ago? If such songs were exclusively from, prominent in, and characteristic of the Black culture, they risked being seen as reinforcement for the fears of sexual prowess, lasciviousness, and miscegenation that walked by night with the xenophobic Klan and lynch mobs. The teens were still a time of lynching and race riots. Perhaps they originated in the half-buzzed humor that seems funny the night before the morning after. Quite probably they were pieces inserted in the market stream for purchase inducing shock value. But, if so, who created the personae? One might ask the same question about Kiss, Megadeth, Skid Row, Pantera, or Marilyn Manson. Bessie Smith seems to have recorded anything she wanted, as did many of the most famous guitarists. They paid the piper and could play the tune. But, did the rest also lead, did they follow, or were they pushed?

Tolstoy (in *Anna Karenina*), as well as the Greeks who preceded him, pointed out that "happy families are all alike; every unhappy family is unhappy in its own way." The latter affords more permutations for pathos, plots, and songs. Society's tastebuds switch from Austen's *Emma* to Shakespeare's *Macbeth* (and back again) for many reasons. The brushes, pens, and tones of art follow the beat. Even country music now enfolds "Achy Breaky Heart" (Cyrus) and "The Whiskey Ain't Workin'" (Tritt). Timing for the blues was perfect. World War I resulted in some nine million dead, and approximately 125,000 American soldiers killed. It ended on the morbid note of the 1918–1919 Spanish Influenza pandemic that resulted in approximately 3 times as many deaths, some six hundred thousand in the United States. The shocks disturbed the nation's view of itself and of life.

Old social patterns were beginning to fracture. People of all colors were on the move. In Chicago, the population had increased by one-third since 1900, but the frustrated Black population had quadrupled. Part of society wanted a music of its own to claim. Part wanted a trip to a foreign country; and it didn't want to worry about its own problems, just listen to someone else's. The color of blues shifted with time and latitude: folk-like country blues, a synergistic fusion of instrument and voice; classic blues, entertaining, sophisticated music and lyrics supported by female vocalists and small bands; and city blues, slicker, harder, crueler. What determines what's popular to whom? The composers? The society? The publishers? It is possibly imprudent and unwise to totally ignore "business" and psychoanalyze blues performers and their society on the basis of lyrics, a time-warped social conscience, and a need to create a romantic vision. Simply put: What sells, plays. It's difficult to know what was in the minds of the very early blues composers and performers. Certainly one of the things in the minds of the record publishers was money. They were well aware of the moods, sensitivities, and mores of the period. Performers of a different race who could push the envelope were a license to stamp bestsellers for Blacks, and some Whites.

Statisticians become concerned when the sampled population is biased. Paul Oliver, and his colleagues, comment: "The roles of talent scouts and music salesmen . . . both in promoting and, by the limitations of their tastes and spheres of contact, in limiting the range of singers they put on wax, has only slowly been recognized."[13] The original mensuration and selection of blues materials generated a long stack of black dominoes, shellac records, that fed back music into the originating environment, changing the creation process by encouraging cloning of successes, and altering the memories of the creation and the creators. Even field studies affected the genre. The force of Heisenberg's Uncertainty Principle is inexorable: measuring something alters it. But the same authors then proceed to psychoanalyze a biased population:

> Throughout blues there runs a strong vein of complaint which sometimes finds expression in words of anger. Frequently it tends to be laconic or passive and occasionally has more than a note of self-pity. If blues was expressive of the human condition of individuals rather than an orchestration of protesting voices, it did not have much to say about personal relationships. Often chauvinistic and blatantly sexual, but gaining from its honesty and forthrightness, blues was affirmative in its glorification of the life-force. Probably three-quarters of recorded blues are about the relationship between the sexes, but the high proportion of these that convey sublimated aggression, bitterness, and disappointment suggests that they are symbolic of more profound psycho-social problems. Seldom does the blues have more than an oblique element of protest which is communicated more by canalizing frustration or anger into statements of broken relationships than through overt declarations of resistance or defiance. . . . Some . . . describe disasters or personal incidents; crime, prostitution, gambling, alcohol and imprisonment have always been popular themes. Many are aggressively sexual, and there is much . . . that is consciously and subconsciously symbolic of the (artist's) perception of his relationship with society.[14]

You can fill in the ellipses with the "blues," or equally with any of the following words—movies, TV, rock, heavy metal, or books. A differential diagnosis of the case isn't clear.

NOTHING BUT THE BLUES

Most histories of the blues are often monophonic paeans that ignore the counterpoint with social, technical, and political surroundings. The blues' beginnings in field shouts, "coon songs," gospel, and Black personal tragedy cannot be denied. The influx of Blacks into the Delta in the late 1800s and early 1900s created a musical mixing pot. Early performers, Black and White, exchanged techniques as they attempted to please their audiences. It involved an awkward triangle of musicians made up from suppressed slave descendants, a rising African-American middle class, and indigenous Whites.

In the possibly apocryphal 1902–1903 encounter at Tutwiler Station by Handy, when he first heard a "lean, loose-jointed Negro" play the music that would label him the "Father of the Blues," one can easily sense the class distinctions between skins of the same color: "His clothes were rags; his feet peeped out of his shoes. His face had on it some of the sadness of the ages."[15] At the same time, somewhat musically segregated White musicians played to racially segregated audiences. This musical potpourri slowly matured in the heat of the Delta sun. But then came change. Agricultural and industrial technology began to push and pull people off the land, and into the cities—first towns like Memphis, and then further north. Some say the music became more sophisticated; others feel it was stained by commercial exploitation.

The first Black-owned publishing company, N. Clark Smith & J. Berne Barbour, was established in 1903. By 1920 there were three more on Tin Pan Alley, including Perry Bradford. "Mayor Crump Blues" ("Mr. Crump Don't 'Low It") was written in 1909, and the derived "Memphis Blues" was published in 1912 by W. C. Handy. That was also the year of Leroy ("Lasses") White's "Nigger Blues" and Lloyd Garret's "Dallas Blues," both titular blues, as well as the Wand/Garrett twelve-bar "Dallas Blues." Some label the Ayer/Brown 1911 hit "Oh, You Beautiful Doll," with its opening twelve-measure format, as the first published blues. Handy's eclectic "St. Louis Blues" was a latecomer in 1914. And then came the Great War.

The need for manual labor to feed the factories led to further migration, and the American melting pot was given a big stir. Black and White were more strongly mixed, and a sharper grayness began to develop. After the Armistice, a heady sense of euphoric release and a desire for personal freedom swept the nation. Society moved at a dizzy pace, despite further tensions created by recession in the early 1920s. The technical world was ready to make things hum, sing, and dance.

The tinfoil phonograph cylinder of 1877 had, by the early 1900s, evolved into a plethora of platters and players: National Gramaphone (Berliner); Victor (Berliner, Johnson); National Phonograph (Edison); Columbia (Bell-Tainter); Vanitrolas; Zonophones; and Polly Portables. Berliner's hard rubber media gave way to Duranoid, a shellac-based plastic. At the turn of the century, Gramaphone's talent scout, Fred Gaisberg, had signed Caruso, and record-making turned serious. In 1917 the Original Dixieland Jazz Band cut its first record. Subsequently, the American Society of Composers, Authors, and Publishers (ASCAP) was formed assuring that someone would be paid for performances. By 1920 lapsing phonograph patents opened the doors to over two hundred "generic" manufacturers. The $75–150 sticker prices began to drop. By the mid-1920s, the box-lid stylus and paper diaphragm speakers, which replaced the large metal and paper horns, made the portable possible.[16]

The New Orleans sound walked in the door of White homes and became a national craze. Mark Thornton writes:

> National prohibition of alcohol (1920–1933)—the "noble experiment"—was undertaken to reduce crime and corruption, solve social problems, reduce the tax burden created by prisons and poorhouses, and improve health and hygiene in America. The results of that experiment clearly indicate that it was a miserable failure on all counts.[17]

Except one: It built a thriving speakeasy culture around jazzmen and bluesmen who brought their sound to Chicago. Record companies capitalized on the captive pool, producing label and generic race records that had the lure of skin color and racy tones. Electronic recording opened up the percussion section of the combo and sounds that used to make the stylus bounce could make the room hop. The treble and bass of recorded music improved.

In 1919 RCA was in a strong position in wireless communication. It held substantial patent rights from the Marconi Company, the DeForest patents of the triode valve, and the Westinghouse patents on heterodyne reception and regeneration. In 1916 its contracts manager, David Sarnoff, had proposed that stations be built for the purpose of transmitting speech and music, and that a radio music box be designed for sale to the general public. In 1920 Horne's Department Store in Pittsburgh began selling Army surplus wireless sets for $10. Westinghouse began mass production and signed on the air with KDKA. Soon the country was listening to more wireless stations than could fit in the bandwidth. By late 1922 there were over two hundred stations and approximately one million receivers in the United States and Canada. By 1924 there were more than fourteen hundred stations in operation in America. But spectrum crowding and business maneuvers darkened the airwaves, and by 1926 there were only approximately eight hundred, as NBC began network consolidation with twenty-five stations. In 1927 it split into the Red and Blue networks, and later started a third. Many homes had access to a radio, and airwaves are colorblind. Hear it, like it, buy it, play it. No wonder in 1927 almost one million phonographs were produced, and approximately one hundred million records sold.[18]

Entrepreneurs saw the opportunities in "cover" artists that swept record buyers into a feeding frenzy that followed certain selected performers. The blues bulge began with the female classic blues singers, but by 1928 Blind Lemon Jefferson, Papa Charlie Jackson, and Mississippi John Hurt had strummed their style and the guitar into the blues. Jackson recorded "Lawdy Lawdy Blues" for Paramount in 1924. The public, Black and White, became attuned to the blues. and scores of male performers were lured to the recording studios. Blind Lemon Jefferson certainly left some of his other musical material behind as he made his first trip to Chicago in 1926, where he cut "Long Lonesome Blues" and "Got the Blues" for Paramount. The Southern songsters' large and varied repertory was chopped to emphasize the blues. But what blues? Mississippi Delta blues—a symbiotic relationship between a harsh guttural guitar and raspy voice; East Texas blues—leaner guitar, breathier, higher voice, more percussive; and East Coast Piedmont blues—more complex, folk music fusion, ragtime stylings. The Delta and Texas styles migrated easily to the city blues. The moans became a flood; and then came the Great Depression. In 1932 only forty thousand phonographs were made, six million records sold. Another boom had become a bust. Free radio and the talkies (*The Jazz Singer,* 1929) became the popular escape. And then came another war.

The blues encysted, survived the 1940s, were revived in the 1960s, then rerevived once more. Along the way, Time's Arrow had lengthened the triangle of artisans into a prism, whose other end represented the various city and regional blues, titular blues, and all the blues' descendants. The faces of this triangular money prism mirrored changing tastes in popular music, the fiscal flights of record publishing houses, and the maw of the communications industries. Performers and songwriters are continuously specularly and diffusely reflected, refracted, bent, and shaped by passage through that prism. Market and money make the music, rather than the music making the market. Taste and technology do the rest. Electric guitars and amplifiers generated acoustic bursitis in the finger-picked runs and ragtime rhythms of Piedmont blues. The American Federation of Musicians' strike in 1942–1943, championed by James C. Petrillo, banned new commercial recording. When Victor and Columbia refused to pay American Federation of Musicians (AFM) royalties, they lost preeminence. The smaller companies that filled the vacuum stressed gospel and rhythm 'n' blues and the Piedmont sounds faded. The hues of the blues changed forever. Most artists change their style to meet the demands of a bulimic, but fickle, producer, press, and public. Big Bill

Broonzy couldn't or wouldn't, and paid the price. B. B. King did, and does, and gains the rewards; but you can occasionally see his soul in his eyes as he plays what is demanded. Time warps all music, but perception of the blues has also been molded by our minds and needs.

BLACK, BROWN, TAN, WHITE, AND GREEN

Jazz is largely an instrumental sound. It could, and did, migrate from Black to White quickly. The lyrical blues evolution proved more difficult. Most White performers originally lacked the experience and vocabulary, and couldn't or wouldn't make the journey. The blues were Black. The White Austin brothers' "Chattanooga Blues" (Columbia 1927) was issued under the race series, and the composers sought "insult" relief damages of $250,000.[19] Other White composers/performers chose blackface pseudonyms. It took World War II, social change, and a different name to create a new White blues minstrel show. With the White rediscovery of blues in the 1960s, the fantasia altered the blues sounds and memories drastically. Musty songs in the music bins, that would never have played well to solely Black audiences, were rehabilitated; and blues' origins were again resculpted. The color of money is always green, but the blues have many shades. Francis Davis comments:

> The blues revivalists of the civil rights era tended to be acoustic ideologues, white liberals in the awkward position of rejecting as tainted goods the amplified blues to which masses of black adults in rural as well as urban areas then still listened. The rigid, qualitative distinction drawn between "country" and ("city") blues must have amused such performers as Lightnin' Hopkins and John Lee Hooker, who were used to changing with the times and giving an audience whatever they perceived it to want. Ironically, by the end of the 1960s, (city) blues was all the rage. It was the country performers who were eclipsed. As Peter Guralnick points out in *Feel Like Going Home,* "To the record producers of the late 1950s teenagers had just about the same status as blacks thirty years earlier and just about the same appeal. They represented a huge but totally unpredictable market subject to the whims and taste and fancy no sane person could possibly predict." . . . You won't get many of them to admit it, but some of the idealistic white men who were going South to hunt for elderly blues singers must have been bitterly disappointed. . . . On records as young men, the singers of the twenties and thirties sounded like black men risking their necks (liter-

ally) to assert their right to be treated as men. . . . What a shock it must have been for the whites to realize that these were men who had survived as long as they had by saying as little as possible around white folks.[20]

NO SUCH THING AS THE BLUES

But we need heroes and heroines, and we create myths to perpetuate some lost part of our existence. To paraphrase Timberlake Wertenbaker: "Myths are oblique images of a yearned for truth reverberating through time."[21] Why else would we recast and deify the bluesmen and -women. Think about the truth and roles of Ned Kelly and Wyatt Earp, or George Custer, and "Chinese" Gordon. Explain Madonna and Michael Jackson. Try to find reality in the reworked histories and mysteries of Son House, Robert Johnson, or Leadbelly. The heroes and heroines of the blues' myths are unusual. Blemishes aren't hidden, they are enhanced. Tragedy is accentuated, made mysterious by convoluted, conflicting tales. A palpable sense of self-guilt often creeps into readers' minds. Perhaps that is the point. It all makes good reading, focuses the attention, and pulls you into the music. The lyrics, harmony, and persona become a synergistic trinity. Of late, it has often had a subliminal or overt social message.

How good were the early bluesmen and women? In his collected essays entitled *Full House,* Stephan J. Gould has written about the right-hand wall that represents the limit of human performance.[22] In areas where we are distant from that wall it is necessary to make temporally relative comparisons of individual achievement. We generally move closer to that wall as knowledge of an area accumulates. Our expectations of performance increase, transcendence is required, and comparisons of noncontemporary individuals gentler. With recent advances in biochemistry and genetics, for example, Pasteur might be labeled incompetent in comparison to Watson and Crick; in his own time Pasteur was beyond the cutting edge. With advances in biogenetics, Watson and Crick might be considered inferior to a brand new Ph.D. On the other hand, once we come within touching distance of the right-hand wall, there is hardly room for improvement. Performance variance decreases around the mean. This is certainly true in many sports, including baseball, male marathon running, and horse racing. In human activities the wall is reached as our understanding and control of the psychomotor and kinetic facets mature, and mind/body limits are reached. In musical performance, which has been near the wall for some time, fingers can only move so dexterously and fast, vocal expression and articulation have reached their limit. Each generation can have its "best," with rigorous absolute standards. Continuous transcendence is not demanded, repetition of maximal excellence is the goal. Evaluations between "the best" noncontemporaries are illusionary. Would you care to claim that Liszt was better than Gould? Or Biggs than Bach? Try comparing Robert Johnson with B. B. King or Eric Clapton.

Yet deification of music performers occurs. The phenomenon is not new. Lisztomania was certainly real. But new ingredients in the fame factory were introduced with the phonograph, radio, and TV. We can admit that blues performers' variance was greater in the early 1900s, although the mean hasn't shifted much. Certainly the luthier's art is currently better than it has ever been. We certainly recognize that a performer's prominence has increasingly become dictated less by open public evaluation and more by controlled and manipulated public exposure. But, the boundary between nostalgia and nostomania is as thin as that between fan and fanatic. Pantheons of the past and present are easy to erect, harder to deconstruct, particularly in popular music. There is no danger, however, unless we begin to believe our dreams.

THE BLUES LINE

Listening to an old 78 r.p.m. recording with all its surface noise in our personal surround-sound entertainment center, walkin' a CD that has more fidelity than it ought, or rompin' in a grassy bowl snaked with a Laocoon tangle of videocamera cables can't bring back what once was. Our skin is too thick, our ears too insensitive, our images too bright, our minds in a different age. I like to play solo blues on an alto recorder as a solitary escape, creating halcyon days. Is that a comfortable venue for the blues? Busking the blues in Bonn, Brussels, and Basel is as close as I can come to the real world of the early blues. The street crowds are a challenge. When the audience starts to fidgit, that's the time to switch it. And the blues always brings them back. The Freie Strasse in Basel, with francs at my feet. Crowds in the rue de l'Aspic in Nîmes, but no coins in the cup. It made me think of the white stubbled brown face reflecting from the wet cement during a cold autumn drizzle in New Orleans, his sax blowing cold blue blues. A man with no audience. A musician more skillful than I. What was he thinking? We can put our mind in grayscale mode, and try to sense in an Ansel Adams world what his blues mood might have been.

The blues notes had been strumming the courses of the twelve-stringed instrument called the musical staff for "quite a spell" before the Depression ended in another war. Where has all the music gone? Some of the primary sources lie partially catalogued in seminal collections such as the Hogan and the Performing Arts Collection of the Library of Congress. Superb transcriptions of the recorded works have been lovingly crafted by the Lomaxes (père et fils), Stefan Grossman, Jerry Silverman, and others. Publishing houses have carried the tune, particularly Hal Leonard, Creative Concepts, and Mel Bay. Sporadic specialty books focus on the heroes and heroines of the blues. For the rest, blow dust off the scattered piles on the floor, gently smooth the wrinkled pages, brush the fly-specks off the covers, and find the blues.

Digging out the old blues is an archeological expedition in melody and lyrics. Until multimedia books are common, we'll have to make do here with just some covers and words that typify the drifting blues. Let's examine some of the strata of those very early years.

LUCY'S BONES BLUES

In 1974 Johanson and Taieb unearthed the most complete *Australopithicus* skeleton yet found. Over forty percent of the skeletal framework is available. The bones belonged to a twenty-year-old female who died about three million years ago. She walked erect, but still retained arboreal abilities. She was named after the popular song "Lucy in the Sky with Diamonds."

> Oh, my music is black,
> Yeah, my music is tan,
> It'll catch the blues any which way it can.

The "Lucy's Bones" of the blues poses a more difficult problem, even though we are closer to the source. Bones survive; sounds fade in the air, paper crumbles, and memories alter. The blues' evolutionary highway is traveled by a triple helix of black, brown, and tan strands whose makeup was described earlier in this chapter: (1) the black songster strand reaching back to West Africa, (2) the growing Black middle-class stretching back for over a century, and (3) the mixed White immigrant American population. Historically the strands are held together by bonds that are sometimes strong, sometimes weak. The relative thickness, robustness, and contribution of each strand varies with time, and the helix takes on tertiary structures that kink and bend along the evolutionary highway, like the proline bends in proteins. A vehicle often out of control, the various blues strands veered back and forth across the racial centerline of musical evolution.

"BLACK-AND-TANS": A RECONSTRUCTION TERM FOR A MIXED BLACK AND WHITE CONSTITUENCY

Our historical dilemma would be solved if the musical equivalent of the Human Genome Project were possible, permitting a complete, week-by-week analysis of the strands. One valuable tool would be a melodic concordance of all the available scores, looking for the musical equivalent of DNA fingerprints among the notes. Science envisages a mapping of the sequence of the three nucleotide bases contained in the some one hundred thousand human genes, involving 10^{10} base pairs. A search involving groups made up from twelve notes in some fifty thousand tunes seems somewhat easier. A six-note sequence would have approximately three million combinations. Software approaches to the musical concordance are possible using a Standard Music Descriptor Language (SMDL). A prosodic verse analysis is within our reach as a result of work done for the emerging digital libraries.

Much of the raw material is available in various collections, but it is unfortunately not in electronic form. Some of the best collections, like submitted copyright materials, are a database management nightmare. Wayne Shirley, of the Library of Congress, has suggested that this source might be scanned for those blues entries showing "1C" notation (submitted but not printed), and "2C" notation (submitted and published).[23] One could then plot, graph, and statistically analyze structure and commercialization of the various blues types. Several of us have manually addressed such an attack and found it productive, but daunting. It is a technique that could fill in the existing time gap between the Jim Crow laws and Handy's reputed "first" publication of a blues tune, and possibly resolve the blues/ragtime coevolution. The fossil record is there, like the remains of *Australopithicus*. But what can be done about material that has vanished, leaving lacunae in the triple helix? The only available approach appears to be suggesting possible connections between extant musical materials and historical knowledge, similar to James Burke's *Connections*.[24]

SPECTRAL COLORS

It seems appropriate at this point to examine more closely the interlocking jigsaw puzzle of technological, societal, and political forces that blended the blues. A musicologist with a passion for blues history must follow a tortuous and disappointing path like the hero of *The Tales of Hoffmann.* The idealized love, or clarity, disappears in a collection of connections that are a snare of scores, poor libraries of lyrics, and lost soundbites. Much of the music wasn't published, many of the lyrics were modified after the fact, and our knowledge of *who* bought *what* sheet music or records *where,* and *who* listened to *what* music on *which* radio stations is incomplete.

Much of the material in this essay was originally collected as the nucleus of a semester-long Undergraduate Honors Colloquium involving students from the humanities, business, social and political science, and the physical sciences at Virginia Tech. It illustrates how tightly intertwined are society, technology, and music. It suggests how music courses can attract a diversity of students and create an historical awareness.

If myths are yearned for truths, imagine a student seminar that discusses the following mixed spectrum:

Were the blues all Black?
How green were the blues? (money and the blues)
Didn't the Whites hear the blues?
Did black, brown, tan, and white mix?
Were the blues "radio"-active?
How blue were the blues?

Some of these points have been reified by repetition, and *le brouillard* is thick. My spectral analysis will assemble data from secondary sources as well as newspaper reports extracted from samplings from the 1906–1928 period, with particular emphasis on the *Indianapolis Freeman* (1906–1916), the *Chicago Defender* (1921–1929), and *Billboard* (1915–1928). Some ten to fifteen percent of the issues were randomly selected. During these periods the national editions of these three weekly publications had, for various times, superb black music and stage critics: Sylvester Russell, Tony Langston, and J. A. Jackson, respectively. Four other influential critics were concurrent: Romeo Dougherty of the *Amsterdam News,* Lester Walton of the *New York Age,* W. E. B. DuBois of *Crisis,* and Theophilus Lewis of the *Messenger.*

The attitudes of these and other critics towards "taste" and intra- and interracial matters were often subtly different, but those of Lewis were unique. He advocated low-down theater for lower-class Black audiences. Anthony Hill has described him nicely: "He recognized the promiscuity of the Roaring Twenties might be temporary, so he wanted to take advantage of it."[25] Lewis' views make interesting reading, and are applicable to certain classes of music and people today.[26] These views were antithetical to those of his compatriots, who are quoted below. The filtering action of the more conservative elements certainly affected what passed to the printed page and may paint a cloud over our perception.

Black, White: The perceived musical elements associated with White ballads and English/Scottish folk tunes in early blues is recognized. Many workers have commented that the small holdings in the Eastern Piedmont would have encouraged twining of the Black and tan strands. Cowley, Lornell, and Spottswood[27] have discussed similarities with West Indian ballad structure evolution, and how a glissade to the blues might have been accomplished. The triangular trade of "the peculiar institution" would support such a view. West African slaves were commonly seasoned in the Caribbean before transport to the United States. Songs like "Aurore Pradere" and "Oh Graveyard!" might be considered an example of "Bluesopithicus."

> I know moonlight, I know starlight. I lay dis body down
> I walk in de moonlight, I walk in de starlight, I lay dis body down
> An' my soul an' your soul will meet in de day,
>   When we lay dis body down.[28]

A typical Anglo-Scottish folk song predecessor might be the traditional Scotch dirge sung by Laurel Massé, formerly of Manhattan Transfer:

> Here I am in sorrow, Here I am in pain;
> Here I am in ruin, Here I am in shame;
> I am left so forlorn, please come encircle me.[29]

Another set of bones—ragtime—started as a random collection of syncopated themes. As it evolved, march and old-world dance materials were absorbed. Three or four themes might be involved, each played and repeated with embellishments, before others entered. The concept is nondevelopmental in the classical sense, and does not involve the improvisation on a theme of jazz. Ragtime was the musical language for the two decades straddling the century mark.[30]

By 1910 everything that was syncopated was called a rag. Sylvester Russell of the *Freeman* described its origin in his year-in-review column of 1908: "The original two-step music of broken-time played without tuition to undeveloped buck and wing dancing by the slaves created the music now called rag-time."[31] It therefore wouldn't be surprising to find rags and blues mixed; Van der Merwe has published a fascinating interpretation of this possibility.[32] In 1896 Ben Harney introduced New York's ragtime craze with "You've Been a Good Old Wagon but You've Done Broke Down" and "Mister Johnson." "Old Wagon" is related to "Mister Frog," dating back before 1880. "Mister Johnson" is related to "Pretty Polly," supporting the contention that Anglo-American song types crept in and out of the early African American repertory. "Mister Johnson" is "a folk tune turning into a twelve-bar blues."[33]

"Harney's rags were only part of a general folk influx of the time. The middle classes neither knew nor cared whether they got their Scotch snaps or pentatonic figures from the black or the Irish." The bluesy element in rags grew steadily. Indeed there are two that some consider the first of the published proto-blues.[34] In Maggio's "I Got the Blues" (1908), a twelve-bar blues in G Major is followed by a section in G minor, ending with a rag riff (see Figure 3.1). Chapman and Smith's "One O' Those Things" (1904) is an earlier blues/rag mix (see Figure 3.2). White's "Original Chicago Blues" (1915) is a later blues/rag amalgam, as is "The Memphis Blues." The tempo of the early rags was much slower than the later virtuoso pieces, as the playing instructions on many of the above mentioned scores indicate. White and Black mind's-ear views of the musical strains were different, but there was a mixed gene pool.

White/Black: In the Delta country the strands separated in the post-bellum period, encouraging a growing individualism in what became "Black blues." This separation would have been accentuated by the tragedies of the Jim Crow laws. Named for an antebellum minstrel show character, these laws were late nineteenth-century statutes passed by legislatures in the southern states that created a racial caste system in the United States. In 1883 the Supreme Court was inclined to agree with White supremacist thinking, and declared the Civil Rights Act of 1875 unconstitutional. In 1896 the Court legitimized the "separate but equal" concept in the case of Plessy v. Ferguson.[35]

During the period 1903–1910, field studies by "song-catchers" E. C. Perrow and H. Odum in Mississippi, and J. Lomax and W. Gates in

I Got The Blues.

A. MAGGIO.

Figure 3.1. A. Maggio, *I Got the Blues* (1908), first page.

Figure 3.2. James Chapman and LeRoy Smith, *One o' Them Things?* (1904), first page.

Texas, found examples of what would eventually be recognized as proto-blues. Many of the lyrics they collected then later turned up on blues records.[36] Bessie Smith and W. C. Handy both reported a new musical sound in the South around 1903. The brown strand of the triple helix drove developing titular blues toward the White side of the highway as the music became popular, appearing in sheet music in the early teens. Sheet music implies a readership with money to spend for instruments and tutelage. "Baby Seal Blues," "Kansas City Blues," and "Dallas Blues" helped spread the blues news toward the darker strands.

Technology, biology, and politics all conspired to change the Black strand in the years between 1917 and 1923.[37] The boll weevil munched its way across the cotton plantations, forcing workers to the cities. By 1908 state legislatures were asking for federal aid to help farmers combat the menace. By 1920 cotton plantations that had produced thousands of bales were producing a few hundred. It would be the mid-1920s before acreage yields would catch up with the preweevil days. The end of World War I brought European demand for cotton, and cotton prices rose, reviving the dream of fields of white gold that had made Mississippi fourth in per capita income before the Civil War. But the boll weevil bred, and the need for Black labor bottomed. The introduction of the International Harvester (IH) row crop tractor hastened the Black exodus. In 1924 IH introduced the first practical two-row row crop tractor. It had been field tested in 1923 to a very responsive audience. By 1928, that company had gained a fifty percent market share, preempting Ford's position in the field. By 1929, IH had a sixty percent share. From a high market share position of seventy-five percent in 1923, Ford sales dropped to a level where it was forced to shift manufacturing operations to Ireland and then to England. The IH tractor was a forward driving tricycle, with an arched rear axle giving a ground clearance of thirty inches. Its wheel spacing allowed it to straddle two forty-inch spaced crop rows, with the front wheel treading the empty space between rows. The unit could deliver 18 HP brake, and 9 HP draw-bar. It displaced both the horse and slave labor from the farm.[38]

Southern lynchings didn't help "keep 'em down on the farm." Lynchings continued after World War I at the following levels: in 1919 there were 76; in 1920, 53; in 1921, 59; in 1922, 51; and in 1923, 29.[39]

Between 1910 and 1920, approximately one-third of a million Black people moved north. In the next decade a larger number followed. Black workers in some of the northern industrialized areas began to have discretionary income for the first time, money to invest in music.

Blues and Green: Existing postwar overproduction of phonographs was exacerbated by the loss of patent control through the *Victor v. Starr* (the Second Court of Appeals, 1922) verdict, opening the market to low overhead companies.

> Victor and Columbia controlled all the patents for lateral (phonograph) recording, in which the needle moved from side to side in the groove. When Edison . . . decided to enter the disc business in 1912 he had no choice but to make "hill and dale" records, in which the needle moved vertically in the groove. Hill and dale records could not be played on Victor or Columbia gramaphones. . . . In 1918 Starr produced lateral-cut disks and Victor immediately brought suit for patent infringement. . . . Eventually the Court pronounced in favor of Starr. Any company was now free to make lateral-cut records.[40]

Columbia's sound ground down toward bankruptcy. Phonograph record marketing groups saw salvation in Black ethnic records at a time when the United States was experiencing an attack of isolationism and European immigration was restricted, eventually by a congressional bill fueled by eugenic pseudoscience. The growing urban black population was the ideal target for "race records." Many of the classic blues straddled the highway. The tensions created by the housing- and labor-induced race riots of the period increased the musical segregation of the harsher country blues.

The trade magazine *Talking Machine World* published an article in 1918 entitled "How Recognition of the Pride of the Race Will Increase Record Sales."[41] In a few years cuts of country and classic blues, sprinkled with the hot spices of bawdy, raunchy tunes, were tastelessly mixed with sermons and gospel. We know roughly how many of these records were sold, but not their demographics. Incidentally, the limitations of these early black platters may have affected the form and feel of the blues. Martin Williams has commented: "Traditionally the improvised music was played as long as the performer could come up with new improvisations. A ten-inch recording could accommodate about four blues stanzas."[42]

RCA took an abortive step toward using polyvinyl chloride for disks in 1932. It has excellent properties. The current phonograph arms were too heavy, however, and caused excessive wear. Shellac was eventually replaced by polyvinyl chloride (vinyl) around 1945 as lightweight pickups became widespread.[43]

Radio broadcasts from the Lyric Theatre in New Orleans in 1922 put Black music on the airwaves. Lonnie Johnson and Putney Dandridge sang blues over Chicago's WATM radio station, Robert Wilkin's aired the blues in Memphis, and Bessie Smith did radio spots in the cities where she performed. Dozens of reports of radio "active" blues airings are found in spot checks of the newspapers of the period. Many of these will be listed and discussed below. It would be nice to know the market penetration of this medium. Try phoning your favorite radio station to determine what music was played a month ago! How many people, and which ones, own copies of Oy music; how many heard it before the German government ban?

The two technologies, radio and phonograph, are synergistic, as disk jockeys (DJs) know. But in 1924 they collided. Victor's sales were down sixty percent, and Edison phonographs were down more than fifty percent. By 1924 there were an estimated three million radio sets in the United States and fourteen hundred stations. The AM band was approximately 500–1,500 KHz. With a modulation of 5,000 Hz, this band would permit only one hundred stations if all were capable of being heard across the United States. With fourteen hundred stations, even at reduced power, the early cacophony on the airwaves was jarring. By 1927 the Federal Communications Commission (FCC) was permitted to assign licenses and frequencies, and regulate power levels.

The world was tuning into radio because of its booming, brilliant sound. The first step for the phonograph's recovery was to introduce electronic recording, where a condenser microphone converted soundwaves into electrical currents that drove the electromechanical cutter of the master disk. The nature of the hearing process, combination tones, and auditory illusions will fill in lower fundamentals, but the timbre of the replayed sound was "metallic." Electronic recording extended the frequency range at both ends: 100–5,000 HZ (F_2–C_8+). At best, the acoustic recording process was limited to the range of 168–2,000 Hz (E_3–C_7). The pressed daughter records could be played on acoustic phonographs, but they often sounded too strident. One solution was a six-foot-long folded (reentrant) horn, and Victor won back part of its losses in late 1925 with the Orthophonic player. Clear sibilants and deep bases resulted. Brunswick produced the first all-electric system—turntable, pickup, amplifier, loudspeaker, and turntable—called the Panatrope, also in 1925–1926. The lateral motions of the stylus in the track created an electrical signal that was amplified, and then fed to an electromagnet at the base of a paper cone, causing it to vibrate in and out.[44]

Toward the end of the decade all the players were electrified, and some took the "brave" step of providing both the phonograph and radio in one housing. At first, however, this was just a shelf to hold someone else's radio set. In 1928, 250,000 phonograph-radios were produced that had a common amplifier. The home entertainment center was on its way.

Black, Brown, Tan, and White: Other colors besides the blues were changing too. In 1918, returning Black servicemen had "seen the elephant," or at least another part of the world. They chafed at their restricted degrees of freedom. When America declared war against Germany in April 1917, only a few Blacks were members of the standing army. The Selective Service Act, applying to all male citizens, led to the eventual induction of some 367,000 Negroes, thirty-one percent of those registered. Only twenty-six percent of the Whites registered were called. The Blacks served in segregated units, and many were assigned menial tasks. Many saw fighting, however, and the 369th was the first American infantry unit to reach the Rhine. The returning Black soldiers brought new experiences and changed attitudes with them. These altered the expectations of a race, and the nature of subsequent race riots in the United States.

Many of the Black veterans became discouraged by continuing racial discrimination. Some rallied around Marcus Garvey's red, black, and green banner: Back-to-Africa. Most struggled at their new home, unsatisfied with the "mind of the South." Race riots occurred in East St. Louis (1917), Houston, Texas (1917), Washington, D.C. (1919), and Chicago (1919), as well as five other cities in 1919.[45] Unemployment, housing, and insensitivity were the triggering issues. In the 1920s, large inward immigration of Blacks and mulattos from the West Indies occurred. Many had a good education, a history of position, and often professional experience. American Black society was changing; so was the White.

Supreme Court decisions were altering the horizon for African Americans. Voting rights (*Guinn v. United States,* 1915), housing rights (*Buchanan v. Warley,* 1917), and jury rights (*Moore v. Dempsey,* 1923) were doors slowly opening. Concurrently, Klan membership and activity increased in the postwar years, and by 1923 it had an estimated membership of approximately two million. Prohibition also opened up new venues. Although the red lights of Storyville in New Orleans and the Levee in Chicago were dead or dim, the vice district of Chicago—twenty square blocks harboring hundreds of saloons, concert halls, and brothels—seethed with activity. Chicago became the scene of the "black-and-tans," nightclubs that employed Blacks to entertain segregated audiences of Blacks and Whites. Chicago's Black Belt was now lit by artificial light, and the Black's own night was bright.

New York's Harlem, a high-density "suburban development" that was desperate for tenants, was seen as an opportunity by Black real estate agent Phillip Payton. It became *the* place. The Harlem renaissance was beginning and soon nightclubs hired Black entertainers to play jazz and blues to White audiences. The bejeweled and the befurred whites flocked to Harlem to hear the great black entertainers at Small's Paradise, Connie's Inn, and the Cotton Club. Some Harlem cabarets maintained a strict nonwhite policy, but many after-hour spots had no racial barriers.[46] "Rafe's Paradise in Atlantic City was a big club with mostly white patrons."[47]

Midnight rambles were common in the 1920s. The blues word was spreading, and it was country, classic, and city—blues hues serving Black, brown, and tan—as well as White. Newspaper reports of various types of contact suggest the stark picture painted of the blues/White segregation has been somewhat overstated. Segregated audiences, "separate but equal" shows, even mixed audiences are reported. Some typical reports appear below and others are appended.[48] Time and geography often hardened segregation, but entertainment helped soften the barriers.

> From an Indianapolis newspaper report: "Community conditions here are such that any colored show, albeit of indifferent merit, would at least make good. It stands to reason that a combo like The Smart Set would be a furor. . . . The audiences were not made up of a single class, thousands of whites jostled and elbowed their black neighbors trying to see what the company had to put on." [*Freeman*, 23 December 1906]

> Sylvester Russell discusses the negro race and the colored theater problem: "One glimpse . . . tells us conclusively that people have no special preference of color regarding places of amusement or performers. White people went to a colored man's theater and the colored man hired white performers to act upon his stage and a mixed race of people went to see the show, but mostly all colored people, because of the theater being located in a colored district. When a new theater was erected by white men in the same colored district, the colored people flocked to the white man's theater. . . . What people wanted was good accommodations, a good show for their money, and a reliable policy of admission. This they have succeeded in getting at the new Grand Theater,

where people can sit where they please, and where the color lines are obliterated." [*Freeman,* 11 May 1912]

A quote from William Allen White of the *Emporia Gazette:* "A Minstrel Show's Lesson—The obvious success of the show (at the Normal Theatre) proved that white people will accept at its true value any artistic offering coming from any kindred, any tribe on this terrestrial ball. The audience accepted the performance not in any patronizing way, not because it was given by colored people, but as a good show." [*Billboard,* 4 December 1920]

"The Sid Perrin's Co. played a special performance for whites after the usual show on Thanksgiving night at the Lyric Theatre New Orleans, and packed the house." [*Billboard,* 18 December 1920]

"The Page," J. A. Jackson: "Three cabarets in Harlem, while ostensibly colored, derive much of their patronage from Broadwayites, who motor to them rather than have the shows brought down town. . . . The practice of presenting midnight shows in otherwise strictly colored theatres in Washington, Indianapolis, Richmond, Cincinnati, and New Orleans and the successful tours of Negro companies of vaudeville artists headed by Mamie Smith and Ethel Waters are mentioned to show that the belated interest in the Negro performance is not local to Broadway." [*Billboard,* 5 August 1922]

"The custom of having special performances for whites originated at the Lyric Theatre in New Orleans. The practice soon became widespread. In 1923 Bessie Smith closed her Atlanta engagement with a midnight special for whites only."[49]

"There were nightly shows and Thursday nights were set aside for whites and coloreds at separate performances. A feature of the presentations were the 'Midnight Rambles'—late shows in which the blues were especially popular."[50]

Letters to Langston from the field are filled with information about vaudeville and comedy shows, and the blues: "Dear Friend, Am writing to inform you that Miss Sarah Martin, the Okeh record blues singer, is having a great success in the Southland. We played a midnight ramble at the Grand (Keith House) to a packed audience." [*Defender*, 10 March 1923]

At the Dreamland Cabaret in the mid-1920s "one could hear Ollie Powers singing with Mae Alix, and press on to the Monogram Theatre to catch Alberta Hunter from Memphis singing with Lovie Austin at the piano. Or there was the chance to hear Bertha 'Chippie' Hill with her abrasive voice singing with King Joe Oliver at the Palladium Dance Hall. Most of these spots were open to white people, and as yet they weren't eyed with the suspicion that they were slumming."[51]

From a report of Cyrena van Gordon, Chicago Civic Opera, who stated: "I would like to hear some real negro jazz." They went to the Palace Theatre on Beale Street, Memphis, and witnessed the performance of The Broadway Rastus Company, who were giving a midnight ramble exclusively for white people. [*Defender*, 7 March 1925]

Blue Blues: Who made some blues blue? How did their off-colors compare with those of other cultures? Were there clashes between Black classes? Newspaper reports of the era have a complex mousseline glass pattern.[52] Let's trace some trails.

The *Freeman* of 27 April 1912 contains a letter to the editor from Paul Carter of the Carter Trio, which discusses his analysis of the source of the "smutty and suggestive" in stage performances. He blames it on the audiences, and presents a theoretical dialogue as follows:

When a performer meets another that has played the theater he intends playing next week, he will ask how things are over there. This will be the answer 'Oh, they like a little smut and things with a double meaning. If you don't put it on you can't make it there.' He then says to himself, 'I guess I'll have to frame up some junk for that bunch.' He then lays aside his music for his regular opening, and when he gets to the theater for rehearsal he will say to the piano player, 'When I come on just play the blues.'

The letter coincides with the following report from the 12 March 1912 *Freeman:* "Baby Seals at the Monograph, Chicago, where Ada Banks sang her latest 'Honey Babe Hun.' Her 'Shake It Babe' was too risky in order to capture." Carter continues:

A great many of the colored manager's cater to only one class. I think
if they would cater to all classes, and demand nothing but up-to-date
acts on the bill, and train the patron in the same way, it would do away
with all the vulgar the performer has to do now to get by.... The
Carter Trio are now playing the Olio Theater in Louisville, and this
manager is a very nice gentleman, but must have had lots of troubles
with performers for in the dressing rooms are more rules printed than I
ever saw in a hotel—rules that are really very good—against fighting
and intoxication, etc. Had he not had trouble with some of them he
would not have those signs up. It is very often a disgrace to see some of
the things performed on the stage. There are young girls [illegible] attending these theaters, and when they see some of these things on the
stage it has a tendency to lead them away from home.[53]

The implied class clash is related to W. C. Handy's unusual comment that, "in a community of cultured white folks there will be found a
similar group of colored people."[54] Carter's letter began by focusing on
one element: the audience. It ends by talking about the performers and
their society. What do other reports have to say? The 21 March 1908
Freeman was sensitive to the issues involved:

Conduct of certain elements of colored patrons to the Park Theatre is
causing no little comment among the better classes of the race . . . this
theatre is the only one in the city allowing the colored people equal
privileges with the white.

The 13 August 1921 *Defender* continues the blue blues theme in one of
the many fascinating letters to Tony Langston:

The first thing a manager puts before us is "Hooten, have you a clean
act? I do not want any smut at all." Afterward it's grand to have him say
"Hooten, you have an act that is really appreciated, especially here
down in the South." Hooten and Hooten, Dreamland Theatre, San Antonio, Texas.

J. A. Jackson, in the "The Page" of the 5 August 1922 *Billboard,* comments:

The American Negro may be regarded precisely as is any other citizen
in the land. There are different types, grades, and classes; and they dif-

fer in degrees of wealth and intelligence. In New York there are two classes of colored entertainment seekers—the mass of workers who seek mediocre entertainment pretty much as do their white prototypes, and the group of intelligent people who shop for their amusement with a full purse, but decline to pay additional charges in the form of mental embarrassment and torture. . . .

The rapid increase of theatres catering strictly to colored patronage with almost all Negro talent has created a situation with some problems that concern the colored artist. To care for these matters, so distinctly different from those of the group playing on the circuits catering to the general public there has been organized the Colored Actors Union.

The 19 August 1922 *Billboard* reprinted a piece from *The Nation,* written by Oswald Garrison Villard, which described changes in other social groups in strong terms:

Berlin had earned the reputation before the war of being more degenerate than Paris. Today, both cities show with pitiful clearness the effect which war has upon womankind and womanhood. 70% of all the paper used in the production of German books is being used for off-color literature. These things . . . are more than ever being considered normal. . . . If one were to stray into six or seven of the plays running in Berlin and should see nothing else, one would be compelled to despair of Germany and believe her new found liberty has degenerated into disgusting indefensible license.

"The Page" of the 16 December 1922 *Billboard* continues:

Some few years back the Queen, a vaudeville house, educated its city with smut. The management used barrel-house acts and the better class of colored folks did not patronize this house. To see a clean show they were compelled to climb to the roof of the Loew or Keith vaudeville houses. But the fight for clean entertainment has been won by the stage manager and with the little help that I give. Acts playing the Queen (now) have to come clean or stay away.

And *Variety* for 2 December 1925 caustically notes:

Scot, Alan, and Lee "hot" singing trio (in *Plantation Review*) inclined to be suggestive in their maneuvers are adequately placed in this café. This is the sort of entertainment that pleases these patrons most.

It would seem that all elements bear the burden for blue blues; *plus ça change, plus ça même-chose.* Popular music becomes popular from the positive feedback in the incestuous circle of performer, audience, and society. Novelty fades fast. This year's fad is next year's failure. As any talentless artist knows, there is only one option: escalate the double entendre. Examine the recent Royal Academy of Arts and Brooklyn Museum exhibit *Sensation.* The piece *Holy Virgin Mary* was a likeness surrounded by dung, an escalation of a crucifix suspended in urine, which is an extension of Marcel Duchamp's signed urinal of 1917, exhibited as *Fountain.* Our view of the prurience of an age, however, also is possibly blurred by the screening process of historical preservation and the human lizard brain. The sensational is more readily preserved, more salaciously savored, and giggled about. Tom Ball summarizes the situation nicely in the forward to his 1995 collection *The Nasty Blues:*

> Within both schools of blues, classic and (country), artists soon began to push the envelope of "respectability." Ma Rainey recorded her (somewhat expurgated) version of "Shave 'Em Dry" in 1924, at which time Bessie Smith's "Nobody In Town Can Bake a Sweet Jelly Role Like Mine" had already been selling well for a year. But the phenomenon was not limited to the blues. As early as 1923 the FCC had already denied airplay to Gershwin's "Do It Again." Of course, the vaudeville tradition has always been far less than squeaky clean. The BBC banned scores of "offensive" records, including such classics as "I'm a Bear in a Lady's Boudoir" by Ukelele Ike, and other scorchers as "Nellie, The Nudist Queen" . . . "Let's All be Fairies," "A Guy What Takes His Time" by the inimitable Mae West, and virtually everything by Sophie Tucker. Country and Western was not without its risqué sense of humor. As early as 1931 the legendary Jimmie Rodgers (The Singing Brakeman) waxed a rude little piece entitled "What's It." Roy Acuff's first record, "When Lulu's Gone," was so offensive it had to be (re)issued.[55]

Many of the bawdy themes in blues were later picked up by White, rural "hillbilly" performers. There are scores of examples of White country hokum being adapted into blues. This racial cross-pollination of musical and lyrical ideas (at least among the working-class southern musicians) was more common than is generally perceived. White upper-classes ignored both traditions equally, and many upper-class Blacks disdained the blues out of concern that the content would contribute to racist stereotypes of Black "immorality." W. C. Handy complained in his autobiography about "the flock of lowdown dirty blues" recordings then currently in vogue: "Just plain smut."

But then, what *is* the blues? LeRoi Jones claims that "The classic blues singers brought the music as close to white America as it could get and still survive. But the music that resulted from this craze had little, if anything, to do with legitimate blues."[56] Who has the right to decide what is the color of the blues? 1920 ads for Pace and Handy's blues reads: "Don't be mislead by imitation blues when the real and original blues may be had from us for the asking" [*Billboard*, 6 November 1920]. A Black Swan Records ad of 1923 for the artist Josie Miles asks,

> Have you ever heard snatches of song sung by Negro section hands on Southern railroads? Do you recall how their plaintive melodies struck a responsive chord in you? How strongly contrasted are these songs springing from the depth of the laborer's soul, to the commonplace dance tunes that we are accustomed to call the blues. [*Defender*, 10 March 1923]

In 1997 Wayne Shirley asked, "What do you call blues—the music that Bessie Smith sang or that loud guitar sound?" Did anything like this academic question bother early blues performers? When it was suggested to him that the music might have been exploited, overused, Shirley's alternate interpretation of the question, implying exploitation of the people, led to the comment:

> That's a myth created by left wing card-carrying members of a self-serving group that feel comforted by such attitudes. Bessie Smith sang what she wanted to sing. Sometimes she didn't even bother to rehearse, as you can tell from some recordings.[57]

Whatever the blues is, we've deified it for a number of reasons: a sense of history and pride, a sense of humanity, or because it is just good listening. It is no coincidence that the White rediscovery of the blues in the 1960s coincided with the civil rights movement, and real or assumed guilt was one factor. It is equally disconcerting and disorienting to read polemics in blues publications and on the Web stating "White men— can't, shouldn't, or won't—play and sing the blues." It is likewise ludicrous that some modern critics refuse to review White performances because "they don't have the suffering in their souls" (cf. Blues World

Figure 3.3. A radio advertisement published in the *Chicago Defender* (1925).

home page: www.bluesworld.com). One wonders what they do with Dvořák or Marcia Ball. Perhaps Eastern European males and Cajun females don't count.

Radio-"Active" Blues: The phonograph certainly was the prime vector for transmission of the blues during the 1920s. But newspaper records suggest that the radio had more effect than has been suggested. By 1927 there were five million sets, and by the early 1930s some twenty million. Black newspapers often ran regular radio columns (see Figure 3.3). The technical level and longevity of the *Defender* column by Ulysses Coates, quoted extensively below, suggests there was a race audience:

"Once you have owned, used, and learned to appreciate a radio scrap book you will never be without one. A scrap book contains station information, technical data, etc." [*Defender,* 10 January 1925]

"If sets which use a variometer to tune the plate circuit fail to regenerate on the higher wavelengths a 25–35 turn honeycomb coil may be placed in series with the variometer to increase the inductance." [*Defender,* 17 January 1925]

An ad for the "Little Wonder Radio Set, complete with tube, $12.98. A one-tube 3 circuit receiving set. Darwal Corp., 799 Broadway, NY, NY." [*Defender,* 17 January 1925]

"Probably the simplest method for controlling regeneration in an RF set employing transformers for the interstage coupling is to use a potentiometer connected across the A battery with the lever connected to the grid return of the amplifier tube." [*Defender,* 28 March 1925]

"The present trend is toward sets using electric lighting current for both filament and plate voltages." [*Defender,* 15 January 1927]

And other newspaper reports suggest that there were indeed people listening.

From a review of Bessie Smith, Beale Street Palace, 1923. "The spirit of the Old South came up from Beale Street at 11 o'clock last night to give the world a concert of Negro folk songs that will be remembered by WMC (Memphis) as long as *midnight frolic* is broadcast from the roof of the Commercial Appeal (building). Bessie Smith . . . gave the air some currents that it will not forget as long as . . . Memphis has a Beale Street. Perhaps the greatest hit Bessie registered last night for WMC was 'Outside of That He's All Right With Me.' She repeated the number upon the request of a large number, who telephoned to the studio and wired from the Memphis territory." WMC was owned and operated by the Memphis Commercial Appeal, and the audience consisted for the most part of White southerners. The performance was repeated in February 1924. In March, the largest race record dealer in Pittsburgh sponsored a radio program on that city's WCAE during Bessie's engagement at the Lincoln and Star theaters.[58]

"Ethel Waters was the first colored entertainer to broadcast over the Times-Picayune radio station in New Orleans in 1923."[59]

WTAM, the *Cleveland Plain Dealer* broadcasting station, puts out an all colored program under the title of "A Night in Dixie." "Air fans have demanded more, and it has reached the point of being a regular event." [*Defender,* 17 January 1925]

"WGBS (NY) had Clarence Williams and his Blue Five performing with vocal assistance from Eva Taylor and Clarence Todd. . . . The opening number was 'Santa Claus Blues' . . . The song of twilight has been dispelled at last by the hilarious blues lights." [*Defender,* 17 January 1925]

"Fletcher Henderson dished out the usual Monday night assignment of syncopation from WHN." [*Billboard,* 8 December 1925]

"Mamie Smith, widely known blues singer, who is appearing at the Beale St. Palace Theatre, Memphis, will this week be heard over WMC radio." [*Billboard,* 18 December 1926]

"Velma Nally, blues singer, returned to Kansas City last week from an eight months tour of the Middle West. Miss Nally resumed her singing over WDAF The Kansas City Star's Station on July 10th." [*Billboard,* 21 July 1928]

"Smiling Billy's Boys play for the Kiwanians (Kinston, NC). The band often gives concerts over radio stations and broadcast Monday evening from station WPTF, Raleigh, NC." [*Defender,* 14 September 1929][60]

And there were other avenues open to advertise the blues:

> "Sarah Martin has the distinction of being the first colored woman to demonstrate songs in a store when she went onto McCrory's in New York boosting the recorded Clarence Williams numbers. Lucille Hageman's records are being featured with displays in department stores in New York and other metropolitan centers." [*Billboard*, 16 December 1922]

> "And Vaughn De Leath (the 'radio girl') sang hits of the day and classical blues over WJZ (1921)."[61]

These waves in the ether suggest that the commonly accepted distribution patterns of the blues might need to be reexamined.[62]

Olio: Paul Oliver has made a punning proposal for what he terms "Past recording and future research . . . Next Week, Sometime?"[63] But sometime may be equivalent to never, or impossible, particularly as the paper of the old blues scores oxidizes. Further research is needed on early sheet music, tracking of first-sale and subsequent distribution, early performances, and demographics. Lynn Abbot and Doug Seroff have recently made a bold step in exploring some of the sheet music and southern vaudeville areas in "They Cert'ly Sound Good to Me."[64]

Before the curtain falls, let's flip through the film of newspapers past, and taste the titles of blues scores, and the progression of the blues mood. These tantalizing reports shrilly ask more questions: "Where did all the sheet music go? Who played them? How common was White purchase of race records?" This potpourri contains many of the titles of songs collected in my own passionate search, a sentimental journey into a personal virtual reality.

> Beginning of a series of ads from Wm. Foster, State St., Chicago, advertising sheet music (15 cents each) for popular hits: "Monkey Rag," "Alexander's Rag Time Band," and "Honey Man," "Oh You Beautiful Doll," "Piano Man," "Undertaker Man," and "Stop Kickin' My Dog Around." [*Freeman*, 20 January 1912]

> May and May at the new Crown Garden: "String Beans has an improvement on the kinds of work he does over that of the others. His blues gets 'em, and his 'Balling the Jack' is his feature. The audience screams for more and he gives them more. At times the yelling was deafening." [*Freeman*, 17 January 1914]

"Prof. Eph Williams and the Silas Green Co., although not a gold band, is the feature of the street demonstrations, and stinging is the applause when they are through pealing forth the silvery strains of the 'Memphis Blues.' A bystander remarked, "Dey play d'em blues, dat's all.'" [*Freeman,* 21 February 1914]

Listing in *Billboard*'s "Song Hints" (Reliable Guide to the Best Songs in the Catalogs of the Leading Publishers): 'The Hesitating Blues' (Pace and Handy Music Co., Memphis, TN)—A hesitation novelty with ginger and go." [*Billboard,* 21 August 1915]

"Miss Lizzie Thompson . . . is stopping the show with the 'Hesitating Blues.'" [*Freeman,* 15 January 1916]

"'I've got the Army Blues,' a real distinctive novelty of the season. . . . The only question is whether a stage song will prove a real seller. . . . Jobbers are already ordering the number before it is in print." [*Billboard,* 15 July 1916]

In the Song Hits listings: "'The Blue Blues' (Francis Newman, Drumright, OK) Featured by Leroy 'Lasses' White; Take a tip, get it." [*Billboard,* 15 July 1916]

In the Song Hits listings: "'The German Blues,' 'It's Neutral' (Lewis Zeeler Music Co., Louisville, KY)—Best burlesque song on the boards." [*Billboard,* 28 October 1916]

The blues rained and reigned in the early 1920s. Tintinnabulous Tin Pan Alley had tinnitus as side-by-side ads for sheet music in the *Billboard* appear: for "Sweet Mama," a riot as a deep "dyed in the wool" blues, Jack Mills, NY, NY; for "Blue Law Sunday Blues," Triangle Music, NY, NY; and for "Dying With the Blues," Arrow Music Co., NY, NY. [*Billboard,* 11 December 1920][65]

The week following, an ad for sheet music from W. C. Handy, writer of "St. Louis Blues," "Memphis Blues," "Yellow Dog Blues," "Beale Street Blues," "Jogo Blues," "Long Gone," and "Shoeboot Serenade." The ad announced the publication of "Loveless Love" as well as "That Thing Called Love" and "Pee Gee Blues." [*Billboard,* 18 December 1920]

This collection, also in a single newspaper issue, featured ads for Mamie Smith's songs: "Don't Care Blues," "That Thing Called

Love," "You Can't Keep a Good Man Down," and "Crazy Blues (30 cents each—Perry Bradford Music Co., Broadway, NY); for GRS Rolls ($1.25), records ($1.25), for sheet music (30 cents) of "Loveless Love Blues" (Pace and Handy Music Co., W. 46th St., NY); and for Lucille Hageman, Colored contralto and the Blue Flame Syncopators: records, rolls and sheet music for "Arkansas Blues," "He's My Man," "Neglected Blues," "Jungle Blues," (Francis Clifford Music Publishing, Chicago), and sold at Williams and Piron (State St., Chicago), and the Vendome Music Shop (47 East 31st St., NY). [*Defender,* 2 April 1921]

A six-column-inch ad for Spencer Williams, and his music, including: "Paradise Blues," "Tishomingo Blues," "Yama Yama Blues," and "Meditation Blues, published variously by McKinley Co. (Chicago), Stern Co. (NY), and Shapiro and Bernstein (NY). [*Defender,* 16 April 1921]

By 1922 everyone was publishing sheet music. Thus ads appeared for "Houston Blues" and "Muscle Shoals Blues" from George Thomas Music Co., Chicago; for "Soldier Bonus Blues" from Randolph Music Co. (Wichita, KA); for "You Can Have Him, I Don't Want Him, Didn't Love Him Anyhow Blues" from Goodman and Rose (NY, NY); and for "Tropical Blues," Charles Roat Co. (Battle Creek MI). [*Billboard,* 5 August 1922]

Bessie Smith's White-only show at the "81" Decatur Street Theatre in Atlanta: "The program was greatly enjoyed by the white people who filled the house after the regular performance. . . . Few white homes are without her records. . . . A prominent white music dealer told a reporter of the Preston News that Bessie Smith's records actually outsell everything else in the catalog." [*Pittsburgh Courier,* 13 February 1924]

Musical scores were often sold at intermissions. At the Frolic Theatre, Birmingham, Alabama, in 1923, "Buzzing" Harris hawked the sheet music for Bessie Smith's "Gulf Coast Blues" in the aisles during intermissions.[66]

Ad for Bessie Smith's: "Sing 'Em Bessie," featuring "Cause They Sound Good To Me," "Sinful Blues," and "Hateful Blues" from Perry Bradford Music Publishing, 1547 Broadway, NY, NY. [*Defender,* 17 January 1925]

A SCRATCHED RECORD CURTAIN

Repetition, the talkies,[67] and then the Depression, drew the needle, scratchily, across the blues record for a while. Decline in discretionary money, and a sense of malaise, made the blues too real to hear with any comfort. In 1924 Jackson, on "The Page," wrote:

> There has been a recent falling off in the demand for blues singers, and there is a reason for it aside from the fact that the record companies have just about plugged these folks so persistently that the public is growing a bit tired of them. There is no mistaking the fact the audiences like the blues style of music. It is the vocal expression of their inner selves. The woman singers of the Race . . . have made fame and fortune for the record companies . . . and the girls, too, have fared well. . . . With the gates opened there came a flood. Every woman who could sing at all became obsessed with the desire to be recorded. The market was flooded with blues records. BUT—and a big BUT—they became a gang of imitators. To see one was to see them all. . . . a low blues number, a change to a slightly better dress while the usually mediocre pianist does a solo bit, then a *risqué* song about "Never Loved, but," with something about "another woman's man." Girls, get some originality about your presentation. [*Billboard,* 13 December 1924]

The male blues guitarists began to rewrite the records and left us "The meanest, moanin'est blues that ever tickled your ears." That phrase was first used in 1923 to describe Gladys Bryant, the Beale Street Mama, but times were changing.

> Listen here mama, I'll be good,
> Make your wine, cut your wood.
> When I do, it wouldn't do,
> I got another, and I don't want you.
> (Blind Lemon Jefferson, 1926)

But poignantly, prophetically, an ad in the 28 December 1928 *Defender,* reads: "Elzadie Robinson sings 'Arkansas Mill Blues'," with the lines:

> When I hear that whistle blow, ther'll be no more work for
>   that man of mine;
> The old pond dries up, the last steam blows the whistle,
> And everybody moves to a new place.

In nine months the stock market delivered the Depression.

Fortunately, the new place still had the blues. Unfortunately, to para-phrase a review of "Who Said Dixie," "When the Lord found out He made the best, He called it Dixie, then took a rest" [*Billboard,* 6 April 1918]. Would that the writers of "the blues" had decided to do what the Lord did." Finding scores is not too difficult; finding good ones is.[68] The multiple blues' tracks waxed and waned on technology, politics, and so-ciety; but they all eventually foundered due to overproduction, overexpo-sure, and overcropping. Records, radio, movies, TV, and CDs—all in their own time—discovered rapidly how to kill songs quickly.

> I want ev'ry bit of it or none at all
> Cause I don't like it second hand
> I want all your kisses now or none at all
> Give me lots of candy, hon, then love is grand
> Mama craves affection both night and day
> I don't like no two-time that is what I say
> I want ev'ry bit of it or none at all
> Cause I don't like it second hand, no
> I don't like it second hand.
> (Clarence Williams and Spencer Williams)[69]

And, as to authenticity, Big Bill Broonzy's standard reply, when asked about authenticity of his material, was: "I guess all songs is folk songs. I never heard no horse sing 'em."[70]

THE BLUES AS SUCH

The difficulty in spectrally analyzing the blues (so to speak) is that dif-fraction and refraction of history, and obsessions with oblique images of the past, make revisionism rife. The present is turbulent, the future dis-concerting; a self-defined past is more comforting. But, imagine if his-tory had been different! What if some mutation had occurred in the triple helix? What if the row tractor had been developed a decade earlier, accel-erating northern migration from the South, leapfrogging the critical country, classic, city dendritic period? What if electric guitars had been developed a decade later, letting the seminal Piedmont blues grow in strength? What if the Supreme Court had swung the other way in *Plessy v. Ferguson,* and the civil rights movement had immediately followed the race riots? What if the record industry had delayed electronic recording beyond 1925, and radio had become the preeminent distribution media?

And then, what if the AFM strike and ASCAP boycott had occurred a
decade earlier, ca. 1932, nucleating a rhythm 'n' blues with roots?[71] Finally, what if the motion picture industry had pressed full-length sound
productions in 1924—after all, in 1923 Lee De Forest's phonovision premiered a two-hour "talkie" at New York's Rivoli Theatre, including performances by Sissle and Blake. Whatever—we'd have to say: It Ain't
Our Blues.[72]

NOTES

[1]Sterling Plumpp, *Blues: The Story Always Untold* (Chicago: Another
Chicago Press, 1989):63.

[2]Some of the signposts are textual: many of the section headings are derived
from seminal reference works on the blues. Some are visual and faded with time.
Early blues sheet music and covers contribute conundrums about published blues
from 1901–1928. Is "I've Got De Blues" (Smith and Bowman, Lyceum 1901) really the first titular blues with "Blues" in the title? Such pieces as "Baby Seals
Blues," "Dallas Blues," "Memphis Blues," and "Jogo Blues" all jockey for a
blues starting position. "I'm Alabama Bound" may seem in a different race. Part
of a schizophrenic genre, some of the pieces are not blues at all. The Black
stereotype cover of "Original Chicago Blues" juxtaposes with the White stereotype figures featured on "Pensacola Blues" and "Jelly's Blues." Did White
graphic artists really have difficulty portraying Blacks in such milieux, or were
the pieces intended for Black and tan audiences? The earliest blues musical score
found to date (Maggio, "I Got the Blues," 1908) is a curious blend of blues and
ragtime. Is it early blues or late ragtime, or a fusion of styles? Puzzling social
themes are represented by cartoons and ads published in 1912 associated with
Baby F. Seals, one of the famous vaudeville and stage performers. The stereotyped cartoons by a Black artist about a Black performer ran in a black newspaper. Seals got his fame, but what strand did the *Freeman* portray? The radio ads
of 1925, and the reality of the boll weevil and row-crop tractor (1921–1924) represent technological and natural forces affecting the Blacks who formed the
blues, forces that have often been neglected in our mystification and mythifica-
tion of the blues and its people.

[3]Paul Dunbar, *Blues,* Chadwyk-Healey English Poetry Full-text Database.

[4]Peter van der Merwe, *Origins of the Popular Style* (Oxford: Clarendon
Press, 1992):88.

[5]The following are bibliographic references that are the best available in English: JoAnn Skowronski, *Black Music in America* (Metuchen, NJ: Scarecrow
Press, 1981); and Mary Hart, Brenda Eagles, and Lisa Haworth, *The Blues: A*

Bibliography (New York: Garland, 1989). Other useful general references have been absorbed over time, forming the mind's memory that supported the writing of the earlier parts of the essay. These include: Samuel Charters, *The Roots of the Blues* (New York: Da Capo Press, 1991); Gerard Herzhaft, *Encyclopedia of the Blues* (Fayetteville: University of Arkansas Press, 1992); Michael Harris, *The Rise of Gospel Blues* (New York: Oxford University Press, 1992); Robert Palmer, *Deep Blues* (New York: Viking Press, 1981); Bruce Cook, *Listen to the Blues* (New York: Scribners, 1973); Gunther Schuller, *Early Jazz* (New York: Oxford University Press, 1968); *Living Blues: The Journal of the American Blues Tradition,* Center for the Study of Southern Culture (University: University of Mississippi); Michael Taft, *Blues Lyric Poetry* (New York: Garland, 1983); Eric Sackheim, *The Blues Line: A Collection of Blues Lyrics* (New York: Grossman, 1969); Paul Oliver, *Blues Off the Record* (New York: Plenum, 1988); and Jeff Titon, *Early Downhome Blues* (Urbana: University of Illinois Press, 1977).

[6] Among other sources, see David Evans, *Big Road Blues* (New York: Da Capo Press, 1987); *Nothing But The Blues,* ed. Lawrence Cohn (New York: Abbeville Press, 1993); and Alan Lomax, *Land Where the Blues Began* (New York : Dell Publishing, 1995).

[7] Charters, *The Roots of the Blues:* 86.

[8] Unidentified. See the sources in Note 6 above.

[9] See the sources in Note 6 above.

[10] Craig Awmiller, *This House on Fire* (New York: Franklin Watts, 1996):52.

[11] Ibid.:58.

[12] Robert M. W. Dixon and John Godrich, *Recording the Blues* (New York: Stein and Day, 1970):126.

[13] Oliver, Max Harrison, and William Bolcom, *The New Grove Gospel, Blues, and Jazz* (New York: W.W. Norton, 1986):155.

[14] Ibid.:168–169.

[15] W. C. Handy, *Father of the Blues* (New York: Da Capo Press, 1985):75.

[16] See Roland Gelatt, *The Fabulous Phonograph* (New York: Macmillan, 1977); and Andre Millard, *America on Record* (Cambridge, UK: Cambridge University Press, 1995).

[17] http://www.cato.org/pubs/pas/pa-157es.html.

[18] http://www.mediahistory.com/time/alltime.html and http://ac.acusd.edu/History/recording/notes.html.

[19] Oliver, *The Story of the Blues* (New York, Penguin Books, 1972):97.

[20] Francis Davis, *The History of the Blues* (New York: Hyperion, 1995):127.

[21] Timberlake Wertenbaker, *The Love of the Nightingale* (New York: Dramatic Publishing, 1989):36.

[22] Stephan Gould, *Full House* (New York: Random House, 1996):129.

[23]Personal communication.

[24]James Burke, *Connections* (New York: Little, Brown, 1980); and the PBS-TV *Connections* (1979) and *Connections 2* series (1991).

[25]Anthony Hill, *Pages from the Harlem Renaissance* (New York: Peter Lang, 1996).

[26]http://www.bobwest.com/ncaat/anthill.html.

The Black critics' response to *Shuffle Along* indicate how difficult it is to grasp the origins of the suggestive sexual humor in the blues. Jackson, DuBois, and Lewis all had their own views of the appropriateness of double entendres, fast paced dancing and scantily clad girls. Lewis recognized the promiscuity of the Roaring Twenties, but his comments don't always ring true. "Reflect for a moment on the hard lot of the poor but prurient stevedore or dramatic critic. He wants his ration of salacious amusement no less than the millionaire. He craves to see attractive women take off their clothes and parade back and forth across the bedroom.

The gay, boisterous, and sinful world of yesteryear has been transformed into one huge lamasery for emasculated monks; but it provides no outlet for the average man's desire for libidinous pleasure except dreams. The world is still gaudy enough for rich men and preachers, of course, for those fortunate fellows are always assured of an adequate supply of private women. But for the luckless ledger clerk or chauffeur, life is a pretty drab proposition. It is to this repressed and sex-starved citizen that the modern musical show brings a royal bounty of color, hilarity and vicarious sin" (Lewis, "Survey of the Negro Theatre—III," *Messenger* 7/10 [October 1926]:302).

[27]http://www.Bluesworld.com/Lornell.htm.

[28]Henry Krehbiel, *Afro-American Folksongs* (reprint; Portland, ME: Longwood Press, 1976):86.

[29]Private concert transcription, 1997. Used with permission.

[30]David Jasen and Trebor Jay Tichenor, *Rags and Ragtime* (New York: Dover, 1989); as well as Tichenour, *Ragtime Rediscoveries* (New York: Dover, 1979) and *Ragtime Rarities* (New York: Dover, 1975).

[31]*Freeman* (6 January 1909).

[32]Van der Merwe, *Origins of Popular Style*, 284–286.

[33]Ibid.:285.

[34]Edward Berlin, *Ragtime* (Los Angeles: University of California Press, 1980):136.

[35]Carl Sandburg, *The Chicago Race Riots* (New York: Harcourt, Brace, and Howe, 1919):97.

[36]Lomax, *Land Where the Blues Began:*75.

[37]http://www.djournal.com/125/weevil.htm and http://www.entercomp.com/users/cybergal/weevil.html.

[38]Ralph Sanders, *Vintage Farm Tractors* (Stillwater, MN: Town Square Books, 1996).

[39]http://rs6.loc.gov/ammem/aap/timelin3.html and http://www.msstate.edu/Archives/History/USA/Afro-Amer/coombs. See also *The Black Experience in America,* as published electronically by its author, Norman Coombs, as part of Project Gutenberg.

[40]Dixon and Godrich, *Recording the Blues:*48.

[41]*Talking Machine World* (September 1918):7.

[42]Martin Williams, "Recording Limits and Blues Form," *The Art of Jazz,* ed. Martin Williams (New York: Oxford University Press, 1959):67–81.

[43]The recording industry faced difficulties three times in the early life of the Blues; in ca, 1920, ca. 1924–1925, and again ca. 1930: from overproduction, the advent of radio, and then the Depression. In the latter case, companies struggled to address the precipitous drop (greater than 90%) in sales volume brought on by loss of discretionary income. A quote from Edward Wallerstein (1891–1970), developer of the LP record, describes one attempt: "RCA had made (LP records) in 1932 and, as a matter of fact, when I became general manager of the Victor Division of RCA on 1 July 1933, my first act was to take them off the market. The idea was good and they might have sold, but there were technical problems. Most of the records were made from Victorlac, a vinyl compound developed by Jim Hunter; the pick-ups available at that time were so heavy they just cut through the material after several plays. The complaints from customers all over the United States were so terrific that we were forced to withdraw the LPs. If you could get a new pressing of one of these records today and play it with a modern lightweight 2–mil pick-up, it probably would sound pretty good.

In 1933 records had fallen into disuse to such an extent that the problem was to find some way to get people to listen to them again. RCA developed at Camden the Duo Jr. player, which could be attached to your radio. There were by this time twenty million radios in U.S., and it seemed to me that this was our big hope in trying for a comeback of the business that had shrunk nationally to probably only $10 million. It worked beautifully, and the little attachment, which was sold at our cost, $9.95, was instrumental in revitalizing the industry. Years later I was able to use this idea again with the LP" http://www.kcmetro.cc.mo.us/pennvalley/Biology/lewis/crosby/lphist.htm. See also Gelatt, *The Fabulous Phonograph;* and Millard, *American on Record.*

[44]"*Talking Machine World* was quick to blame the record slump of 1924–1925 on a failure to innovate in the face of new technology, and was optimistic that the new sound of recordings would win back an audience that had been lost to radio and motion pictures" [*Talking Machine World* 23 (15 January 1927):29, 90].

[45]Consider *Beauharnais v. Illinois,* 118, 343 U.S. 25. In 1900, the total population of Chicago was 1.8 million, the Black population some 31,000. By 1910 the total population had risen to 2.4 million, the Black population to forty-seven thousand. By 1920 the total population was three million, the Black population 115,000. By 1930 the respective figures were four million and 250,000. The Chicago riots, triggered by a racially induced injury at a swimming area, resulted in thirty-five killed, five hundred injured. See also Special Committee Authorized by Congress to Investigate East St. Louis Riots: H.R. Doc. 1231, 65th Congress 2nd Session, 11. See also the Chicago Commission on Race Relations, *The Negro in Chicago:*75.

[46]Chris Albertson, *Bessie* (New York: Stein and Day, 1972):112.

[47]Ethel Waters with Charles Samuels, *His Eye is on the Sparrow* (New York: Doubleday, 1951):94.

[48]The Western Vaudeville and B. F. Keith–Orpheum Circuits booked acts for colored audiences who could watch from the peanut galleries in the segregated theaters, but there was a need for a theater chain for Negroes. This the Theatre Owners Booking Agency (TOBA) provided (1909).

"When black musicians appeared before white customers (in Manhattan) they did so . . . in the 'black and tans' or visit(ed) elite nightclubs. Connie's Inn was a major site . . . but its fame was overshadowed by that of the Cotton Club. Its building had originally been owned by Jack Johnson, the first black heavyweight boxing champion. From 1922–1935 the club presented black musical shows for whites. For Africans, jazz thrived in white-owned clubs like Chicago's Lincoln Gardens, where the audience were segregated. Harlem's Savoy Ballroom was also white owned and patronized, although there were some black dancers. South Side Chicago's 'Stroll' around 35th and State St. also saw white customers, although blacks dominated. Harlem's Lenox Avenue, Pittsburgh's Hill District, and South Central Avenue in Los Angeles were by and for black people" [*Jazz in American Culture,* Burton Peretti, Ivan R. Dee, Bel Canto, (Chicago 1997), 45–47].

[49]Hill, *Strategies for a Renaissance: The Role of Early Writers in Shaping Black Theatre,* http://www.bobwest.com/ncaat/anthill.html. See also Albertson, *Bessie:*1.

[50]Oliver, *The Story of the Blues:*95.

[51]Oliver, *The Story of the Blues:*75.

[52]Oliver, *Screening the Blues* (New York: Da Capo, 1968, 1989):78.

[53]*Freeman* (27 April 1912).

[54]Handy, *Father of the Blues:*127.

[55]Tom Ball, *The Nasty Blues* (Fullerton, CA: Centerstream Pub., 1995; Hal Leonard distributor):4.

[56]LeRoi Jones, *Blues People* (New York: William Morrow, 1963):92.

[57]Personal communication.

[58]Albertson, *Bessie:*101.

[59]Waters, *His Eye is on the Sparrow:*60.

[60]In 1922 Fletcher Henderson scored huge success at the Lyric Theatre in New Orleans, and in radio broadcasts originating from it. In 1923 New York's WNH broadcast his music. The first Black musicians to be broadcast with regularity over network facilities were bandleaders Duke Ellington and Noble Sissle. The disk jockey concept was pioneered by Jack L. Cooper who first aired "The All Negro Hour" over WSBC in Chicago in 1929. His first efforts were live variety with local Black talent, but he soon switched to recorded music to reduce costs. By the turn of the decade he had a stable of African American DJs working on Black-appeal programs broadcast over two stations. Similar programs came to other cities in the 1940s: Memphis, WDIA, Nat Williams; Detroit, WCHB, Martha Stienberg; Baltimore, WBEE, Maurice Hulbert. The first Black-owned radio station was Atlanta's WERD (1950), owned by J. B. Blayton [*Encyclopedia of Afro-American Culture and History* (New York: Simon and Schuster, 1996)].

[61]De Leath was the first woman singer to gain recognition over the radio. A concert singer from her teens, she made her first appearance on radio in January 1920 over De Forest's experimental station singing "Swanee River." In 1921 she helped open WJZ. She sang songs like "I'm Just Wild About Harry" (Sissle–Blake), "Nobody Knows What a Red-Headed Mama Can Do" (Mills–Fain) and many classic blues, which she recorded for Okeh, Gennett, Edison, and Columbia earlier.

[62]Paul Oliver has summarized readily available statistics on record production and apparent utilization [Oliver, *Songsters and Saints* (Cambridge: Cambridge University Press, 1984):103]. One study (1927–1934) around Atlanta suggested that nineteen percent of the 323 rural black homes studied had phonographs, none had radios, but twenty-three percent had pianos or organs. A similar study in 1920 in Macon County, Alabama, of 612 Black families, showed that twelve percent had phonographs, and 4.5 percent had organs or pianos. A 1935 study of a reputed sample of twenty-five thousand Black families throughout the South had a more complicated set of results—phonographs being favored in rural areas, radios in urban areas, and piano ownership correlated with rising income. What of fiscal reality?

Ads in the *Freeman* for 1912 show: *Big Music Book,* thirty-five pieces, $3.00, Victor-Victrola Phonographs, $10–150, and used pianos and player pianos, $95–385. Ads in the *Freeman* in 1914 show Victor-Victrolas for $15–200 and Victors for $10–100, and discontinued or refurbished pianos and player pianos for $150–500. Ads in the *Defender* during 1923–1925 show that radio sets were approximately $15–100 depending upon the quality and reception potential. In the mid-twenties *Defender,* ads from Vocalion were offering free portable phonographs to those who purchased one hundred records by mail at prices of seventy-five cents each. Typical Chicago wages then were $0.50–1.00/hour. This purchase/use arena deserves a more thorough evaluation.

[63]Oliver, *Songsters and Saints:*109.

[64]Lynn Abbott and Doug Seroff, " 'They Cert'ly Sound Good to Me,' Sheet Music, Southern Vaudeville, and the Commercial Ascendancy of the Blues," *American Music* 14 (1996):402–454.

[65]Tin Pan Alley's native songwriters, White and Black, poured the blues out in the late 1910s and 1920s: "The Alcoholic Blues" (1917, Laska–von Tilzer), "Left Alone Blues" and "Blue Danube Blues" (1920–1921, Kern), "Home Again Blues" and "Schoolhouse Blues" (1920–1921, Berlin), "Wabash Blues" (1921, Ringle–Meinken), "Wang, Wang Blues" (1921, Wood–Mueller), "Yankee Doodle Blues" (1922, G. Gershwin–De Sylva), "Lovesick Blues" (1922, Mills–Friend), "Hometown Blues" (1923, Ringle–Coots), "The Half of It, Dearie, Blues" [Lady, Be Good!] (1924, Ira Gershwin), "Washboard Blues" (1926, Parish–Carmichael), "How Long, How Long Blues" (1929, Ann Enberg–Carr), and "Bye, Bye Blues" (1930, Hamm, Bennett, Gray)—the last of which became the signature for Bert Lown and the Hotel Biltmore Orchestra. In 1926 the "Birth of the Blues" in *George White's Scandals of 1926* featured Margaret and Dorothy McCarthy singing "The Memphis Blues" and the "St. Louis Blues."

[66]Albertson, *Bessie:*127.

[67]The silent film was not silent. Before 1928 movies were accompanied by sound effects, live music, live singers, actors, and phonograph records. The French Phon-Cinema toured during 1900–1901, and the French dominated the sound movies of the first decade of commercial motion picture. The first significant U.S. success in making the silent movies "talk" occurred in 1923, when Henry Stoller and Harry Pfannenstiehl used separate electric motors to drive the camera and disc recorder, coupling them to achieve synchronization (*Vitaphone v. ERPI,* 1933, pp 357–362). A sixteen-inch platter that recorded from the inside toward the rim, like modern CDs, was used. It rotated at 33⅓ rpms to extend the playing time to match reel length. Short test films were made. Although the motors were synchronized, there was still the phonograph's manual starting process to contend with upon playback. Coincident with the German demonstration of a soundtrack on film, Lee DeForest showed that the intensity of a light beam could be modulated by the current from a microphone, and record the sound image photographically on the edge of the film. Synchronization was automatic. His short Phonofilms were shown in 1923, and William Fox used a derived technique to make short newsreels. Meanwhile, General Electric developed a technique

that used the sound energy to change the width of the sound strip on the film, and Western Electric developed a method that changed the strip's density. The goal was full-length feature sound synchronization.

Western Electric chose in the short run, however, to pursue sound disks of traditional nature. Warner Brothers licensed the technology, and the Vitaphone Corporation was formed in 1925 to provide musical accompaniment to movies. Musical synchronization was more forgiving than the problems speech presented. Vitaphone's *Don Juan* of 1926 was received well by the audience, but executives were cautious. But radio kept eating into the silent movies' market share. The *Jazz Singer* of 1927 had moments of disk recorded speech that were lip-synched, and the audiences cheered. By 1928 the move to disk soundtracks became a flood. Over one thousand installations of Western Electric disk sound systems were made. But synchronization was still a problem.

In 1927 GE's variable area system on film was used to make RKO's *Wings*. Although Germany's UFA studio produced the first film with an optical soundtrack, the *Jazz Singer,* 1927, was the first popular "talkie." Western Electric's variable density system was used in a 1929 full-length feature. By 1930 film soundtracks had silenced the "silents," and the blues were also entering a dark night.

[68]Score sources include the William Ransom Hogan Jazz Archive, Tulane University, New Orleans (the finest collection of printed and manuscript music, recorded sound, and oral history; some fifty thousand pieces of popular sheet music; will photocopy at about fifty cents/page); and the Archives of American Folk Songs, Library of Congress (some one hundred thousand recordings, vast, loosely catalogued sheet music). Published sources include Jerry Silverman, *110 American Folk Blues, Compiled, Edited and Arranged for Voice, Piano, and Guitar* [an excellent starting point] (New York: MacMillan, 1958); *All-American Blues,* Vols. 1–2 [a superb catholic collections of country and city blues; 160 scores] (Ojai, CA: Creative Concepts, no date); *The Book of the Blues,* ed. Kay Shirley [over one hundred classic, country, and city blues] (New York: MCA Music, 1963); *Bessie Smith, Empress of the Blues* [a collection of sophisticated City Blues] (New York: Schirmer, 1975); *Best of the Blues Series* [consisting of individual volumes for Sonny Boy Williamson, Slim Harpo, John Lee Hooker, Howlin Wolf, Jimmy Reed, B. B. King, Elmore James, Bobby Bland, Junior Parker, Johnny Ace and Little Walter] (Ojai, CA: Creative Concepts, no dates); and Stefan Grossman, Stephan Calt, Hal Grossman, *Country Blues Songbook* (New York: Oak Publications,1973), *Texas Blues* (New York: Oak Publications, 1984), *Reverend Gary Davis/Blues Guitar* (New York: Oak Publications, 1974), and *Ragtime Blues* (New York: Oak Publications, 1970). Finally, many superb collections from Mel Bay Publishing, Dailey Industrial Park, Pacific, MO, 63069.

[69]Library of Congress, Special Collection, Typescript Lyrics; shelf number M 1630.2.W.

[70]Quoted in a *Wall Street Journal* column (13 November 1997) by Martha Bayles, author of *Hole in Our Soul: The Loss of Beauty and Meaning in American Popular Music* (New York: Free Press, 1994).

[71]Strikes by the American Federation of Musicians (AFM) from 1942 to 1943, banning new commercial recording, and boycotts of radio networks by the American Society of Composers, Authors, and Publishers (ASCAP) beginning in 1940 changed the direction of popular musical sound. As indicated earlier, Victor and Columbia lost market position in recordings due to the AFM strike, opening the window of opportunity for smaller companies with new sounds. The ASCAP boycott led 256 stations to form a consortium that led to the formation of their own copyright organization, Broadcast Music Incorporated (BMI). Their compass needle pointed not to printed music, Broadway, and Tin Pan Alley, but to performance styles, vocalists, and southward. The needle swung from swing, a new rhythm was added to the blues, and the color was bleached from race records.

[72]Robert Kimball and William Bolcum, *Reminiscing with Sissle and Blake* (New York: Viking Press, 1973):43.

This work was nurtured by various editors, librarians, musicologists, and colleagues: Ben Dunham (American Recorder), Michael Saffle; Wayne Shirley, Charles Sens, Elizabeth Smith, Sarah Streiner, Neil Gladd (Library of Congress); Anita Haney, Marilyn Norstedt (Virginia Tech), Scott Silet (Univ. of Virginia), Lynn Abbot (New Orleans), Samuel Floyd (Center for Black Music Research, Columbia College), Karen Rege (Winterthur), Jerry Silverman (New York) and Ron Earp (Virginia Tech). The research was facilitated by access to the University air-shuttle service, sponsored by the Research and Graduate Studies Division, and staffed by Regina Young (scheduler), and Phil Harmon, Joe Garst, and John Gunter (pilots).

NB: While this article was in press the following book came to the author's attention, one quite synergistic with the views presented here: Tony Russell, *Blacks, Whites and Blues* (New York: Stein & Day, 1970).

CHAPTER 4

Some American Firms and Their Contributions to the Development of the Reproducing Piano

KENT HOLLIDAY

Reproducing pianos were originally invented and developed at the beginning of the twentieth century by the Welte-Bockisch firm in Freiburg, Germany. Many refinements and innovations in the field of piano performance reproduction were accomplished, however, by a host of American firms that came into existence a decade or so after the reproducing instruments' inception. Before discussing these firms and their unique contributions to reproducing piano design, it would be advisable to preface our discussion with a brief overview of the inventions and principles that led to the concept and design of reproducing pianos.

During the nineteenth century, means were developed to accurately record visual and aural events. Joseph Niepce's invention of the camera in the 1820s and Edison's cylinder recorder in 1877 inaugurated early attempts at preserving these events. Crude as these attempts were, they pointed significantly toward twentieth century scientific and empirical outlooks. They allowed one to reproduce something with a minimal intervention of subjective interpretation. It is through such early experiments that we know more precisely how a specific musical performance sounded. The prime objective was the meticulous reproduction of an event as witnessed by its observer.

The clockwork music provided by a music box and the performance given by a reproducing piano share mechanical similarities: both operate from a digital storage and retrieval system. A music box, however, does not actually reproduce a piece of music as recorded by a performer of that music. Rather, by means of its pinned barrel mechanism, it gives us a direct presentation of the notes themselves, with no nuances beyond the correct pitches occurring at proper intervals of time.

A reproducing piano, on the other hand, presents not merely notes but a particular interpretation of these notes. By means of a perforated piano roll, we are able to hear not only the correct pitches and rhythms, but also those elements that comprise the expressive rendering of a piece. The representation by such an instrument actually conveys an individual pianist's interpretation of a musical composition. It reenacts the expression the pianist puts on the face of the music.

To achieve the reproduction of sound there are three necessary elements: a means for recording sound, a medium to carry the sound, and a means for reproducing what was recorded. Eighteenth-century attempts at preserving keyboard performances fulfilled only the first two of these elements, as the third presented a formidable challenge to the technology existing at that time.

One such early attempt to record keyboard improvisations was the piano-harpsichord patented in 1780 by the English inventor Joseph Merlin. (Merlin is more famous for his invention of the wheelchair and roller skate.) His piano-harpsichord bears the inscription: "Josephus Merlin Privelegiarus Nove Forte Piano No. 80 Londini 1780." It recorded which notes were played and how long they were held. This was achieved by means of sixty-one graphite pencils marking the notes and durations on a continuous paper belt driven by a clockwork mechanism. The paper belt had to be transcribed back into standard musical notation to decipher what had been played. How fortunate it would be for us if the young Mozart or Beethoven had improvised on this ingenious instrument! Alas, no such recordings have been discovered.

The origins of the player piano mechanism, like many inventions of a revolutionary nature, are in doubt. Certainly, the pneumatic principle used in player pianos can be traced back as far as the early nineteenth century. Joseph Marie Jacquard, a silk-loom designer, utilized perforated cardboard patterns in order to reproduce the patterns to be woven. The adaptation of a musical instrument to Jacquard's perforated cardboard principle was patented by Claude Felix Seytre in 1842. Seytre described his idea in detail in his "patent for an invention of five years," but no existing instrument is known.

Attempts at activating player piano mechanisms by other than air vacuum pneumatics were tried with some success. Power by means of cranks, springs, water motors, or hot air engines was not uncommon. One such instrument, the Antiphonal, patented by Alexandre Debain in

1846, enjoyed popularity for many years. Instead of utilizing a paper or cardboard medium, Debain used rectangular wooden planchettes in which iron pins were inserted. When a crank was turned, these pins contacted the instrument's keys through a system of jacks, and notes were produced.

Many of the early piano playing mechanisms were what are called cabinet style or push-up players. The name comes from the fact that the device was literally pushed up to a conventional keyboard, contacting it through pneumatically controlled wooden "fingers" covered with felt or soft leather. One of the earliest push-up type player pianos was the Pianista, patented by Napoleon Fourneaux of Paris in 1863. When situated with its fingers over piano keyboard, the Pianista was played by turning a crank, which caused pneumatic motors to activate the fingers. Music to be played was stored on a pinned barrel, similar to that found in a music box. The Pianista was exhibited at the Philadelphia Exposition in 1876.

In addition to the planchette and barrel, music was stored on perforated cardboard rectangles folded accordion fashion into a book. This principle was no doubt derived from the patent by Seytre and the earlier experiments of Jacquard. Forerunners of perforated music rolls, cardboard books were popular for many years as a means for controlling not only pianos but much larger mechanical instruments—orchestrions, for example, which were large mechanical organ—including additional instruments such as glockenspiels, drums, cymbals, and triangles.

One problem with perforated cardboard books was the size and space they required in order to contain compositions of more than a few minutes in length. A solution to this problem was the invention and patent by the Welte Company of Freiburg i.Br. in 1887 of the perforated music roll. A roll of thin paper took up a minimum amount of space compared to cardboard books, and one Welte roll could play for up to thirteen minutes. Shortly after composing the *Children's Corner Suite,* Claude Debussy recorded the entire work on one Welte reproducing roll; the same piece would have occupied at least three gramophone record sides at that time.

The general acceptance of the perforated music roll confirmed the widespread adaptation of pneumatic principles for powering reproducing piano mechanisms. Capable of performing remarkable technical feats at moderate operating pressures, vacuum devices proved to be more practical than mechanical ones used earlier in the century. The flexibility in working pressures of the vacuum pneumatic system promoted the design of reproducing pianos along the same lines as the earlier player pianos, though far more sophisticated applications of the vacuum principle were utilized.

Almost at the same time that Welte produced his perforated music roll, the American G. B. Kelly invented a remarkable wind motor, utilizing slide valves to open and close ducts to a pneumatic bellows. Used to power the drive system for the music roll, the wind motor was the basic heartbeat of player and reproducing pianos. With few exceptions, wind motors continued to be used in this capacity until replaced by the electric motor in the late twenties.

Up until the turn of the century, cabinet or push-up players were more common than self-contained player pianos. The compact cabinet player designed by Americans Edward White and William Parker, and the popular Pianola by E. S. Votey, saw wide acceptance around 1900 before being superseded by interior playing mechanisms. Still, push-up type reproducing instruments were constructed on a limited basis well into the twentieth century by such firms as Welte and Sons.

Most player pianos played what was known as a designed roll, which was a hand-punched paper roll perforated according to a traditionally printed music score. Not capable of a wide range of differences in dynamics, most players produced only two levels: loud, and not so loud. Sensitive musicians of the day must have deemed this not so good! Little wonder the designers sought a subtler instrument to convey expression as the listening public's taste graduated from ragtime to the delicate shadings of Impressionism.

The basic principles of the reproducing and player pianos are similar, both operating from a set of pneumatics controlled by a vacuum pressure system. The subtle capabilities of the costly reproducing pianos, however, set them far above their cruder forerunners as instruments of superior musical refinement. Delicate shadings in dynamic levels and multiple uses of the pedals were reproduced, through vacuum pneumatics, with a precision previously unknown.

A piano roll is basically a digital system; each note the piano is capable of playing is individually coded as either "on" or "off" in function. The longer the corresponding slots or series of holes in the paper roll, the longer the duration of a note.

Player and reproducing pianos differ in their abilities to vary dynamic levels in the notes they play. Most player pianos' hammers travel their normal distance and play loudly, or are lifted closer to the strings by a hammer rail and, having less distance and time to gather speed, play more softly.

The reproducing piano, on the other hand, is capable of playing at many dynamic levels. The change from one dynamic level to the next can be almost instantaneous or can gradually take place over a designated period of time, as in a crescendo or decrescendo. Individual notes or groups of notes can be accented, and a melody line can be made to stand out from accompanimental figures. The challenge to distinguish melody from accompaniment, a process known as theme isolation, intrigued inventive minds early in this century. Many musicians still dispute whether this was ever satisfactorily accomplished.

In 1904 Edwin Welte and Karl Bockisch introduced to the musical world one of the first reproducing pianos, a cabinet player called a Vorsetzer, a "fore-sitter" or "sitter-in-front-of."[1] When placed in front of an ordinary piano with its felt-covered wooden fingers engaged over the keys, the Vorsetzer was able to reproduce with great accuracy a performance recorded by a famous artist of the time.

For the next three decades some of the finest minds in Europe and the United States grappled with the technological challenge of how best to record and reproduce what transpires when a great artist plays. Ideal reproduction involves reenactment of an original performance down to the most minute detail. A tremendous amount of complex technical hardware requires a humanization of the mechanical elements so that they function to perfection without extraneous noise.

Many American firms undertook the task of designing and marketing reproducing instruments during the first three decades of the twentieth century. Through survival of the fittest, some manufacturers enjoyed considerable success during the Golden Age of the reproducing piano, while others fell into oblivion. The firm of M. Welte and Sons continued to be a leader in the production of reproducing pianos and piano rolls. Prior to World War I, Welte established a company in the United States that built instruments according to a license that allowed the American firm to use Welte patents. The American instruments, originally called Auto Deluxe Welte Mignon Reproducing Pianos, were more commonly known as Welte Licensees (see Figure 4.1).

Welte-Mignon means "little Welte," and was so named because it was comparatively small alongside the colossal orchestrions that Welte also manufactured. The name prompted Ignace Paderewski to state that the only fault he could find with the Mignon was its name, which was misleading as to the "immense effect of the instrument and its great artistic importance."[2]

After World War I the original Welte-built Welte Mignon and the

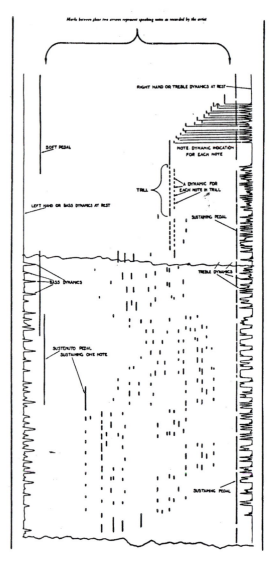

This photograph of a section from an original recording of Chopin's Etude in F Major shows how every detail of the artist's playing is graphically recorded while he plays. ¶With this absolutely authentic "tone picture" as a guide, the making of records for Welte Mignon (Licensee) Reproducing Pianos is free from every vestige of guesswork. Nothing is added or substracted that the artist does not himself put into his music, so that the record is not a mere approximation, but an exact reproduction of his playing. ¶What may be called the "film of the music camera" receives impressions of every detail of both his fingering and pedaling. ¶The exact position of every note played is fixed by faint vertical lines corresponding in number to the keys on the piano. The staggered lines on the extreme right and left are the means by which the mechanism, like the delicate needle of the seismograph that records the slightest tremor of the earth, graphically indicates exactly the degree of pressure with which the artist struck the keys, thus faithfully recording the finest shading of his interpretation.

Figure 4.1. A Welte-Mignon recording of a Chopin etude.

American Welte Licensee were both manufactured in the United States. Competition between the two was inevitable, but by that time there were two more serious contenders for the American market, the Aeolian Corporation's Duo-Art Reproducing Piano, and the American Piano Company's Ampico system.

The Aeolian Corporation's reproducing piano was originally known as the Duo-Art Pianola and appeared on the market in 1913. Later dubbed simply the Duo-Art, the mechanism was installed in Steinway pianos as well as in instruments made by the Aeolian Company itself. With distributors in the United States and Europe, and with recording studios in New York and London, the Aeolian Company soon achieved worldwide acclaim. Aeolian established schools of instruction for servicing Duo-Art reproducing mechanisms in many American cities.

In its 1972 service manual describing the operation of the Duo-Art reproducing mechanism, the Aeolian Company claims that the instrument is built on an entirely different mechanical principle from any other device of its kind. Actually the Duo-Art system differs from its competitors not so much in mechanics as in concept.

Instead of merely dividing the keyboard into an upper and lower section for treble and bass expression control, the Duo-Art expression system is designed to accommodate theme and accompanimental notes. It is very logical that an instrument intended to faithfully reproduce as much of the human element as possible in a performance should be so designed. In at least ninety-five percent of piano pieces written before 1900, theme and accompaniment elements are juxtaposed. Theme, or the single melodic line, usually stands out louder than accompaniment, accompaniment being the contrapuntal or chordal configurations which lend a necessary harmonic contest to the melody. Duo-Art control of theme notes is independent of accompaniment notes. By means of theme control, a melodic line may be made to stand out clearly above an accompaniment, whether sounding in the bass, middle, or treble register. At the same time, any degree of power may be given to the accompaniment. The Duo-Art expression system is directly linked to thematic and accompanimental elements in the music itself instead of to a mere physical division of the keyboard into left and right.

As in the Welte Licensee system, the amount of vacuum reaching the pneumatic stack is controlled by a sliding knife valve covering a port leading to the vacuum pump. The amount of air permitted to be withdrawn through this port depends on how much of it is covered by the knife valve. Unlike the Welte system, this valve is controlled by a set of four pneumatics, called accordion pneumatics, which are connected by a rod to the heel of the sliding knife valve. Each of these four accordion pneumatics collapses a different distance, in multiples of two. The smallest pneumatic, 1A, closes one-sixteenth of an inch; pneumatic 2A closes one-eighth of an inch; pneumatic 4A closes one-fourth of an inch; pneumatic 8A closes half an inch. These pneumatics are activated by four large slots in the bass and treble ends of the tracker bar, set above the regular note holes. Each slot leads through a pouch block and valve box to the specific accordion pneumatic that it controls. There are sixteen dynamic gradations available in the Duo-Art system, and these are obtained through the accordion pneumatics, working singly or in combination, to open the knife valve any desired degree. A chart showing these combinations of accordion pneumatics and the resultant dynamic gradations is shown below:

Pressure #1 zero setting adjusted to play piano as softly as possible
Pressure #2 Holes in tracker open #1   Accordion pneumatics collapsed #1–1/16"

" #3 " " " " #2	"	" "	#2–2/16"
" #4 " " " " #1–2	"	" "	#1–2–3/16"
" #5 " " " " #4	"	" "	#4–4/16"
" #6 " " " " #1–4	"	" "	#1–4–5/16"
" #7 " " " " #2–4	"	" "	#2–4–6/16"
" #8 " " " " #1–2–4	"	" "	#1–2–4–7/16"
" #9 " " " " #8	"	" "	#8–8/16"
" #10 " " " " #1–8	"	" "	#1–8–9/16''
" #11 " " " " #2–8	"	" "	#2–8–10/16"
" #12 " " " " #1–2–8	"	" "	#1–2–8–11/16"
" #13 " " " " #4–8	"	" "	#4–8–12/16"
" #14 " " " " #1–4–8	"	" "	#1–4–8–13/16"
" #15 " " " " #2–4–8	"	" "	#2–4–8–14/16"
" #16 " " " " #1–2–4–8	"	" "	#1–2–4–8–15/16"

Note that the zero degree setting makes no use of accordion pneumatics whatsoever. Playing at this setting would be as soft as possible, with theme sounding only a small degree louder than accompaniment. The setting of the theme dynamic level is dependent upon the setting of the accompaniment level; at whatever volume the latter is sounding, the theme will always be one degree louder (see Figure 4.2).

The dynamic levels set for the accompaniment expression unit normally control volume for all the notes playing except when theme notes occur. The theme expression unit is switched on by pairs of tiny holes, commonly called "snakebites," at the moment more thematic power is desired. These paired holes are about half the size of ordinary note holes found in the tracker bar. Being smaller, they provide extreme speed and precision in attach and release of dynamic power, at the same time admitting a sufficient quantity of air, because of their pairing, to get the job done. The original concept of "snakebite" perforations goes back to 1900, when J. W. Crooks invented his Themodist, which used paired note

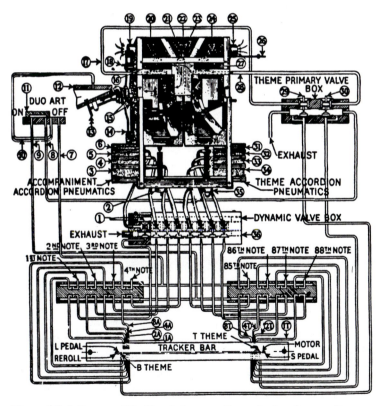

Figure 4.2. A diagram of the Duo-Art pneumatic mechanism for recording dynamic variations.

holes to achieve accentuation, though otherwise incapable of dynamic control.

Many Duo-Art grands were equipped with a pneumatically controlled key frame shifting device. Varieties in timbre achieved through differing positions of the soft pedal could be duplicated through such a key frame shifting mechanism.

The American Piano Company, maker of Ampico, employed two substantially different systems in their instruments. These two systems are known as the Model A and the Model B Ampico. The Ampico system, originally named the Stoddard-Ampico after its inventor, Charles F. Stoddard, evolved from early production models brought out in 1913, into the popular Model A Ampico. The Model A Ampico system was installed in many brands of uprights and grands, and was the most widely sold system the company produced. In 1919 the "New Ampico," Model B, appeared. Due in large part to the brilliant design innovations by Clarence Hickman, the Model B was the result of years of planning and careful experiments dealing with piano touch and tone production.

The Model A Ampico borrowed several designs from the Amphion Company of Syracuse and was one of the most widely marketed reproducing pianos ever to be sold. Originally designed with a step system of dynamic control similar to the Duo-Art, Ampico added a crescendo pneumatic to gain a smoother response in crescendos and decrescendos.

Vacuum in the pneumatic stack is controlled by the regulator valve, which is attached by a rod to three intensity pneumatics. Each of these pneumatics exerts a different pulling power on the regulator valve because of its different location on the lever attached to the regulator valve connecting rod. The pneumatic secured near the lever's fulcrum, number one, has the least influence on the valve, and the one attached furthest from the fulcrum, number three, has the most. The effect of these intensity pneumatics, used singly or in combination, is to quickly bring about an increase or decrease in playing power. There are seven intensity levels available, and the correlation between these levels and the pneumatics producing them is shown in the table on page 115.

The use of the three intensity pneumatics alone will not provide a smooth crescendo or decrescendo, however. This effect is achieved by balancing the downpull of the intensity pneumatics on the regulator valve with a spring pneumatic controlled by a crescendo pneumatic. The crescendo pneumatic is regulated by a set of valves for fast and slow crescendo. When operating, there is always a lower amount of air pressure in the crescendo and spring pneumatics of the Ampico A system.

Intensity of Playing	Intensity Valves Open	Holes in Tracker Open
No. 1	None	None
No. 2	No. 1	No. 2
No. 3	No. 2	No. 4
No. 4	No. 3	No. 6
No. 4	No. 1, No. 2	No. 2, No. 4
No. 5	No. 1, No. 3	No. 2, No. 6
No. 6	No. 2, No. 3	No. 4, No. 6
No. 7	No. 1, No. 2, No. 3	No. 2, No. 4, No. 6

The spring pneumatic, controlled by the crescendo pneumatic, will pull up to counteract the downpull of the three intensity pneumatics (see Figure 4.3).

With the Ampico A system it is possible to reproduce accents within a long crescendo line. Whereas the crescendo pneumatic causes a gradual increase in volume, the three intensity pneumatics determine the correct amount of accentuation for each note as directed from holes at either end of the tracker bar. There are two dynamic expression mechanisms in the Ampico A, one for each half of the keyboard.

When the Model B Ampico system was brought out, it was called the "New Ampico." Due in large part to the design innovations by Clarence Hickman, the Model B was unique in the use of lighter, less cumbersome materials. In many respects it represented a simplification of principles that seemed to require increasingly complex mechanisms.

The regulation of air pressure drawn from the pneumatic stack in the Ampico B is controlled by a thin rubber cloth pouch (A), acting as a membrane over a celluloid grill (B). The amount of suction that the pouch will permit to be withdrawn from the stack is determined by four regulating pouches (0, 2, 3, 6), each of which is controlled by intensity and crescendo valves. Because of the lightness of the pouches in the Model B, the system had about one-thousandth the inertia of the regulating system found in the Model A Ampico. Consequently its response to changing levels in intensity was much faster and more flexible.

The use of scientific methodology to investigate what actually does take place when a piano is played was the basis for many of the innova-

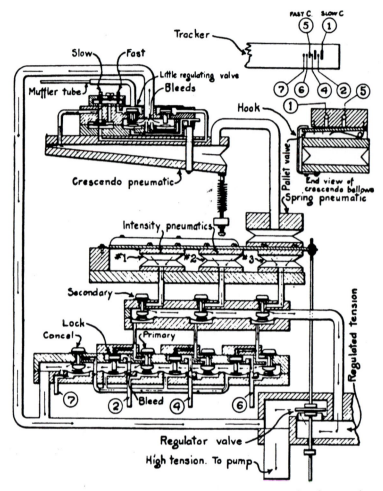

Figure 4.3. A diagram of the Welte-Mignon pneumatic mechanism for recording dynamic variations.

tions found in the Model B Ampico. Hickman observed that less force is required to attain a specific loudness when the sustaining pedal is on, as the dampers are already raised, than when the pedal is off. Automatic reduction in suction in the Model B pneumatic stack complied with this whenever the sustaining pedal was in use.

Until the Model B Ampico, most reproducing piano rolls were

driven by an air motor that operated off the piano's vacuum pump; however, air motors were found to be unsuitable in maintaining an even speed when longer music rolls were used. Since the Model B Ampico played rolls lasting up to thirty minutes, electric motor drives were used on all production models.

Other innovations found in the Model B Ampico included variable ball-bleed valves, which enabled greater speed in response to the valve blocks; braking devices for compact rewinding and maintenance of even tension on the paper roll as it crossed the tracker bar; and a tracking system that could be used with rolls of various widths and that regulated their centering across the bar within five-thousandths of an inch.

The Model B Ampico used many devices that represented the state of the art in reproducing piano design and construction. In 1929 financial conditions in the United States changed drastically and the general interest in reproducing instruments began to wane. Consequently, the Ampico B was never produced in great quantities, and a good instrument today is a "rara avis" indeed. At the end of the Golden Age of reproducing pianos, around 1930, the American Piano Company was forced to merge with its former competitor, Aeolian, makers of the Duo-Art.

Several other American reproducing systems were ingenious in design. The Artrio-Angelus, or simply Angelus as it was commonly called, was produced by the Wilcox and White Company of Meriden, Connecticut from 1915–1921. Similar to the Duo-Art system in many respects, it made use of paired holes called melodant perforations that were used for accentuation, much the same as the "snakebites" invented by Crooks at the turn of the century.

Many great pianists, including Harold Bauer, Ossip Gabrilowitsch, and Leopold Godowsky, made rolls at their Meriden recording studio. Firm believers in the motto "whatever is worth doing is worth doing well," the company issued a thirty-roll set of Godowsky playing his *Triakontameron;* lasting nearly six hours, *Triakontameron* was a piece of ambitious length even for modern long-playing records.

The Angelus expression mechanism consists of three sets of expression chambers, called bass accompaniment intensity control, solo intensity control, and treble accompaniment intensity control. Each expression chamber has a set of intensity valves that control an expression pneumatic. The bass and treble accompaniment controls have three small valves and one large one, while the solo intensity control consists of four small valves and one large one. Each of the thirteen intensity valves is governed by expression holes in the tracker bar.

Air is drawn from the left and right portions of the pneumatic stack into the bass and treble control sections and out through the middle solo section to the vacuum pump. If all the expression holes in the tracker bar are sealed by the paper roll, the thirteen intensity valves will be closed, and the only vacuum reaching the playing section is that which passes through the regulator B-R, S-R, and T-R. This will produce the softest level of volume that the piano can play. The small valves in the intensity control sections permit gradual increases in intensity, while the large openings produce an instant increase in loudness for maximum effect.

Generally, the middle or solo governor determines the general playing level, and the bass and treble governors control the relative power of bass and treble halves of the keyboard. Because of their connective design, the treble, solo, and bass sections of the Angelus system function interdependently.

A melody can be made to stand out over an accompaniment by permitting air to flow from the right side of the pneumatic stack through the large intensity valve into the solo expression section and out to the pump. Only one or two of the small intensity valves of the bass accompaniment side need be open, and the bass side of the pneumatic stack will not contain as great a vacuum. A melody can be made to stand out any number of degrees louder than an accompaniment by means of these intensity valves controlled by expression perforations in the music roll.

The Solo Carola Inner-Player, made by the Cable Company of Chicago, introduced a unique system for control of dynamic levels using the pneumatic principle. Most uprights and some grand pianos have a soft pedal arrangement whereby a rest rail, on which the hammers normally lie, can be raised closer to the strings. When a hammer that has been carried closer to the strings is activated, it does not have as much distance to gather speed as when in normal rest position. Thus it plays more softly, and with less effort on the pianist's part. The Solo Carola, billed as the "most marvelous musical invention of the century,"[3] featured a unique tracker bar in which a row of long, vertical openings, called solo slots, was located immediately above the usual row of eighty-eight note holes. Each solo slot was connected to a small pneumatic which individually controlled the distance of each hammer from the strings. Before striking, each hammer was individually set a correct distance from the strings in direct proportion to the amount of volume desired (see Figure 4.4).

Advertisements for Solo Carola maintained that it was the only reproducing piano on which any of the eighty-eight notes could be struck individually or simultaneously with varying degrees of power.[4] The prin-

Figure 4.4. An advertisement for the Solo Carola "Inner Player."

ciple would have provided a remarkably simple solution to the problems
of theme isolation had it worked as well as its manufacturers claimed.
Not many pianists made rolls for the Solo Carola, and it never gained the
popularity of Ampico and Duo-Art.

Many reproducing pianos had provisions for semi-automatic operation, enabling the owner to control such things as expression, pedaling,
and rubato. With automatic expression controls overridden, the music
roll supplied only the notes, and it was up to the "player" to use taste and
good judgment in putting an expression on the face of the music. In some
instruments, the tempo could be varied by means of foot pedals or a
tempo control lever, such as the tempanomic lever in the Duo-Art system. Dynamics also were controlled by means of levers or buttons.

For some, the presence of these semi-automatic expression devices
is a humanizing element, allowing one to participate in a music-making
experience, although with surrogate fingers. (It has even been suggested
that the music-making capabilities of a competent player-pianist can ex-
ceed those of a top artist because the attention can be focused on phrasing and expression rather than on the mechanics of hitting the correct
notes.) For others, reproducing instruments are our only true connection
with pianism of the past, and as such should not be sullied with the addition of "idiot levers."

The invention of Welte and Bockisch represents a significant shift
from direct presentations of the designed roll format of player pianos to
more exacting representations of artists' interpretations by reproducing
pianos. The expressive capabilities of most reproducing pianos utilize
principles described in the original Welte-Bockisch patent. Control of
differing dynamic levels is achieved by varying a basic level of vacuum
that activates the pneumatics for individual notes. Since increased loudness is achieved by greater speed of the hammer striking the string, this
increased speed can be brought about by introducing a greater vacuum
into the pneumatic that activates the hammer. A pianist uses various
amounts of muscle and weight for playing loud or soft notes; in a reproducing piano, atmospheric pressure is put to work, through an increase or
decrease in vacuum, to accomplish the same task. Perforations in the
paper roll run over corresponding ducts in the tracker bar to achieve
these different dynamic levels.

Likewise, pneumatic technology for reproducing intricacies of pedaling reached a new zenith in the late 1920s. Since subtle use of damper
and *una corda* pedals was considered by many to be one of the hallmarks
of early twentieth-century pianism, reproducing these features was unquestionably of great importance. Even the uncommon use of the

sostenuto or middle pedal could be faithfully simulated. The three principal reproducing piano mechanisms, Welte, Duo-Art, and Ampico, all used different pneumatic means to bring about these ends.

By the 1920s it is quite likely that microphones were used, perhaps in conjunction with filters, to electromagnetically record dynamics at upper and lower registers of the piano's range. Whatever method was used at this time, there is a marked improvement in the quality of expression recorded on the American Welte Licensee rolls from those numbered seven thousand and up.

Whether or not the original Welte process had the technology to record dynamic levels automatically is not known. It is likely that many decisions concerning dynamic levels were made by a Studio Master, or Artist and Recording (A & R) man. The importance of the Studio Master or A & R man as an artist in his own right should not be underestimated. As "interpreter of the interpretation," he had immense responsibility for seeing that a recording, as he perceived it, was as faithful to an original performance as possible. A vast amount of musical knowledge was needed, as well as familiarity with the technical processes used to translate the master roll into a final salable product.

In the author's interview with the noted English pianist Frank Laffitte, who recorded rolls for Duo-Art Aeolian in the 1920s, the following description of a recording session emerged:

KH: Would you please describe the room in which you made your recordings?

FL: It was not a large size room. The piano was in the middle of the room and Reginald Reynolds, the Studio Master, was sitting to one side at a kind of console.

KH: What kind of piano was it? Were you aware, when playing it, of any differences in its mechanical action due to electrical connections leading to the recording apparatus?

FL: It was a Weber grand, a beautiful piano, about drawing-room size. I was not aware of anything in the action different from the usual. For me it was a concert. It had to be like as concert performance. Reginald Reynolds, who of course was a very first-class musician and who was at the recording session, turned toward me and said, "Yes, it's a concert forever."

KH: Did you ever get to see the recording apparatus in the control room?

FL: No. Nobody ever knew what went on in there. However, I remember there was a large metal hosepipe, which came from underneath the piano and connected with the recording machine in the control room.

KH: Was the console that Reginald Reynolds sat at able to notate dynamics?

FL: Probably. But this was not of prime importance. What counted
tremendously was phrasing, rhythm, and pedaling.

KH: Did you have an opportunity to hear your rolls before release to the
public?

FL: Yes. They made a master roll, and then they made a roll which we
heard.

KH: When you heard the proof copies of your rolls, did you want to
make any corrections or alterations?

FL: No. Apart from correcting a wrong note or changing the speed, you
couldn't make alterations. There was no cheating. Of course, one
could always repeat a performance, but I never had any trouble like
that. I was always very particular and self-critical to a degree. If
you're not self-critical, other people will jolly well criticize you.

The recording apparatus that Mr. Laffitte never saw was a machine
designed to punch perforations in a master roll notating precisely the
notes that the pianist played, including correct phrasing and pedaling.
The Weber grand on which he gave his "concert forever" was equipped
with electrical contacts that triggered solenoids in a punching block. The
recording machine was located in an adjacent room, or often on another
floor, because the process of the punches perforating the paper roll was
incredibly noisy.

The console at which the Studio Master sat consisted of two knobs,
one for theme and one for accompaniment. Each knob controlled fifteen
increments from soft to loud and cut slots into the roll corresponding to
the dynamics that the Studio Master perceived. General dynamic levels
were recorded in this way during the playing of a piece, the Studio Master following a musical score. Themodist perforations for accentuation of
the melody were added later, the snakebites being punched by hand. Occasionally, during a recording session, a gramophone record would be
made as well. Recorded simultaneously during the cutting of the roll, it
was used later for reference in checking dynamic levels and for locating
accentuations.

Once the master roll was cut and had been edited to the satisfaction
of the artist and the Studio Master, it was transferred onto a wide stencil
that ran approximately five times the length of the master roll. The stencil, being five times the length of the master roll, was ink-marked according to the perforations in the master roll and later punched out by hand.
In punching the stencil by hand it was necessary to add what is known as

bridging to insure stability in the rolls cut from the stencil. If a note, or series of notes, is held by the performer for a length of time, the roll would have either a very long slot or a series of holes equidistantly spaced representing that note. By the use of *bridging* or *contiguous punching,* a series of short slots alternate with round holes in the paper, which gives the same musical effect, but that makes the roll stronger and allows the paper to hold up better over the years.

In a later process Duo-Art recorded performances by marking the stencil directly with ink, eliminating the need for cutting a master roll initially. Once the stencil was punched it served as a template or model from which the final rolls were cut. Because of its great length and speed at which it was run, the stencil provided extreme precision in the duplication process. When fed into a punching machine, the perforations in the stencil passed over a tracker bar similar to ones found in player pianos themselves. The tracker bar activated a set of pneumatics and solenoids that controlled punches that plunged down into a cutting die. The contiguous perforations in the high speed stencil were duplicated exactly by punching copies in up to ten roll sheets at once, all running at the slower speed of the original master roll. This process ensured that thousands of copies could be produced that were almost identical in precision and accuracy.

Capturing the expression of an artist's performance is the essential goal in every reproducing system. The secretive aura of early recording sessions makes it difficult to evaluate today what methods were used. Welte's claims about automatic expression recording may have been true, or may have been exaggerations contrived to regain an expanding market that the Welte firm once monopolized. Validity of the Welte process for needing expression must remain an intriguing enigma for speculation by generations to come.

We know far more about the techniques used for recording expression at the close of the Ampico dynasty in the late 1920s than we know about methods used during the first two decades of this century. The only device used for automatically recording dynamics that can be thoroughly documented is the spark chronograph; there may have been other means, but we have no proof of this today. It is unfortunate that the highly sophisticated Model B Ampico system, which followed the invention of the spark chronograph by about three years, came too late to capture the playing of many of the great pianists early in this century. The Model B Ampico could not effectively play the earlier Model A rolls because of differences in dynamic coding. The B Ampico had a single crescendo mechanism that would not respond to separate bass and treble coding.

About nine hundred Model B Ampicos were manufactured, but relatively few classical rolls were produced for it.

One of the top A & R men at Ampico, who prefers to remain anonymous, revealed that before the spark chronograph was developed, it was necessary that pianists recording rolls *believe* every expressive aspect of their playing was being recorded. Many pianists recorded pieces on which they built their reputations as concert artists. It was imperative they feel assured that every nuance and subtlety of their playing was being recorded in as precise a manner as possible.

Expression was often recorded by a Studio Master stenographer, who represented the dynamic levels in the music score by means of lines called "hills" and "dales." A trial run was made usually for the benefit of the stenographer beforehand if a phonograph recording by the artist if the particular piece was available. The pianist may not have been aware of this. After the actual recording session, the piano roll was produced with approximate dynamics and played for the performing artist and technicians.

Many reproducing rolls bore the signatures of performers as endorsements of accuracy and faithful replication of their playing. The "John Hancock" of an artist, however, may have signified nothing. Some signed on the dotted line immediately after the recording session without ever hearing their roll played back. Others insisted on hearing the roll many times and made necessary changes until their highest expectations were met. Among these were Percy Grainger, Josef Hofmann, Fritz Kreisler, Moritz Rosenthal, and Sergei Rachmaninoff. Rachmaninoff was so enthusiastic about the first roll he cut for Ampico that the company provided him with an Ampico reproducing piano for his home in New York, where he could hear and judge for himself the rolls that he made before they were released to the public. (The enormous sound and variety of tone that Rachmaninoff was capable of could never be captured on the gramophone disc. Pedal effects, which are barely noticeable in the gramophone recordings, are marvelously clear in reproducing roll performances. A striking three-record set of Rachmaninoff's playing was released in the 1970s by London, played on an Estonia concert grand employing an Ampico A mechanism.)[5]

Comparison concerts, in which a pianist and a reproducing piano played successively on the same program, were popular in Europe and the United States. Leopold Godowsky inaugurated a series of concerts on 5 June 1919, when he played before an audience of three thousand at the Trinity Auditorium of Los Angeles. His incredible pianism, and the reproduction of it by an Ampico A system in a concert grand, entranced the audience. A music critic from the Los Angeles papers said:

> Enthusiasm broke all bounds at the conclusion of the Chopin Ballade in A Flat, and when the artist returned and bowed his appreciation of the plaudits, the great piano on the platform, as though supercharged with vitality and magnetism of the soloist, suddenly began, apparently of its own volition, to reproduce note for note the number exactly as the pianist had given it. Thus the Ampico reproducing piano was introduced to the great audience and its faithful discharge of so brilliant a responsibility is something for artists and music patrons alike to consider. Shadings, evanescent rhythms and dynamics were presented exactly as the artist himself had given them but a moment before. The house sat spellbound as the marvels of this great invention were revealed.[6]

Ernest Newman describes a famous London concert in which the eminent French pianist Alfred Cortot was performing a Liszt *Hungarian Rhapsody*. At midpoint in the piece Cortot stopped playing and a roll recorded by himself took over. It was said at the time that with your eyes closed, you couldn't tell which was which.[7]

Philip Hale, newspaper critic for the *Boston Herald,* was exuberant about a comparison concert he attended. "In some instances the Ampico surpassed what had just gone before, and thus did justice to the pianist when he had fallen below his own standard."[8]

The renowned American pianist Rudolph Ganz once "conducted himself" playing two Liszt concertos on the same program. Ganz played the Concerto in A Major first, seated at the keyboard of a Steinway grand. After taking his bows, he was handed the baton and proceeded to conduct from the podium the Concerto in E-flat Major. A Duo-Art mechanism inside the Steinway played a roll Ganz had previously recorded, coming in on cue by means of a button that he activated with his left hand, while wielding the baton with his right. Ganz described the occasion with his inimitable sense of humor: "Nothing was told in the paper as to how it was done. The people could see the keys coming up and down, just as if somebody was playing on it . . . oh, I remember it was quite a thrill and the trouble was, at the end I had to shake hands with myself."[9]

An interesting comparison between the Welte, Duo-Art, and Ampico A mechanisms was issued by the American Piano Company

during the early 1920s when highly competitive advertising reached a
new intensity (see Figure 4.5). The disadvantages of the Welte expression pneumatic and the Duo-Art accordion pneumatic systems, as perceived by Ampico, are first pointed out. This is followed by a tabular
comparison of all three brands in regard to specific musical and technical
aspects of piano playing. The basic criticism of the Welte expression system is that it is incapable of giving a sufficient and clean-cut accent to a
note or series of notes in a musical phrase. Either the loudness of an accent is sacrificed for its instantaneous occurrence at the proper time, or it
has to be anticipated, causing a slight swelling and diminishing in volume before and after it sounds.

This is indeed a drawback of any reproducing system using a single,
large expression pneumatic. For the modern listener who really wants to
know what DePachman sounded like in 1910, accented passages such as
those occur often enough in Classical and Romantic music to be vexing
when heard on such a reproducing instrument.

The accordion pneumatic type reproducing system used by Duo-Art
is taken to task in the Ampico comparison for its inability to reproduce
smooth crescendos and diminuendos originally created on the piano by a
succession of notes played in a widely variegated series of dynamic
steps. Since an increase or decrease in volume is digitally produced (no
pun intended), successive notes, as information bits, are given increments of varying intensity and this creates the illusion of smooth
crescendos and diminuendos. What the Ampico Piano Company critic of
Duo-Art implies is that the sixteen volume levels available through the
fixed steps of the accordion pneumatics are not enough levels to portray
all the subtleties of intensity that a sensitive pianist can produce.[10]

Some might find this objection to the Duo-Art system picayune.
Sixteen different dynamic levels are certainly sufficient to give a very accurate reproduction of a master's performance. As an experiment, persons with pianistic ability should attempt playing a single chord or note
at sixteen different dynamic levels ranging from *ppp* to *fff*. The minute
variations in intensity from one degree to the next are barely perceptible.
Similarly, in the visual arts, one might examine a photographic portrait
with a microscope and object to the grain of the negative and the paper it
was printed on. Viewed normally, the portrait yields a highly accurate
photographic likeness of a particular person.

As in the Duo-Art accordion pneumatic type system, the earliest
Ampico system for dynamic control used sixteen steps in volume level.
This mechanism was dropped in favor of the Model A Ampico, which

The Problem of Reproducing Variations
in Tone Volume

In a reproducing piano, all variations in tone volume—accents, crescendos, diminuendos, trills, and nuances—are caused by changing the air tension inside the player action.

The greater the air tension or air exhaustion inside the player action, the stronger is the pressure of the outside air and, consequently, the greater is the force behind the movement of the striking pneumatics (the individual pneumatics for each note); and this force determines the tone volume.

The amount of air tension in the player action is determined by the movement of a regulator valve.

The movement of this regulator valve in turn is controlled by one or more pneumatics, which are connected with the expression holes in the tracker bar, and in which the air tension is varied as the expression holes are opened or closed.

Chart of Piano-Playing

I—*Expressionless Playing*	*Found in playing of:*	III—*Playing with Finished Expression.*	*Found in playing of:*
Striking the right notes. Maintaining perfectly even time and rhythm.	Pupils learning to play the piano. Mechanical player-pianos.	Subtle accenting. Smooth crescendos and diminuendos. Accenting combined with crescendos and diminuendos. Nuances (delicate pulsations of tone-volume). Subtle pedal effects. Blending of tones with sustained tones and overtones. Singing tones. Individual phrasing and interpretations. The power to strike any note with any force at any time.	Great pianists. The Ampico.
II—*Playing with Partial Expression*	*Found in playing of:*		
General loudness or softness of tone-volume. Emphasis on melody in contrast with accompaniment. Harsh accenting. Crude crescendos and diminuendos. Elementary pedal effects. Individual variations in rhythm.	Ordinary amateur pianists. Player-pianos with expression mechanism, when played by skilled operator. Most reproducing pianos.		

On the succeeding pages will be found charts showing the methods of securing variations in tone volume employed by the Duo-Art, the Welte-Mignon, and the Ampico, so that a comparison is easily understood and visualized.

Figure 4.5. A comparison of Ampico, Duo-Art, and Welte-Mignon mechanisms for recording dynamic variations (*continued on next two pages*).

Tabular Comparison of Reproduction by Ampico and Duo-Art

Piano Playing Effects	The Artist	The Duo-Art	The Ampico
I—*Tone Volume* Smooth crescendos and diminuendos. Perfect control of accenting. Nuances.	Produces tone - volume ranging from the softest to the loudest through his ability to strike any string at any time with any desired degree of force. He can thus bring forth at his will smooth trills, crescendos, and diminuendos, subtle or brilliant accents, and delicate pulsations (nuances) ; and he can combine these elements in such a way as to create the contrasts and gradations of tone-volume that best express his personality and his interpretation of the composition.	Reproduces variations in tone-volume by means of a series of four accordion pneumatics, which control the air-tension behind the hammers. By using these pneumatics, either singly or in combination, the Duo-Art can play *sixteen fixed degrees* of tone-volume, *but it cannot reproduce the subtle intermediate gradations of tone between these steps.* Consequently, the Duo-Art is limited in reproducing smooth crescendos and diminuendos because these are built up with a *series of steps* instead of with a *gradual* swelling or diminishing of tone-volume, such as characterizes artistic playing. The Duo-Art is also limited to *only one fixed degree* for accenting the melody above the accompaniment being played at the time.	Re-enacts variations in tone-volume by means of both a crescendo pneumatic system and an instantaneous accent pneumatic system, which it has the exclusive right to use *in combination* to control the air-tension behind the hammers. These systems may be operated *independently* for their separate effects, or *concurrently* for their combined effects. Consequently the Ampico can re-enact smooth crescendos and diminuendos, instantaneous accents, and the most delicate shadings of tone-volume. *It can strike any note at any time with any degree of force, and it is the only instrument on the market that can do this.*
II—*Tone Colour* Pedal effects. Singing tone.	The artist is able to sustain tones through lifting the dampers from certain strings or groups of strings. For this purpose he may hold down one or more keys for a brief period, or he may use with wonderful rapidity and delicacy the damper and sostenuto pedals. The subtle pedal effects and the singing tones thus produced blend with and colour succeeding tones in an infinite variety of beautiful effects.	The Duo-Art possesses a limited ability to operate the damper-pedal, but not with the rapidity and sureness of a skilled artist. It has no other means of lifting the dampers from the strings. Consequently it fails to reproduce the subtle pedal effects and singing tones which constitute one of the chief distinctions of superlative piano-playing.	The Ampico is able to lift any damper from any string for any period of time within the command of an artist. It accomplishes this both through its control of the pedals and through its patented system of lengthened perforations on the recording. It can thus re-enact even the artist's most delicate effects of tone-blending and tone-colouring.
III—*Phrasing* Variations in time. Variations in rhythm.	The artist is able, through minute variations in the time of striking notes and through variations in time and rhythm thus produced, to give his individual phrasing and interpretation to a composition.	The Duo-Art method of recording with a cutting mechanism fails to register with the necessary exactitude the slight variations in the time of beginning notes, which is an essential element in an artist's individual phrasing.	The Ampico is able to re-enact the artist's individual phrasing and interpretation through its exact method of recording the beginning of notes with a marking mechanism, and through the responsiveness and precision of its balanced regulation of dynamic control.

Figure 4.5 (*continued*)

Tabular Comparison of Reproduction by Ampico and Welte-Mignon

Piano Playing Effects	The Artist	The Welte-Mignon	The Ampico
I—Tone Volume Smooth crescendos and diminuendos. Perfect control of accenting. Nuances.	Produces tone - volume ranging from the softest to the loudest through his ability to strike any string at any time with any desired degree of force. He can thus bring forth at his will smooth trills, crescendos, and diminuendos, subtle or brilliant accents, and delicate pulsations (nuances); and he can combine these elements in such a way as to create the contrasts and gradations of tone-volume that best express his personality and his interpretation of the composition.	Reproduces variations in tone-volume by means of a single expression pneumatic, on each side of the piano, to control the air-tension behind the hammers. The *one* pneumatic is used to control both the crescendos and the different degrees of accent required, and it is limited to a *fixed rate* of collapse for accenting, of either two or nine seconds. Consequently, the Welte - Mignon lacks proper control in reproducing crescendos and lacks speed and accuracy in accenting. As a result, the Welte-Mignon reproduces *only approximately* the constant variations of tone-volume in the artist's playing and misses much of the beauty of such playing.	Re-enacts variations in tone-volume by means of both a crescendo pneumatic system and an instantaneous accent pneumatic system, which it has the *exclusive* right to use *in combination* to control the air-tension behind the hammers. These systems may be operated *independently* for their separate effects, or *concurrently* for their combined effects. Consequently the Ampico can re-enact smooth crescendos and diminuendos, instantaneous accents, and the most delicate shadings of tone-volume. *It can strike any note at any time with any degree of force, and it is the only instrument on the market that can do this.*
II—Tone Colour Pedal effects. Singing tone.	The artist is able to sustain tones through lifting the dampers from certain strings or groups of strings. For this purpose he may hold down one or more keys for a brief period, or he may use with wonderful rapidity and delicacy the damper and sostenuto pedals. The subtle pedal effects and the singing tones thus produced blend with and colour succeeding tones in an infinite variety of beautiful effects.	The Welte-Mignon possesses a limited ability to operate the damper-pedal, but not with the rapidity and sureness of a skilled artist. It has no other means of lifting the dampers from the strings. Consequently it fails to reproduce the subtle pedal effects and the singing tones which constitute one of the chief distinctions of superlative piano playing.	The Ampico is able to lift any damper from any string for any period of time within the command of an artist. It accomplishes this both through its control of the pedals and through its patented system of lengthened perforations on the recording. It can thus re-enact even the artist's most delicate effects of tone-blending and tone-colouring.
III—Phrasing Variations in time. Variations in rhythm.	The artist is able, through minute variations in the time of striking notes, and through variations in time and rhythm thus produced, to give his individual phrasing and interpretation to a composition.	The Welte-Mignon recordings fail to register with exactitude slight variations in the time of beginning notes; and in addition, its dynamic control system is lacking in the responsiveness and precision requisite for exact reproduction of an artist's phrasing.	The Ampico is able to re-enact the artist's individual phrasing and interpretation through its exact method of recording the beginning of notes with a marking mechanism, and through the responsiveness and precision of its balanced regulation of dynamic control.

Figure 4.5 (*continued*)

balanced a regulator valve between crescendo and intensity pneumatics. This easily solved the problem of handling sudden accents. Ampico designers felt that seven steps were all that were necessary for reproducing loud accentuations.

The criticism of Duo-Art's inability to produce accentuation of the melody louder than one fixed degree of intensity above the accompaniment is certainly valid. Thematic material, particularly in late Romantic and early twentieth-century music, often requires dynamic levels several degrees louder than the accompanimental level in order to fulfill the composer's intentions. The music of Rachmaninoff, Scriabin, and Prokofief, for example, requires considerable difference in intensity between theme and accompaniment much of the time.

Ampico's tabular comparison states that the Duo-Art method of recording with a cutting mechanism fails to register slight variations in time at the beginning of notes with necessary exactitude. It is true there is more inertia in a recording machine using punches than there is in a machine using marking pens. The use of a cutting mechanism, however, did not seem to impair the beginning of notes and phrases according to those who recorded for Duo-Art. In the 1920s Duo-Art developed a second type of recording process in which a stencil was marked directly with ink.

One element of reproduction that Ampico took great pains to accurately represent was pedaling. Many subtle overtone effects are obtained when the damper pedal is used allowing all the strings to vibrate sympathetically. The damper pedal can be applied by different degrees, lifting the dampers only slightly from the strings for wonderful half-pedal effects. The sostenuto, or middle pedal, catches certain dampers and holds them off the strings, while the *una corda,* or soft pedal, moves the whole action over so that the softer parts of the felt covered hammers strike the strings with marked differences in the overtones produced. In most uprights the hammers are moved closer to the strings by a hammer rail and consequently do not move as far before striking.

Ampico master rolls had extensive markings on the side margins showing exactly when the dampers lifted from the strings and when they were returned. There were also indications that showed how fast the hammers were lifted from the strings or returned to them, and how deeply the dampers sank into the strings. In transferring these subtle effects to a mechanically operated pedal system, Ampico used a patented process of "bleeding" certain notes through extended note perforations. If a half-pedal effect was used, those notes whose dampers would be slightly raised in the original performance were sustained during playback by extended perforations in the music roll. The pneumatic mechanism controlling the damper pedal could not distinguish different degrees of half-pedaling. (Alas, Josef Lhevinne maintained there were at least four such degrees!)[11] An approximate half-pedal effect was recreated, however, by extending the note perforations. Neither Duo-Art nor Welte gave such careful attention to matters of pedaling, and the Welte firm was sometimes criticized for releasing rolls in which pedaling was smeary and imprecise.

Difficulties in reproducing soft pedal effects have never been fully explored, perhaps because of the many variables in hammer size, weight, and condition from one piano to the next. The lifting of the hammers by means of a rail in an upright does not produce the same variety in timbres as a shift in locus of the felt hammer tip in a grand piano. This lack of accurate reproduction of *una corda* tonal effects may be the only major shortcoming in the quest for reenacting the pedaling of past artists.

The challenge of accurately isolating a theme and voicing it so it stands out against an accompaniment is a problem that plagued designers even into the 1930s, when the popularity of reproducing pianos was past its prime.

Most reproducing pianos utilized two expression mechanisms, one controlling the treble half of the keyboard, and one accommodating the bass. The keyboard was usually divided between E-flat and E above middle C. If, as in most instances, melodic material occurred in the upper half of the keyboard and accompanimental figures in the lower half, there was no difficulty getting the melody to stand out more loudly than the accompaniment. More vacuum was introduced in the right half of the pneumatic stack by its expression mechanism than in the left half. Similarly, if melody occurred in the lower keyboard area and accompaniment in the upper part, a reverse of these vacuum levels brought the theme to the fore.

Occasionally both theme and accompaniment notes occur simultaneously and exclusively in the lower or upper regions of the keyboard. Then the problem of theme isolation becomes more of a challenge. An example in which this difficulty appears is the beginning of the Andante movement from Beethoven's Sonata in f minor, Op. 57, the *Appassionata*. This beautiful theme and variations begins with chords in the low register of the piano, the theme set in the top voice. Since both theme and accompaniment material are on the same side of a divided stack, the problem is how to make the theme sound louder than the accompaniment. By setting holes for the theme slightly ahead or behind accompaniment holes on the roll, a different pressure can be introduced almost instantaneously in the stack to make the melody stand out more. Welte usually set the theme ahead or behind approximately two holes, while Duo-Art and Ampico delayed or advanced theme holes by a distance of one hole. By delaying theme holes rather than advancing them, the accompaniment provided a masking effect that made time discrepancy between theme and accompaniment virtually unnoticeable.

In the Aeolian system, themodist or "snakebite" perforations are used to emphasize the melody, but again, only if those melody notes precede or follow the other notes in the chord by a fraction of time. In order to be affected by themodist perforations, melody note holes must occur slightly earlier or later than note holes for the rest of a chord. Rudolph Ganz actually felt it was more realistic to separate theme notes by preceding or succeeding accompaniment notes in such a manner. This process fails, however, to give us an accurate portrayal of who may have actually played that way.

The ideal reproducing system would be capable of simultaneously isolating a theme against its accompaniment. An ingenious solution to the problem of theme isolation was arrived at by Gordon Iles of Aeolian in England. Iles designed a tracker bar featuring two rows of holes, one for accompaniment, and one for theme. The accompaniment row of holes could be instantaneously switched on or off, while the row of holes for melody was activated by themodist perforations at the sides of the roll.

Such a system provides for a row of melody and accompaniment notes simultaneously sounding together, with a difference in dynamic level of a fixed degree. A desirable feature of this system was that rolls cut for it could be played on the standard pianola and could activate its expression mechanism in the usual way.

Another means for isolating themes was designed by Aeolian in which a tracker bar with a single row of holes was used. Each hole had three individual functions: (1) every hole represented a given note, (2) every hole canceled the note playing power of the hole on its left, and (3) each hole was switched by the hole on its left to theme playing intensity. In a composition such as the Brahms *Intermezzo,* Op. 117, No. 3, where a melody is straddled on both sides by accompaniment, each theme perforation served to accentuate the melody note, at the same time having its own note playing power canceled by the theme perforation to its immediate right.

Perfection in theme isolation devices came too late to be a commercial success. Despite the immense amount of research that went into design of theme isolation devices, the cost for producing and marketing such devices was prohibitively expensive, especially after the Depression.

Accuracy in reproducing a past performance depends not only on the recording process used and on the reproducing instrument playing it back, but also on the condition of the roll itself, whether it be an original or a third-generation copy. Ideally the collector will seek a reproducing roll that is one of the original lot cut from a stencil taken from the master roll. Since these original rolls are produced in limited numbers and are subject to wear, copies are often made from them. A copy made from an original roll will lose some accuracy, perhaps as much as eight percent. If a copy is then run from the first generation copy, another eight percent accuracy is lost and the result will be slightly less than eighty-five percent accurate. It is always preferable, though not always possible, to have a copy run from the original stencil. The superior speed and wider spacing of perforations in the stencil will usually produce a more accurate result than roll to roll copying in the ratio of one-to-one.

The figure marked at the beginning of each roll, divided by ten, designates the roll's speed in number of feet per minute. Tempo 80 means a roll should run at the rate of eight feet per minute. Tempo 50 means a roll should run at the rate of five feet per minute. The number marked by the manufacturer can be regarded as accurate, but it was not uncommon for technicians to adjust reproducer vacuum and speed settings on the high side. Perhaps this was part of the faster-louder mania that ravaged ragtime during the Flapper Era. Vacuum and speed adjustments can be easily checked, however, on a reproducing piano by using a test roll issued by the manufacturer.

One criticism of the paper roll was that it could be easily altered. Wrong notes could be amended by taping over corresponding note holes and punching new holes in correct locations on the master piano roll. Expression coding could be changed in a similar way. Copies of the original roll, however, revealed none of the editing that preceded their release.

How much editing individual companies may have done before issuing their piano rolls is not verifiable. The standards maintained by Welte, Duo-Art, and Ampico were exceedingly high, not only because of the integrity of the artists who recorded for them, but because they were in competition with each other. Some master rolls were withheld despite considerable editing, perhaps in the belief that "you can't make a silk purse out of a sow's ear."

Despite considerable advertising by each firm lauding their own technology, it is apparent that all reproducing systems have strengths and weaknesses intrinsic to their basic design. No one system can be placed on a pedestal above the others. The technological advantages some manufacturers realized in the late 1920s are offset by the fact that some of the most interesting recordings were made with earlier systems on rolls that could not be played on the later reproducers.[12]

The notes themselves, with attendant rubatos, phrasings, and articulations, are most important in preserving a pianist's style. Most of the reproducing systems described give satisfactory results in these respects. Dynamics and pedaling give a reasonably accurate account of what went on in the recording studio, especially in the case of composer-pianists, such as Rachmaninoff, who were fastidious in reworking a roll to their ultimate satisfaction.

Since a Studio Master was often responsible for notating dynamics and pedaling in the piano score as a work was performed, early recording sessions partook of a subjective element. Despite tremendous efforts of early designers and manufacturers to achieve perfection in recreating a pianist's performance, what ultimately resulted from a recording session may have been more a subjective depiction of an artist's playing rather than an objective photograph of it. Given the subjective element in painted portraits, the artist's presentation of a person often reveals more of a subject's character than does a photographic representation of the same. Many reproducing rolls may not be photographs, as such, of an artist's playing. Instead, they are to be regarded as veritable portraits of great artistic worth.

The reproducing piano in the United States was an important addition to the living-room parlor where most social interactions transpired. Not only did it provide music for enjoyment, but it represented the rising faith in the machine as an instrument of benefit to mankind even in the province of the arts. If Henry Ford could build a horseless carriage to transport an individual from east to west coast, why not build a musical machine to transport one's soul to the rapturous climes of a musical Mt. Olympus as well? Originally a rich man's source of enjoyment, reproducing pianos became increasingly available to the American middle-class homeowner at an affordable price.

The musical significance of the reproducing piano had been succinctly stated by Josef Hofmann almost eighty years ago. Writing a testimonial for M. Welte and Sons, he said: "The incomparable Welte Mignon art piano has opened an eventful future before the musical world. Henceforth the player piano will be on a level with the productive artist in regard to the imperishability of his work. What a loss it means to us not to have had the reproducing piano long ago! But what a blessing it will prove to future generations!"[13]

As reproducing instruments proliferated in the 1920s, however, the number of qualified servicemen became more thinly spread. Because of intricate mechanisms employed in reproducing systems, needs for periodic adjustment and maintenance were great; these often went unfulfilled. The sad consequence was that many people came to believe that reproducing systems were crude devices at best. Some went so far as to have their pianos gutted of the reproducing elements altogether, so they might be played solely in the ordinary manner.

By 1930 the reproducing piano was on the wane for a number of reasons. The Depression following the 1929 stock market crash affected numerous potential buyers. Many of the wealthy who were unscathed by bankruptcy delayed purchasing such luxuries as reproducing pianos to see how the money tide might flow.

Further, the gramophone was coming into its own as acoustic recordings and record players were replaced by electric ones. Not only were gramophone records more convenient to handle and store, but the discs and machines themselves were more compact and considerably less expensive than the cumbersome reproducing instruments. Moreover, the gramophone could play back not only piano selections, but vocal and orchestral performances as well.

No doubt a number of wealthy persons purchased reproducing pianos solely for prestige. During the 1930s infatuation with the motorcar was prevalent in Europe and the United States. Many believed "you are what you drive." Doubtless for such people the reproducing piano couldn't compete with such a mobile prestige item. By the mid-1930s, despite some remarkable innovations in design, the demand for reproducing pianos trickled almost to a standstill, and interest in these instruments lay dormant for decades.

Only in the 1980s did reproducing pianos begin to make a comeback, this time using sophisticated electronics to measure hammer velocity and pedaling instead of vacuum pneumatics. Phoenix-like, interest in these instruments and a commercial market for electronically digitalized versions of the classical piano rolls has risen once again. A new era, girded by increasingly innovative technological advances, heralds a fresh interest in America for the preservation of present and past keyboard performances for generations yet to come.

NOTES:

[1]*Welte Mignon's Artists' List:*161.

[2]Ibid.:3.

[3]Q. David Bowers, *Encyclopedia of Automatic Musical Instruments* (Vestal Press; Vestal, NY, 1977):340.

[4]Ibid.:340.

[5]London Records (Historic) Record No. 425964–2 LM (ADD).

[6]*The Great Piano Roll Mystery,* BBC 3.

[7]Ibid.

[8]Ibid.

[9]Ibid.

[10]*The American Piano Company Comparison Chart:*24.

[11]Josef Lhevinne, *Basic Principles in Pianoforte Playing* (reprint New York: Dover, 1972):47.

[12]Bowers, *Encyclopedia of Automatic Musical Instruments:*273.

[13]More detailed information about various reproducing designs and systems can be found in my book *Reproducing Pianos Past and Present* (Mellen 1989). The following sources also contain valuable information about reproducing pianos: Alexander Buchner, *Mechanical Musical Instruments* (London: Batchworth, 1955); Alfred Dolge, *Pianos and Their Makers* (Covina, California, 1911); Larry Givens, *Re-enacting the Artist* (Vestal, NY: Vestal Press, 1970); John McTammany, *The Technical History of the Player* (New York: Musical Courier Co, 1915); Arthur W. J. G. Ord-Hume, *Pianola/The History of the Self-Playing Piano* (London: Geroge Allen and Unwin, 1984): Albert Protz, *Mechanische Musikinstrumente* (Kasel: Bärenreiter, 1943); and William Braid White, *Piano Playing Mechanisms* (New York: Edward Lyman Bill, 1925). Finally, I also consulted the following sources in preparing this essay: The American Piano Company Comparison Chart, AMPICO (New York, New York, 1925); *The Ampico Magazine* (Winter, 1920); Patent Records; service and repair manuals; and a personal interview with Frank Laffitte, Berkhamstead, England (17 July 1978).

CHAPTER 5

Dances, Frolics, and Orchestra Wars
The Territory Bands and Ballrooms of Kansas City, Missouri, 1925–1935

MARC RICE

Throughout the 1920s and 1930s Kansas City, Missouri, was the focal point for the travels of the territory bands: African American jazz ensembles that toured the cities and towns of the South- and Midwest. These bands were of central importance in the Black culture of this city, both as entertainers and as markers of Black pride and identity in a hostile, segregated region. In the early 1920s the territory bands played for African American charities, holiday events, political and social organizations, and other affairs unique to the Black communities. By the late 1920s the bands also were performing for White dances, thus introducing Black music to a segregated audience.

Much of the research into the territory band phenomenon has focused on either the orchestras themselves, in terms of their personnel and performance itineraries, or the connections between the orchestras and the illicit gambling and alcohol industries generated predominantly by White politicians and criminals.[1] Certainly there was a connection between criminal elements and the bands, particularly in Kansas City. There was another aspect in the history of these orchestras, however, that requires further examination: the relationship of the bands with the city's Black communities. In Kansas City there was extensive racial segregation and discrimination against Blacks, and the African American communities constantly strove to achieve autonomy in this situation. The territory bands were a vital part of this struggle.

During the 1910s and 1920s, many cities witnessed a rapid increase in their African American populations, as the result of a large migration of Blacks from the south to the north, and from rural to urban centers. In

137

Kansas City, the Black population rose from 23,704 in 1910, to 30,893 in 1920, and to 42,005 in 1930.[2] African American residence, however, was confined to approximately twenty-three square blocks, in the northeastern section of the city. As Charles Goodwin, a guitarist with several territory bands remembered:

> It was known that this is the line where Blacks stop . . . this was my boundaries and I know this is where I am supposed to live, and I didn't like it. But there wasn't nothing too much you could do about it, only try not to put yourself in a position to think that you were a lower type person because of the place where you had to live.[3]

Threats and violence were one means by which African American housing was restricted. Until the late 1920s bombings and bomb threats were commonly reported in the city's African American newspaper, the *Kansas City Call.*[4] In 1922, for example, a Black disabled veteran was confronted by fourteen White men as he moved into a home at 21st and Park,[5] and the home of a Dr. Bruce on 26th street was bombed twice.[6]

Political maneuvers were another means by which Whites segregated Black real estate. For instance, in 1926, a group of Whites called the "Linwood Improvement Association" petitioned Kansas City's Parks Board to create a park along 26th Street, the southernmost border of the Black district. The group wanted the park to serve as a "buffer zone" between White and Black neighborhoods. The plan would have required the condemnation of sixty-two African American homes, which was rejected by the board after a protracted battle.[7]

The segregated African American district served as a perfect area for the establishments of illicit bars and nightclubs offering alcohol, gambling, and prostitution, three activities that were illegal in the 1920s and early 1930s. Historians of jazz in Kansas City have concentrated on such venues, which were supported by and provided profits to the corrupt city government. Three issues need to be addressed, however, to fully complete the picture of jazz in Kansas City, and in the Southwest as a whole. First of all, many of the city's Blacks resented the presence of illegal activity connected to the illicit venues in their neighborhoods. Second, many African Americans did not patronize the clandestine venues, but many more did attend the large formal dances that they themselves organized. Finally, the illicit bars were not the jazz musician's main source of income; that came from the formal dances held in venues that could accommodate many more patrons.

The bars and nightclubs that featured criminal activity were supported by the policies of the city government, which was controlled by Tom Pendergast from 1925–1938. The Pendergast government established a system whereby a bar or nightclub owner could openly provide alcohol, gambling, and prostitution, if a portion of the proceeds went into the pockets of government officials. From 1928–1932 Johnny Lazia served as a liaison between Pendergast and the nightclub owners. The control of politicians over this industry is revealed by Jerome T. Duggan, a city counselor member of that era:

> I remember I was assigned to represent the directory of liquor control. And I found out up there that . . . to get a liquor license you'd have to order your beer from Johnny Lazia, [order] your mix, you had to order a certain towel service. Everything was designated where you had to do business. If you'd go up there and apply for a license, you'd be turned down. But when you came out of that office, there'd be a man there waiting, saying "You're having trouble getting that license? Well I can fix that for you. Sign these orders, and order these supplies." They had the fix on everything.[8]

The typical venue that featured illegal activities in the 1920s and 1930s was a small, two-story structure, with a room for listening and dancing to jazz, and another room for gambling. One of the most notorious bars in Kansas City was the Yellow Front, where a sixteen-year-old boy named Fred Hicks was a frequent patron. As Hicks remembered seventy years later, the Yellow Front was far from the most illustrious building in the Black district:

> [The Yellow Front] was an old house, and this house leaned like the tower of Babylon. It must have been well built, because you don't find a house leaning, and as many people as they had going in this club, dancing and jumping around, that would remain standing.[9]

Hicks recalled that the activities at the Yellow Front, and the class of people who patronized it, also were not the most respectable of the community:

> Now upstairs is where they did the dancing, all the entertaining and stuff. Below was where they shot dice, played cards, and all that kind of carrying on. . . . It was a different type that went in those places. . . .

Down on that end of town was sort of on the low-brow. Guys that had
been out of society, had done wrong things, they'd hang down there,
they wouldn't hang with the best.[10]

The involvement of venues such as the Yellow Front with illegal activities brought serious criminal and gangster problems to the African
American neighborhoods. In 1929 fifty Blacks were murdered in the
city.[11] The same year Felix Payne, who owned the Subway Club, was
kidnapped by "business partners" and ordered to produce $20,000 in
cash within a specified length of time.[12] During this same period, Ellis
Burton, the owner of the Yellow Front, was accused of hiring a thug to
assault an organizer of the Brotherhood of Sleeping Car Porters.[13]

Clearly, places such as the Yellow Front were not always safe. According to musician Booker T. Washington, "They were drinking nothing
but corn whiskey there. And they get full of that and people start shooting
at each other, and take a knife at each other."[14] But there was a large seg-
ment of the Black population that did not partake of the illegal activities
offered at these places. As Woodie Walder, a saxophonist in Kansas City
for many years, stated, "If they wasn't [respectable] I didn't know
nothin' about 'em because I'd stay away from bad company. That's what
my people always said; don't run with bad company."[15]

Certainly there were African Americans who patronized places like
the Yellow Front; but there were many others who resented the criminal
element that such venues, and their political supporters, brought into
their community. These opinions appeared often in the *Call*. As one editorial summarized the situation,

ties between the police and the racketeers endanger us most of all the
elements that make up the city's population.... Our residence
district ... suffers the contamination of white vice resorts.... So long
as an officer [is] expected to contribute funds to the [political] party in
power, his own initiative, and sometimes direct orders from superiors,
made him a collector from the rackets which prey upon the community.[16]

African Americans in the city also resented the image that illegal activities gave to their neighborhood. For instance, after an election in
1928, in which most Black voters supported the Democratic party in
power, the White newspaper the *Kansas City Star* stated that this support
was "to protect crap games." The *Call* responded:

One daily paper [white] quoted politicians as stating that Negroes voted for the protection of their crap games and night life on Twelfth and Eighteenth Sts. . . . Even the fertile imagination of the reporter who wrote that twaddle would hardly charge the women who handle family finances and the host of church members with voting "to protect crap games." . . . Their operators and their customers are too few to effect the thousands of Negro voters ("Analysis of Vote Figures Shows Vice Had Little Effect on Negro Ballots").[17]

It is clear from this commentary that many of Kansas City's Blacks did not patronize the gambling and drinking establishments. Also seen in this quote is a glimpse of the many social structures that made up the city's Black culture. Many of the "women who handle family finances" belonged to ladies auxiliaries; many of the "host of church members" also were members of fraternal lodges and/or charity organizations. These groups danced and listened to jazz, but in a quite different context than that of the bar or gambling parlor.

The various African American social groups in the Southwest organized and attended large, often formal dances, which had little connection to any criminal element. In Kansas City the Freemasons, the Knights of Pythias, and Elks Club had African American chapters. There were also locally based men's groups, such as the Beau Brummels and the Cheerio Boys. In addition there were women's groups, including the Forget-Me-Not Girls, the Nit-Wit Club, and the Delta Sigma Theta sorority of Lincoln University in Jefferson City, Missouri. Dances that were not sponsored by social organizations were sponsored by the musicians themselves; the Black Musicians Local 627 had an annual dance that featured four or more of the city's best bands.

These dances were held not in small, decrepit buildings, but in large, elegant dance halls. In Kansas City there were two such ballrooms that were frequently used by African Americans: the hall at the Labor Temple, and the Paseo Hall. These buildings were White-owned, but were located in the Black district. African American dances there were usually held on Sundays or weekdays; presumably Fridays and Saturdays were reserved for Whites.

Even though the dance halls were owned by Whites, these events were organized solely by and for African Americans. They were a place for safe, respectable recreation, "where uncertain teenagers, clerks, shopgirls, and young workmen were gentlemen and ladies for the evening."[18] The ballrooms also enriched the community spirit. As Hazzard-Gordon discovered about dance halls in other communities, those in Kansas City reinforced ethnic and class ties.[19] The dances were a communal effort, and a source of pride for this community.

The Labor Temple was near the center of Kansas City's African American district, which was 18th and Vine. From this point Black businesses, entertainment venues, and residences were located for several blocks in any direction. The Labor Temple was located on a corner two blocks east and four blocks north of 18th and Vine, on 14th and Woodland. Its primary function was to serve as a meeting place for the city's various labor unions, both White and Black. On the second floor of the Labor Temple was a ballroom that could accommodate approximately eight hundred people. On certain days it was opened to Blacks, and represented one of the first and most luxurious dance venues available to them. As Hicks recalled, "The Labor Temple was an upstairs affair. It wasn't too large but it was large enough to give a dance . . . all night dances. You'd like to go there about twelve o'clock, dance till about five in the morning. That's where the people went."[20]

According to Hicks, three dancing halls were established in rapid succession for the use of African Americans during the early 1920s. The first two were the Lydia and the Labor Temple, which, if the advertisements in the *Call* are an indication, were used frequently until the early 1930s. The third ballroom was The Paseo Hall, which first admitted Blacks in 1925. According to Hicks, the Paseo Hall was the most extravagant in the city available to Blacks. It was also the dance venue featured most prominently in the press during this time.[21]

The Paseo Hall was located on the corner of 15th and the Paseo, three blocks north and one block west from 18th and Vine. Hicks remembers that the decor was certainly much different from that of the nightclubs and gambling parlors such as the Yellow Front. Furthermore, Hicks makes class distinctions about those who attended dances at the Paseo Hall, which contrasted markedly with his referral to the Yellow Front patrons as "lowbrow":

> The Paseo Hall, that's the classiest, where the elites would go. It was a beautiful place. You'd see oak floors like glass. They had the crystal ball in the ceiling that sparkled the place all up. They had booths that you could sit around, if you wasn't dancing. They had a bandstand on the west side of the hall. . . . [at the Paseo] you got to have ties and suits on. You don't come in there anyway. You got to have your best on.[22]

In comparison to nightclubs such as the Yellow Front, there was little illegal activity at the ballroom dances. Ironically, an arrest of twenty-five people for drinking after a dance supports this claim. As the *Call* reported the incident, the revelers were in search of a drink, after a sober affair:

> Among those arrested were several couples in evening dress who had come to the hotel after the closing of a smart formal dancing party given by one of the leading professional organizations of the city. These people, as parties frequently do, had come to the hotel seeking to "break loose" in an after party, following the severely dignified, full-dress affair. They were among the first to be loaded into the wagon.[23]

Virtually every week in Kansas City during the 1920s and 1930s American social groups, or the musicians themselves, organized ballroom dances. These affairs may be categorized into several types. Holidays, in particular Christmas and New Year's Eve, and also Easter, Mother's Day, and Halloween, were celebrated at the dance halls, with special decorations and themes. There were frequent charity dances, benefits for African American schools and hospitals, or political causes like the National Association for the Advancement of Colored People (NAACP), the Pullman Porters, or the musicians' unions. There were affairs featuring nonmusical elements, for instance a tennis or basketball exhibition preceding a dance, the awarding of special door prizes, and even the shooting of movies. Also important were the battle of the band contests, which "pitted" two or more orchestras "against" each other. In addition to these events there were the regularly scheduled dancing nights. Such dances provided steady employment for the bands, and carried no special connotations.

By the early 1920s dances were held at the Kansas City ballrooms to celebrate most holidays. Quite often these dances were organized as benefits for a cause, such as the Halloween Dance of 1923 at the Shriner's hall in Kansas City, Kansas, which raised money for a children's home. As with many other dances, the hall for this affair was decorated in the spirit of the holiday, and the dancers wore costumes.[24]

The nature of the Halloween holiday, with its connection to costumes and pagan ritual, suggests a good opportunity for a dance. Indeed, the Halloween dances were an annual affair. But other and even minor holidays also were celebrated with dances. In 1929, for instance, Mother's Day was celebrated with the appearance of Terrence "T."

Holder's Eleven Clouds of Joy at the Paseo Hall. The Holder orchestra
was a territory band based in Tulsa, and during this time they only played
once or twice a year in Kansas City. The article advertising the event ran
a long quote from George E. Lee, who stated "I believe that T. Holders
[*sic*] and his Eleven Clouds of Joy are absolutely the hottest Negro orchestra in the United States.[25]

Labor Day also was celebrated with dancing. In 1929 the Labor Day
dance was held at the Paseo Hall, and featured a territory band from St.
Louis led by Oliver Cobb. The ad for this event provided great detail
about the musicians, which demonstrates the style of publicity and also
the importance of having guest musicians. Supplying the "holiday dancing menu" was cornetist Cobb, "the man who out-Armstrong's Louis
Armstrong," his "drummer and cymbalist extraordinary" Lester Nichols;
Eddie Johnson, the "wizard of the piano and accordion," and Benny
Jackson, "who can make a banjo do things it shouldn't."[26]

Easter was a special day in the African American communities, and
after parades, church services, and dinners there was dancing. For example, in 1926 a "Big Easter Frolic and Dance" was held at the Paseo Hall,
with music provided by the Bennie Moten Orchestra. At this affair a diamond ring and a gold watch were given away as door prizes. According
to the ad for the occasion, new dances were to be introduced, and the organizers promised "to make this the biggest affair of the year."[27]

Thanksgiving 1927 was celebrated at the Paseo Hall with the distribution of free turkeys. This dance was organized by the Triangle Club, a
group of government employees. The turkeys were to ensure a large attendance, as the ad indicated:

> When the happy hour for dinner is here—and you smell the odor of
> that famous turkey—and you are all happy around the family table—
> ain't that a grand and glorious feeling! No wonder we are expecting a
> big crowd! With a FREE Turkey and the best dance of the year. How
> could we keep 'em out? And remember Bennie Moten's Orchestra will
> be there with some new music. Come![28]

The most elaborate holiday dances were held during the Christmas
season, and special activities and decorations marked the celebrations.
For instance, on Christmas Day 1926, and New Year's Day 1927, the
Labor Temple ballroom was transformed into a "French Cabaret—one of
those Montmarte cabarets that the boys of the A. E. F. talk about." The ad
(see Figure 5.1) gives a brief description of "this beautiful dance hall

Figure 5.1. An advertisement in the *Kansas City Call* (24 December 1926).

with its mammoth crystal ball." The phrase "don't forget our regular SUNDAY NIGHT DANCES" indicates the continuous dancing and steady employment for the dance orchestras at the Labor Temple Ballroom during this time.[29] Similar dances were held on 25 and 26 December 1927 at the Paseo Hall. According to the ad for this event, "this cabaret dance will be an exact duplicate of the night life in New York City, featuring numerous singers and dancers. [There will be] presents for everyone attending this mammoth affair." The Moten Orchestra was the featured attraction, but clearly there were additional entertainers as well.[30]

By the early 1920s the presentation of dances was an important method of raising money for charity. The dances were organized by three basic social groups: men's clubs, ladies' auxiliaries, and political organizations. There were also three general causes: the African American poor of the city, the health and social institutions, such as the Niles Orphan's Home, the Wheatley Provident Hospital; and political groups, such as the NAACP, the Brotherhood of Sleeping Car Porters, or the Republican Party.

The most prominent men's groups involved in charity functions were the Elks, the Masons, and the Beau Brummels. In 1922 the Elks began holding annual dances in early December for the benefit of the poor. That particular event featured Bennie Moten's first group, a trio called the B. B. and D., which was proclaimed the "Elks Official Orchestra" and was held at the Labor Temple.[31] The Elk's dances became even more important with the onset of the Depression, as the dance of 1930 raised enough money to provide baskets of food and coal for about five hundred families.[32]

One of the most extravagant benefits of the 1920s was the weeklong fair organized by the local African American Masonic Lodge in 1926. As Figure 5.2 shows, different activities were planned for each night of the week, several contests and prizes were awarded, with a costume night on Tuesday. The bands featured were the best in the city, including George E. Lee's and Bennie Moten's orchestras, and a military band. The location of the fair, at Lincoln Hall, also indicates the nature of the event: Lincoln Hall was used for vaudeville in the early 1920s, and for shows that combined vaudeville and movies in the late 1920s and early 1930s. It was patronized almost exclusively by Blacks and was the Kansas City stop for the T. O. B. A. shows.[33]

The Beau Brummels was a local men's club with an involvement in raising money for various charities. The club also held annual benefits, which often combined dancing with skits and carnival booths. For exam-

Figure 5.2. An advertisement in the *Kansas City Call* (3 December 1926).

ple, an ad for a dance held in 1925 announces a "Vaudeville Review, Carnival, and Dance" with the Bennie Moten Orchestra. This event, held at the Labor Temple, benefited the Niles Orphan's Home and a group called "Allied Charities."[34] The Beau Brummels were the largest (or at least sponsored the most dances) of several men's charity groups, with names like the Bachelor Boys, the Cheerio Boys, and the Sans Souci. There also was a Council of Men's Clubs, which administered all these groups.[35]

The Wheatley Provident Hospital was one of two hospitals available to African Americans, and the only one in the African American district. Beginning in 1919 a women's group called the "Wheatley Provident Hospital Auxiliary No. 1" organized an annual benefit for the institution, which became increasing elaborate as the popularity of dancing grew during the 1920s. By the mid-1920s, and in conjunction with this benefit, there was a fashion show, with "beautiful costumes, spectacular ensembles, [and a] gorgeous setting," combined with dancing music provided by either the Moten or Lee orchestras.[36] By 1930 the benefit had expanded to include a circus, with "200 Performers," including a snake charmer, a tightrope walker, and a bearded lady. All this in addition to the fashion show, which by 1930 exhibited "137 models, 24 ballet dancers, 10 soft shoe dancers, and 25 toe dancers."[37]

The Delta Sigma Theta sorority of Lincoln University also held benefit dances for the hospital. In 1926 they gave a "College Cabaret" at the Labor Temple, including a "college girls interpretation of modern cabaret with song, dance, and snappy review." The music of the Moten Orchestra was heard in alternation with performances by the sorority members, which included songs and Charleston dancing exhibitions. According to an article published in the *Call,* the event was very well attended.[38]

The benefit dances both provided assistance and served to unite the Black communities of Kansas City. This unification is clearly demonstrated by the many benefits for political causes, such as the benefit dance for the Brotherhood of Sleeping Car Porters, held in 1928. The Brotherhood was a very strong Black union; thus, the ad for this affair includes much political commentary. The *Call*'s readers were urged to buy tickets whether they attend or not,

> **Because**—you will be fighting against the oppression of All laboring Negroes;
> **Because**—you will be helping directly the upkeep of churches, fraternal and social organizations;
> **Because**—you will be aiding in the general education of our children the country over;
> **Because**—only organized Negro resistance will successfully overcome organized white unfairness.[39]

This dance was held at the Paseo Hall, with music by the Bennie Moten Orchestra.

The Kansas City chapter of the NAACP was organized about 1922, and an important task of this group each year was to raise money for the national fund. According to its president, John L. Love, in the 1920s the group

kept the Stiles brothers from being returned to Arkansas peonage, it
has provided guards for homes threatened with bombing, it helped fi-
nance the most important case in Kansas City involving the right to
purchase and occupy homes, it has been active in cases of the miscar-
riage of justice . . . it has sought to protect our womanhood . . . and demanded the prosecution of lynchers.[40]

The NAACP also sponsored dances to raise funds. One such dance,
given in 1927, featured costumes and a "Greenwich Village" theme. Although the ad is not quite as elaborate as some from this period, the unusual rhyme scheme distinguishes it from others.[41]

A dance event took place in 1928 that challenges, if not refutes, the
theory that jazz in Kansas City was completely dependent upon the city's
political corruption. The political party in power, and the main benefi-
ciary of gambling and liquor distribution, was the Democrat Party. In
1922 most of the city's Blacks voted for the Republicans, but by 1928
about half were voting for the Democrats. Just before the November
elections in 1928, a rally for the Republican Party was staged by African
Americans with the head of the Elks, and member of the Republican
Party, J. Finley Wilson, delivering a speech. The interesting aspect is that
the Bennie Moten Orchestra provided the entertainment for this affair,
thus performing for the rivals of those who controlled the nightclubs.[42]

Another genre of dances may be termed "special events." These
were affairs with extramusical aspects featured as part of the entertainment, in addition to dancing. Athletic exhibitions, contests for the
dancers, the filming of movies, and celebrations for the achievements of
the bands themselves were frequently part of the festivities at the Black
ballrooms.

Athletic exhibitions occasionally prefaced dancing at the Labor
Temple and Paseo halls. For example, in 1923 there was a basketball
game between the *Kansas City Call* Athletic Club and the Kaw Valley
Athletic Club at the Labor Temple, followed by dancing to the Bennie
Moten Orchestra. As the ad announced, those in attendance witnessed "a
basketball game and dance for one admission."[43] Another example was
a dance preceded by a tennis exhibition in 1927. The exhibition featured
a series of matches, culminating in a demonstration by Eyre B. Saitch,
the African American singles champion. The audience was encouraged
to dress up, as "two prizes [were] given for the best sport costumes on the
floor." The Moten Orchestra concluded the affair.[44]

A very important event in the African American culture of the city was the opening day of the season for the Kansas City Monarchs, the Negro League baseball team. In 1929 this event was celebrated with a dance at Paseo Hall, with the entire team in attendance (see the illustration on the following page). The ad clearly demonstrates that the team was part of the community, with remarks like, "would you know the ball players in their street attire? See if you can pick them out among the crowd. . . . Meet the new ones along with the old timers." An appeal to the single ladies of the community seems to be made with the phrase "Some are married. Some are not; some not quite—but all fine fellows and worth meeting." The comment "Hear the Rinky Dinks blow those 'hateful' Monarchs blues" hints at the style of music heard at the dance, and the probability that the Downs Orchestra had at least one piece in their repertory named for the team.[45]

Contests and costume competitions were a popular part of the ballroom affairs. Perhaps the most unusual contest was a combination "Cabaret Dance" and live rooster race, held in 1927. This was held at the Paseo Hall, with music supplied by the Moten Orchestra. Six "trained fast roosters" were supplied by the organizers of the event, but contestants also were encouraged to "bring on your [own] roosters."[46] Another example of a contest was the "Girls Popularity Contest," also held at the Paseo Hall in 1927.[47] There also were frequent costume competitions, usually associated with themes. A dance in 1929 was called "Kiddies on Parade," during which the Lee Orchestra "intend[ed] to 'Stomp It' for you 'Children'." The dance offered "one 'good shot' for Grownups to be Kids again," and a "big cash prize for the best kiddie costume."[48]

A few months after the "Kiddies" dance there was another affair with a "Wigwam" theme. Attendants were informed that "Chief George Lee" would provide a night of "Heap Big Whoopee!!" The dancers, labeled "squaws and braves" were instructed to

> bring your ball and chain and put them in your teepee. Bundle up your cares and worries for this special night. Get that back to nature feeling when the bands starts throbbing torrid syncopation. Camp grounds will be laid at Paseo Hall, decorated for the occasion with wigwams and Indian fixin's [*sic*]. Bows and arrows will be waiting for you. Revel, dance, stomp, 'till the night gets long and the day's not far![49]

The production of a movie at Paseo Hall in 1927 was an unusual, but very important event. The Pathé company came to Paseo to make "a

Super Movie Picture of the Negroes of Greater Kansas City—Social—
Business—Civic" during five consecutive nights. The ad (see Figure 5.3)
demonstrates the Pathé company's appeal to the pride of African Americans, with phrases such as "History making! Will you be a part of it?"
and the description of the film as "Educational—Refined—Interesting. A

Figure 5.3. An advertisement in the *Kansas City Call* (18 March 1927).

picture everyone should be in." The ad also provides important details of the Black social organizations. Even the gender roles of the community can be seen: Those in charge of enrolling the various clubs and committees were all women; those assisting the cameramen, with the exception of Mrs. Ida Becks, were all men.[50]

Special dances were often held in honor of the orchestras themselves.[51] When the bands won an award, a celebration dance was held; when they went out of town, a farewell dance fit the occasion; when they returned to Kansas City, they were welcomed back with a large reception and ball. If the ads in the *Call* provide an accurate picture, the Moten and Lee bands in particular were extremely popular, and were often the guests of honor at the affairs for which they entertained.

In December 1926, the Moten Orchestra made its first records for the Victor label. This was an achievement, because it was the first band from the Southwest to record for a record company with national distribution, and was the only band to be recorded regularly. In addition, the orchestra had just switched to Victor from the smaller Okeh label, itself the "race record" division of the General Phonograph Company. The *Call* announced the occasion with much fanfare:

> It's Bennie Moten's Victor Orchestra now. In three years this hustling musician has brought his organization to real national recognition. . . . This is the first colored orchestra to record popular numbers and the second to record anything for the Victor Co., who just recently decided to feature the colored musicians.[52]

The Moten recordings were released in Kansas City in March 1927. As is common today, there was a record release party, with a celebration dance at the Paseo Hall. The ad requested that the Black public "all turn out and give Bennie and his orchestra a rousing welcome. The first colored orchestra outside of New York to record for Victor. It has taken Bennie years of effort to reach his goal." From the time of this ad until the end of the Moten Orchestra's career in 1935, the band was advertised in the *Call* as "Bennie Moten and his Victor Recording Orchestra."[53]

A month after the Victor dance, Moten was awarded a "$500 Loving Cup" by the American Recording Artists. Naturally, such an occasion called for a dance at the Paseo Hall. The ad for this event featured a picture of the trophy, and the caption "Let's turn out and give Bennie three cheers for this Great Honor bestowed upon him." An important feature of the ad is the description of the entertainment: "Dainty Girls singing Steaming Hot Blues." Clearly foxtrots and schottisches were not the only dances performed at the Paseo Hall.[54]

The Moten Orchestra made their first tour of the Northeast, including Harlem and upstate New York, in 1928.[55] Upon the orchestra's return to Kansas City in September, a dance was held that filled the Paseo Hall to near-capacity. The *Call*'s review of the evening indicates the popularity of the orchestra within the African American communities:

> That Kansas City's music and dance lovers are glad Bennie Moten and his orchestra are back was vividly illustrated . . . when 1,700 people crowded into Paseo hall to hear and see what the boys had brought back in the way of syncopation, after their nine months absence. Apparently, from the reception given the orchestra, the boys brought back plenty. . . . [They] showed their pleasure in being back again by rendering the latest music with such an improvement in style that encore after encore was necessary to satisfy the huge crowd.[56]

During the absence of the Moten Orchestra from Kansas City, the Lee Orchestra filled the void, and achieved a comparable popularity with the public. In fact, a biographical article about Lee was published in the *Call* in June 1928, under the title "The *Call*'s Success Stories: Men and Women Worth While."[57] When the Lee Orchestra departed in July for a long tour, a farewell dance was given at the Paseo Hall. The *Call*'s announcement of the occasion illustrates the affection of the community for this band:

> We remember the club dances, all the public dances and the tight contests which they have played for the last twelve months; they were just too hot! This last dance, in which they bid us adieu will be tighter than that. There will be a prize given away by Mr. Lee himself, a souvenir just to remember. Paseo Hall has been the scene of some torrid rehearsals the last few days, and a real Farewell Dance program will be yours. This is good-bye.[58]

The Paseo Hall was a witness to many band battles during this time. There were at least five well-established orchestras active in or near Kansas City in the late 1920s: the Moten Orchestra, the Lee Orchestra, Chauncey Downs and His Rinky Dinks, Jessie Stone's Blue Serenaders, and Paul Bank's Syncopating Band. It was the custom for two or more bands to schedule a musical dual at a ballroom, in order to establish superiority in a territory, and to draw a large audience. Such events offered the crowd the excitement of a contest, and also continuous music.

The publicity for the territory battles that appeared in the *Call* was quite elaborate. For example, when the Moten Orchestra met the Blue Serenaders in January 1927, the newspaper ad made the contest appear to be a heavyweight prizefight:

Bennie Moten Musical Crown in **Danger**
$500 Side Bet—Bennie Posts $250.00. Stone's Money is Up.
Bennie Says—
  "This contest is going to be a horse race. [It] is going to be a bloody battle of jazz music. There can be no dead heat. I am going to win . . .
Stone Says—
  "I have heard much of Moten's orchestra and if he beats me he'll know he has been to a dog fight. I am going to grab those honors if I have to blow Bennie out of the hall."[59]

This ad is just one aspect of the publicity for the battle. Above the notice is an article that gives a fictitious account of an arrest of the Moten Orchestra:

Bennie and the boys were taken before the captain and charged with having the finest orchestra in the west. . . . Bennie was charged with being a real piano player and Lomar [*sic*] Wright was charged with getting more jazz notes out of a cornet than anyone else. Thaman [*sic*] Hayes was charged with being the hottest trombone player in Missouri. Woodie Walters [*sic*] was charged with playing more jazz with the clarinet than the man that made them. Harlan Lenard [*sic*] was charged with making the people cry with such mournful tunes. . . . When leaving [the captain] told Bennie to wine [*sic*] that contest next Thursday night at 15th and Paseo between he and Jess Stone.[60]

The publicity campaign was effective, for "hundreds [were] turned away," from the event. The *Call* announced that Paseo Hall was filled to capacity for the battle, although the "winner" was not revealed:

The largest crowd that ever attended an entertainment in Kansas City stormed the doors of Paseo Recreation Hall last Thursday night for the orchestra contest between Bennie Moten's Victor Recording orchestra and Jesse Stone's Blue Serenaders. People began arriving as early as 7 P.M. and long before midnight the management was forced to close down the ticket window.[61]

The publicity for the battles often played upon territory rivalries to engage the interest of the audience. An ad for such an event described a musical "war" between Kansas and Missouri. Chauncey Downs, "Mr. Kansas," was quoted as saying "All Kansas will be there expecting us to win and they will not be disappointed." The reply of George Lee, "Mr. Missouri," was "We are going to give them the beating of their young lives and make them like it. So let's all pull together for 'old Missu'." As this ad demonstrates, Paseo Hall dances sometimes drew audiences from outside of Missouri.[62] Occasionally bands from outside of the Southwest visited Paseo Hall during national tours. The ads for these events featured less combative rhetoric, and emphasized the abilities of the visiting band and their popularity in other venues. A local orchestra was usually present at such an affair, but the focus of the evening was clearly upon the visitors. The price of admission for these dances was raised from the usual fifty cents to seventy-five cents.

In February 1927 the Fletcher Henderson Orchestra appeared at the Paseo Hall during its first tour of the West. The *Call*'s ad for the dance demonstrates the importance of this event (see Figure 5.4). The band is depicted in glowing terms, as the ad is filled with reports of the orchestra's popularity in other places, including revues from other African American newspapers. The comments solicited from important members of the community also provided a selling point.[63] In addition, an accompanying article portrays Henderson as a model of a successful orchestra leader: "Fletcher Henderson, the director of the famous aggregation, is reputed to have grown wealthy off the excellent entertainment furnished by his orchestra, and is said to occupy one of the finest homes owned by Negroes in New York."[64]

Although the Moten Orchestra was present at the dance, the role of Bennie Moten is distinctly defined as assisting, not battling, the visitors. One of the telegrams, apparently from Henderson, politely asks Moten to "favor us with several numbers," a much more respectful tone than that used for typical battle announcements. The local band battles were often serious competitions for the favors of the dance community, but Moten did not have to defend his territory from a New York orchestra. Clearly, the Henderson ensemble was treated as a special guest.

In July 1930, the Ellington Orchestra was traveling through the West

Figure 5.4. An advertisement in the *Kansas City Call* (11 February 1927).

on its way to Hollywood to make an "Amos 'n' Andy" movie.[65] They gave a dance at Paseo Hall that, in contrast to the Henderson engagement, was billed as "The Greatest Battle of Bands ever staged from New York to San Francisco," with the George E. Lee Orchestra. The *Call*'s ad for the affair did emphasize the achievements of the guests, stating:

In the appearance of Duke Ellington and his world famous jungle band, favorites of New York and all the east, the management of Paseo Hall feels that it is offering the dancing public of Kansas City one of those unrivaled treats which comes only once in a great while. . . .

Duke and his boys will amaze you. SEE, HEAR, and FROLIC while these mighty masters of musical magic play for you the weird arrangements which have set New York by the ears![66]

George Lee also received acknowledgment, however, as "America's greatest ballroom entertainer—the undisputed king of the West who meets them all!"

The guests from New York were treated well by the host community. When the Ellington Orchestra visited again in 1934, the Depression Girls, a ladies' auxiliary, held a banquet in Duke Ellington's honor that drew "1000" guests, including Ellington and his father. There were decorations, a tap dance exhibition, a fashion review of sports clothes, and an imitation of Cab Calloway by one of the Depression Girls.[67] A few nights later Mr. and Mrs. Banks had a private dinner for the Ellington Orchestra, which included quail, guinea hens, and rabbits.[68]

By 1928 the Black orchestras of Kansas City began to play for White-only dances, in ballrooms like the El Torreon and the hall at the segregated Fairyland Park. In 1929 the Paseo Hall hosted a White ensemble for the first time, Jack Owen and his Atcan Aces. The publicity in the *Call* for this event reveals the pride that the African American communities felt for their bands, as the Lee Orchestra prepared to challenge the Owen group. An article announcing the event provides the usual combative rhetoric between the bandleaders. Especially for this battle, however, the guest orchestra represented "outsiders," as Owen's appeal for a "square deal from the audience" indicates:

Are Negro orchestras superior to white orchestras? This long debated question will have a show-down next Thursday night. . . .

Both leaders are confident of victory. Jack Owen . . . says in part "You may say for me that I have no fear of the outcome of this contest. . . . All I ask is a square deal from the audience. I am confident of receiving that. We welcome this opportunity to play before a Negro audience and they may be assured that we will do our best."

George E. Lee said last night that he didn't want any favoritism shown him because he was playing a contest with a white orchestra. "I

will beat them on my merits. There never was a white orchestra born
that can stomp it out like we do. . . ."[69]

The phrase "are Negro orchestras superior to white orchestras" ex-
emplifies the meaning of this battle, or at least the point of appeal for the
dancing public. For the prospective audience, the purpose of the dance
was not to answer the question of which ensemble was better, but
whether an orchestra's ability was race-determined. The *Call*'s ad for the
dance (see Figure 5.5) illustrates this fact. In the top right corner, the
phrase "White people dance to colored orchestras, now's your chance to
dance to a white orchestra" is clearly an effort to address the reader's desire for some retribution. The comments of Owen and Lee, a debate of
the question "Are Negro orchestras the Best?," also are provocative.
Owen's initial statement, "I believe that as a whole the white orchestras
of this country are superior to the Negro orchestras" must certainly have
created some interest among the Black dancing community. In response,
Lee replies "Now listen folks, give them a square deal—then stand back.
We'll lick them, don't you worry," and concludes with the comment,
"Yours for the race." The phrase in the lower right corner, "Are Negro orchestras superior to white orchestras? These are some of the questions
that will be answered. . . . Let's all be there to give George and his boys
the support they deserve," leaves no doubt as to the marketing scheme of
this dance, and the sensibilities of the audience.[70]

The Black musicians' union of Kansas City, AFM Local 627, staged
the most elaborate band battles. The annual ball held for the union's benefit presented the best Black orchestras of the city in competition with
each other. These battles were very important as a showcase for the musicians. As Pearson writes, they were used by booking agents to determine
the best and most popular bands to book.[71] A good performance meant
future prosperity for a band; a bad showing could be the start of hard
times in the city.

Local 627 originated in 1917, during a time when few musicians
supported themselves exclusively through music. The union grew as the
popularity of dancing grew. In 1928 the *Call* reported that membership in
the union had risen from eighty-seven to three hundred in one year, as
"Negro musicians who have in the past been forced to go to larger cities
in order to earn a living are staying at home and doing well."[72] In fact, all
members of the city's dance orchestras belonged to the union.

The first annual union ball was given in December 1929. Six bands
appeared at the Paseo Hall, including those of Moten, Lee, Andy Kirk,

First Time Ever a Contest Between a White and Colored Orchestras in K.C.

White People Dance to Colored Orchestras, Now! Your Chance to Dance to a White Orchestra.

BLACK & WHITE Orchestra War!

JACK OWEN and his

Atcan Aces

GEORGE LEE and his

Novelty Singing Orchestra

Jack Owen and his Atcan Aces are in the forefront of America's greatest dance orchestras. In the finest dance palaces, on the radio, records and stage they have scored overwhelming successes. They hail from sunny California and all the warmth and color of that cheerful land is reflected in the brilliance of their melodies. Kansas City wins the opportunity to hear them as they return from a recording in New York City. You are going to enjoy Jack Owen and his Alcan Aces. They can play and will play. Come out this coming Thursday.

Are Negro Orchestras the Best?
"No," says Owen "Yes," says Lee

Jack Owen
Come to Paseo Hall Thursday!

George E. Lee

George E. Lee and his Novelty Singing Orchestra need no introduction to the southwest. That they are greatest race musical aggregation ever assembled in this part of the country admits of no doubt. But they are against the contest of their lives when they meet Jack Owen and his Aces. Can they win? Are Negro orchestras superior to white orchestras? These are some of the questions that will be answered next Thursday night at Paseo Hall. Let's all be there to give George and his boys the support they deserve.

No advance in admission — 50c

No advance in admission — 50c

Thurs. - March 14 - Paseo Hall

Figure 5.5. An advertisement in the *Kansas City Call* (8 March 1929).

Paul Banks, and Walter Page.[73] The following year there were eight bands, all for fifty cents admission. As the *Call* stated, "The Musicians Union dances are different and better than the ordinary run because they offer the cream of the local orchestras playing continuously in pitched battle where each does his best."[74] The comments of the band leaders appeared with this ad (see Figure 5.6), and illuminates the combination of humor and braggadocio that was employed to peak the public's interest.[75]

The story of Thamon Hayes's Kansas City Rockets illustrates the importance of the union battles for a band's fiscal success. Their career began in early 1932, with constant rehearsals and new uniforms bought in preparation for a battle with the Moten Orchestra at the union ball. From all indications, the Rockets beat the Moten band handily. According to the critic for the *Call*, "If I heard one person in the balcony comment on the good work of this band, I heard a dozen. . . . Their zippy novelty style, up to the second melodies, and unusual arrangements drew a great hand from the crowd."[76] It is probably no coincidence that immediately after this dance, the Rockets signed a sixteen-week contract to play the segregated Fairyland Park, the city's most lucrative summer engagement, and one previously held by the Moten Orchestra.[77]

During the summer months of the late 1920s and early 1930s African Americans moved their dancing affairs from the indoor venues to the ballroom at Liberty Park. Liberty was the city's only park to admit Blacks on a regular basis. It featured a pool, a miniature railroad, rides, and picnic grounds, and the Dreamland Palace, where the orchestras—in particular, the Moten Orchestra—performed.[78]

The exact dates of the Moten Orchestra's performances at Liberty Park cannot be determined. The ads in the *Call* indicate, however, that they played at the park on a regular basis during the summer months. One such ad announced that the orchestra performed for public dances every Tuesday, Thursday, and Sunday night at the Dreamland Palace during June 1926. Other nights were available to clubs, lodges, and private dances. According to the *Call,* these events were "like a circus but better, more momentous."[79] There were also special occasions and holidays at the park that featured an orchestra for an entire week. For example, in August 1925 a weeklong "Big Beauty Contest and Mardi Gras" was held. The Moten Orchestra was an important part of the entertainment, since it performed every night. As the *Call* announced, "The dance lovers of Kansas City know what that means."[80]

The African American holiday "Juneteenth" also was celebrated

Figure 5.6. An advertisement in the *Kansas City Call* (2 May 1930).

each year at the park with the Moten Orchestra. This holiday, which originated in Texas, held particular appeal for the people with family ties in that state. In 1926 the *Call*'s advertisement for this event mentioned that "last year fifteen thousand people came to the Liberty Park barbecue so you had better come early." The entertainment included Abu SaHatta, "the world famous mystic whose answers to questions have mystified thousands. See him in his rifle shooting stunt, done blindfolded."[81]

Liberty Park was owned and operated by whites, and was administered by the city government. The Moten Orchestra, however, also performed at the Dunbar Park, in Kansas City, Kansas, which, according to the *Call,* was the only park in the area owned by African Americans. In July 1926, the Orchestra performed for a "$1500 Beauty Show and big Apron and Overall Carnival." The attractions were staged "by some of our best people," a phrase that implies a sense of pride, and indicates that this was a respectable event. The festivities included Buck and Wing dancing, Charleston dancing, shadow boxing, and roller skating.[82]

In addition to providing the African American communities with places to dance, the ballrooms also were the primary source of income for the territory bands. In fact, the illicit nightclubs and gambling houses were places where the musicians would go to jam and socialize when their real job was finished. According to Woodie Walder, a clarinetist with the Bennie Moten and Thamon Hayes Orchestras, "We would get off at 12 [P.M.], would go have a jam session somewhere . . . generally [at] a club. [No pay, but] you'd just get alot of fun out of it and that was it."[83] As Jessie Stone commented on the nightclubs, and the relationship of crime to jazz,

> I didn't work in those places exclusively, and the same music that I played in those places I played for parties, wedding, and things like that, so I don't know that it could be said that the crime era had alot [*sic*] to do with supporting the music or the music supporting the crime area.[84]

The music and dancing styles presented in Kansas City's African American ballrooms changed greatly during the decade of the 1920s. In particular the Charleston and related genres, brought into the ballrooms by the Moten and Lee orchestras in the mid-1920s, had a great impact upon the dancers and musicians that extended beyond a change in musical taste. This transition in dance styles in fact created yet another way in which Blacks achieved autonomy from White segregation. In 1920 there was no opportunity for a Black orchestra in the White community; however, by the end of the decade, the new styles of Black music had become popular in the White communities of Kansas City. This newfound enthusiasm for Black music among Whites led to the first instances of the city's segregated venues hiring African American orchestras and dance instructors.

In the late 1910s and early 1920s, the African American ballrooms of Kansas City were, as Hazzard-Gordon has written, the provenance of the "elite" class.[85] The styles of the "elite" dances were recalled by Lawrence Denton, a local musician. As he remembered, the music and dancing in African American ballrooms at this time was quite formal:

> The floor manager called the sets, called the dances. See, they had a dozen different dances. Seaside Scottishe, all different kinds of Schottisches and the Imperial Gavotte and they all danced the same kind of dance . . . in unison. And the floor manager would call it. He'd call the set and he'd go over there and he'd break away. You go over and dance, swing your partner around and then you'd come back. Had a lot of waltzes in them days. Spanish Waltz, Waltz Oxford, and all them dances . . . he called it. Said "next is such and such a dance. Waltz Oxford." Everybody would line up and then the band would hit up the piece.[86]

The "elite's" taste in ballroom dancing eventually gave way in the mid-1920s to that of the working-class migrants from the South. As Emery points out, the Charleston, which appeared in the city's African American ballrooms around 1925, has roots in Black southern culture.[87] These new styles represented a transition from formal dance music, based on European styles, to styles influenced by the music and dance of the Black, rural South. This transition is illuminated by Kansas City dancer and pianist Sam Price, who described the process by which this music became a part of the Black community, and its adoption by the local musicians:

> I was shining shoes, because this was in 1923 or 1924 when the Charleston craze was popular and I was a Charleston dancer, and I'd shine shoes there and people would want the Charleston king to shine their shoes. . . . I did the Charleston, and I became a famous Charleston dancer locally. I think dancing and the music ran parallel because from the dancing I started playing the music.[88]

The importation of the Charleston from the street corners to the African American ballrooms began to occur by 1925. An ad in the *Call* for a "Charleston Wedding" demonstrates the immediate popularity of the dance. The event, which took place in May 1925, was a benefit organized by "The Twelve Charity Girls" at the Paseo Hall; it featured the Moten Orchestra, which provided music for "the sensational amusement event [that] everybody is talking about."[89] After this time, waltzes and schottisches are never again mentioned in the *Call*'s ads; instead terms such as "Charleston" or "Steaming Hot Blues" are used.[90]

By 1928 the desire of Whites to dance to the Charleston led to the first employment of African American musicians in White dance halls. Jesse Stone, whose Blues Serenaders had their most profitable year in 1928, recalled:

> I used to teach the Charleston just before the dance would start. I would get out, I had four of the other guys who were like Lieutenants of mine and I would step out in front and would teach it to them. This was a drawing card. This was very popular among the white dancers, because, when the Charleston first came out they couldn't do it. They looked to the black people to teach them to do it, so we got a lot of jobs for the fact that we could advertise Charleston lessons. . . . There's never been a dance as popular as the Charleston was.[91]

The Bennie Moten Orchestra also profited by the popularity of Black music among Kansas City's White dancers. By the autumn of 1928, they were performing frequently at the segregated El Torreon ballroom.[92] In 1929 they were hired to perform for the summer at the segregated Fairyland Park. This was an important event, for it meant that the orchestra could not maintain its regular engagement at the African American Liberty Park.[93]

The employment of the Moten Orchestra at Fairyland Park foreshadowed a transition for the African American ballrooms. In the late 1920s and early 1930s, the employment of Kansas City's Black orchestras in White venues increased significantly. The jobs in the White halls were more stable and more profitable for the bands, because of a tremendous economic advantage that the White community held over the Black community in the city. Thus, the jobs at Fairyland Park and El Torreon began to draw the Black orchestras away from their neighborhood ballrooms.

There were other factors that also led to the decline of the African American ballrooms of Kansas City. As their reputations grew, the territory bands native to the city made more extensive trips away from home. For instance, the Moten Orchestra spent much of the early 1930s on the East Coast. In addition, the Great Depression and the fall of the Pendergast regime in 1938 contributed to the decline of the city's African American economy, which in turn negatively affected the ballroom business.[94] As Fred Hicks said, "It just killed us. We didn't have any more business. We had all kinds of business, like barbershops, pool halls, restaurants, hotels, and so forth, and after the war [World War II] all our business just went to nothing."[95]

Although Kansas City's African-American dance halls failed to prosper after the early 1940s, they certainly left a legacy. In addition to the nightclubs and gambling parlors, the ballrooms were important places in the development of jazz from its early styles to Swing. The dancers in attendance witnessed the orchestras as their musical skills grew, in response to audience demand and strong competition. In an effort to win the approval of the dancers, the bands defined new standards for virtuosic improvisation, and the sophistication of the arrangements steadily evolved. The affairs at the Paseo Hall and Labor Temple in the late 1920s and early 1930s indeed were an integral part of the creation of new possibilities for jazz.

NOTES

[1]For information concerning the relationship between jazz and politics in Kansas City, see Franklin S. Driggs, "Kansas City and the Southwest," *Jazz: New Perspectives on the History of Jazz by Twelve of the Worlds's Foremost Jazz Critics and Scholars,* ed. Nat Hentoff and Albert J. McCarthy (New York: Da Capo Press, 1959); Nathan W. Pearson, Jr., *Goin' to Kansas City* (Urbana: University of Illinois Press, 1987); and Ross Russell, *Jazz Style in Kansas City and the Southwest* (Berkeley and Los Angeles: University of California Press, 1973).

[2]*Statistical Abstracts of the United States.*

[3]Charles Goodwin, interview, Kansas City Jazz Historical Collection, Western Historical Manuscript Collection, University of Missouri, Kansas City, Kansas City, Missouri, 12 April 1977. For more on the career of Goodwin, see Pearson, *Goin' to Kansas City:*224.

[4]The *Kansas City Call* was a weekly African-American newspaper that was issued on Fridays. Roy Wilkins, the future leader of the NAACP, was the paper's most prominant editorial voice at this time. The other newspapers used in this essay are the White *Kansas City Star,* the city's main daily newspaper, and the *El Torreon News,* a newsletter advertising events at the El Torreon ballroom.

[5]"Bombs for Crippled Vets Home," *Kansas City Call* (29 April 1922):1.

[6]"Home Bombed Again," *Kansas City Call* (8 December 1922):1.

[7]"Park Board Flatly Refuses to Take Homes," *Kansas City Call* (5 December 1926):1. See also Roy Wilkins, *Standing Fast: The Autobiography of Roy Wilkins* (New York: Viking Press, 1982):63.

[8]Jerome T. Duggan, interview, Reform Oral History Collection, Western Historical Manuscript Collection, University of Missouri, Kansas City, Kansas City, Missouri, 15 April 1988.

[9]Fred Hicks, personal interview, 16 May 1996. I interviewed Mr. Hicks for several hours on two consecutive days. He has lived in this neighborhood his entire life, and now resides near the corner of 19th and Highland. He attended Lincoln High School, and has had many types of employment, working most frequently as a hod-carrier. He also served as an Army cook in World War II. In addition, he was the custodian for over twenty years of the building that housed the Musician's Local 627, now the Mutual Musician's Foundation. This building, on the corner of 19th and Highland, is across the street from his current residence.

Mr. Hicks was introduced to me by Ray Reed, a resident of the neighborhood and a member of the Musician's Foundation. Ray is a taxicab driver, with the dream of bringing the music of the Moten Orchestra back to the neighborhood. In fact, he leads his own ensemble, which he calls the New Bennie Moten Orchestra. While speaking with Ray at the Musician's Foundation, I told him of my desire to interview people who witnessed the Moten era. Ray pointed to an elderly gentleman sitting on his porch across the street. This was Hicks. Our first interview began on this porch thirty seconds later and lasted for two hours. Our second interview occured at the Musician's Foundation the next day, and lasted over three hours.

[10]Hicks, personal interview, 16 May 1996.

[11]"Fifty Murders Here During 1929," *Kansas City Call* (3 January 1930):1.

[12]"Wealthy Clubman 'Taken For Ride'," *Kansas City Call* (4 January 1929):1.

[13]"Totten Assailant is Convicted," *Kansas City Call* (19 July 1929):1.

[14]Quoted in Pearson:99.

[15]Woodie Walder, interview, Kansas City Jazz Historical Collection, Western Historical Manuscript Collection, University of Missouri, Kansas City, Kansas City, Missouri, 29 April 1977. Significantly, when interviewed, Walder had no recollection of the Yellow Front, even though he was in his late teens and early twenties, and was a musician in Kansas City's Bennie Moten Orchestra at the time of its existence.

[16]"Killing the Graft," *Kansas City Call* (10 January 1930):11.

[17]"Analysis of Vote Figures Shows Vice Had Little Effect on Negro Ballots," *Kansas City Call* (28 March 1930):1.

[18]Russel B. Nye, "Saturday Night at the Paradise Ballroom: Or, Dance Halls in the Twenties," *Journal of Popular Culture* 7 (Summer 1973):18.

[19]Katrina Hazzard-Gordon, *Jookin': The Rise of Social Dance Formations in African-American Culture* (Philadelphia: Temple University Press, 1990):129.

[20]Hicks, personal interview, 16 May 1996.

[21]Hicks, personal interview, 16 May 1996.

[22]Hicks, personal interview, 16 May 1996. Mr. Hicks's use of the term "elites" does not mean that the dances were strictly segregated by class. As a teenager Mr. Hicks patronized both the dance halls and gambling parlors such as the Yellow Front. It is likely that a substantial portion of the Black population patronized both types of venues. According to Oliver Todd, a musician active in Kansas City from the 1930s until the present, it was common for some dancers at a Paseo Hall dance to go to the gambling parlors and nightclubs afterward. Personal phone conversation, 6 June 1996.

[23]"Hostelry Cafe Hides Liquor," *Kansas City Call* (25 February 1927):1.

[24]"Halloween Dance," *Kansas City Call* (26 October 1923):7.

[25]"T. Holder and his Eleven Clouds of Joy," *Kansas City Call* (10 May 1929):5.

[26]"Labor Day Frolic," *Kansas City Call* (30 August 1929):8.

[27]"Big Easter Frolic and Dance," *Kansas City Call* (2 April 1926):7.

[28]"Turkey Free!," *Kansas City Call* (11 November 1927):6.

[29]"Follow the Crowd—Holiday Dances," *Kansas City Call* (24 December 1926):6.

[30]"Two Big Holiday Dances," *Kansas City Call* (23 December 1927):5.

[31]"Annual Charity Ball," *Kansas City Call* (1 December 1922):7.

[32]"Proceeds from Elks Annual Charity Dance," *Kansas City Call* (5 December 1930):7.

[33]"Let's Go! Masonic Charity Fair," *Kansas City Call* (3 December 1926):7. For more on the TOBA shows, see Thomas L. Riis, "Pink Morton's Theater, Black Vaudeville, and the TOBA: Recovering the History, 1910–30," *New Perspectives on Music: Essays in Honor of Eileen Southern*. ed. Josephina Wright and Samuel A. Floyd Jr. (Warren, MI: Harmonie Park Press, 1992).

[34]"Beau Brummel Vaudeville Review," *Kansas City Call* (17 April 1925):4.

[35]"Benefit Dance Next Monday Night," *Kansas City Call* (13 June 1930):8.

[36]"9th Annual Fashion Show," *Kansas City Call* (8 April 1927):7.

[37]"Fashions in a Garden," *Kansas City Call* (18 April 1930):5.

[38]"S. R. O. sign looms for College Cabaret," *Kansas City Call* (2 April 1926):2.

[39]"Brotherhood of Sleeping Car Porters Monster Benefit," *Kansas City Call* (28 September 1928):5. Emphasis in original.

[40]"NAACP will seek fund of $5,000," *Kansas City Call* (19 April 1929):1.

[41]"Greenwich Village Dance," *Kansas City Call* (22 April 1927):7. Paseo Academy is the original name of the Paseo Hall.

[42]"Is the Republican Party Tired of the Negro?," *Kansas City Call* (2 November 1928):7.

[43]"Basket-Ball—Dance," *Kansas City Call* (12 January 1923):4.

[44]"Indoor Tennis Exhibition and Dance," *Kansas City Call* (18 February 1927):6.

[45]"First Annual Monarch Home Coming," *Kansas City Call* (17 May 1929):8.

[46]"Rooster Race," *Kansas City Call* (6 May 1927):7.

[47]"Girls Popularity Contest," *Kansas City Call* (25 February 1927):8.

[48]"Kiddies on Parade," *Kansas City Call* (25 January 1929):5.

[49]"Wigwam Dance," *Kansas City Call* (16 August 1929):5.

[50]"Pathé Movie Week," *Kansas City Call* (18 March 1927):7.

[51]The orchestra leaders may have held dances in their own honor, as the exact relationship between the dance promoters/organizers and the bandleaders has yet to be defined (there is little information available to define it).

[52]"Bennie Moten Makes Records for Victor," *Kansas City Call* (17 December 1926):4. The Moten Orchestra released ninety-six instrumental recordings, and six for which they accompanied blues singers. Their first twenty recordings were made for Okeh from 1923–1925; the rest were made for Victor from 1925–1932. The term "race record" was used by record companies for recordings by African American artists. For more information concerning the "race records," see Ronald C. Forman Jr., "Jazz and Race Records, 1920–1932: Their Origins and their Significance for the Record Industry and Society" (Dissertation, University of Illinois, 1968).

[53]"Victor Dance," *Kansas City Call* (4 March 1927):4.

[54]"Loving Cup Dance," *Kansas City Call* (1 April 1927):7. Capitalization as in the original.

[55]According to Driggs:203, the orchestra played a long engagement at the Paradise Ballroom in Buffalo. An article in the *Call* annouces that they also played at the Hotel Statler in New York, the Twentieth Century Club in Buffalo, a prom in Geneva, New York, and the Roseland Gardens in Harlem ("Bennie Moten's Home-Coming Dance!," *Kansas City Call* (7 September 1928):7.

[56]"Moten's Band Draws Crowd," *Kansas City Call* (14 September 1928):7. This ad announced that the promoter for the dance was William Little, one of the few times that a promoter is mentioned for an event. Mr. Little was not a member

of the Moten Orchestra, and his name appears in the *Call* in the early 1930s as the leader of his own group, Bill Little and his Little Bills.

[57]"Boy Violinist Grows Up," *Kansas City Call* (8 June 1928):7.

[58]"Farewell Dance," *Kansas City Call* (5 July 1929):5.

[59]"Bennie Moten musical crown in Danger," *Kansas City Call* (28 January 1927):5; emphasis in original. This ad is published in Pearson:134, where it is erroneously dated as ca. 1928.

[60]"Bennie Moten Faces the Night Captain," *Kansas City Call* (28 January 1927):5. The correct spellings are Lamar Wright, Thamon Hayes, and Woodie Walder. According to Driggs:195, the bandleaders often did the promotional work for their bands. This may be true, but the fact that the names of musicians who had been with Moten for several years are misspelled suggests that someone other than Moten had written this article.

[61]"Hundreds Turned Away," *Kansas City Call* (1 February 1927):5.

[62]"War! War! Kansas vs Missouri," *Kansas City Call* (11 January 1929):5.

[63]"Mighty Monarch of Melody," *Kansas City Call* (11 February 1927):7. Homer Roberts owned one of the most successful Black businesses, a car dealership. Carl Beckwith was the sports editor for the Call, and covered the Monarchs for many years. Felix Payne, the gambler and nightclub entreprenuer, was very well known, if not necessarily admired by all.

[64]"Fletcher Henderson, Gotham Dance King," *Kansas City Call* (11 February 1927):1.

[65]For more on this tour and the movie, see John Edward Hasse, *Beyond Category: The Life and Genius of Duke Ellington* (New York: Da Capo Press, 1995):128–129.

[66]"The Greatest Battle of Bands," *Kansas City Call* (25 July 1930):7.

[67]"The Depression Girls Entertain," *Kansas City Call* (5 January 1934):5.

[68]"Mr. and Mrs. Phillip Banks Entertain," *Kansas City Call* (5 January 1934):5.

[69]"Black—White Music War," *Kansas City Call* (8 March 1929):8.

[70]"Black & White Orchestra War!," *Kansas City Call* (8 March 1929):2.

[71]Pearson:162.

[72]"300 Members are in Union of Musicians," *Kansas City Call* (14 September 1928):7.

[73]"Musicians 1st Annual Ball," *Kansas City Call* (29 January 1929):7.

[74]"Zowie! Monster Battle of Bands," (2 May 1930):7.

[75]"Band Leaders who will Battle at Paseo," *Kansas City Call* (2 May 1930):7. The commentators from top to bottom on the page are: Bennie Moten, George E. Lee, Paul Banks, Andy Kirk, Jasper (Jap) Allen, Bill Little, Elmer Payne, and Julius Banks.

[76]"Musician's Open House," *Kansas City Call* (6 May 1932):7.

[77]"Thamon Hayes and Band to Play at Fairyland Park," *Kansas City Call* (6 May 1932):7. For much more concerning the Rockets career, see Pearson, 154–162.

[78]"Whoop-ee! Liberty Park Opens," *Kansas City Call* (14 May 1925):7.

[79]"Liberty Park—Dancing, Swimming, Fun," *Kansas City Call* (25 June 1926):7.

[80]"Kansas City on Tip-Toe," *Kansas City Call* (28 August 1925):8.

[81]"Texans June 19th Celebratin'," *Kansas City Call* (18 June 1926):5.

[82]"$1500 Beauty Show." *Kansas City Call* (16 July 1926):5.

[83]Walder, interview.

[84]Jesse Stone, interview, Kansas City Jazz Historical Collection, Western Historical Manuscript Collection, University of Missouri, Kansas City, Long Island, New York, 15 June 1977. For more on Stone's careeer, see Pearson:226.

[85]Hazzard-Gordon:117.

[86]Denton, Lawrence, interview, Kansas City Jazz Historical Collection, Western Historical Manuscript Collection, University of Missouri, Kansas City, Kansas City, Missouri, 3 June, 1977. For more on the career of Denton, see Pearson:224.

[87]Lynne Farley Emery, *Black Dance: From 1619 to Today* (Princeton, NJ: Princeton Book Company, 1972):227. See also Marshall Stearns and Jean Stearn, *Jazz Dance: The Story of American Vernaculary Dance* (New York: Schirmer Books, 1968), 109–110.

[88]Sam Price, interview, Kansas City Jazz Historical Collection, Western Historical Manuscript Collection, University of Missouri, Kansas City, Kansas City, Missouri, 19 February 1977. For more on the career of Price, see Pearson:226.

[89]"Loving Cup Dance," *Kansas City Call* (1 April 1927):7.

[90]"Charleston Wedding," *Kansas City Call* (24 April 1925):7.

[91]Jesse Stone, interview.

[92]"2 Bands Thurs.," *El Torreon News* (27 October 1928):1.

[93]"Fairyland Park," *Kansas City Star* (9 May 1930):30.

[94]For more concerning the decline of the Kansas City bands, see Pearson:184–195.

[95]Fred Hicks, interview.

CHAPTER 6

Thomas A. Dorsey and the Development and Diffusion of Traditional Black Gospel Piano

TIMOTHY M. KALIL

Thomas A. Dorsey (1899–1993) fused various early twentieth-century piano styles to create traditional Black gospel piano around 1930. His influence in the codification and dissemination of the genre took place first in Chicago, and thence spread to other parts of the country. Traditional Black gospel piano music of the kind developed and disseminated by Dorsey dominated gospel music accompaniment until ca. 1965, whereupon it was either supplanted or co-existed with contemporary Black gospel piano.[1]

The traditional Black gospel piano style developed by Dorsey is homophonic and usually accompanimental in purpose. Improvisation, based mainly on blues elements, is one of its important features. In traditional gospel piano playing, the structure of the piece remains intact: melody notes are played by the right hand but not as such; instead, they are presented embedded in chords or displaced rhythmically against chords. Accompanimental notes are played by the left hand, mostly in the form of octaves, boogie-woogie (hereafter, boogie) basses, modified stride, or a combination of all three. There are two general categories of playing: metered or isometric, and nonmetered (parlando-rubato); the latter is more ornamented than the former. Most gospel renditions feature "meter modification" where, for example, a piece in $\frac{3}{4}$ and $\frac{4}{4}$ time respectively is compounded into $\frac{9}{8}$ and $\frac{12}{8}$.

Amid the chaos of the post-Civil War era, there emerged on a large scale, the Institution of the Black Church, a church controlled by African Americans.[2] To be sure, this Institution had its roots in the "hush harbors/brush arbors" (secret meetings) and/or the more demonstrative services of the "praise cabins/praise houses/pray's houses" of the mid-to-late slave era.[3] The music of this post-Civil War Black Church consisted mostly of spirituals, revival hymns, lined hymns, moans, and chanted prayers and sermons.

During the post-Reconstruction period and during the early decades of the twentieth century, many Blacks began migrating to the urban north in large numbers. For example, between 1910 and 1920, Chicago's Black population grew from ca. 44,000 to 109,000, or an increase of ca. 150 percent.[4] Because of discrimination in housing, urban Blacks settled in enclaves (e.g., Cleveland's near East Side) that mushroomed into the Black neighborhoods that still are extant.

Almost overnight, Black ministers witnessed their congregations changing from assimilated northern Blacks to migrant, unassimilated Deep Southern Blacks. In Chicago, for example, many of the migrants were from Mississippi.[5] Several composers began writing gospel hymns that spoke to the "Black urban experience." One such composer was the Rev. Charles A. Tindley (1856–1933) of Philadelphia whose lyrics have references to twentieth-century urban living. Furthermore, his music encouraged improvisation (so dear to the African American) by leaving "space/time" between the notes of the hymn. He also widely published his music. As such, he is considered by many to be the "Progenitor of Black Gospel Music."[6]

Dorsey, however, mixed blues elements with the Baptist hymn to create an identifiable African American genre entitled "(traditional) Black gospel music" ca. 1930. Dorsey, a former blues and jazz musician (known as "Georgia Tom") used and encouraged the use of blues improvisational techniques. In the process, his music gave Black migrants a sense of identity, pride, and concomitantly, became a "symbol of ethnicity."[7] Furthermore, in 1932, he founded the first convention dedicated to Black gospel music (the National Convention of Gospel Choirs and Choruses or "Dorsey Convention"), the first Black gospel publishing house (he eventually owned three publishing houses in Chicago), and in 1941, the first Black gospel school of music. The musical "vehicle" that he created is the more improvisational Black "gospel song" not gospel hymn which is generally performed "as is."

Dorsey also created a Black gospel piano style to accompany his gospel songs. Combining elements from the music of the Sanctified church, 1920s Chicago blues and jazz, and the Baptist hymn, he created an identifiable style of (traditional) Black gospel piano playing in

Chicago ca. 1930. As such, he is also known as "The Father of Traditional Black Gospel Piano."

While Dorsey is the recognized Father of traditional Black gospel piano, his student, Roberta Martin ("Miss Martin") of Chicago also was influential in the codification and diffusion of the genre. The Dorsey–Martin Chicago "School" of traditional Black gospel pianists/ organists included Lena McLin, Julia Whitfield, Robert Anderson, Willie Webb (piano and organ), Lucy Collier, Louise Overall Weaver (organ), Charlene Willis, Mildred Falls, James Cleveland, Alex Bradford, Dolores Chandler, and Gwendolyn Cooper Lightner. Today, Chicago pianists such as Ronald Barrett, Sylvester Harper, Stanley Keeble, Charles Pikes, and Edward Robinson keep the traditional style alive. Although each traditional player ultimately uses Dorsey as a basis, his/her own musical experiences and preferences also influence each pianist. Therefore, each traditional player since Dorsey pays homage to him by appropriating the basics set down by him. States McLin:

> Dorsey was the model for Clara Ward and Roberta Martin. They sought after him. They kept up on what he was doing. They were similar to him in that they tried to get his style early on. Then they went their own ways. At first they tried to imitate what he was doing.[8]

Gospel piano generally accompanies a soloist, ensemble, or choir of voices. In most churches, the piano is used in conjunction with the organ (since mid-century). Whether solo or duo (in conjunction with the organ), the style remains the same. Taken as a whole, gospel musicians are viewed as "ministers of music." While a minister preaches the gospel verbally (which in many churches evolves into chanting and /or singing), gospel musicians "preach" the gospel musically. Currently, traditional Black gospel piano and contemporary Black gospel piano (developed ca. 1965) co-exist in most Black churches. Traditional Black gospel piano is the focal point of this discussion.

THE ROLE OF THE SANCTIFIED CHURCH IN
THE TRADITIONAL BLACK GOSPEL PIANO MOVEMENT

In the 1890s Bishop C. H. Mason founded the Church of God in Christ (hereafter, COGIC), the largest of all the Pentacostal-Holiness or Sanctified denominations. After its leaders attended the lengthy Azusa Street

Revival in Los Angeles in 1907, the denomination "instituted their own highly emotional services." These were "characterized by speaking in tongues (glossolalia), shouting, trances and visions, and suitably emotional music, often improvised, and sung in a highly emotional style."[9]

These spontaneous and emotional services, where the ultimate goal was the "blessing in the Holy Spirit," were conducive to highly rhythmic music. Unlike some African American denominations, instruments were welcomed in Sanctified churches. The instruments these churches used included "secular" instruments such as guitar, piano, and percussion (mainly tambourines). These instruments could potentially supply the highly rhythmic music needed for COGIC's emotional and demonstrative services. The late Mattie Moss Clark, former International President of the Music Department of COGIC stated:

> The guitar, piano, and percussion were always in the Church. My mother, Mattie Moss Ramsey, played piano and guitar in her Sanctified church in the 1890s. The saxophone and other instruments came much later, in the 1920s and 1930s, while the organ was [used] even later than that—the 1940s.[10]

The instrumentalists best suited to produce this type of highly rhythmic music and who, in turn, influenced the style of music in the Sanctified church, were secularly oriented musicians. Concomitantly, the initial meetings (1890s) of the denomination were in Lexington, Mississippi near blues country (the Mississippi/Yazoo River Delta).

After 1900, the headquarters of COGIC was moved to Memphis near the focal point of black popular music in that city—Beale Street. Thus, the early COGIC elders drew initially upon the musicians from these areas. According to Paul Oliver: "In this musically rich area the appeal of a church which encouraged playing instruments in church was considerable and the new denomination spread rapidly."[11]

As blues and jazz musicians increasingly played both Saturday night dances and Sunday morning services, the stylistic lines between sacred and secular tunes gradually became blurred. For example, religious songs such as "Just A Closer Walk With Thee" and "When The Saints Go Marching In" also could be heard on the early jazz bandstand. To be sure, the guitar was the most important blues instrument while the piano was the premier barrelhouse instrument. For our purposes, the barrelhouse style is important because Dorsey, a barrelhouse player, mixed this type of blues with elements of the Baptist hymn in his development of traditional Black gospel piano around 1930.

BARRELHOUSE BLUES PIANO

The barrelhouse style entered the Sanctified church via early twentieth century barrelhouse players such as Will Ezell, Eurreal "Little Brother" Montgomery (hereafter Little Brother), and (possibly) "Georgia Tom" (Dorsey), who did double duty as sidemen on recordings of the Sanctified church and played in barrelhouses (blues clubs). The latter will now be discussed.

At the turn of the nineteenth century, lumber and turpentine camps were big business in the Deep South, especially western Louisiana and eastern Texas. These camps employed mainly African-American male labor. Among the various "box-car" shacks of the lumber camps was one that functioned as a dance hall, gambling den, and whorehouse for the men: the barrelhouse or makeshift tavern. In short, the barrelhouse provided a psychological release for the workers on weekends. These rough-and-tumble spots, where shootings were common, were replete (usually) with out-of-tune pianos. A style of piano playing called barrelhouse (blues) evolved that fit in with the ever-present noise, dancing, drinking, and sex: a loud, percussive, and rhythmic-oriented style played with a heavy accented beat.[12] Barrelhouse piano, as exemplified by Little Brother, employs the following ostinato figures in the left hand:

1. simple stride basses (alternation of root, chord, fifth, chord),
2. single notes, grace notes, octaves, and chords,
3. "walking" basses (single notes or octaves in mostly conjunct motion), and
4. rhythmic-harmonic (chordal) figures that "fit the hand."

The right hand plays "blues licks" (cliched figures), such as:

1. grace notes, tremolos, "crushed" chords (chords that include accented nonharmonic tones),
2. repeated and parallel single notes, chords, and octaves,
3. repeated and parallel thirds, and sixths, and
4. secondary dominant sevenths and unresolved secondary dominant sevenths.

The barrelhouse style features use of the blues, mixolydian, and diatonic scales, heavily accented beats, and "breaks" (as used here, temporary suspension of time). Two examples of the barrelhouse piano style may be found respectively on pages 176 and 177, a transcription of Little Brother's "Vicksburg Blues No. 2" (see Figure 6.1) and "Georgia Tom's" (i.e., Dorsey's) rendition of "M and O Blues–Part I" (see Figure 6.2). Blues characteristics in "Vicksburg" include repeated notes, repeated chords, and "crushed notes" (see mm. 19–22, right hand). "M and O" features blues elements such as the following (see final chorus):

1. a left hand consisting of repeated octaves; also, grace notes are played that accents the chords,
2. a right hand consisting of repeated chords and crushed chords,
3. heavily accented beats in $\frac{4}{4}$,
4. percussive use of the piano, and
5. secondary dominants.

THE PROTOTYPE OF TRADITIONAL
BLACK GOSPEL PIANO

Although Dorsey was a barrelhouse player in the 1920s, he did not develop the prototype for traditional Black gospel piano. In the first

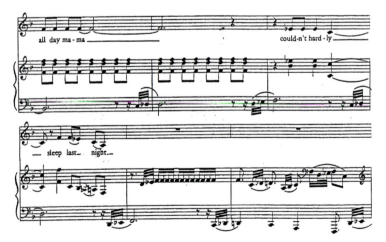

Figure 6.1. *Vicksburg Blues* No. 2, as played by Little Brother Montgomery, mm. 18–23 ($\frac{4}{4}$ time). Transcription by Eric Kriss.

Figure 6.2. *M and O Blues–Part I,* as played by "Georgia Tom" (Thomas A. Dorsey), final chorus, mm. 1–6. Transcription by the author.

decades of the twentieth century, pianists of the Sanctified church, for example, Elizabeth Cooper, Charles Beck, Louis Hooper, and especially Arizona Dranes, did develop a prototype for the genre. These pianists were the first to fuse the barrelhouse blues elements of Ezell and Montgomery with sacred Black song accompaniment; thus, Dranes and the others provide the link between Dorsey and the secularly oriented elements of the Sanctified church.

A Baptist, Dorsey learned the style by occasionally attending Sanctified services in Chicago and by listening to the recordings of Dranes. Furthermore, these provided comfort and solace for the young Dorsey who "tried-out" many of his new gospel compositions in Sanctified and also Baptist churches, accompanying song demonstrators/evangelist Mahalia Jackson. Dorsey states: "Yes I pat with them [Sanctified church members] . . . dance with them. . . . If I can put some of what she [Dranes] does and mix it with the blues, I'll be able to come up with a gospel style."[13] Dorsey's traditional Black gospel piano style thus has its roots in the playing of Dranes. Horace Boyer tells us that "the most famous of the blind singers was Sister Arizona Dranes; her piano style was a model for that of the first gospel songs recorded by Dorsey."[14]

In the 1920s, Arizona Juanita Dranes (ca. 1905–1957) of the Dallas–Fort Worth area was invited by the Okeh Record Company of Chicago to record her evangelistic playing and singing. She concertized in Chicago's Sanctified churches and "storefronts" (a commercial premise used as a temporary place of worship) and later in Texas and Tennessee. Storefronts proliferated on Chicago's South Side, and it was here that the majority of the COGIC denominations were housed.

The Chicago concerts were organized by Okeh with the promotion/ sale of her records in mind. These recordings targeted the "race" (African-American) market. The transcription of "Lamb's Blood Has Washed Me Clean" on this page (see Figure 6.3) exhibits certain barrelhouse elements in Dranes' playing. In the instrumental interlude (mm. 11–13, right hand) of "Lamb's Blood," one sees blues elements such as flatted thirds and repeated chords in the left hand and repeated octave basses.

Certainly one of the chief differences between the styles of Dranes and Dorsey is that the former's gospel piano renditions do not "swing," as her eighth notes are played evenly (i.e., as written). Instead, Dorsey's gospel piano renditions have the swing (two eighth-notes realized as quarter-note/eighth-note triplet) and improvisational quality of 1920s jazz and blues.

DORSEY AND THE DEVELOPMENT OF
TRADITIONAL BLACK GOSPEL PIANO

One important musical result of the "Great Migration" of sixty-five thousand Deep Southern Blacks to Chicago during World War I (an increase of ca. 150 percent) was the development of traditional Black gospel piano by Dorsey ca. 1930.[15] In short, the development of the genre could not have occurred at any other time or place.

Encouraging the migration were articles, advertisements, and headlines (sometimes fabricated to increase readership) in one of the most important Black newspapers of the early twentieth century: the *Chicago Defender,* a thirty-two-page weekly with city and national editions. Nationally, this paper had a large readership in Mississippi. Such an "inciteful" paper prompted southern authorities to suppress it. This had the opposite effect of making the newspaper a status symbol to read, as Blacks smuggled and defiantly read the *Defender*. This paper was started in 1905 by Robert S. Abbott, himself a southern migrant who was attracted initially to Chicago by the World's Fair of 1893. In addition to the

Figure 6.3. *Lamb's Blood Has Washed Me Clean,* as played by Arizona Dranes, instrumental interlude, mm. 11–13. Transcription by author.

Defender, advertisements describing the wealth and abundance of the city could also be seen by Black southerners in the Sears and Roebuck catalogues that began circulating in 1896.

Southern musicians, wary of finding work in a new city, were encouraged by the advertisements of nonmusical or industrial employment (the "day-gig") in Chicago that could supplement their entertainment careers. For example, steel production, packing houses, and rail/sea shipping industries proliferated in the city. At one time or another, Dorsey (who worked in a Gary, Indiana steel mill), Albert Ammons, Meade "Lux" Lewis, and Jimmy Yancey all worked in nonmusical jobs. Thus Chicago became synonymous with the North.

Also facilitating this migration was the Illinois Central Railroad that ran directly from New Orleans to Chicago and had "tie-ins" from various smaller southern lines. Many Mississippi/Yazoo Delta musicians used the Pea Vine Line, which intersected the Illinois Central near the confluence of the Yazoo and Mississippi rivers. Furthermore, when Louis Armstrong was called to Chicago in 1923 by Joe "King" Oliver," the former traveled via the Illinois Central.

Although Dorsey was a well-known party pianist in Atlanta from 1911 to 1916 (he migrated to Chicago in 1916), the emerging "Jazz Age" in Chicago (1920–1930) provided more career opportunities. Dorsey and other Deep Southern musicians viewed Chicago as the "Promised Land" and concomitantly brought to the South Side of Chicago the blues and jazz they formerly played respectively in the Mississippi/Yazoo Delta and New Orleans.

Because of discrimination in employment and housing, most of these migrant musicians settled on Chicago's Black South Side in an eight-square-mile area known variously as the "BlackBelt/Bronzeville/ Black Metropolis."[16] On the South Side, entertainment was centered in "The Stroll" or "Black Broadway" at 35th and South State streets. In this hub of nightlife, Dorsey worked at "black-and-tans" (integrated nightclubs and theaters such as the Grand and Monogram). At the latter two, Dorsey (also known as "Georgia Tom") led "Ma" Rainey's (the "Mother of the Blues") Wild Cats Jazz Band (1923–1926).[17] White jazz ensembles, such as Chicago's "Austin High Gang," also visited this area to receive their "music lessons."

The city of Chicago also was a locus for music publishing, booking agencies and tours, radio and newspapers (the *Chicago Whip* and the *Defender*), recording, and music education. As such, Dorsey worked as an arranger for Brunswick and Paramount records, was signed with the

Theater Owners' Booking Association (TOBA), and recorded with the famous "classic" blues singers of the era. Dorsey also attended the Chicago College of Composition and Arranging. Chicago's entertainment industry, like Kansas City and New York's, functioned under the umbrella of the alliance between music and politics.[18] Furthermore, mobsters, such as Al Capone, were well-known supporters of jazz.

Although Dorsey was a key figure in Chicago's Jazz Age, he was also exposed to the music of the Baptist church. Informally, his first keyboard lessons were with his mother, Etta Plant Spencer Dorsey, a sacred music accompanist. Also, his father, Rev. Thomas Madison Dorsey, was a Baptist minister in Villa Rica, Georgia.

Many times during the decade of the 1920s, Thomas A. Dorsey, the bluesman, considered devoting his energies solely to religious composition. Some of his best gospel songs were written then: "If I Don't Get There," "How About You?," and "If You See My Savior, Tell That You Saw Me"—the latter written after a long illness in 1926.

Inspired by an improvisatory rendition of "I Do, Don't You?" by W. M. Nix at the 1921 National Baptist Convention (held in Chicago), Dorsey briefly became director of music at Chicago's New Hope Baptist Church. Finally, in 1932, he embarked on a new career as a gospel music composer. This was due to economic, spiritual, and personal factors. Encouraged by the powerful Lucie Eddie Campbell, head of the music division of the 1930 National Baptist Convention (held in Chicago), Dorsey's composition, "If You See My Savior, Tell Him That You Saw Me," was a hit and catapulted him into the limelight. Dorsey himself, however, states that "we saw the blues waning, going out. And I didn't start writin' [*sic*] gospel songs because of that. I started writing because of a definite spiritual change in me and my world of operations."[19] The spiritual change resulted from the death of his wife and baby in 1932. Dorsey's greatest song, "Precious Lord," was the result of this tragedy. Dorsey affirms: "If my baby and my wife . . . if that hadn't happened, I wouldn't be doing what I'm doing now."[20]

Although he left the blues life per se, Dorsey's blues training was utilized in his development of gospel blues on piano: traditional Black gospel piano, ca. 1930. This mixing of blues with Baptist hymn elements was facilitated by the following similarities between the two genres, respectively. First, the forms are fixed: the twelve-bar blues and the verse (eight measures)—chorus (eight measures) of the gospel song form. Second, the forms also are strophic, as the music remains the same and the words change upon repeat. Third, the harmonies employed are mainly diatonic. Fourth, the phrases are largely symmetrical. Fifth, the texts are expressive of powerful emotions, often those of sadness and loss. Finally, the piano (and/or guitar in blues) is the basic accompanying instrument.

Most blues and jazz are written on lead sheets, that is, a skeletal structure consisting of melody and chords. Most blues and gospel musicians use the score as a point of departure for improvisation. When the young Dorsey saw the fixed structure of the hymn, it was but a short step to apply the same blues imrpovisational techniques that he had used in blues and gospel songs. Dorsey declares that "the music doesn't have anything to do with the gospel. I could take the blues and put it to music and sing it. I could put some gospel words to it and it wouldn't be no more degrading than the song out of the hymn book. It is the message that counts, not the music."[21]

Dorsey is known for his Black gospel songs (sung mainly by semi-professional choirs/soloists, improvisation expected, and texts that relate to the African-American urban experience, not gospel hymns (congregational singing mainly, sung as written, and generic, inspirational texts). At the time, however, that he was contracted to conduct the Ebenezer and Pilgrim Baptist Church choirs in 1931 and 1932, respectively, he had only published a handful of gospel songs. Therefore, Dorsey's early repertory consisted mainly of using blues improvisational and performance techniques on what was ready and available, and familiar: the Baptist hymn. Rev. Robert Johnson Smith whose father (Rev. J. H. L. Smith) first introduced Dorsey's music at Chicago's Ebenezer Baptist Church in 1932, states: "My father wanted Thomas Dorsey's music because he knew Dorsey's music closely resembled music he had heard down South in Alabama. Dorsey had a secular music background and he brought that with him into the church."[22]

It seems highly probable that Dorsey's experience with Ma Rainey and other classic blues singers made him comfortable with singers and choirs, in general. Continuing this line of thought, he must have learned the dramatic power of a song and how to "sell a song" from Rainey and other vaudeville singers, as seen in his performance of "Precious Lord" and "The Lord Will Make A Way Some How" in the documentary movie *Say Amen, Somebody*.[23] States Dorsey: "I took the stuff out of show business and put it in this and gave more life to it."[24]

From 1963 to 1984, Channel 7 in Chicago (WLS-TV, an ABC affiliate) televised led *Jubilee Showcase*—a weekly (Sundays) series featuring all the Chicago Black gospel "greats" (except Mahalia Jackson). Sid

Ordower produced the series. The one hundred programs were made into videos and graciously donated to the Chicago Public Library (Harold Washington Branch) by Ordower.[25] Dorsey and Martin performed on these programs. Dorsey is heard accompanying vocalist "Brother" John Sellers on several numbers. Other musicians on this date include Willie Dixon, Weaver, Faith McBride, and Joseph Norfleet. The piece that Dorsey and Sellers collaborated on were: "I've Got to Live the Life I Sing About in My Song," "I'm Coming Back Home To Live With Jesus," and "Today."

In "I've Got to Live the Life I Sing About in My Song" (see Figure 6.4) there are many influences from the blues. The work is in $\frac{4}{4}$ meter and all four beats are heavily accented. Bars 1–6 employ "shuffle rhythm" (i.e., triplets based on quarter-note–eighth-note figures). In this arrangement, the piano and guitar repeat the chords in shuffle rhythm to such an extent that these chords become a kind of ostinato bass. This piece eventually features other blues elements, such as repeated and parallel thirds, octaves, and chords (right hand). Other noteworthy blues characteristics include a percussive timbre, use of blues, mixolydian, and diatonic scales, use of primary chords, and swung eighths.

"I'm Coming Back Home To Live With Jesus" also has influences from the blues. The piece is set in $\frac{4}{4}$ meter, which includes heavily accented beats on all four pulses. The left and right hands participate basically in the same chords with the same shuffle rhythm found in Example 6.4.

"Today" is nonmetered (parlando-rubato) and in slow tempo. The texture is chordal and, for dramatic purposes, Dorsey plays arpeggios, octave arpeggios, broken chords, tremolos, and accented or sustained chords. As stated earlier, nonmetered playing is more ornamented than metered playing, as it follows the nuances of the lyrics and spontaneity of the singer. Concomitantly, there are many changes in feeling and tempo. Although slow nonmetered pieces do not include many blues elements in general, Dorsey maintains the use of riffs (short, rhythmic-harmonic figures) of this piece.

Figure 6.4. *I've Got To Live The Life I Sing About In My Song,* as played by Dorsey, verse 1, mm. 1–6. Transcription by the author.

Ca. 1930, then, Dorsey combined elements of blues and hymn playing to create traditional Black gospel piano. While Dorsey is the recognized "Father of traditional Black gospel piano," his student, Martin of Chicago, also was influential in the diffusion of the genre.

As stated above, the Dorsey–Martin Chicago "School" of traditional Black gospel pianists included McLin, Julia Whitfield, Anderson, Willie Webb (piano and organ), Collier, Weaver (organ), Cleveland, Bradford, Gwendolyn Cooper Lightner, Charlene Willis, Mildred Falls. Today, Charles Pikes, Stanley Keeble, Ronald Barrett, Sylvester Harper, and Edward Robinson keep the traditional style alive in Chicago. In their playing, these pianists continue to use the blues elements that form the basis of traditional Black gospel piano playing.

Although each player ultimately Dorsey as a basis, each pianist also is influenced by his/her own musical experiences and preferences. Therefore, each pianist traditional pianist since Dorsey pays homage to him by appropriating the basics set down by him.

Lena McLin, niece of Dorsey, gospel composer and musician, classical composer, educator, ordained Baptist minister and honorary doctoral recipient (Virginia Union University, 1977) affirms: "Uncle 'Tad' had a difficult time teaching people to play gospel piano. When he played, everyone wanted to imitate him and they came to his church (Pilgrim Baptist) and studio to learn it.[26]

McLin's historical in traditional Black gospel piano stems from her playing, which corroborates Dorsey's style; thus, one can speak of a core style of traditional Black gospel piano playing.[27] She was born in Atlanta, Georgia in 1929; she lived with Dorsey from 1933–1942 and again in 1952–1953. At the Dorsey home, she often accompanied famous gospel singers, including Sallie Martin and Mahalia Jackson. McLin, therefore, witnessed the birth of traditional Black gospel music/piano in the 1930s. She worshipped with Dorsey at Pilgrim Baptist Church and played piano there on the fourth Sunday concerts: "I play like Dorsey. It's the traditional style which is more blues-oriented than jazz [oriented]. . . . The anointing of the Holy Spirit is important to my playing.[28]

In McLin's rendition of "I've Got To Live The Life I Sing About In My Song" (see Figure 6.5, mm. 1–4)," blues elements include boogie figures in the left hand, such as "walking basses," octaves, and open fifths and sixths. The right hand features blues influences, such as secondary dominant sevenths and repeated chords. In general, one sees flatted sevenths, flatted thirds, and the shuffle rhythm from the blues.

Figure 6.5. *I've Got To Live The Life I Sing About In My Song,* as played by Lena McLin, verse 1, mm. 1–4. Transcription by the author.

THE MARTIN AND ANDERSON SOUNDS

Roberta Martin began her gospel career under Dorsey's tutelage at Ebenezer Baptist Church in the early 1930s. She created the "Roberta Martin Singers" from a group at Ebenezer initially formed by Willie Webb called the "Self-Organizers." From the 1930s to the 1960s, this group included influential singers and pianists/organists such as Collier, Webb, Anderson, Cleveland, Bradford, and Weaver. From the 1940s to the 1960s, Martin's influence via composing (ca. seventy songs), arranging, publishing, recording (Apollo and Savoy labels), performing, teaching, and spiritual comforter was pervasive. Many gospel singers viewed Martin as a "mother" figure. Because of her varied activities, the "Martin" sound became well known, imitated, and codified in mid-century gospel circles. It was know as "classic gospel music" and "defined an entire musical era. Miss Martin is known for a sweet ensemble sound, well-planned arrangements, and lyrics that sympathetically and gently speak to the African-American urban plight.[29]

It is generally thought that Martin is a more classical and ensemble-oriented player than Dorsey because she provides vocal support not only chordally but melodically. "Ride On, King Jesus" is instructive (see Figure 6.6). In the introduction and mm. 1–10 of chorus 1, one sees trademarks of the "Martin" piano sound, such as introductions, endings, counterpoint, "lead-ins" (scale runs between vocal entrances), and piano "responses" to the singers "calls." In addition, the vocal and instrumental texture is basically integrated. Often Martin's right-hand chords and vocal line are homorhythmic.

Figure 6.6. *Ride On, King Jesus,* as played by Roberta Martin, introduction, m. 1; chorus 1, mm. 1–4. Transcription by Horace Boyer.

Horace Boyer writes:

Martin was careful with harmonic and dynamic nuances, which she incorporated into gospel style. From 1935 until her death in 1969, she stressed three elements in her playing: richer harmonies (including secondary dominants and seventh chords) connected by single-note motives in the right hand; percussive-like "bomb" in octaves assigned to the left hand; and a less-rigid, but at the same time, more complex use of chords. To support the singers, she followed the melody with the chords, often doubling the melody on the piano. While independent melodic development is not a feature of contemporary gospel piano, "breaks" and "riffs" normally associated with brass instruments in the jazz idiom, are common. Whenever the soloist or singers drop out for a beat, the piano fills in the silence with a short motive, chord, and of late a short scalar run. This practice was derived from the style of Roberta Martin.[30]

Robert Anderson spread the style of traditional Black gospel piano via groups he founded, such as the "Robert Anderson Gospel Caravans," which included the young James Cleveland. Taken over by Albertina Walker (and called the "Caravans" or "Vans") in the 1950s, this group featured singers such as Inez Andrews, Shirley Ceasar (the "singing preacher"), and Dorothy Norwood. These women became gospel stars in their own right in the 1960s and were important in the transition from traditional gospel to contemporary gospel (1965–present).

Anderson's rendition of "Precious Lord" (see Figure 6.7) uses many "classical" ornamentations. Like his longtime mentor Martin, Anderson's playing has classical" leanings. Her influence is especially strong in his nonmetered playing, for example, "Precious Lord." Classical characteristics include grace notes (measure 6), arpeggios (measure 7), anticipations (measure 14), a neighboring tone (measure 24), and a turn (measure 24). To be sure, Anderson's metered playing is a catalog of blues techniques. For example, his playing of "The Lord Will Make A Way Some How" (see Figure 6.8) features boogie basses (measure 1, not shown), shuffle

Figure 6.7. *Precious Lord,* as played by Robert Anderson, mm. 1–7. Transcription by the author.

Figure 6.8. *The Lord Will Make A Way Some How,* as played by Robert Anderson, verse 1, introduction, mm. 1–11. Transcription by the author.

rhythm (measure 1), a blues "lick"/cliché (measure 1), and an unresolved secondary dominant seventh (measure 4). A $\frac{12}{8}$ blues "feel" and repeated chords from the blues (measure 8, not shown) are also seen.

THE DIFFUSION OF TRADITIONAL BLACK GOSPEL PIANO

With regard to traditional Black gospel piano, a unique situation exists. The genre was not known or documented until Dorsey arrived on the gospel music scene circa 1930. In the "Among the Churches" section of the *Defender,* words such as "gosepl music," "gospel chorus," "gospel choir," or "gospel piano," are not mentioned until mid-1932. Although the first gospel chorus was organized at Ebenezer Baptist Church by Dorsey and Theodore Frye in 1931, the respectability of the genre was not assured until a second gospel chorus was organized at another "established" (middle- and upper-class members or those aspiring to same) church, Pilgrim Baptist by Dorsey in 1932. From that point on, the traditional Black gospel piano style was "infectious" and spread throughout most of the nation. By the 1940s, gospel choruses were a mainstay of most South Side churches.[31]

With Dorsey at the center of this style, the genre spread outwardly at first to his students and thence to other regions of the country via traveling song demonstrators/evangelists such as Sallie Martin and Mahalia Jackson. Dorsey accompanied many of these individuals. His itinerary included the major cities of the country. While in these cities, he influenced gospel singers such as Willie Mae Ford Smith of St. Louis (known as "Mother" Smith) and Clara Ward (Philadelphia).

This entire process of diffusion also was facilitated by Dorsey's founding of the aforementioned Dorsey Convention, the first Black gospel music publishing house, and the first Black gospel school of music. At these conventions, performers and choir directors learned the style firsthand from Dorsey and his "students" such as Roberta Martin, McLin, and Dorsey's longtime accompanist at Pilgrim Baptist, Julia Whitfield. Therefore, the style diffused from Dorsey, the centerpoint in Chicago, to regional cities such as Los Angeles, which in turn became major gospel music cities (discussed below). Furthermore, gospel tours, gospel music radio stations, and recordings also were crucial to the dissemination of the nascent genre.

Traditional Black gospel piano also diffused because it spoke to the African American urban experience in early twentieth-century America via lyrics and musical style. To be sure, the Great Migration created African American areas in other urban areas outside of Chicago. In these areas, African Americans were linked by similarities in education and socioeconomics. Concomitantly, traditional Black gospel piano became a symbol, then, for ethnicity and racial pride.

Los Angeles, like Chicago, was receptive to and the focal point for many musical developments only after large numbers of African Americans migrated there after World War II. Pianist Gwendolyn Cooper Lightner from Chicago was one of the migrants who became influential in the Los Angeles gospel music scene after settling there in 1946. In Los Angeles, Lightner's role in the diffusion of the traditional Black gospel piano is exemplary, as she was one of the Chicago "pioneers" who brought the genre to that city in the 1940s. Although she did not formally study with Dorsey, she was an early attendee at his conventions, became an avid follower of his music, and played piano on his concerts in Chicago, Milwaukee, and Los Angeles. Asserts Lightner:

> Dorsey created the basic style. He is the roots of this style. I am known as the "Queen of West Coast gospel piano." When I came here in 1946, gospel piano as we knew it in Chicago did not exist. I brought the gospel beat started by Dorsey in Chicago.[32]

Figure 6.9 demonstrates Lightner's traditional playing of "I'm So Glad Jesus Lifted Me." Blues elements include four accented beats in $\frac{4}{4}$ meter, dominant and secondary dominant sevenths (mm. 1 and 7 respectively), and repeated octaves and chords (throughout transcription).

To summarize: Although Thomas A. Dorsey was not the first to use blues elements in Black gospel music/piano, he was the first to publish and promote it on a large scale. Thus the title given him by music scholars, "The Father of Traditional Black Gospel Music," is deservedly his. States Willie Webb: "Dorsey wrote down what was already existing 'out

Figure 6.9. *I'm So Glad Jesus Lifted Me,* as played by Gwendolyn Cooper Lightner, introduction, mm. 1–2; verse, mm. 1–8. Transcription by author.

there.' He was not the first to use blues elements, but he was the first to write it down, publish it."[33] At the close of the twentieth century, traditional Black gospel piano joins ragtime, blues, and jazz piano as one of Black America's most important musical contributions.

NOTES

[1]Biographical information on Dorsey is given by Timothy M. Kalil in "The Role of the Great Migration of African-Amercians to Chicago in the Development of Traditional Black Gospel Piano by Thomas A. Dorsey, Circa 1930" (Ph.D. dissertation, Kent State University, 1993). See also Michael W. Harris, *The Rise of Gospel Blues: The Music of Thomas Andrew Dorsey in the Urban Church* (New York: Oxford University Press, 1992).

[2]Eric Lincoln and Lawrence W. Mamiya, *The Black Church in the African American Experience* (Durham N.C.: Duke University Press, 1990).

[3]*Ain't Gonna Lay My 'Ligion Down,* ed. Alonzo Johnson and Paul Jersild (Columbia: University of South Carolina Press, 1996):8–38.

[4]*Chicago Commission on Race Relations: The Negro in Chicago: A Study of Race Relations and a Riot* (Chicago: University of Chicago Press, 1922):106.

[5]James R. Grossman, *Land of Hope: Chicago, Black Southerners, and the Great Migration* (Chicago: University of Chicago Press, 1989):Appendix B; 6; 155.

[6]Horace Boyer, "Charles Albert Tindley: Progenitor of Black-American Gospel Music," *The Black Perspective in Music* 11/2 (1983):103–132.

[7]Mellonee Burnim, "The Black Gospel Music Tradition: A Symbol of Ethnicity" (Ph.D. dissertation, Indiana University, 1980).

[8]Lena McLin, interview by author, 1 March 1992, Chicago, field notes, author's private collection, Ashtabula, OH.

[9]Boyer, "Gospel Music," in *The New Grove Dictionary of American Music.*

[10]Mattie Moss Clark, telephone interview by author, 13 January 1993, Ashtabula to Detroit, author's private collection, Ashtabula, OH.

[11]Paul Oliver, *Songsters and Saints: Vocal Traditions on Race Records* (New York: Cambridge University Press, 1984):172.

[12]Kalil, "The Twelve-Bar Blues as a Vehicle For Variation in the History and Performance of Jazz Piano" (Master's Thesis, Kent State University, 1989):6–14.

[13]Boyer, interview by Bernice Johnson Reagon (1993), broadcast 21 May 1994, Washington, D.C., National Public Radio, "Wade in the Water: African-American Sacred Music Traditions."

[14]Boyer, "Gospel Music."

[15]August Meier and Elliott M. Rudwick, *The Making of Black America: Essays in Negro Life and History* (New York: Atheneum, 1974):Vol. II; 174.

[16]*Chicago Commission on Race Relations:*108.

[17]Jon T. Robinson and Wendy Greenhouse, *The Art of Archibald J. Motley, Jr.* (Chicago: Chicago Historical Society, 1991).

[18]James Lincoln Collier, "Jazz," in *The New Grove Dictionary of American Music.* See also Mark H. Haller, "Policy Gambling, Entertainment, and the Emergence of Black Politics: Chicago from 1900 to 1940," *Journal of Social History* 24 (1991):719–139.

[19]See also Thomas A. Dorsey, "Living Blues Interview: Georgia Tom Dorsey," interview by Jim and Amy O'Neal (1974–75), Living Blues, 20:16–34.

[20]Dorsey, "Present at the Creation," interview by Howard Reich (Chicago, 27 May 1990), *Chicago Tribune,* section 13:14.

[21]Dorsey, interview by John Hasse (Chicago, 1976), Archives of Traditional Music, Indiana University, accession #76–133–F/B cassette 1534, tape 7.

[22]Robert Johnson Smith, interview by author, 16 August 1992, Chicago, field notes, author's private collection, Ashtabula, OH.

[23]Willie Mae Ford Smith, The Barrett Sisters, Dorsey, Sallie Martin, and the O'Neal Twins, *Say Amen, Somebody,* produced by George T. Nierenberg, Pacific Arts Video Records, 1983, PAVR-547, Carmel CA, released, 1983, copyright, 1984, videocassette.

[24]Dorsey, interview by John Hasse (Chicago, 1976), Archives of Traditional Music, Indiana University, accession #76–133–F/B cassette 1533, tape 6.

[25]Dorsey, Jubilee Showcase (cassette 12, show 1, 4 JS-64), producer, Sid Ordower, Chicago Public Library, Harold Washington Branch, 1992.

[26]McLin, interview by author, 1 March 1992.

[27]Kalil, *The Role of the Great Migration of African-Americans to Chicago:* 128–134.

[28]McLin, interview by author, 1 March 1992.

[29]Kalil, *The Role of the Great Migration of African-Americans to Chicago:* 144–153.

[30]Boyer, "Contemporary Gospel Music: Part I: Sacred or Secular?" *The Black Perspective In Music* 7/1 (1979):32–33.

[31]McLin, interview by author, 14 September 1992, Chicago, field notes, author's private collection, Ashtabula, OH.

[32]Gwendolyn Cooper Lightner, telephone interview by author, 29 March 1993, Los Angeles, field notes, author's private collection, Ashtabula, OH.

[33]Willie Webb, interview by author, 10 February 1992, Chicago, field notes, author's private collection, Ashtabula, OH.

CHAPTER 7

Western Swing
Working-Class Southwestern Jazz of the 1930s and 1940s

JEAN A. BOYD

The first European settlers viewed Texas as a vast, endless, boundless place where land and sky continued virtually uninterrupted as far as the eye could see. It was the promise of land and more land that ultimately brought people to Texas; and even though twentieth-century urbanization has brought changes, it is still the land that draws people to the Lone Star State. The land in all of its expanse and diversity has molded Texas culture, for in Texas human society and art are closely tied to the land.

Larry Willoughby, in his book *Texas Rhythm, Texas Rhyme,* has painted a colorful picture of western swing seeping off the plains and prairies and into the dance halls of the Southwest. Western swing was rural jazz that evolved out of the various ethnic streams that combined to form the unique culture of Texas.

The Mexican-Texan contribution to western swing was the emphasis on dance and dance music, and the traditions of violins and guitars as the primary instruments that accompanied dancing. The energetic rhythms and even the flavor of Mexican music in Texas, especially that of ensembles like the *mariachi,* certainly influenced western swing bands. African Texans contributed blues patterns and melodic inventiveness, polyrhythms, and "swing," as well as the focus on improvisation essential to western swing. From the Anglo traditions came the fiddle tunes, breakdowns, and instrumental style on which western swing musicians built—and from which they diverged. German immigrants established the organized dance scene, built dance halls, and added their waltzes, polkas, and accordions to the mix that became western swing.

Like all jazz, then, western swing came about as an amalgamation of diverse cultural and musical elements. The premise of this essay is that the mixing and molding that resulted in western swing could only have occurred in a rural setting, and that western swing was created and became pervasive in the Southwest specifically because of the area's rural character. Western swing music and musicians were tied to their landscape, and the audience for their music was comprised of farmers and ranchers who rebelled (and still rebel) against the forces of urbanization. Western swing thus defies the accepted notion that jazz is inherently urban Black music, because western swing was created in a rural context for rural, White, working-class Southwesteners.

SPANISH IMMIGRANTS AND THEIR MUSICAL INFLUENCE

Spanish interest in Texas was fueled by rumors of incredible treasure, such as the Seven Cities of Cibola, supposedly sighted in 1531 by an Indian slave to Nuño de Guzman, governor of New Spain. Although Guzman's expedition uncovered only an impoverished tribe of Native Americans living on the northern plains of Texas, the myth survived. In 1540, Francisco Vasquez de Coronado, governor of Nueva Galicia, led an expedition that carried him to the present Arizona-New Mexico border before he turned back empty-handed and reported to King Charles I that there was no reason for Spanish colonization to the north.

Whereas these and other explorers added little to the Spanish treasury, they expanded Spain's land holdings in the New World. By 1563, the frontier of New Spain extended from Santa Barbara, on the headwaters of the Conchos, which flowed into the Rio Grande, to East Texas. Much of this territory was harsh and inhospitable, but as Douglas Kent Hall has observed:

> The Spaniards were the perfect people to conquer it. The Iberian peninsula where they were bred and raised, with its own austere mountainous terrain and high desert plateau, prepared them for the hardships they had to face.[1]

The conquistadors had little to do with the colonization of Texas. That job was undertaken by zealous Franciscan missionaries, who had accompanied the explorers and seen the greater treasure of human souls to be won for the Roman Catholic Church and Spanish civilization. Although the Franciscans experienced little success in bringing the indigenous population of Texas into the church, they made great strides toward establishing the major industry of the area, cattle ranching. Spanish cattle and horses adapted easily to the New World. By 1560, northern Mexico teemed with cattle, many of them running wild. Within twenty years of their initial exploration of Texas, the Spaniards had large herds grazing in three main areas: San Antonio, Nacogdoches, and between the Rio Grande and Neches rivers in South Texas.

The Spaniards brought not only the cattle and horses, but also the ranch system that made livestock raising a profitable enterprise. Since the full-blooded Spanish considered cattle-handling beneath them, they put non-Spaniards—Indians, Negroes, mestizos—on horseback and trained them in the methods of cattle management, thus creating the *vaqueros,* or cattle-handlers. Cattle were raised for food, hides, and tallow.

By the beginning of the seventeenth century Spain had gone bankrupt supporting her far-flung empire, and land constituted the only remaining form of wealth for the crown. Spanish colonists in New Spain procured land grants from the government and amassed huge land holdings as a means of achieving political and social influence. The central institution of this land holding aristocracy was the *hacienda,* ruled by the *hacendado* (lord of the *hacienda*). The term "hacienda" stems from the Spanish verb "hacer," meaning "to do," and identified an income-producing enterprise. There were cattle *haciendas,* lumbering *haciendas,* and mining *haciendas,* all representing economic and social stability. As the power of the Spanish monarchy decreased, the New World *hacienda* system began to resemble the feudalism of the European Middle Ages, with the *hacendado* ruling everything and everyone he could see, and the *vaqueros* reduced to a state of serfdom through a strategy of low pay, loans, and indebtedness that kept generations of workers tied to the same *hacienda.* Thus was established the caste system of powerful landowners and powerless laborers that existed in Texas even after the demise of Spanish and Mexican rule. The essential point to be made is that the sociopolitical-socioeconomic system that prevailed in Spanish Texas was tied to the land and to what the land could produce. Consequently, Spanish culture in Texas, including art and entertainment, sprang from the land and from a nonurbanized and nonindustrialized lifestyle.

Spanish colonists introduced into Texas the musical instruments used to accompany dancing and the concept of dancing as a primary means of entertainment. Violins and guitars provided the music for *fandangos.* The *fandango,* originally the name of a type of Spanish dance, was a "festive gathering colored by gay strains of music, sinuous dancing, drinking, gambling, eating, and an overall commotion that gave the occasion an aura of both good and evil."[2] *Fandangos* were held at any time of the year, and in almost any context, as street dances, in private homes, and makeshift *fandango* halls. Spanish colonists made the activity of dancing, certain dances (like the two-step), and instruments such as the violin and guitar integral to Texas culture, and they influenced the ranch dances, fiddling and guitar styles, and eventually the dance hall scene that became significant in the lives of Anglo Texans.

Less rowdy than the *fandangos* were the *bailes,* which usually took place in more isolated, rural settings and brought together families and friends for miles around. Organizers would smooth and pack dirt dance floors, arrange wooden benches, set up lamps, and hire guitarists, violinists, and sometimes accordion players to provide music.

Dancing was an essential aspect of life among the Spanish inhabitants of Texas, as it was a means of escaping the hardship and drudgery of frontier life. Dance historian Betty Casey says that Spanish dances

> were performed with much flair and foot stomping. Among the Mexicans in Texas there were rowdy public *fandangos* patronized by the lower classes and elegant affairs, diligently chaperoned by older women. *Fandangos* added a bright note to the arduous, often dull and dreary lives of many Texas settlers of other ethnic origins.[3]

OTHER NATIONALITIES AND MUSICAL INFLUENCES

The largest group of non-Spanish settlers in Texas consisted of Anglos from the United States, who had been trickling in for years, but who began to create large colonies in the 1820s. By the end of summer 1824, the Mexican government had issued 272 land titles to individuals in Stephen F. Austin's colony; and by the end of 1831, Austin's colony had grown to 5,665 people and included several new towns: Washington on the Brazos, Independence, Columbus, Hempstead, and San Felipe de Austin.

Anglo-Americans were drawn to Texas by the promise of large quantities of extremely cheap land at a time when land prices were rising steadily in the United States. Most of the Anglos were farmers, some planters with slaves. Many were literate, honest, hard-working. They came from Louisiana, Alabama, Arkansas, Tennessee, and Missouri, thus imposing a southern outlook on Mexican Texas. There were conditions imposed by the Mexican government—land had to be improved within two years of settlement, colonists had to profess to be Catholics, all slave children born in Texas had to be freed at age fourteen—but these were easily ignored because the Mexican government did not interfere in Anglo colonial affairs.

Mexican dictator Santa Anna's refutation of the liberal Mexican Constitution of 1824 and his attempts to collect taxes and duties from which Anglo Texans had been exempt, coupled with a long-standing racial prejudice against all people of color—Native Americans, Negroes, Mexicans—led to the Texas Revolution of 1827–1835, and the founding of the Republic of Texas in 1836. Once Anglo Texans had won their independence from Mexico, they systematically excluded Mexican Texans from all political, economic, and social processes. The annexation of Texas by the United States and the Mexican War that followed ten years later further widened the gap between Anglo and Mexican Texans, and strengthened animosities on both sides.

Despite significant differences between Mexican and Anglo cultures in regard to language and folklore, religion, political systems, types of housing, and even food, Mexican Texans had established a socioeconomic system based on land ownership that was highly compatible with Anglo intentions of building individual domains safe from government interference. Americans had moved west not only to acquire cheap land, but also to escape government regulation; and when Anglo Texans took up arms against Mexico, it was to fend off government involvement in their lives. Anglo Texans demanded and won freedom from centralized governmental constraints, and the right to do with their land as they saw fit, a right that in Texas is taken for granted even today.

Hard-working and mostly literate, family oriented, politically active, religious, male-dominated—all have been documented as character traits of Anglo-Americans who settled in Texas. Did these people make time for entertainment? They played as hard as they worked, despite moral outcries against pleasurable activities. National and religious holidays were times of celebration, as were marriages and even funerals. There were competitions in all manner of skills, as well as sewing bees, church dinners, and choir rehearsals. Circuses, country fairs, and traveling tent shows occasionally spiced up life for Anglo Texans. And Anglo Texans, like their Hispanic neighbors, enjoyed dancing. In fact, there were times when dancing was the only available entertainment.

It was not always easy or convenient for Anglo Texans to dance. There were physical obstacles, like great distances, lack of facilities, mud, fire, and the threat of hostile Indian attack. But Spanish Texans had already established the pattern with their *bailes* and *fandangos,* and Anglo families likewise negotiated treacherous roads and mere trails to reach designated farm or ranch houses, staying for several days, dancing and socializing. Even cowboys at distant cow camps enjoyed occasional dances when a group of ladies would crowd into a wagon and travel to meet them. The cowboys would treat their lady friends to a meal from the chuckwagon, then spread a wagon sheet over the prairie dirt, and the dancing would begin.

Anglo settlers brought a variety of dances to Texas: schottisches, waltzes, mazurkas, jigs, polkas, lancers, quadrilles, cotillions, and germans. These mixed with Spanish dances that were already in place, and new Texas dance steps evolved. Like their Spanish predecessors, Anglos danced primarily to violin music. Larger towns like San Antonio, Galveston, and Austin had wind bands, string bands, and Mexican bands to accompany dancing, but the fiddler and his music remained the mainstay of dancing in nineteenth-century Anglo Texas. Fiddlers were much in demand, and their presence in a community prompted instant dancing.

Texas fiddlers played a repertory of tunes, many of British origin, which had been passed through oral tradition since the eighteenth century. Most British and American fiddle tunes were formally comprised of two similar melodic strains, one of which was higher in range. When fiddlers played for dances they repeated the two strains until the dancers tired. The best Texas fiddlers could improvise upon the two strains of a fiddle tune, piling variation upon variation, keeping the tune always fresh and still familiar. Improvisation was a skill acquired through necessity and inspired by the African American population in Texas; and improvisation along with syncopated, energetic rhythms and lively tempos also learned from the Black inhabitants distinguished the Texas fiddle style from that of the Southeast.

This distinctive fiddle style is still recognizable today. Texas swing violinist Carroll Hubbard recounts his background in fiddle music, starting with his grandfather in the 1920s, who often played solo fiddle for dancing, always in full, toe-tapping swing. And he remembers that his father taught him to improvise on breakdowns. "I've played in a lot of different ways," says Hubbard, "lots of breakdowns. That's the way I grew up. Daddy said, 'Play it different—paint a different picture every time.'"[4] For Texas fiddlers, the test was not in being able to play a fiddle tune accurately, but in being able to vary it and make it contagiously danceable.

The fiddle was the most frequently recorded country instrument of the 1920s and 1930s, and the first fiddler to be recorded was Alexander Campbell (Eck) Robertson from Amarillo, Texas, whose "Sallie Goodin" (1924) became a regional hit. The fiddle was the primary melody instrument of the string (fiddle) bands, consisting of fiddle, banjo, and/or guitar, and bass, that played for dancing in the Southwest; and it was the central melody instrument of the western swing bands that emerged in the 1930s and 1940s.

The land of Texas drew large numbers of European immigrants in the nineteenth century, especially from German-speaking areas. German colonization in Texas began in 1831, when Friedrich Ernst and Charles Fordtran by-passed a large German settlement in Missouri for the promise of virtually free and inexhaustible land in Texas. Though life in Texas was a struggle, Ernst wrote a glowing report to friends and family in Oldenburg encouraging further German immigration to Texas.

The largest movement of Germans to Texas began in 1842, under the supervision of the Mainzer Adelsverein, a society comprised of five sovereign princes and sixteen other aristocrats. Three shiploads of Germans arrived in Galveston in December 1844, and traveled by wagons and ox-carts to a designated site named New Braunfels, after its founder Prince Carl of Solmes-Braunfels. After 1847, the Adelsverein declined as an agent for transplanting Germans to Texas, but German immigrants continued arriving to fill up what came to be called the "German Belt."[5]

Whereas the Anglo pioneers who settled in Texas tended to distance themselves from their neighbors, the Germans congregated in well-organized communities. Social historian Richard A. Bartlett comments:

In spite of their growing love for their new country, the Germans nevertheless tried desperately to retain their cultural heritage. In this they had the advantage of a language of their own. In addition they were very literate, and a goodly number of them were trained in the arts and professions. All over the West there were German Liederkrantz [i.e., singing] clubs and Schiller societies ... Turnverein[e]—societies combining gymnastics and physical fitness with liberal, even free-thinking ideals—flourished in most American cities. There were breweries bearing German names . . . and occasional mining engineers and metallurgists who had graduated from the School of Mines at Freiburg. There were numerous German-language newspapers. Yet the power of the predominant American culture was such that the Germans were overwhelmed.[6]

Germans were absorbed into the basic mix that emerged as the people of Texas, but their indelible and unique mark continued on in improved farming and ranching techniques, emphasis on public education in the state, the creation of literary societies, theatrical societies, athletic societies, fraternal organizations, and singing societies. German musicians filled roles as composers and teachers in Texas. Pastor Adolph Fuchs left Kolzow, Mecklenburg, in the fall of 1845. Among Fuchs's friends was August Hoffmann von Fallersleben, composer of the words to "Deutschland über Alles." Fallersleben wrote a going-away song for Fuchs entitled "Der Stern von Texas," and he also made a collection of thirty-one Texas freedom songs, *Texanische Lieder,* and wrote an opera libretto, *In beiden Welten* (In Two Worlds). Once he had arrived in Texas, Pastor Fuchs adapted many of Fallersleben's Texas poems to German folk tunes, and composed his own settings for others. He was also a violinist, pianist, and singer, and taught music at Baylor College in Independence, Texas.

It was the German tendency to organize into societies and clubs that greatly affected the entertainment industry in Texas. For Germans, as for Mexicans and Anglos living in Texas, dancing was an integral part of recreation and socialization. Given their bent for organized activity, German Texans, not surprisingly, formed the first dance clubs. The pervasiveness of Germans in organized dancing in Texas was attested to by the fact that the label "German Club" was used to identify any dance club, even when no German Texans were involved. By the early 1900s, "german" was a common way of denoting a large ball or dance that lasted for several hours and included a midnight meal. In early Texas days there was even a complex circle dance called the german, which though it was actually of French origin, was so named because it was a community- and family-oriented dance. Even the dance hall scene in Texas owed much to the enterprise of German Texans.

All of the different nationalities who made their way to Texas participated in a rural society, and their folk arts stemmed from the circumstances of rural life. As late as 1910, there were no Texas cities with populations over one hundred thousand, and San Antonio, without significant industry, was the largest Texas town. Although the second half of the twentieth century brought urbanization, Texas in 1940 was still predominantly rural. The single event that changed the lives of all Texans and sped the migration from farms to cities was World War II, which brought wartime industry and a strong military presence to the state. Thus, with the exception of San Antonio and Galveston, Texas cities can be regarded as twentieth-century phenomena. Explains T. R. Fehrenbach in his interesting book about the Texas persona:

> [Texas cities] grew up basically as mercantile, distribution, or financial centers for the country side, or as ports of entry. And until well past the middle of this century, they were peopled primarily from the surrounding rural areas, from old American agrarian stock. In most cases they became metropolitan areas, some fifty in all, without the development of manufacturing industry.[7]

In Texas, city dwellers were only slightly removed from the farms and ranches; and though they assumed new occupations in town, they did not immediately acquire urban attitudes, culture, or musical tastes. Urban Texans retained rural Texas socioeconomic structures, including racial separation and a class division based upon the differentiation between property owners and hired labor, with property owners controlling most facets of business and society. This basic ruralism was an essential component of Texas popular music, especially of western swing, which emerged in the 1930s.

In its point of origin, western swing confounds the accepted notion that jazz is an urban phenomenon. Western swing was country jazz, created on country instruments in rural settings or in towns that were extensions of those rural settings, for entirely White audiences who were closely tied to the land through farming, ranching, or the distribution of produce. Some of these Texas agriculturists became affluent and important, others barely scraped by and exerted no influence, but all retained their ties to the land and to the cultural traditions born there. Western swing grew out of those rural traditions. This amalgam of country music and jazz, this western swing, was the most pervasive music in Texas in the 1930s and 1940s, and far outweighed mainstream horn jazz in terms of commercial success and lasting popularity.

COMING OF AGE: HONKY-TONKS, DANCE HALLS, AND RANCH DANCES

Western swing steel guitarist Tommy Morrell calls western swing "prairie music,"[8] which speaks to the fact that it was created for the entertainment of rural folk—farmers and ranchers—who made their livings off the land. The audience for western swing was White, Protestant, conservative, and hard-working, and western swing was the music with which they identified. Parallels can be drawn between western swing and its audience and Texas-Mexican *conjunto* music and its audience. Both types of dance music emerged on the Texas scene at the same time and appealed to similar classes, though different races, of people.

In his book *The Texas-Mexican Conjunto: History of a Working Class Music,* Manuel H. Peña argues that the accordion-led *conjunto* ensemble and its repertory of polkas was the music of the politically disenfranchised, socioeconomically deprived Texas Mexican laborers who had no property. *Conjunto* artists avoided the popular music and swing jazz of the dominant White race in order to create a music that impoverished, rural Texas Mexicans could identify as their own. Upwardly mobile, educated, urbanized, property-owning Texas Mexicans, who were attempting to assimilate into White culture, adopted a style of music that openly imitated White popular music and swing jazz. Whereas rural, White Texans were not politically helpless like their Mexican neighbors, they were strongly tied to the land and to the traditions of the land, and they were a working-class people. Western swing was the working-class music of working-class, rural White people, as *conjunto* music was the working-class music of working-class, rural Texas Mexicans. Upwardly mobile, urbanized White Texans regarded western swing not as jazz, but as "hillbilly" music while embracing the music of both regionally and nationally known swing bands, predominantly consisting of horns.

Like *conjunto* musicians, western swing musicians emerged from the people they entertained. Largely self-taught, they frequently escaped the drudgery of farm and ranch work through their music. But they did not abandon the rural community of folk from which they sprang, and, therefore, like their *conjunto* cousins, most western swing musicians gained only regional acclaim and never garnered national recognition.

Dancing was the primary recreation of rural Texans of all races, and Texas possessed the venues that promoted dancing and dance music. Texas was a prime location for honky-tonks after the repeal of Prohibition in 1933, because Texas was one of the states that allowed for county local-option elections to determine the legality of liquor and beer sales. County-line taverns, honky-tonks, sprang up along the lines between wet and dry counties all over the state. Even when economic times were hard during the 1930s, many rural Texans owned vehicles in which they could escape to local honky-tonks, especially on Saturday nights, to relax and drink away their Depression Era troubles. Some honky-tonks catered to families and advertised more wholesome atmospheres, but most were dives with dance floors. Jukeboxes provided the music for dancing during the week, but on weekends, many honky-tonks featured local bands, usually western swing bands in those that catered to Whites. Some larger Texas towns offered clubs and ballrooms, but these were populated predominantly by rural folk who had relocated to town in search of jobs, and by city folk who served the needs of agriculture, and thus traditional ideas of dancing and dance music prevailed. This explains why the better western swing bands could draw larger crowds than the mainstream horn bands, even those of national renown, like the Benny Goodman or Harry James bands. It was not until World War II brought many people from out of state into Texas that the demand for the big horn bands began to equal that for western swing.

Texans also promoted dancing through dance clubs, still called German Clubs even after 1900. So popular was dancing in the state that dance entrepreneurs built large dance halls capable of accommodating hundreds of couples. One of the longest lasting of the German clubs was the San Antonio German Club, founded in the 1880s and chartered by the state of Texas in 1936, as a benevolent society dedicated to the promotion of the social welfare of the citizens of Bexar County. Other old dance clubs were the German Club of Kerr County and the Germania Farmers Verein, founded in Anhalt, Texas, in 1860 and still active in 1908, when its members constructed a new dance hall.

In West Texas, where ranches incorporated thousands of acres in order to maintain large herds of cattle and horses, the ranch dance became an extremely important social institution, drawing entire families and ranch hands for many miles. Some of these ranch dances became organized functions that occurred regularly at specific times and places, such as the Matador Ranch Valentine Dance, held every Saturday night beginning in the 1890s at one of the large ranches—Matador, Pitchfork, Moon, or McAdams.

Some communities assumed the role of dance promoters, as in the case of Crider's, located originally in a field west of Hunt, Texas. Beginning in 1925 and continuing for a number of years, dances were held there after rodeo performances. County fairs, for example the Heart of Texas Fair and Rodeo in Waco, Texas, often hire bands and provide a sheltered dance area.

The short list of legendary Texas dance halls, some of which are still in operation, is a long list indeed: Austin's Double Eagle and Broken Spoke; Monahans's Green Lantern; Grand Prairie's Old Sadie Hawkins; Comfort's El 87; Helotes's Floore's Country Store; Fischer's Fischer Hall; Bandera's Cabaret; Luckenbach's Luckenbach Hall; Abilene's

Ponderosa Ballroom; Longview's Rio Palm Isle; Lubbock's Red Raider and Cotton Club; El Paso's Caravan East; Amarillo's Caravan Club; Goliad's Schroeder Hall; Gruene's Gruene Hall; Fort Worth's Pickin' Palace, Billy Bob's, Gateway, and Cowtown U. S. A.; Dallas's Longhorn Ballroom and Palms Danceland; Pasadena's Gilley's; Kerrville's Long Branch; Anhalt's Anhalt Verein Hall; Mexia's Cowboy Club; Waco's Terrace Club. Add to these more famous halls the countless local SPJST halls, Sons of Herman halls, Veterans of Foreign Wars halls, Knights of Columbus halls, and many more, and Texas emerges as the land of a thousand dance halls, most of which featured western swing in its heyday. The multiculturalism, the socioeconomic climate, and the abundance of dance venues in Texas made Texas the logical birthplace for western swing.

THE 1930s: FROM TEXAS STRING TO WESTERN SWING

Before western swing was clearly defined in the early 1930s, dance music for the numerous Texas venues was provided by fiddle bands comprised of fiddle, guitar, and/or banjo, and bass. Some of these fiddle bands bridged the gap between oral tradition folk music and western swing. For example, Prince Albert Hunt's Texas Ramblers out of Terrell, Texas, featured Hunt as a superb breakdown fiddler whose improvisations on traditional tunes resulted in a jazz-like flavor to the band. Hunt learned to improvise by listening to Black musicians. His band was popular in Dallas from the late 1920s until his death in 1931. Another fiddle band, the East Texas Serenaders, included bass player Henry Bogan, whose improvised and rhythmically exciting bass figures added a jazz element to this Texas string ensemble. The Serenaders recorded for Brunswick and Decca from 1927 to 1934, and enjoyed a large following around their hometown of Lindale, Texas.

Prince Albert Hunt's Ramblers and the East Texas Serenaders were but two of the best examples of the grassroots fusion of traditional country music and jazz affecting most Texas fiddle bands in the late 1920s and early 1930s. The first full-fledged western swing band was the creation of pop singer Milton Brown, from Fort Worth. Brown began his career as lead vocalist in the Wills' Fiddle Band. Brown first met fiddler Bob Wills and guitarist Herman Arnspiger in the spring of 1930 at a house dance in Fort Worth. When Wills heard Brown sing, he invited him and his younger brother Derwood (guitarist) to join the band. The Wills Fiddle Band, with featured vocalist Milton Brown, began playing every Saturday night at Eagles Fraternal Hall in downtown Fort Worth. They spent much of their time at Kemble Brothers Furniture Company listening to the latest pop and jazz record releases and expanding their repertory.

In the summer of 1930, the Wills Fiddle Band won a fiddle contest for which they earned radio air time on Fort Worth station KFJZ, then on the more powerful Dallas station WBAP, where they were billed as the Aladdin Laddies after their sponsor, the Aladdin Lamp Company. Their appearances on WBAP increased the band's exposure, and soon they were appearing at Crystal Springs dance hall and swimming pool near Fort Worth. For the Crystal Springs job Bob Wills hired additional musicians—banjoist Clifton "Sleepy" Johnson and a second fiddler, Jesse Ashlock.

In late 1930, Wills, Arnspiger, and Brown, with the help of their friend, furniture store owner Ed Kemble, convinced Burrus Mills to sponsor a radio program on KFJZ. Since Burrus Mills produced Light Crust Flour, the band assumed the identity of the Light Crust Doughboys. They broadcast for the first time in January 1931. To W. Lee O'Daniel, general manager of Burrus Mills, the Doughboys simply worked at the mill and played on the side, until he observed that their radio program had brought about an increase in the sale of Light Crust Flour. O'Daniel took over as band manager and emcee, making all of the performance arrangements, appearing on the radio broadcasts, and even writing song lyrics and inspirational speeches.

On 9 February 1932, the Doughboys, consisting of Sleepy Johnson (guitar/banjo), Derwood Brown (guitar), Bob Wills (fiddle), and Milton Brown (vocals), recorded two sides on the RCA Victor label. The two songs released, "Sunbonnet Sue" and "Nancy Jane," were traditional and did not sell well. At this point the Light Crust Doughboys was just another of the many fiddle bands that worked in Texas, and probably not even among the best.

Seeking more exposure and a wider audience for the band, O'Daniel moved them to WBAP, where they were given a prime-time slot at 12:30 P.M. After six months on WBAP, they were also broadcasting over stations WOAI in San Antonio, KPRC in Houston, and on Southwest Quality Network stations KTAT in Fort Worth and KOMA in Oklahoma City. The Doughboys' show was so popular that O'Daniel built a state-of-the-art studio at Burrus Mills and raised each musician's salary to $25 per week. The Light Crust Doughboys became the best-known fiddle band in Texas and Oklahoma, but Milton Brown wanted to make a different kind of music. When O'Daniel demanded that the Doughboys restrict their playing to the daily radio broadcast and personal appearances, and that they refuse dance jobs, Milton Brown and his brother Derwood bolted from the band.

In September 1932, Milton Brown organized the Musical Brownies and molded them into the first western swing band. He started his band with Jesse Ashlock playing fiddle, Ocie Stockard on tenor banjo, Wanna Coffman slapping his upright string bass, brother Derwood on guitar, and himself providing the vocals. Then he began to hire the players that brought a definite jazz sound to the Brownies. Brown's first major addition was Fred "Papa" Calhoun, whose blues-tinged improvisations gave a definite jazz flavor to the Brownies. Calhoun gained immediate attention as the first jazz pianist to play in a string band. Early in 1933, Brown hired formally trained violinist Cecil Brower, whose horn-like phrasing and heavily syncopated choruses added a sharp edge to the Brownies' sound. In combination—first with Jesse Ashlock and then Cliff Bruner—Cecil Brower created the first example of harmonizing twin fiddles, working together like a pair of horns.

Then in 1934, Milton Brown took the unprecedented step of adding jazz trombonist and guitarist Bob Dunn playing a relatively new instrument, electric steel guitar. Dunn could play rapid-fire single-string solo choruses, or back the other players with large chords so that he sounded like an entire section of harmonizing saxophones. With these additions Milton Brown put together the prototype western swing band—two fiddles, banjo, bass, steel guitar, and piano, which he supplemented with his own melodious pop vocal styling and occasional scat-singing. Journalist Kevin Coffey notes that "[Milton Brown] was a smooth pop singer from a family of string band musicians. His father fiddled, brother Derwood picked guitar; Milton merged these with heavy doses of jazz and blues . . . and occasional touches of mariachi and Tin Pan Alley cowboy."[9]

Although the Musical Brownies looked like a fiddle band, with the exception of the piano and steel guitar, its sound and method were far removed from country music. The Musical Brownies improvised ensemble and solo choruses on the popular tunes of the day. Their sound was not that of a typical country band; the Brownies were emulating the big swing bands and doing it on string instruments. The Brownies played pops, both current and standard, as well as heavy doses of jazz and pumped-up blues. A cowboy song or a sentimental waltz would crop up occasionally, but the Brownies was essentially a young, hard-driving band.[10]

Milton Brown revolutionized Texas fiddle band music, and created a western swing band that other Texas ensembles emulated. His Musical Brownies became the most popular and influential dance band in Texas between 1932 and Milton's death in 1936. They had a large and avid following of people who attended their dances and bought their records. They were the first to record western swing, in 1934, on the RCA Victor/Bluebird label. In 1935 and 1936, they recorded for Decca, and in the brief two-year period from 1934 to 1936, released one hundred tunes. Had Milton Brown not died at the age of thirty-three, he would have achieved the national prominence that was later afforded to Bob Wills, Spade Cooley, Tex Williams, and others who built on his model.

Milton Brown created the standards for instrumentation, rhythm, improvisation, and repertory that distinguished western swing from traditional fiddle band music, and hundreds of southwestern fiddle bands followed his lead. Many of these bands achieved only local importance and recorded infrequently, if at all, while others, like Bob Wills and His Texas Playboys, the Spade Cooley Band, and Tex Williams and His Western Caravan gained national recognition. But all of these western swing bands flooded southwestern and California dance halls, honky-tonks, and radio airways with western swing, the music which spoke to working-class, rural White audiences.

THE 1940s: EVOLUTION AND MIGRATIONS

Western swing evolved and yet remained remarkably stable over the two decades of its greatest popularity. By the late 1930s, Bob Wills had added a complete horn section to his nucleus of strings, essentially integrating two bands into one. This aggregate of players made the Texas Playboys one of the most versatile big bands in the business, capable of performing everything from fiddle tunes and blues to large, complex swing band arrangements. Brass and reeds shared melody lines with fiddles and guitars, took jazz choruses, filled in breaks behind other instruments and singers, and sometimes played duets with fiddles. The Texas Playboys recorded on the Vocalion, Okeh, and Columbia labels, and outsold other artists on those labels. Art Satherly, A & R man for Columbia, estimated that Bob Wills's records were playing on three hundred thousand jukeboxes and being heard by millions of Americans daily. The Playboys was also drawing in the thousands to their dance engagements.

California-based western swing leader Spade Cooley added accordion, large harp, and eventually horns to his band, and played compli-

cated arrangements. When vocalist Tex Williams left Cooley's organization to form his Western Caravan Band in mid-1947, he stayed with
strings, but added accordion and large harp, and later a drummer who
doubled on marimba. The better western swing bands were constantly
updating their sound and repertory.

But modernization did not diminish the unique and basically rural
character of western swing, which remained distinct from mainstream
horn jazz because of the prominent place given to fiddles and guitars,
both standard and steel. The fiddle was the lead instrument in any western swing band, even those with horns, and every other instrumentalist
adjusted to the fiddlers' stylings and preferences for sharp keys. There
also were rhythmic differences between western swing bands and horn
bands. Western swing was dance music, with the emphasis on a clearly
discernible and uncluttered beat pattern. Western swing bands tended to
use a highly syncopated rhythmic bass (i.e., $\frac{2}{4}$ time signature), moving to
the more relaxed swing-four (i.e., $\frac{4}{4}$ time signature) only to back certain
soloists. This gave western swing bands more rhythmic drive and an
overall more aggressive character than most horn bands.

The amount of improvisation also was significantly different between western swing and mainstream horn bands. Most of the nationally
known horn bands were populated by reading musicians who were more
comfortable with scores than with long stretches of solo or collective improvisation. But western swing musicians were largely self-taught non-
readers who improvised out of necessity and the need to express their
individuality in their music. Western swing fiddle legend Cliff Bruner
talks about the importance of improvisation in the creation of western
swing. "These tunes would come out [on records and radio] and I'd just
improvise on them and play them. I'd set my own style; there were many
different fiddle men who set a style of playing."[11] Fiddle and guitar players who "set their own styles" were influenced by their local musical
scenes—the blues and Cajun music in South Texas, traditional fiddle
tunes, Tin Pan Alley pop, and big bands in central and north Texas, Mexican dance music in west Texas—but all were creating their own unique
interpretations of the swing jazz heard on records and radio. Western
swing musicians retained more individuality of musical expression than
did many of their mainstream horn contemporaries, because individuality was ingrained in them from their rural roots.

Texans have a powerful sense of who they are, of time and place,
and of their past. Few states in the union possess as colorful and intense a

history as Texas. Texans are imbued with and shaped by their history, and this strong sense of the past causes them to be traditionalists, conservatives, and proud of it. But there also is a contradictory strain of adventurous individualism that runs through the character of the native Texan, and an adamant belief in the sanctity of privacy. That no governing body, state, federal, or labor union, should infringe upon the rights of individuals in the privacy of their domains remains the inviolable belief of most Texans.

Western swing came into existence and remained stable in the face of modernization because of this Texas mindset, with its contradictory strains of traditionalism and individualism. Western swing musicians kept the country instruments and some of the oral repertory that was part of their musical past, but screamed their individuality through the adventurous jazz improvisation that was the essence of their present.

Western swing thrived in Texas and elsewhere in the Southwest during the 1930s and 1940s, and migrated to new locations as southwesterners did. The route of migration was westward to California. The first massive wave of relocation to California occurred in the 1930s when farmers hard-hit by Depression and dust bowl conditions in West Texas, Oklahoma, Kansas, and Missouri fled to the fertile valleys of central California in an effort to recreate their lives in a more hospitable environment. The second exodus from the Southwest to California was prompted by California's thriving defense industry during World War II. The southwesterners who migrated to California transplanted their culture and music—their western swing—so that when, for example, Bob Wills and His Texas Playboys arrived in Hollywood in 1940 to work on the first of several feature films, they could pack large California dance halls like Venice Pier with thousands of displaced southwesterners. They had a ready-made, homegrown audience, as did Donnell Clyde "Spade" Cooley, the fiddler from near Pack Saddle, Oklahoma, who became a major figure in West Coast swing. Western swing was so popular in California that Bob Wills moved his band there and found more than enough work, while his brother Billy Jack had a similarly large following of avid fans for his band in northern California, and Spade Cooley with his band hosted the most popular program on early California television. In the Southwest and California, western swing bands always outdrew the major horn bands, a trend that continued until the Big Band Era fell victim to economics, unionization, and rock 'n' roll.

JAZZ FOR WHITE, WORKING-CLASS, RURAL AMERICANS

Record company executives of the 1930s and 1940s did not know how to classify improvisation created by country string bands, and so they labeled it "hillbilly" and "folk." But western swing musicians never perceived of themselves as "country pickers"; they were jazz musicians, fulfilling the entire process that is jazz. Jazz is not a type of music, as the Italian Renaissance madrigal is a type of music; rather, it is an approach to making music that involves personal interpretation, improvisation, and a unique sense both of rhythm and sound production. Western swing musicians have been denied their rightful places in jazz studies because of this misidentification with hillbilly music, and as jazz historian Gunther Schuller admits,

> [they] . . . have never been given credit in any jazz-writing either for their jazz leanings or their efforts on behalf of guitar amplification. Players like "Zeke" Campbell, Bob Dunn, and Leon McAuliffe [all guitarists] were very much in a jazz groove and by the mid-[1930s] certainly far removed from any of the older guitar, mandolin, banjo vertical "finger-pickin'" country styles.[12]

Although western swing cannot be classified as country music, it thrived first in the rural scene that gave rise to country music, where self-taught fiddlers and guitarists combined elements of blues, Big Band swing, polka music, traditional country music, Mexican music, and even Cajun music into a unique brand of rural jazz that became the most popular dance music of the entire Southwest and California in the 1930s and 1940s. The vast majority of western swing musicians were born and raised in the rural Southwest. They picked up their respective instruments and learned to play by the trial-and-error method. They acquired their repertories by listening to live performances of older music and record and radio performances of newer music. They practiced without instructors to correct or to prevent them from developing totally individual voices. And they learned the band business through on-the-job training, sharing techniques, tunes, and jazz licks. As Cliff Bruner explains:

> We learned to just improvise, and still sticking with the melody, we'd doctor it up a little bit. I think it puts a lot of beauty onto a tune. I don't care if it's a breakdown or "Stardust," it still comes from the heart and you're just ad-libbing, and you're doing something different that somebody else is not doing. You're playing it from your own thinking.[13]

Western swing musicians mostly emerged from rural backgrounds, and music was their means of escape from the drudgery of farm and ranch work. Times were hard and money scarce, but musicians could make more money in a few hours playing for dances than they could working sixteen-hour days on farms and ranches in the blistering heat of the Texas summers. Cliff Bruner and his young musician friends hopped freight trains after school let out each year; they were in hopes that their travels would put them into situations where they could earn money playing in bands rather than sweating in the fields. Cliff recalls,

> I was trying to get anywhere, didn't make a difference where, if I could get a chance to play my fiddle. And to make a long story short, we always ran into some fellows that felt just like I did, and we were always trying to start a band and looking for the rainbow to get us off the farm and we just nearly starved to death.[14]

Cliff Bruner's stories capture the experiences shared by most western swing musicians, and although some made it off of the farms and ranches, and into the dance halls and recording studios, they never forgot their rural roots and their people. Western swing was down-home, earthy dance music which provided a unique interpretation of the sounds, techniques, and repertory of swing jazz on typically country instruments. Western swing was a working-class southwestern dance music intended to meet the needs of White, working-class, rural people. And even though western swing migrated to other parts of the country, it retained the dual strains of thought that defined the southwestern character: a strong sense of tradition and a heady adventurousness.

NOTES

[1] Douglas Kent Hall, *The Border: Life on the Line* (New York: Abbeville Press, 1988):18.

[2] Arnold De Leon, *The Tejano Community, 1836–1900* (Albuquerque: University of New Mexico Press, 1982):172.

[3] Betty Casey, *Dance Across Texas* (Austin: University of Texas Press, 1985):11.

[4] Carroll Hubbard, Interview by Jean A. Boyd, 20 January 1993, transcript, Baylor University Oral History Institute, Texas Collection, Baylor University, Waco, TX.

[5] Glen E. Lich, *The German Texans* (San Antonio: The University of Texas Institute of Texan Cultures, 1981):38.

[6]Richard A. Bartlett, *The New Country: A Social History of the American Frontier, 1776–1890* (New York: Oxford University Press, 1974):154–155.

[7]T. R. Fehrenbach, *Seven Keys to Texas* (El Paso: University of Texas Press, 1983):83.

[8]Tommy Morrell, Interview by Jean A. Boyd, 29 June 1993, transcript, Baylor University Oral History Institute, Texas Collection, Baylor University, Waco, TX.

[9]Kevin Coffey, "Is Bob Wills Still the King?" *Fort Worth Star Telegram* (9 March 1992), section E 2.

[10]Ibid.

[11]Cliff Bruner, Interview by Jean A. Boyd, 14 August 1991, transcript, Baylor University Oral History Institute, Texas Collection, Baylor University, Waco, TX.

[12]Gunther Schuller, *The Swing Era: The Development of Jazz, 1930–1945* (New York: Oxford University Press, 1989):65.

[13]Bruner, Interview.

[14]Ibid.

APPENDIX: A BIBLIOGRAPHIC SURVEY
OF SOUTHWESTERN SWING

For information concerning the Spanish presence in Texas and the rest of the Southwest, consult the following books and essays: Francis Edward Abernethy, "The Spanish on the Moral," in *The Folklore of Texas Cultures,* ed. by Francis Edward Abernethy and Dan Beaty (Austin, TX: The Encino Press, 1974); Douglas Kent Hall, *The Border: Life on the Line* (New York: Abbeville Press, 1988); Arnold De Leon, *The Tejano Community, 1836–1900* (Albuquerque: University of New Mexico Press, 1982); David Mountejano, *Anglos and Mexicans in the Making of Texas, 1836–1986* (Austin: University of Texas Press, 1987); and William D. Wittliff and Joe B. Frantz, "Vaquero: Genesis of the Texas Cowboy," in *The Folklore of Texas Cultures,* ed. Abernethy and Beaty.

The Spanish mission system in Texas is the topic of Thomas P. O'Rourke, "The Franciscan Missions in Texas, 1690–1793" (Ph.D. dissertation, The Catholic University of America, Washington, D.C., 1927). Musical contributions made by the Spanish colonists to Texas are mentioned in Arnold De Leon's book, and in several specialized studies: Brownie McNeil, "Corridos of the Mexican Border," in *Mexican Border Ballads and Other Lore,* ed. by Mody C. Boatright, Publication of the Texas Folklore Society (Austin, TX: Capital Printing Co., 1946);

Americo Paredas, "The Mexican Corrido: Its Rise and Fall," in *Madstones and Twisters,* a publication of the Texas Folk Society, ed. by Mody C. Boatright, Wilson M. Hudson, and Allen Maxwell (Dallas: Southern Methodist University Press, 1958); and Manuel H. Peña, *The Texas-Mexican Conjunto: History of a Working-Class Music* (Austin: University of Texas Press, 1985).

An excellent general introduction to the major European immigrants to the American West, is Richard A. Bartlett, *The New Country: A Social History of the American Frontier, 1776–1890* (New York: Oxford University Press, 1974). Information on Anglo cowboy culture and music can be found in David Davy, *Cowboy Culture: A Saga of Five Centuries* (New York: Alfred A. Knopf, 1981); Ron Tyler and Langmore Bank, *The Cowboy* (New York: William Morrow and Co., Inc., 1975); and John T. White, *Get Along, Little Dogies, Songs and Songmakers of the American West,* with Foreword by Austin E. Fife (Urbana: University of Illinois Press, 1975). A brief discussion of the British and American fiddle tune tradition can be found in Bruno Nettl, *Folk and Traditional Music of the Western Continents* (Englewood Cliffs, NJ: Prentice Hall, 1990):68–70.

Accounts of German immigration and influence in Texas include: Theodore John Albrecht, "German Singing Societies in Texas" (Ph.D. dissertation, North Texas State University, Denton, Texas, 1975); Glen E. Lich, *The German Texans* (San Antonio: The University of Texas Institute of Texan Cultures, 1981); and Hermann Seele, *The Cypress and Other Writings of a German Pioneer in Texas,* trans. by Edward C. Breitenkamp (Austin and London: University of Texas Press, 1979; originally printed in 1936).

The lives of African Americans and Louisiana Cajuns in Texas are recounted in Gordon Baxter, "Cajun Lapland," in *The Folklore of Texan Cultures,* ed. Abernethy and Beaty; see also Alfreda Iglehart, "Waco Jive," Jo Lyday, "Jumbalaya"; and Beaty; Lorece P. Williams, "Country Blacks," all in the same volume.

General discussions of the sociopolitical and cultural life of Texas can be found in Walter L. Buenger, *Secession and the Union in Texas* (Austin: University of Texas Press, 1984); T. R. Fehrenbach, *Seven Keys to Texas* (El Paso: University of Texas Press, 1983); George Fuermann, *Reluctant Empire* (New York: Doubleday and Co., Inc., 1957); and Rupert N. Richardson, Ernest Wallace, and Adrian N. Anderson, *Texas the Lone Star State,* 3rd ed. (Englewood Cliffs, NJ: Prentice Hall, 1970).

The rich musical fabric of Texas is documented in Ellen Walker Rienstra and Judith Walker Linsley, *Music in Texas: Frontier to 1900*

(Beaumont, Texas: Beaumont Heritage Society, 1980); and Larry Willoughby, *Texas Rhythm, Texas Rhyme: A Pictorial History of Texas Music* (Austin: Tonkawa Free Press, 1990). The story of dance in Texas is told in Betty Casey, *Dance Across Texas* (Austin: University of Texas Press, 1985). The history of country music is best told by Bill C. Malone, *Country Music, U.S.A.* (Austin: University of Texas Press, 1968).

For more information concerning western swing consult the following: Kevin Coffey, "Is Bob Wills Still the King?" *Fort Worth Star Telegram* (9 March 1992), section E 2; Tom Dunbar, *From Bob Wills to Ray Benson: A History of Western Swing* (Austin, TX: Term Publications, 1988); Charles R. Townsend, *San Antonio Rose, The Life and Music of Bob Wills* (Urbana: University of Illinois Press, 1976). Finally, my own book, *The Jazz of the Southwest, An Oral History of Western Swing* (Austin: University of Texas Press, 1988), is based on some fifty interviews with western swing musicians and explores the origins, development, and performers of western swing.

Transcripts of the following oral history interviews may be obtained from the Institute for Oral History, Baylor University, Waco, Texas: Maurice Anderson (steel guitarist), Louise Rowe Beasley (bassist), Bobby Boatright (fiddler), Jim Boyd (bassist, vocalist), Clyde Brewer (fiddler), Cliff Bruner (fiddler), Clarence Cagle (pianist), Truitt Cunningham (bassist, vocalist), Dean Moore (vocalist), Johnny Cuviello (drummer), W. E. "Smoky" Dacus (drummer), Glynn Duncan (bassist, vocalist), Cliff "Skeeter" Elkins (pianist), Joe Frank Ferguson (bassist, vocalist), Ken Frazier (guitarist), Benny Garcia (guitarist), Tommy Perkins (drummer), Johnny Gimble (fiddler), Ray "Curle" Hollingsworth (pianist), Carroll Hubband (fiddler), Curly Lewis (fiddler), Leon McAuliffe (steel guitarist), Marvin "Smokey" Montgomery (banjoist), Tommy Morrell (steel guitarist), Bob Murrell (guitarist), Leon Rausch (bassist, vocalist), Buddy Ray (saxophonist), Eldon Shamblin (guitarist), Al Stricklin (pianist), Jimmy Thomason (fiddler), Dallas Williams (widow of Tex Williams), and Luke Wills (bassist, vocalist).

CHAPTER 8

The Art of Noise
John Cage, Lou Harrison, and the
West Coast Percussion Ensemble[1]

LETA E. MILLER

HENRY COWELL AND THE MODERN DANCE

"Up to this year, in my experience as a music publisher," wrote Henry Cowell in 1933, "I have never been offered any work for percussion instruments alone. This season I have been offered fifteen."[2] Cowell immediately published the two he found most compelling: William Russell's *Fugue for Eight Percussion Instruments,* and Edgard Varèse's *Ionisation.* In 1936 he issued a collection containing six more works.[3]

By 1940 the number of percussion compositions had grown so numerous that Cowell felt the need to identify various "sources" or "schools." These he reduced to four. The earliest was the work of the Italian futurists (e.g. Francesco Balilla Pratella and Luigi Russolo), who "gave the world what were then considered earsplitting demonstrations. They also issued manifestos on how important it all was."[4] The futurists' approach, said Cowell, was "in essence artificial, the basic idea being to create, ready-made and without gradual development . . . a highly complex and sophisticated art-form." The culmination of their movement was the work of Varèse.

A second source was the expansion of the percussion section of the traditional orchestra. Here Cowell pointed to the work of Percy Grainger, where percussion functions as "an incident, to enhance and punctuate . . . orchestration." The third school arose from "direct experience . . . [with] primitive percussion rhythms," particularly apparent in the music of a group Cuban composers, José Ardévol, Alejandro Caturla, and Amadeo Roldán, who were "in close contact with the native Afro-Cuban music."

215

Finally, Cowell concludes, "our newest Pacific coast group" comes by their interest in percussion through modern dance. Here Cowell cites Ray Green, Gerald Strang, John Cage, and Lou Harrison.

Extensive as is Cowell's list of influences, he omitted an extremely important one: himself. Cowell was a major force in the development of the percussion orchestra through his publications of modern music, his teaching, and his own compositions. His *Ostinato Pianissimo* for percussion octet, for example, was composed in 1934 (though not performed until 1943).[5] By the time of his 1940 article, Cowell also had written *Pulse* and *Return,* as well as several works for percussion and piano. As for Cage and Harrison, the stimulus for their percussion compositions came not only from dance, but also, in large measure, from Henry Cowell.

For years Cowell had worked closely with dancers, and through these interactions had sought a relationship between the two arts that would respect both as independent and equally viable elements in a collaborative composition. In 1934 Cowell published an article, "How Relate Music and Dance?"[6] in which he traced the history of music/dance interaction from tribal ceremonials (where sound induces "the proper rhythmical urge") to the latest modern dance styles. In "primitive dance" as well as the "cultivated music of the Orient," he noted, the drummer(s) functions as conductor. But in modern times, such "interpretive dance"—where music governs movement—has come "under bad repute."

In an attempt to counteract this domination of the sound element, modern dancers had focused on the music's dramatic sweep without close adherence to rhythmic particulars (as in the work of Isadora Duncan), or, in the extreme, had even danced to silence. But Cowell felt that the music for Duncan's dances (set to "classical masterpieces") was "so interesting that it tended to distract the audience from the dance. One missed the primitive relationship of the movements to the actual beat." On the other hand, he was equally dissatisfied with some recent dance music for percussion, which merely replicated "primitive sounds" without connection to movement. Instead Cowell strove for a contrapuntal relationship between the two arts, which he explored in some works for Martha Graham: "The music rises to its point of interest when the dance is quiescent," he explained, "and then the music dies down in interest while the dance rises."[7]

Cowell discussed such issues in a series of articles during the next few years: for instance, "Relating Music and Concert Dance" (1937), in which he proposed his "elastic form" (to be discussed below); and "East Indian Tala Music" (1939), in which he described ways in which tala could serve as a compositional resource for new approaches to large-scale form-building. In "New Sounds in Music for the Dance" (1941), he even advocated the exploration of "highly varied and deliberately rough or incomplete tonal gamuts, for each instrument,"[8] arguing that the tone colors of standard instruments had become so refined and the instrumentalists so skilled in controlling them that the music was complete in itself: "too complete, too entirely adequate and self-reliant. . . . There is nothing that is necessary for the dance to add." By the time Cowell wrote this essay, the percussion ensemble repertory had become extensive enough for him to champion it as the ideal medium for dance. Its "instrument tones . . . contain a combination of sound-noise elements with tone elements. The combined possibilities are almost infinite . . . yet the tones are never perfect enough as pure tones to be entirely complete. It takes the added element of the dance to make a complete whole—or perhaps it would be fairer to put it the other way about, as it is usually the percussion tone which completes the dance."

During the period in which these articles were written, both John Cage and Lou Harrison came under Cowell's influence. While Cage was in New York in 1934, he took classes from Cowell at the New School, including "Primitive and Folk Origins of Music" and "Creative Music Today."[9] Harrison took Cowell's "Music of the Peoples of the World" at the University of California extension in San Francisco in the spring of 1935. Although both composers were aware of recent European and American music for percussion ensemble, the impact of Cowell's teaching was profound. In 1959 Cage reflected, "Henry Cowell was for many years the open sesame for new music in America."[10] Harrison speaks of him with similar reverence, noting that "for at least two or three generations of American composers he was a kind of 'central information booth'."[11] In a recent retrospective, Harrison summarized Cowell's effect on those he encountered: "Brushing aside plain academicism, he stretched out the minds of everyone towards music shunned by Eurocentric schools, and stimulated hearing abilities by confronting them with other instruments, other tonalities, and other ways of making music."[12]

CAGE'S EARLY WORK WITH PERCUSSION (LOS ANGELES, 1935–1938)

John Cage's first known percussion works were written in Los Angeles in 1935–1936. The direct stimulus was a comment by avant-garde filmmaker Oskar Fischinger (1900–1967), whom Cage met through the art agent and patron Galka Scheyer.[13] One day Scheyer brought Fischinger to hear some of Cage's music, and Fischinger invited Cage to work with him on a film. During the course of the project, Fischinger remarked that "everything in the world has a spirit which is released by its sound,"[14] a comment that begged experimentation. "The next day I began writing music . . . to be played on percussion instruments," said Cage.[15]

Though Fischinger was the catalyst, Cage had been moving in this direction for some time. He had been trying his hand at twelve-tone music, but found himself dissatisfied with the results. "I admired the theory," he confessed, "but I did not like its sound."[16] Cage tried enhancing the rhythmic component of his serial works by "dividing the row into a series of static, non-variable motives and giving each motive its own ictus pattern. This brought the element of rhythm into an integral relation with that of pitch." Nevertheless Cage realized that serial composition, "in making use of the instruments which had been developed for tonal music . . . , had continually to be written negatively rather than straightforwardly: it had always to avoid the harmonic relationships which were natural to the tonal instruments . . . ; I was convinced that for atonal music new instruments proper to it were required."[17]

In 1935 Cage completed a percussion quartet with "no idea what it would sound like, nor even what instruments would be used to play it."[18] Only then did he convince three nonmusicians to try it out with him. Cage and his wife Xenia Andreyevna Kashevaroff (an Alaskan Russian-Orthodox priest's daughter whom he had swept off to Yuma, Arizona, and married in a sunrise service at 5 A.M. on 7 June 1935)[19] were studying bookbinding in Santa Monica with Hazel Dreis. Cage persuaded the bookbinders' group to become percussionists and learn his new piece. First they used "whatever was at hand: we tapped tables, books, chairs, and so forth."[20] From there they moved to pots and pans, then to instruments Cage had gathered in junkyards. After several weeks, they settled on a collection of found and foraged instruments supplemented by a pedal timpani and a Chinese gong (though the *Quartet* was later published with unspecified instrumentation). The following year he composed a percussion trio for tom-toms, bass drum, bamboo sticks, and graduated pieces of wood.

In succeeding years, Cage increasingly became convinced that rhythm should function as the dominant element in music. These elements, he often said, could be reduced to four: pitch, timbre, amplitude, and duration. But since duration alone characterizes both silence and sound, "a structure based on durations (rhythmic: phrase, time lengths) is correct (corresponds with the nature of the material), whereas harmonic structure is incorrect (derived from pitch, which has no being in silence)."[21]

Cage did not create percussion music in a vacuum. He had heard Varèse's *Ionisation* (1931) and William Russell's *Three Dance Movements* (1933), and was well aware of the Italian futurists' attempts to incorporate machine sounds in musical compositions.[22] Percussion, for Cage, meant "sound inclusive of noise," not merely struck instruments. "Just as modern music in general may be said to have been the history of the liberation of the dissonance, so this new music is part of the attempt to liberate all audible sound from the limitations of musical prejudice."[23]

Though the bookbinders apparently took delight in this liberation, the reception from musicians was much cooler. Schoenberg declined an invitation to hear Cage's percussion music,[24] and others greeted his experiments with similar skepticism. On the other hand, dancers welcomed his work. "Modern dancers were grateful for any sounds or noises that could be produced for their recitals," he recalled years later.[25]

A commission from the University of California, Los Angeles (UCLA) Physical Education Department stimulated Cage to write music for an aquatic ballet. (When he found that the swimmers had trouble hearing the music, Cage tried dipping the large gong in the water and was entranced by the resultant sliding tone. The pitch change of this "water gong" was irrelevant to the swimmers; time alone mattered to them— and the time remained unchanged.) With his aunt Phoebe James (Cage's piano teacher), he also taught an extension course for UCLA entitled "Musical Accompaniments for Rhythmic Expression," which met for fifteen sessions from January–May 1938.[26] "Every source of sound entered the musical accompaniments provided by aunt and nephew—from balloons squeezed with wet fingers or jiggled with rice inside to radiators struck with tynes."[27]

At the end of the 1938 spring semester Cage decided to seek work in northern California. He and Xenia headed for Carmel where Xenia's sisters (Sasha and Natalya) were part of an engaging social circle that included both John Steinbeck and Ed "Doc" Ricketts. Leaving Xenia in Carmel, Cage drove to San Francisco in search of employment. On his agenda was a visit to another young composer, who, according to Cowell, held similar interests in percussion and dance.

Lou Harrison was busy composing at the Steinway upright in his small railroad flat apartment on Francisco Street when Cage arrived. He answered the door to find a slender young man, five years his senior, standing outside. "Hello, my name is John Cage," said Cage. "Henry Cowell sent me."[28]

HARRISON: PERCUSSION AND DANCE
IN SAN FRANCISCO (1935–1938)

Lou Harrison had been living in San Francisco since his graduation from Burlingame High School in December 1934. After taking Cowell's course in world music in the spring of 1935, Harrison approached his teacher for private composition lessons (to which Cowell readily assented). Instruction began in September 1935.

During the same period (late 1935 or early 1936), dancer Carol Beals contacted Harrison to write music for a new choreography concerning a major labor strike in San Francisco the previous year. That work stoppage, which brought business activity in the city to a virtual standstill for three days in July 1934, capped years of wrangling between the longshoremen and the California shipping industry. A strike by port workers, supported by seamen, teamsters, and others, had led to strike-breaking measures by industry, which in turn prompted street battles in San Francisco, the death of two longshoremen, and sympathy walk-outs by other unions, ushering in a general city strike. Beals and her husband, Mervin Levy (later Leeds), were friends of the strike leader, Harry Bridges.[29]

Beals had originally approached a lawyer and amateur composer friend to write the music for her dance, but he declined, recommending instead "a young musician out at State College. So Lou arrived one day on my doorstep. He looked like a teenager but he talked like an adult. We hit it off from the beginning."[30] The music Harrison composed for Beals—his first work for percussion and his first for dance—was scored for a single player (himself). *Waterfront—1934* premiered in the boxing ring at the longshoremen's headquarters. Harrison sat below the ring surrounded by his percussion instruments, the dancers swinging out over him as they leaned on the ropes.

Another performance was staged on 17 May 1936 at the Dance Council of Northern California's Second Dance Festival.[31] Beals and Levy had founded the Dance Council in September 1934, after returning from a year in New York where Beals had studied with Martha Graham. "San Francisco's dance [situation] was down in the dregs," Beals recalls. "There were no performing places. The city said, 'You can't perform here and you can't perform there.' We had to get an organization together to see what could be done about dance in San Francisco. So that's what we did."[32] By May 1936 the Dance Council included over a hundred members representing some twenty dance groups. With a governing board and seven standing committees, it sponsored a lecture-demonstration series, a concert series, a workshop project, and the annual dance festival. At the conference-dinner following its first festival in March 1935, speakers included Henry Cowell as well as music and dance critic Alfred Frankenstein. Cowell even spoke at one of the council's regular membership meetings in 1936 on "Current Developments in Writing Music for the Dance."

Cowell also taught percussion at Ann Mundstock's dance studio on Sacramento Street. Mundstock had come to San Francisco in 1926 from Germany, where she had worked with Rudolph von Laban; she opened her own studio in 1932.[33] By 1936 she was offering classes in technique and dance composition (taught by Welland Lathrop), Laban choreography (Mundstock), and "percussion study" (Cowell).[34] The following summer, Munstock employed Gerald Strang, who was at UCLA, to teach music composition for the dance.[35] Lou Harrison and Carol Beals took a course in Labanotation in this period, probably at the Mundstock studio.

Through Beals, Harrison became an integral part of the modern dance community of San Francisco. She taught him the basics of Graham technique, and he began to compose music for a number of dancers in the Bay Area. The Dance Council's third festival, on 2 May 1937, featured an experiment in collective choreography—*Changing World,* a cycle in eight episodes developed by nine collaborators, including Harrison. He wrote the music, helped with the choreography, performed on three instruments, and even left the quartet of musicians to dance in one scene. Like *Waterfront—1934,* the work's subject was political: Part 1, for instance, featured sections such as "Women Walk Free," "All Religions are One," and "City" (which included the "Intellectuals," the "Workers," the "Night Lifers," and the "Country People"). Harrison scored his music for two pianos, three percussionists, and recorder (he played all three instruments at various times during the performance), along with a "voice" in one scene, and a "declaimer."

The following April, Harrison danced the part of Winter in an opera by Oakland composer Harvey Raab at the War Memorial Opera House. Frankenstein panned the production in the next day's *San Francisco Chronicle,* saving his only compliments for the staging, costuming, and the "good ballet led by Lenore Peters Job."[36] Job, one of the directors and choreographers for *Changing World,* ran the Peters Wright School of

Dancing on Sacramento Street, founded in the teens by her sister Anita Peters and Peters's husband, Dexter Wright. As a child, Carol Beals had studied at the Peters Wright School and during the 1930s she taught ballet and children's classes there. (Among her young students was the daughter of strike leader, Harry Bridges.)[37] Harrison composed several pieces for Job's productions during this period,[38] as well as other works for percussion: for instance, the unpublished (and unauthorized) *We are Always Winter*—a brief encomium to the wonders of spring for speaking chorus and three percussionists (playing a battery of three woodblocks, three gongs, and three drums).

In the fall of 1937, when he was but twenty years old, Lou Harrison went to work for Mills College in Oakland as dance accompanist.[39] He was employed not by the music department, but by the physical education department, which at the time supervised the dance curriculum. The main dance instructor was Tina Flade, who had come to Mills in 1934 and built a rigorous program by the time she left after the summer session of 1938. Trained in Dresden as a concert pianist, Flade changed her focus to dance after watching a performance by Mary Wigman, whose technique contrasted sharply with that of Martha Graham. (Wigman focused on the relationship between the dancer and the physical environment in contrast to Graham's torso-oriented approach.)

Harrison's main assignment was to accompany Flade's classes, improvising on piano or percussion. It taxed both his imagination and his patience: he recalls, for instance, once spending an entire day improvising over the four-note motive c' a d' g (from the stage call "We want Cantor" for comedian Eddie Cantor). For Flade's own choreographies, Harrison would watch the dance, take down the "counts," and write complementary music. Flade, however, was wont to improvise herself, changing her steps (and hence the counts) from session to session. Harrison would bring in his new composition only to find that it didn't fit. Puzzled, he recorded her steps in Labanotation. At the following rehearsal, when they reached a point of noncoordination, he said, "Tina, according to my notes, what you did here was this" and stood up and danced the section for her. "Oh yes," she responded. "I do recall something of the sort."[40]

The process eventually settled into a fixed form, and a number of Flade's choreographies with music by Harrison appear on programs of the time. In fact, his Prelude for Grandpiano (16 September 1937), which was published in the *New Music Quarterly* for July 1938, was premiered as a dance work with Flade.[41] On the same program, Harrison accompanied (on piano or percussion) dances by Veronika Pataky and Bernice van Gelder (both from the Wigman School),[42] Lenore Peters Job, and Carol Beals.

Summer sessions at Mills College brought notable artists to campus in a variety of fields. Beginning in 1934, for instance, the dance curriculum featured Hanya Holm, director of the New York Wigman School and "one of the Big Four of [the] Bennington [School of the Dance]."[43] In addition to dance classes, Holm taught a course in "percussion (music in relation to the dance)."[44] Henry Cowell was also a member of Mills's summer staff. Once Lou Harrison began to work at the college, he also became heavily involved in its summer session activities, and during his first year (26 June–6 August 1938) made several important connections in the dance world, one of which enabled him to find a job for his new friend John Cage.

BONNIE BIRD, MILLS COLLEGE, AND
THE CORNISH SCHOOL (1938–1939)

In the summer of 1938, Mills College brought dancer/choreographer Lester Horton up from Los Angeles and Graham-trained dancer Bonnie Bird down from Seattle. Bird had just completed her first year on the faculty of Seattle's Cornish School, where she succeeded Welland Lathrop, who, as we have seen, had taught at Ann Mundstock's studio in San Francisco.[45] Bird stayed at Mills only for the first two weeks, but brought along two of her best students, Dorothy Hermann and an emerging talent, Mercier Cunningham. Horton stayed for the full program and brought his own assistant, the now renowned Bella Lewitzky.

Lou Harrison, for his part, was kept very busy during the six-week session. On Mondays, Wednesdays, and Fridays, he collaborated with Flade in teaching an hour-long class on "dance composition." "Miss Flade approaches the problems of composition from an analysis of movement," notes the course description in the summer session brochure.[46] "Relations of gesture and movement, of pantomime and dance. Mr. Harrison will offer material in the classic dance forms of the 16th and 17th centuries in relation to modern music and dance." On Tuesdays and Thursdays Harrison taught his own percussion course, offering "elementary instruction in the technique of percussion accompaniment." Advanced students also had the opportunity to work with him three days a week in the afternoon: course "S260" presented students with "advanced problems for percussion composition," the "results" to be used in the production of the "Workshop group," which was run by Lester Horton four evenings each week. On Thursdays, when Horton's workshop did not meet, students and faculty attended discussion sessions. At one of these (21 July) Harrison presented a lecture on "Modern Music for Modern Dance," which he had given three months earlier during Mills's dance festival.[47] At another, Bird gave a recital, and at a third she spoke on "Martha Graham's Approach to Dance."

When she first accepted the position at Cornish in the fall of 1937, Bonnie Bird had found the dance situation frustrating. "I expected I would have to start reconstruction from the bottom up," she said, "but I never realized how barren the bottom could be."[48] There were only five dance majors enrolled in the program. By the time she came to Mills in June 1938, however, she was more upbeat: three of her students had proven quite exceptional—Dorothy Hermann, Syvilla Fort (who would later become supervising director of the Katherine Dunham School in New York),[49] and Merce Cunningham. At the same time, Bird's composer-accompanist Ralph Gilbert, who had previously worked with Lathrop, moved to New York to accompany Martha Graham.[50] Thus Bird was on the lookout for a new accompanist. She first offered the job to Harrison, but, satisfied with his work at Mills, he declined.[51] In his stead he recommended John Cage.

Cage recalls the offer as one of several that came from Harrison's connections. "I . . . went up to San Francisco to meet Lou [because] I knew that he shared with me the love of the modern dance; and I needed a job," said Cage in 1992. "Through Lou in San Francisco in one day I got eight jobs," he added, no doubt with some hyperbole.[52] Cage chose the position at Cornish because Bird described to him a "closet full of percussion instruments,"[53] among them a collection of Chinese gongs, cymbals, tom-toms, and woodblocks belonging to German dancer Lore Deja.[54] By the fall John and Xenia Cage had moved into a small apartment in Seattle.

Cage immediately set about organizing a percussion ensemble, which presented three concerts at Cornish in 1938 and 1939 (9 December 1938; 19 May 1939; and 9 December 1939). The 1938 concert, as he proudly stated in later years, was the "first complete percussion concert in America."[55] Among those he recruited for his group were pianist Margaret Jansen and eurythmics instructor Doris Dennison, both of whom later moved to San Francisco with the Cages. The second and third concerts also included Cornish student Imogene Horsley, who would later become a recognized musicologist and scholar of Renaissance and

Baroque music.[56] For his first Seattle concert Cage programmed his own trio and quartet from Los Angeles (1935–1936), along with three pieces published by Cowell in the 1936 percussion collection: Ray Green's *Three Inventories of Casey Jones,* Gerald Strang's *Percussion Music for Three Players,* and two of William Russell's *Three Dance Movements.*

Cowell was fond of Green's music and published his percussion and piano/vocal works in the *New Music Quarterly* and *Orchestra Series* (1934 and 1936). Like Harrison and Cage, Green had worked with dancers, including May O'Donnell (a member of the Graham troupe whom he married in 1938) and Graham herself.[57] His *Three Inventories of Casey Jones,* which uses folk song material, calls for five graduated pop bottles, two drums, two cymbals, four gongs, a large bottle containing four or five marbles, and piano. Bird developed a dance to it depicting Casey as "a company fellow who, having driven his famous engine too fast around a bend and crashed, found himself in 'the other place' instead of heaven because he was not a union man."[58]

William (Bill) Russell, one of the two composers whose percussion works had first attracted Cowell's attention, performed both jazz and Chinese music. From 1934 to 1940 he toured with Pauline Benton and Robert Youmans as the musician in the Red Gate Players, a group that mounted Chinese shadow puppet plays.[59] Benton, daughter of the president of the University of the Philippines, had for years studied the shadow plays of rural China. On 23 October 1939, her small group appeared at Mills College and among those in the audience was Lou Harrison. Years later—long after he had returned to California in 1953 from his ten-year residency on the East Coast—Harrison helped Benton revive the group, with himself as music director. Russell moved to New Orleans in 1940, where he wrote about and recorded jazz, eventually becoming jazz-archive curator at Tulane.

In this first Seattle concert, Cage programmed only the first and third of Russell's *Three Dance Movements*: a "Waltz" in $\frac{7}{4}$ and a "Fox Trot" in $\frac{5}{4}$. The four players of these pieces handle a large assortment of instruments: triangles, a dinner bell, a bottle, an anvil, cymbals (finger, suspended Turkish, suspended Chinese, and two-handed varieties), tom-toms, small and large wood blocks, slapstick, and various drums. In the middle of the "Fox Trot," Player No. 1 breaks the bottle (*sffffz*). Another performer plucks the strings of a piano with a fork or plays tone clusters ranging from a third to the entire keyboard. (The middle movement, "March," which Cage added on later programs, contains the following instruction for the pianist: "Use a board [4 ft. long, 1 in.

by 4 in.] to play all black or white keys. In final bar, tremolo by rocking board from black to white keys; for final chord use all keys on piano.")[60]

Gerald Strang, who had studied composition and counterpoint at the University of California, Berkeley, managed the *New Music Quarterly* during Henry Cowell's four years in San Quentin prison. (Cowell was incarcerated in 1936 on a morals charge; soon after his release in 1940 he was granted a full pardon by the governor of California.)[61] Strang, who lived in Los Angeles, also assisted Schoenberg for fourteen years as a copyist and an editor of some of the theoretical works. Like the other composers featured on Cage's first program, Strang had developed close links with modern dance. In fact, the percussion trio that Cage performed in December 1938 was designed specifically for music/dance interaction, as Strang stated in his introductory notes to the score: "The aim in composing the Percussion Music has been to write pieces possessing a musical value in their own right, yet suitable for dancing, and capable of performance by a small number of reasonably well equipped and trained dance percussionists."[62]

Meanwhile, Harrison continued his collaboration with dancers in the San Francisco area. The 1938 Mills summer session ended on 5 August with a performance of *Conquest,* a Horton dance about the triumph of native Mexican culture over Spanish influence. Lewitzky starred as the "spirit of the people" and Harrison wrote music for piano, percussion, conch shell, and some type of flute (probably recorder or ocarina; the score, partially improvised at the time, no longer survives). He also helped design the decor.

After the 1938 summer session, Flade was replaced at Mills by Marian van Tuyl, for whom Harrison composed a number of works during the next two years (including *Uneasy Rapture* for piano and percussion, written before 2 May 1939). Van Tuyl also requested a composition from Henry Cowell, which he wrote in "elastic form" and entrusted to Harrison to realize. On one of Harrison's visits to San Quentin, Cowell described how Harrison was to assemble the phrases of this work (*Ritual of Wonder*) to fit the requirements of Van Tuyl's dance.[63]

Cowell had discussed the concept of elastic form in an article published in the *Dance Observer* in January 1937, and had essayed the concept in several works: one for three melody instruments and two percussionists (1936), and another for oboe, clarinet, and percussion written for Martha Graham and premiered in July 1937. His object was to "establish a meeting ground for musical and dance composition, in which the dance will be more definite than usual in form . . . and the music will be less rigid than usual."[64] He recommended that phrases should be expandable by lengthening or shortening individual notes; that sections should be written so as to be repeated, rearranged, omitted, or varied at will; that the instrumentation should be adjustable (hence the advantage of percussion); and that the length of the entire work should be flexible.

In this same period Harrison also began to write percussion music that was independent of dance: for instance, substituting the percussion ensemble for the traditional orchestra in concerti. In 1939 he completed a *Fourth Violin Concerto* (for violin and one percussionist) and a *First Concerto* for flute and two percussionists, the latter work premiered two years later at Bennington College by Otto Luening, with Henry Cowell and Frank Wigglesworth playing the two ostinato percussion parts.[65]

As Cage prepared for his second percussion concert at Cornish (19 May 1939), he determined to solicit new works from composers throughout the country. Some, like Virgil Thomson, never responded to his request.[66] Others happily complied. Among the pieces Cage received and programmed were *Pulse* by Henry Cowell, *Three Movements* by Johanna Beyer (a shadowy figure who was featured in Cowell's 1936 percussion collection, and who helped him manage the *New Music Quarterly*),[67] and the *Fifth Simfony* and *Counterdance* by Harrison. Harrison wrote both works to order, completing the *Simfony* on 8 March and *Counterdance* on 29 March. The latter was intended to have a companion movement preceding it, entitled "Passage through Darkness," but Harrison did not finish it in time. Although he envisioned its form and instrumentation (including several alarm clocks), "Passage" was not written until 1982 for his sixty-fifth birthday celebration at Mills.[68]

Cage was especially taken with the *Counterdance,* which he programmed repeatedly in future years. In a letter postmarked 20 April, he told Harrison, "Your Counterdance is excellent. Wish you would send the 1st movement. The Simfony is coming into shape. I'm working on it again tonite. I hope you will be pleased with the way we do it."[69]

Not everyone was convinced by Cage's efforts, however. One reviewer even compared the music to "a trolley going down the street," recalled Xenia Cage years later.[70] And on 14 February 1939, Theresa Stevens wrote in a talent column in the *Seattle Star*: "Percussion Music! . . . It has been hurting our eyes to see the words together in print. It's been hurting our ears just to hear them mentioned and it took us two

weeks to gather enough courage to call John Cage for help."[71] Cage
agreed that "P—M—," as Stevens called the unmentionable sounds, was
a poor term; a better one, he said, was the "Art of Noise." Stevens found
that appellation hardly more palatable, taking refuge in a "whiff of
smelling salts" and a long listen to "that new Brahms recording." On the
other hand, she had to admit that Cage was "an awfully nice person" and
her interest was more than a little piqued by the prospect of his May concert. (Stevens seems to have been primarily interested in Xenia—whose
photograph appears in her column—and in the Cages' bookbinding
work, an exhibit of which was on display at the Cornish School from
9–22 February.)

Despite his recollection of sharing with Harrison a "love of the modern dance," Cage confessed that his work at Cornish could at times become quite tedious. In that same letter of 20 April he told Harrison, "I
have the possibility of a job in Taos this summer. Director of music, if
you please; also cooperating with Alice Sherbon, dancer. I wouldn't get
paid very much if at all; but it would be a step away from accompaniment—drudgery which I hate." He also noted that "Henry [Cowell] suggests that we have a percussion festival at the Fair this summer
[presumably the Golden Gate Exposition, held on Treasure Island in
1939], cooperating with Ray Green."

Their percussion festival at the Exposition never took place, but a
lively concert was held nearby at Mills on 27 July. The summer of 1939
was an unusual one for Mills College: the entire Bennington School of
Dance moved its operations to the West Coast from 1 July to 11 August.
They brought their own faculty and staff, including composer Louis
Horst. Dance faculty at Mills that summer included Martha Graham,
Doris Humphrey, Charles Weidman, and Hanya Holm; among the teaching assistants were José Limón, Louise Kloepper, and Katherine Man-
ning (who would later work with Cage in Chicago). Cunningham came
from Seattle for a second summer at Mills and was enticed to New York
to work with Graham. Among all this activity, Harrison also convinced
the college to bring Cage to Oakland to present a program of "modern
American percussion music," including the first movement of Cage's
Quartet, Harrison's *Counterdance,* and selections from Beyer's *Three
Movements,* as well as works by Franziska Boas (*Changing Tensions*)
and William Russell (*March Suite, Studies in Cuban Rhythms,* and *Three
Dance Movements*—the last with its "March" added). Alfred Franken-
stein enthusiastically reviewed the performance in the *San Francisco
Chronicle:*

> That Western concert music has much to learn from its orchestra step-
> children, the percussion instruments, was suggested last night at Mills
> College. . . . One might almost say that the modern dance discovered
> the possibilities of the battery for the Western world. . . . [Of course]
> we are still very far from the subtlety of rhythmic speech the Arabs and
> Indians get out of their little hand drums or the symphonic grandeur of
> the Balinese percussion orchestras.[72]

Nevertheless, Frankenstein was taken with Russell's *Cuban Rhythms* and
Three Dance Movements, Harrison's *Counterdance,* and Cage's *Quartet.*

SPREADING THE CREDO (FALL 1939–SPRING 1940)

During Cage's second year at Cornish (1939–1940), his percussion ensemble grew both in size and in competence. Twelve players performed
on the Third Percussion Concert (9 December 1939), compared to seven
the previous May, and a group of twenty-three sponsors is listed as well,
including the painter Mark Tobey and "Mr. John Steinbeck," who, according to an article in the *Seattle Times,* "visited Mr. and Mrs. Cage last
summer."[73] Programmed were Cowell's *Pulse,* now coupled with the
companion piece *Return,* and Russell's *Fugue* for eight players—one of
the two initial percussion pieces published by Cowell. The group also
added to its repertory Amadeo Roldán's *Ritmicas V* and *VI,* Mildred
Couper's *Dirge* for two pianos tuned in quarter tones, and a new work by
Cage, *[First] Construction in Metal* [*sic*].[74]

Cowell had actively championed the music of both Roldán and
Couper. As early as 1930, he reviewed a New Music Society concert that
featured, among other works, Roldán's *Ritmicas,* conducted by "Mr.
Pedro Sanjuan [who] came all the way from Havana . . . to make his
[conducting] debut in San Francisco." About Roldán's work Cowell
wrote: "If intoxicants are all prohibited by law, then surely this delightful, rhythmic, undulating bit of Afro-Cuban music is a forbidden pleasure."[75] Cowell featured music by Roldán (conductor of the Havana
Philharmonic) in the *New Music Quarterly* in 1934, and six years later
published a tribute to him and his colleague Alejandro García Caturla in
Modern Music following the untimely death of both composers (Roldán
was thirty-eight, Caturla thirty-four). "Nowhere else in America has the
native African rhythm been so well preserved as in Cuba," wrote Cowell
in 1940, "and no other composer [besides Roldán] has made so significant a development of these ritualistic and secular rhythmic modes."[76]

Mildred Cooper (1887–1974), who married Impressionist landscape painter Richard Hamilton Couper (thus becoming Mildred Cooper Couper), taught at the Mannes School from 1915 to 1927 and later moved to Santa Barbara where she helped found the Music Academy of the West. She wrote several quarter-tone works, including *Xanadu, Dirge,* and *Rumba.*[77] Cowell published *Dirge* in January 1937.

The other new work on the concert, Cage's *Construction in Metal,* for thundersheets, orchestra bells, "string piano" (Cowell's term for playing the strings of a regular piano), sleigh bells, cow bells, temple gongs, brake drums, cymbals, anvils, and gongs, was the first of three such pieces Cage would compose for percussion ensemble during the years 1939–1941. It is also the first work to use what he called a "micro-macrocosmic" rhythmic structure, that is, one in which the proportions of larger sections mirror those of their component parts. The piece, with its sixteen units of sixteen measures and its phrase organization of $4 + 3 + 2 + 3 + 4$ ($= 16$), has been analyzed repeatedly (including by Cage himself), and I will therefore refrain from repeating such an analysis here. Suffice it to say that the compositional process Cage utilized for the first time in this work—a method often called his "square root" form—set the stage for his later percussion works, including a joint composition with Lou Harrison written in 1941. In later years Harrison used Cage's square root form as a teaching tool.[78]

The December 1939 concert at Cornish also featured an endorsement of percussion music by Cowell, phrased in quasipolitical terms:

> I honestly believe and formally predict that the immediate future of music lies in the bringing of percussion on one hand, and sliding tones on the other, to as great a state of perfection in construction of composition and flexibility of handling on instruments as older elements are now.

This statement calls to mind a similar manifesto that Cage delivered at a meeting of the Seattle Artists League, most likely on 18 February 1940, though the year has repeatedly been given erroneously as 1937.[79] Cage later titled his talk "The Future of Music: Credo"; its basic text (which was accompanied by extensive interpolated glosses) reads as follows:

> I believe that the use of noise to make music will continue and increase until we reach a music produced through the aid of electrical instru-

ments which will make available for musical purposes any and all sounds that can be heard. Photo-electric, film and mechanical mediums for the synthetic production of music will be explored. Whereas, in the past, the point of disagreement has been between dissonance and consonance, it will be, in the immediate future, between noise and so-called musical sounds. The present methods of writing music, principally those which employ harmony and its reference to particular steps in the field of sound, will be inadequate for the composer who will be faced with the entire field of sound. New methods will be discovered, bearing a definite relation to Schoenberg's twelve-tone system and present methods of writing percussion music and any other methods which are free from the concept of a fundamental tone. The principle of form will be our only constant connection with the past. Although the great form of the future will not be as it was in the past, at one time a fugue and at another the sonata, it will be related to these as they are to each other through the principle of organization or man's common ability to think.

Cage expanded on the role of percussion music as a catalyst in effecting a revolution in Western music in an article published in the *Dance Observer* in the same month as his third Cornish School percussion concert:

> Percussion music is revolution. Sound and rhythm have too long been submissive to the restrictions of 19th century music. . . .
>
> At the present stage of revolution, a healthy lawlessness is warranted. Experiment must necessarily be carried on by hitting anything—tin pans, rice bowls, iron pipes—anything we can lay our hands on. Not only hitting, but rubbing, smashing, making sound in every possible way. . . .
>
> The conscientious objectors to modern music will, of course, attempt everything in the way of counter-revolution. . . . But our common answer to every criticism must be to continue working and listening, making music with its materials, sound and rhythm.[80]

Cage's 1939 *Dance Observer* article was but one in a series of six suggested by Louis Horst and featured in the journal from October 1939 through March 1940 under the general heading "Percussion Music and its Relation to the Modern Dance." Contributors included William Russell ("Hot Jazz and Percussion Music"), Henry Cowell ("East Indian Tala Music"), Cage ("Goal: New Music, New Dance"), Franziska Boas ("Fundamental Concepts"), and Lou Harrison ("Statement").

The list of sponsors for Cage's Third Percussion Concert suggests that he had begun to convince others of his ideas as well. And he spread his creed more widely by taking his percussion show on the road. In January 1940 the "Cage Percussion Players" (John and Xenia Cage, Doris Dennison, and Margaret Jansen) presented programs at the University of Idaho, the University of Montana, and Whitman College in Walla Walla, Washington, featuring selections from their repertory: Russell's *March Suite, Studies in Cuban Rhythms,* and *Three Dance Movements;* Green's *Inventories of Casey Jones;* two of Beyer's *Three Movements;* Cage's *Quartet;* and Harrison's *Counterdance.*[81] The Idaho audience was particularly shaken: Cage called them "extremely hysterical."[82] (In later years the group would joke about the question period after this concert, during which an elderly audience member asked, "Have you ever played for the intelligensia before?")[83] On 14 February the group appeared at Reed College in Portland, adding Cage's *Second Construction* to their program.

While Cage was busy drumming up support for percussion music in the Northwest, Harrison continued to explore the same medium in San Francisco. Following his *Counterdance* and *Fifth Simfony* (March 1939), he wrote *Bomba* (15 May 1939: five percussionists), *Rune* (15 January 1940: six percussionists), and *Canticle [No. 1]* (21 June 1940: five percussionists).[84] He also continued to write concerti with percussion orchestra: in addition to the flute and violin concertos cited above, Harrison started another one for violin and percussion, which he ultimately completed in 1959.[85] Undated (and unauthorized) works from this same period include several similar pieces: a *Prelude* for cello and two percussionists, *Song Project No. 2* for voice and percussion, and a *Viola Concerto* (viola and percussion). After Hitler invaded Poland in September 1939, Harrison responded to the news by beginning a Mass for unison chorus with percussion. The opening melodic figure in the "Kyrie" was his own "cry of anguish," its percussion accompaniment evoking a heavy military march. In the "Gloria," on the other hand, he projected a message of hope through an accompaniment of diverse bell sounds designed to create a great chime.[86] Surviving programs from the time also show Harrison appearing frequently with dancers at Mills, in San Francisco, and elsewhere in the Bay Area. Between 2 April and 10 June 1939, he took part in at least eight programs, including a concert with Van Tuyl at the Golden Gate Exposition on Treasure Island.

It was at this Exposition (specifically, at the Dutch East Indies Pavilion) that Harrison for the first time saw a Balinese gamelan. True, he had heard recorded gamelan music in Cowell's class and been entranced by its sound, but the effect of the live Indonesian percussion ensemble in the idyllic setting in the midst of San Francisco Bay was riveting. The implications for his later work composing for (and building) gamelan, a highly sophisticated percussion-based ensemble, were profound indeed.

Against this background, Harrison's article in the *Dance Observer* (March 1940) marks a watershed. As his first published essay, it not only represented the opinions of a now seasoned percussion composer, but also heralded the beginning of his literary work, which would blossom in the 1940s to over three hundred reviews for the *New York Herald Tribune* and essays in *Modern Music, Listen, View,* and other periodicals.

Harrison began his 1940 essay with a tribute to two of the strongest influences on his own work: Charles Ives and Henry Cowell, both of whom, he claimed, were "interested more in rhythm and melody than in harmony."[87] In terms of pitch relations, Harrison noted that for Ives "the focal tone or group of focal tones need not lie among the tones of the mode"; and for Cowell "that all or any of the tones of the mode may be sounded simultaneously along the progression of the melody and not only allow all functions within the melody to remain evident but even enforce these functions." As for rhythm, it "is more vital and important than it has been in many a century. This has led to a fine and simple vigor in Cowell's work and a nervous yearning in Ives' multiple linear music." Music, said Harrison, is "idealized movement" wherein one learns to deal with "stress, duration and velocity." Only one other art poses similar challenges: dance.

In the second part of the article, Harrison addressed practical concerns of the contemporary composer, noting the "great gaps" that had developed among composer, executant, and audience. "It should be sufficiently obvious," he wrote, "that the only music which may be considered creative and therefor [*sic*] important today is being pursued by a small group of inadequately supported amateurs." Bemoaning the difficulties of arranging for public performance, Harrison recommended that the safest route for the composer ("as far as . . . probable actualization goes") was to write for the human voice or for percussion. His experiences, like those of Cage, had shown that the specification of found or foraged instruments, far from discouraging performances, actually stimulated them by involving the amateur, who "still reigns with his clear and vigorous head on his shoulders and his anxious hands on a drum."

Harrison and Cage would soon test that hypothesis together.

THE SUMMER OF 1940

At the end of the spring semester 1940, Bonnie Bird resigned from the Cornish School.[88] So did John Cage. He and Xenia decided to move to San Francisco, and Doris Dennison and Margaret Jansen chose to come along as well.

For its part, Mills College hosted a summer residency of faculty from the Chicago School of Design, the former Bauhaus group headed by painter and photographer László Moholy-Nagy (1895–1946). Harrison arranged for the college to bring both Cage and Lester Horton again as well.

By this time, Harrison and Cage had each accumulated a sizable collection of percussion instruments. In July 1940 Cage compiled an inventory of his, listing nearly a hundred different items including (in addition to the expected ones) one saw blade, one hand saw, one egg beater, ten thunder sheets, two forks, three brake drums, three metal discs, one lion's roar, and one washtub.[89] Ten varieties of bells, five types of cymbals, various kinds of drums and whistles, a conch shell, and other soundmakers are detailed as well.

Staff for Mills's dance program in the summer of 1940 included Marian van Tuyl, Louise Kloepper ("teaching assistant to Hanya Holm"), and José Limón (billed as a "teaching assistant to Charles Weidman"), among others. The musicians on the dance staff were Harrison; Esther Williamson [Ballou], who had graduated from Bennington College in 1937 and was then a "fellow in music" at Mills; and Cage, described as "Musical Director, American Dance Theatre, Seattle" and "director of his own group of percussion players." The American Dance Theatre, brainchild of Bonnie Bird, had been founded in January 1940. Over eighty young people aged fifteen to twenty-two auditioned for the opportunity to participate in a ten-week daily training program in technique and composition. Of these, a third were selected for a festival in May, in which Bird featured the sixteen most advanced participants along with several of her own students from Cornish. The music ranged from Bach to new compositions by Cage, including a work entitled *Imaginary Landscape No. 2* (subsequently rejected, and unrelated to the later work with the same name).[90]

At the 1940 summer session at Mills, Cage and Harrison each taught a basic course in percussion daily ("a study of types of sounds, use of instruments, percussive scoring of rhythmic patterns, and elementary percussion composition"). They also offered a more advanced class,

"Percussion for Accompanists," which supplemented the basic class by adding "work in analysis of rhythm, study of percussive scoring, and percussion composition." Alone, Harrison taught still a third daily course, "Musical Composition for Dance," which offered students the opportunity "to solve actual problems in conjunction with the classes in dance composition."[91] While the basic course was designed for dancers, the more advanced ones (along with a class by Esther Williamson in keyboard improvisation) were geared to musicians, requiring "a background in harmony, a knowledge of musical form and analysis, and some experience in working with the dance."

Six performances were also on the schedule for the six-week session. The program of 6 July featured the Horton dance group with music by Harrison, including two new works: *16 to 24,* about disenchanted youth, and *Something to Please Everybody,* a loosely organized revue among whose movements was an "Aphrodisiac" danced by Bella Lewitzky. Harrison, who wrote bluesy music to accompany the number, describes it as "a mock strip-tease for the tired businessman," and the following day's *San Francisco Chronicle* carried a review by Frankenstein headlined "At Mills—Strip Tease!" (He described Lewitzky's number as "an uproarious burlesque of burlesque.")[92] The following week Mills presented a dance concert by May O'Donnell (wife of Ray Green), who had been featured in her debut solo recital in San Francisco five months earlier.[93] And on 18 July, Harrison, Cage, and William Russell gave a joint concert of percussion music (see Figures 8.1 and 8.2).

The Bauhaus people helped with the concert's stage, designing a multilevel set-up that included knotted rope ladders in which the musicians could hang beaters not currently in use. Frankenstein was able to attend only the dress rehearsal, but reviewed it nevertheless, mentioning plans for a "choreography of moving lights" (which Harrison does not recall).

This time the performance attracted national, as well as local coverage: in *Time Magazine, Modern Music,* and the *Dance Observer* as well as the *San Francisco Chronicle.* "At California's Mills College last week," began the article in *Time,*

> summer-school students filed on to a stage before a Picasso-like background of musical scales, picked up an assortment of bells, whistles and drums, and let go with everything they had. With ordered gusto they banged, rattled, beat, blew, stomped and rang their way through [the works on the program]. . . . When they had finished, the audience gave percussive approval.[94]

Figures 8.1. Photo from the *Oakland Tribune,* 18 July 1940, appearing with the announcement of that evening's percussion concert at Mills College. Front, left to right: Doris Dennison, Margaret Jansen; rear, left to right: Lou Harrison, John Cage, Xenia Cage. (Photo courtesy of the *Oakland Tribune.*)

The seventeen "percussors," as Cowell called them in an article in *Modern Music,* included not only students from the Mills summer session but also Cage, Harrison, Russell, Dennison, Jansen, and Xenia Cage, as well as Irving Morrow, consulting architect for the Golden Gate Bridge[95] (to whom they assigned the siren in José Ardévol's *Suite;* police permission was required for its use). Morrow, a friend of Harrison's, had designed the San Francisco home of Harry and Olive Cowell (Henry's father and stepmother), as well as a series of listening rooms for Wilson's Record Library in San Francisco, where Harrison worked. He recalls that for these rooms Morrow used "two panes of glass of different thicknesses and of such slight misalignment as prevented resonance between them."[96]

PERCUSSION

PROGRAM

INTERMISSION

PULSE •
dragon's mouths, woodblocks, drums, tom toms, rice bowls, temple gongs, cymbals, gongs, pipe lengths, brake drums.
COWELL

2ND CONSTRUCTION ••
sleigh bells, rattle, maracas, wind glass, snare drum, tom toms, temple gongs, tam tam, thundersheet, gongs, string piano.
CAGE

CHICAGO SKETCHES* •••
3525 S. Dearborn   washboard band
222 N. State   including suitcase,
5507 S. Michigan   string drum, cans,
4726 S. State   tub; piano; drums,
cowbells, cymbals,
woodblocks; fingersnaps & foot-stomps.
RUSSELL

CANTICLE* ••••
sistrum, woodblocks, bells, rattles, dragon's mouths, temple gongs, flower pots, cowbells, guiro, wind glass, triangle, cymbal, brake drum, tam tam, thundersheet, drums, muted gongs.
HARRISON

SUITE* •••••
Allegro moderato   sirens, bells, hand-
Adagio   claps, claves, guiros,
Fuga: allegro   maracas, triangle,
anvils,cymbals,slap-
stick, police whistle, tam tam, drums, gong, piano.
ARDEVOL

RITMICAS V AND VI ••••••
En tiempo de 'son'
En tiempo de 'rumba'
claves, cowbells, quijadas, guiro, maracas, bongos, drums, marimbula.
ROLDAN

★ **DIRECTION**
JOHN CAGE
LOU HARRISON
WILLIAM RUSSELL

★ **PROGRAM NOTES**
JOSÉ ARDEVOL, a Spaniard, lives in Havana where, in 1934, he founded the "Orquesta 'da camera' de la Habana" of which he is conductor. AMADEO ROLDAN (1900-1939) was born of Cuban parents in Paris. In 1932 he was appointed Conductor of the Philharmonic Orchestra of Havana.

★ **PLAYERS**
PHOEBE APPY
XENIA CAGE
JOHN CAGE
MARIAN CONSTABLE
DORIS DENNISON
NORMA T. DORFMAN
GERRY EGBERT
RENATA GARVE
LOU HARRISON
MARGARET JANSEN
MARINA LEE
IRVING MORROW
LAURA JEAN NAST
LAURA PICCIRILLO
WILLIAM RUSSELL
EVELYN SEMENZA
GWENDOLYN THOMAS
*Première performance.

★ **DESIGNERS**
SETTING
GORDON WEBBER
STAGE MANAGER
MARGARET THOMSON
CREW
MARJORIE HAWORTH
KATHRYN-LEE HOLCOMB
LEROY BINKLEY

"I honestly believe and formally predict that the immediate future of music lies in the bringing of percussion on one hand, and sliding tones on the other, to as great a state of perfection in construction of composition and flexibility of handling on instruments as older elements are now."
HENRY COWELL

THURSDAY, JULY 18, 1940, 8:30 P.M., LISSER HALL, MILLS COLLEGE

Figure 8.2. Program from the percussion concert at Mills College, 18 July 1940.

The program featured several works from Cage's previous concerts: Cowell's *Pulse* and Roldán's *Ritmicas,* for instance, and Cage's *Second Construction*. But there were new works as well, including premieres of Ardévol's *Suite,* Russell's *Chicago Sketches,* and Harrison's *Canticle* [*No. 1*]. Cowell's proclamation on the "future of music" reappeared as well. But he must have meant the "future of Western art music," wrote Frankenstein,

for the music of the Orient and of "primitive" American peoples have
long since developed percussion and "sliding tones" to an extremely
sophisticated degree. . . . Experimental shafts do not always strike pay
dirt, and some of the things played last night may not turn out to be the
final metal. . . . But there is drama and power and excitement in much
of the music played . . . and the palette of tone color set forth was end-
lessly fascinating. . . . There was something epical . . . in seeing
William Russell pound on a suitcase in his "Chicago Sketches" for the
delicious thud that only a suitcase can provide.[97]

Cage's *Second Construction* is a quartet, with three of the four players assigned four instruments each: Player No. 1: seven variously pitched
sleigh bells, Indian rattle, two small maracas, wind glass; Player No. 2:
snare drum, two maracas, five tom-toms of different sizes, three temple
gongs; and Player No. 3: five muted gongs, tam-tam, water gong, thundersheet. (Player No. 4 has only one instrument: the piano.) Harrison's
Canticle, composed in four hours on 21 June, is a quintet with similarly
diverse instrumentation: sistrum, three woodblocks, three high bells,
gourd rattle, three dragon's mouths, three large glass bells, a wooden rattle, three clay bells, three large cowbells, Indian wooden rasp, glass
windbells, triangle, suspended Turkish cymbal, large bell, "very large
tam-tam," large thundersheet, three high drums, three muted gongs, and
three low drums.

Despite the pitch range available in his instrumentation, Cage's
orientation remained primarily temporal. He again used his micro-
macrocosmic form, but with less rigidity than in the *First Construction:*
the proportions of larger and smaller sections are not always identical.[98]
Harrison's orientation is more consciously melodic, exemplifying his
comments in the *Dance Observer* on the importance of melody and
rhythm over harmony (a concept strongly advocated by Cowell). Indeed,
Harrison's music consistently shows a lyric bent; even his dissonant
counterpoint and serial compositions of the 1940s and early 1950s are
decidedly melodic. His formal organization is less balanced than is
Cage's; neither is it controlled by mathematical relationships. At the
same time the governing form in Harrison's work is more audible: an
opening forty-four-measure section introduces thematic material that is
varied in four shorter sections to follow. The composition's overall shape
is more classical than that of Cage's work: *Canticle No. 1* rises to a dynamic crest about two-thirds of the way through, followed by a clear re-
capitulation. Harrison's emphasis is less on devising proportional

relationships among the sections than on exploring contrapuntal possibilities inherent in his thematic material.

In his influential article "Drums along the Pacific" (*Modern Music,* 1940), Henry Cowell used the Mills performance as a springboard for a discussion of the origins of percussion music. Citing the "extraordinary interest" in the medium that had "developed on the Pacific coast," Cowell listed the concert's complete catalog of instruments and then delineated the four "schools" of composition cited at the beginning of the present essay: "It is irrelevant, for the moment" he said, "to evaluate the compositions performed [at Mills] as good or bad, important or unimportant. Let it be sufficient to note that all were serious attempts showing considerable variety."[99] Yet even in 1940, after the veritable explosion of percussion music during the previous seven years (much of it published by himself), Cowell still sensed a need to defend the basic concept: "Why is it more reprehensible to write for four percussion instruments than for two violins, viola and 'cello?" he asked. "The string quartet may at times be quite boring as a combination of instruments. Percussion alone may prove monotonous, but is less apt to, because it is still in a state of experiment."

COLLABORATION (1940–1941)

After Cage moved to San Francisco in 1940, his collaboration with Harrison intensified. Poet Elsa Gidlow, who met Harrison through a mutual friend, Sherman Slayback, attended some of their joint practice sessions in a loft on Jackson Street, fascinated by their ensemble of "brake drums . . . buffalo bells, [and] a dozen other exotic instruments."[100] Harrison set to music several of Gidlow's poems, including *May Rain* (1941), in which the solo voice is accompanied by tam-tam and a piano prepared with screws inserted between its strings—a technique Cage showed Harrison during one of their practice sessions. Cage's development of the prepared piano was stimulated by both percussion and dance: when space restrictions at Seattle's Repertory Playhouse prohibited the use of a percussion ensemble to accompany Syvilla Fort's *Bacchanale,* he sought a substitute using solo piano. During one of Bird's dance classes at Cornish, he discovered that he could imitate many of the percussion sounds he desired by inserting various objects into the piano strings.[101]

Despite the number of instruments they already owned, Cage and Harrison continually sought more. "John was constantly on the telephone trying to raise money to buy percussion instruments," recalls

Xenia.[102] They purchased metal pipe in hardware stores, ceramic flower pots in nurseries, and delicate porcelain bowls in Asian import stores. The music stores typically offered a wide selection of ocarinas (globular flutes), which Harrison favored for their delicate timbre. And in a store on Market Street, they bought a bright green *quijada* (the jawbone of an ass), painted with flowers. Cage also built a replica of a Mexican *teponazli,* a slit-drum traditionally made from a hollowed log with a series of H-shaped cuts. He made his version from a wooden box with a cover.

For years Harrison had frequented the Chinese opera productions in San Francisco and knew not only the stores in the area, but also the people. He had also learned to bargain effectively:

> I remember the day John Cage and I bought our big tam-tams in China-town. We paid $45 apiece and had tea as well. Today, of course, it's just a one-price tourist business. But in those days, if you started to bargain with a Chinese merchant you were invited to tea.[103]

Then there were the junkyards, which yielded, among other treasures, the surprisingly decorous-sounding brakedrums. Prewar drums were made from spun steel and afforded a lovely ringing sound when suspended from their axle holes. (After the war, the automobile industry began using cast iron, which is more machinable but less resonant; Harrison still maintains a collection of prewar drums, which he happily loans to those wishing to play his music.) The brakedrums also could be laid flat and hit with mallets. "John and I considered them the trumpet section of the percussion orchestra," Harrison recalls.[104]

Cage also enhanced his connections with Mills in this period. In the College's Extension Education brochure for Spring 1941, he is listed as teaching "Percussion: Systematic examination and organization of new sound materials," with special emphasis on "sound in relation to the modern dance."

By May 1941 Harrison and Cage were ready to present a joint concert. They rented the California Club auditorium on Clay Street for 14 May (Harrison's birthday) and sold tickets for fifty cents apiece (a quarter for students). Performers included Harrison, John and Xenia Cage, Dennison, Jansen, and two new members: Elizabeth Hall and pianist Brabazon Lindsey, another Seattle transplant. (Lindsey studied at the Cornish School during the time Cage taught there, although she is not listed as a member of his percussion ensemble.) Some familar pieces reappear on the program (Cage's *Trio* and *Quartet* and Harrison's *Canti-*

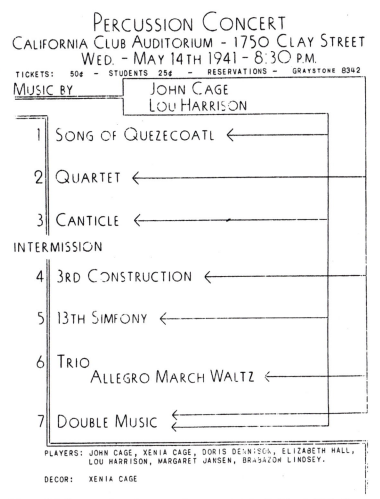

Figure 8.3. Program from the percussion concert at the California Club, San Francisco, 14 May 1941.

cle), but there are also four new works: *Song of Quetzalcoatl* and *13th Simfony* by Harrison, the *Third Construction* by Cage, and a joint composition by the two of them: *Double Music* (see Figure 8.3).[105] Xenia Cage built a large mobile that hung over the stage and swayed "like a dancer," with "a kind of breath rhythm."[106] In the following day's *San Francisco News,* Emilia Hodel described a "bewildering array of instruments, including everything that can be tapped, from cymbals, drums, Oriental gongs and bells to washtubs filled with water, paint cans, water tumblers and iron wheel hubs."[107] Frankenstein attended as well, commenting afterwards on the "enormously rich and varied range of color, rhythm and dynamics," although he found "the whole style . . . better calculated to dance accompaniment than to concert performance."[108] He also noted (correctly) that the absence of more "conventional instruments" such as timpani, xylophone, and snare drums, reflected both economic constraints and technical limitations on the part of the performers. "Who could afford timpani?" says Harrison. "And besides, none of us could roll."[109]

Double Music, now a staple of the percussion ensemble repertory, was written quickly with a minimum of collaboration. Cage and Harrison agreed on a total duration (which translated into two hundred $\frac{4}{4}$ measures), instrumentation (all metal at Harrison's request, in admiration of Cage's *First Construction*), and basic figurations (rhythmic motives that could be combined in various arrangements, with rests of corresponding lengths). The two composers then went about the compositional process independently, Cage writing the parts for the first and third players, Harrison for the second and fourth. Cage used his micro-macro system, dividing the two hundred measures into fourteen sections of fourteen (with a four-measure coda), each section subdivided into units of 4 + 3 + 2 + 5. Harrison decided on twenty-one units of nine and one-half measures, adding the extra half-measure at the end. When they completed their individual parts, the two composers put them together "and never changed a note."[110] Students of aleatoric composition may see this process as a foreshadowing of chance music, but Harrison gives a more prosaic explanation: "We didn't need to [alter anything]. By that time I knew perfectly well what John would be doing; so I accommodated him. And he did the same for me, too."[111]

Since Cage and Harrison had just enough money to fund the recording of one piece, they allowed the audience the choice by conducting a poll at the end of the program. The winner was Harrison's *Simfony #13* (not "#3," as Cage stated in several later interviews). John and Xenia Cage, Harrison, Dennison, and Jansen recorded the nine-minute work at the Photo and Sound Company in the Sherman-Clay building in San Francisco and issued the recording that fall.

Meanwhile, Cage had read Edgard Varèse's "Organized Sound for the Sound Film," published in *The Commonweal* in December 1940. "We must unmuzzle music," Varèse exhorted, "if we are to allow it to perform its function of arousing people and making them feel. . . . We

now are in possession of scientific means not merely of realistic reproduction of sounds but of *production of entirely new combinations of
sound,* with the possibility of creating new emotions, awakening dulled
sensibilities. Any possible sound we can imagine can be produced with
perfect control of its quality, intensity and pitch."[112] Varèse's definition of
music as "organized sound" struck a responsive chord in Cage; in fact,
the article had such a profound effect on him that he typed it out in its entirety.[113] Years later he recalled, "I had previously defined [music] as the
'organization of sound.' I saw that I had used three words whereas Varèse
had used two. So it seemed to me perfectly reasonable for us to call this
[new recording] 'the first recording of organized sound.' So we did." And
they sent a copy of the record to Varèse, who responded, "Please desist
from using my term."[114] (Later in New York, Varèse's wife explained that
her husband was concerned about his work becoming confused with that
of Cage and Harrison.)

Frankenstein, who seemed to always have his finger on the pulse of
new music, reviewed the *Simfony #13* recording in the *Chronicle*.[115] "For
several years past," he began,

> John Cage and Lou Harrison . . . have established a kind of citadel of
> [percussion ensemble music] under the wing of the Mills College
> dance department. This movement started with dance accompani-
> ment . . . although Harrison has written some extremely interesting
> concert pieces. . . . There is nothing freakish or strange about [this]
> work; it is, rather, an exhilarating lyrical study. . . . It is almost impres-
> sionistic compared to the annihilating roar and rage of the only other
> recorded piece of this type, the notorious "Ionization" of Edgar [*sic*]
> Varese.

For years the score of *Simfony #13* was thought to have been lost
until a copy was uncovered in the course of research for the present
writer's book, *Lou Harrison: Composing a World*.[116] In 1997, for a concert celebrating Harrison's eightieth birthday, he heard the piece for the
first time since 1941.

THE END OF THE WEST COAST
RESIDENCY (SUMMER 1941–SUMMER 1942)

Lou Harrison and John Cage collaborated on one final West Coast percussion concert before Cage left for Chicago and then New York (where
he arrived in the summer of 1942). On 26 July 1941, in collaboration

with Marian van Tuyl, Cage organized a performance in Mills College's Lisser Hall entitled "Percussion, Quarter Tones, Dance, Electric Sound." Advance publicity billed the program as a sequel to the previous year's event: "John Cage, whose percussion concert last summer proved so successful, has arranged a program this year of even greater and more spectacular variety."[117] He and Van Tuyl created *Horror Dream,* focusing on a choreographer's "fantastic dreams" about the "hazards of performance." The music was *Imaginary Landscape No. 1,* composed at Cornish in 1939 and prerecorded at Sherman Clay's Photo and Sound studio, using cymbals, piano, and "re-recordings of constant and variable frequencies."[118] The lengthy program also featured some old favorites: Roldán's *Ritmicas,* Cage's *Third Construction,* Russell's *Three Dance Movements,* Couper's *Dirge* (along with her *Rumba*), and Harrison's *Simfony #13.*

Although the Mills performance was the last of their West Coast concerts, it was not the end of the Harrison–Cage friendship, collaboration, or exchange of ideas—or of either man's composition and performance of percussion works. In both Chicago and New York, Cage continued to mount percussion concerts with many of the same pieces he had programmed at Cornish or in the Bay Area. In March 1942, for example, Cage's Chicago percussion group performed twice, at the Arts Club and at the University of Chicago's Mandel Hall. He programmed Harrison's *Canticle* on both concerts and the *Counterdance* at the Club, along with older works and his own *Imaginary Landscape No. 3.* (The *Imaginary Landscapes* use electronic sounds. The first, composed for Bonnie Bird, used test tone recordings from which Cage created sliding tones by varying the turntable speed. Perhaps the most well known of the set is *Imaginary Landscape No. 4* [*March No. 2*] scored for twelve radios, premiered in 1951.) In May 1942 Cage composed *City Wears a Slouch Hat* for percussion and voices, to accompany Kenneth Patchen's CBS radio play of the same name.

The 18 March concert at the University of Chicago featured a particularly eclectic repertory: wedged between Holst's *St. Paul's Suite* for strings and Beethoven's *Romanze* in F Major for violin and orchestra were Harrison's *Canticle* and Russell's *Three Dance Movements.* (Works by Saint-Saëns, Bach, Abert, and Dvořák followed.) Cage created a sensation with his six-member percussion orchestra, as he had two weeks earlier at the Arts Club where a somewhat larger group played to "a packed house, slightly confused by it all, but hysterical with applause."[119] Reviewers were both fascinated and bewildered, highlighting special effects such as the breaking of the beer bottle in the middle of

Russell's "Fox Trot" and the board-assisted full-keyboard tremolo in his "March."[120]

Probably the most famous of Cage's percussion concerts, however, was the one held in New York City at the Museum of Modern Art (MOMA) on 7 February 1943. The event was given full-court press in *Life,* complete with photos of the ensemble and many of the individual players.[121] Cage programmed his own *Construction in Metal* and *Imaginary Landscape #3,* Harrison's *Canticle* and *Counterdance,* and Roldán's *Ritmicas V* and *VI,* along with premieres of Henry Cowell's *Ostinato Pianissimo,* Ardévol's *Preludio à 11,* and Cage's own *Amores.*

In portions of this last work (scored for prepared piano and percussion trio), Cage experimented with a new concept of rhythmic organization—one he had learned from Harrison in San Francisco: predetermining the number of attacks within a given structural division. Harrison would later describe the process as "ictus control." Always a systematizer, Harrison devised a compositional method of controlling the number of "strikes" in a particular time unit irrespective of their metric position, thus permitting manifold realizations within the confines of strict rule. In his 1971 *Music Primer* he presented an example of the process using an ictus pattern of 3, 5, 5, 7, 4, and 3 strokes in successive measures:

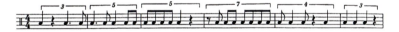

Figure 8.4

Among the performers in Cage's MOMA concert was dancer/choreographer Jean Erdman (wife of writer Joseph Campbell), whom Cage met shortly after arriving in New York. In the early 1930s Campbell had lived in Carmel, where he became close friends with Xenia Cage's sisters. He met Xenia in 1932 when he took a boat trip from Tacoma to Juneau with her brother-in-law Jack Calvin and Ed Ricketts. (Xenia joined them for the final leg from Sitka to Juneau.)[122] When John and Xenia Cage needed a place to stay in New York in the summer of 1942, Xenia called Campbell. Since he and Jean were about to leave for Bennington for Jean's work with the Martha Graham Company, Campbell invited the Cages to stay in their apartment.[123] Grateful for their generosity, Cage soon began to compose for Erdman's dances: he wrote *Forever and Sunsmell,* a solo dance (with music for voice and percussion duo), and *Credo in Us,* a duet for Erdman and Cunningham accompanied by tin cans, gongs, electric buzzer, tom-toms, piano, and phonograph or radio. They presented both works at Bennington College in August 1942 and in New York in October of the same year, and Cage later arranged for a visit to the Arts Club of Chicago the week after the New York MOMA concert.

Meanwhile Erdman devised a new choreography in her studio imitating the bird dances of the Balinese. She asked Cage for music, but busy preparing for the MOMA performance, he had no time to write another piece. Instead he suggested Harrison's *Counterdance,* which Erdman found ideal, both in style and in length. She called the dance "Creature on a Journey," and programmed it repeatedly in future years.[124]

While Cage was busy carrying the percussion credo to the East Coast, Harrison remained in San Francisco for another year, composing percussion music and working with local dancers. The period is marked by an extraordinary increase in the number of his percussion works. In addition to *Simfony #13, Song of Quetzalcoatl,* and *Double Music,* Harrison also wrote *Labyrinth #3* in 1941, which calls for eleven percussionists playing ninety-four instruments. (It would not be performed until January 1961, when Paul Price and the Manhattan Percussion Ensemble presented it at a Town Hall concert in New York.) In 1942 Harrison added to the repertory *Canticle #3, Suite for Percussion, Canticle #5,* and *Fugue,* all before he departed for Los Angeles at the end of the summer.

Although Cage was no longer in San Francisco, Harrison continued their percussion concert series alone with a performance at the Holloway Playhouse in the Fairmont Hotel on 7 May 1942. The *Chronicle* published an advance article in its magazine section the previous Sunday, complete with a cartoon of Harrison playing drums, bells, and bottles (see Figure 8.5). According to the *San Francisco News* review, the hall was packed.

Frankenstein, as usual, reviewed the concert for the *Chronicle.* "About once a year," he began, "Lou Harrison gathers together a collection of drums, rattles, gongs, bells, ratchets, Chinese blocks and old tin cans, trains a cohort of performers, and gives us the latest on the art of music for percussion instruments. Last night . . . he presented the report for 1942."[125] Frankenstein assessed the music as "partly fascinating, partly rather monotonous, and sometimes a little bit comic." He was especially taken by Cowell's "highly dramatic" *Return* (the companion piece to *Pulse,* programmed on Cage's third Cornish concert), and with "two neat little studies in rhythm" by Johanna Beyer. Harrison had corre-

Figure 8.5. Cartoon by Antonio Sotomayor depicting Lou Harrison playing his percussion instruments, from the *San Francisco Chronicle,* 3 May 1942. (Reprinted with permission of the *San Francisco Chronicle.*)

sponded with Beyer for some time: in 1939, for instance, she sent him several of Cowell's orchestral pieces, hoping he could convince Pierre Monteux to program them with the San Francisco Symphony (Monteux played Harrison's overture to the *Trojan Women* on a Standard Oil Broadcast on 13 June 1940); and in 1940 she solicited a letter of support for Cowell's parole board.[126] The two pieces by Beyer that Harrison presented in 1942 are designated as premieres, though it is not certain from which work they were taken: perhaps two of the three movements of her *Percussion Suite* from 1933.

Frankenstein was also impressed by Harrison's new *Canticle #3* (particularly by the ocarina), although he found the work far too long. (It "was very effective," he wrote, "but unfortunately . . . [it] sounded like 'Canticles 3 to 150' before it was over.") The problem, though, might well have been one of tempo, necessitated by the technical limitations of the amateur players. Professional percussionists today typically play the piece much faster than the tempo suggested on the published score.[127] Harrison, however, took Frankenstein's comments to heart and for several later performances authorized large cuts. *Canticle #3* illustrates Harrison's lyrical side particularly effectively, contrasting quiet sections foregrounding the winsome ocarina with fortissimo percussion outbursts. (The ensemble also includes a guitar that functions primarily as a rhythm instrument, having only strummed bar chords that can be played by an amateur.)

Less to Frankenstein's taste was a new piece by Cage entitled *Fourth Construction:*

> Some of the most unorthodox of Harrison's instruments are among his best. Brake drums from junked automobiles, for instance, make marvelous tuned gongs. . . . But there is almost a touch of burlesque about a piece like John Cage's "Fourth Construction," which was played last night, and which calls for an orchestra made up very largely of half-gallon cans.
>
> Almost anything goes if it makes an interesting plink, plunk or thud, but sometimes the lack of melodic interest gets on your nerves.[128]

Harrison not only recalls blowing a huge conch shell during Cage's piece, but also remembers assembling for its performance an instument comprised of a large spring attached to a phonograph pick-up, which made "a melodious roar."[129] Cage wrote *Fourth Construction*—later retitled *March (Imaginary Landscape No. 2)*—in Chicago in April 1942 and dedicated it to Harrison.[130] The work is unrelated to his earlier *Imaginary Landscape No. 2,* premiered at Cornish in 1940 and subsequently withdrawn.[131]

The evening ended with a new dance, *In Praise of Johnny Appleseed,* choreographed by Carol Beals and Bodil Genkel and set to music by Harrison for three percussionists (Dennison, Jansen, and himself), which he composed in a style inspired by Cowell's elastic form. Phrases can be played in any order, and repeated or omitted at will. In this work, as in *Canticle #3,* one of the percussionists is called upon to play a simple flute, a solution that though economical, is only effective in a group with someone of Harrison's performance versatility. In 1976 when he recopied the score, Harrison added precise instructions for building the instruments. For the flute, he writes, select "any reasonable . . . length of bamboo or cane" and bore a mouth-hole and six fingerholes "at unpremeditated distances from the blowhole, end of flute, and one another. Use any pleasing sequence of tones out of this beginning." The marimba should be made from "randomly cut lengths . . . of 1" x 4" good redwood or similar wood," strung at their nodal points over a box resonator or tin cans.[132]

Meanwhile Beals continued her crusade for modern dance in San Francisco. A year earlier she and Genkel had joined forces with Letitia Innes to form the Modern Ballet Group, a collaborative effort aimed at presenting programs "free to the public and free from commercialism."[133] (See Figure 8.6.) Innes, a member of a "social-registered family," was able to secure the use of the outdoor stage at Sigmund Stern Grove. "Mrs. Stern, who put up the money for Stern Grove, had no use for modern dance," recalls Beals. "But Letitia said, 'I'll see what strings I can pull.' She proceeded to string-pull and we got our permission. It was the first time a dance program had been given there and they had the largest turn-out they ever had for any affair."[134] On 24 August 1941 the Modern Ballet Group presented three works, among them the premiere of Harrison's *Green Mansions* for piano, recorder, and percussion, with choreography by Innes. The ever-present Frankenstein was there and commented that the score was in Harrison's "best dynamic vein."[135] As usual, Harrison filled multiple roles: He not only performed the music, but also danced the role of Abel, who represented "man's quest for perfect beauty and love."[136]

The following summer Beals and Genkel, now heading what they called the "Modern Ballet Theatre," presented *Johnny Appleseed* at the Grove, together with two works from their 1941 appearance. This time Harrison remained with the musicians, performing as a member of the San Francisco Percussion Orchestra.

Although his reputation was now well established, Harrison was nevertheless growing restless in San Francisco. Cage had already headed East and Cowell was living in New York. Harrison, too, felt the need to move beyond the opportunities offered in the Bay Area. Immediately following the 9 August Stern Grove performance, he and his partner William Brown (a dancer who played the leading role in *Johnny Appleseed*) drove to Los Angeles where Brown danced with the Lester Horton company (and

Figure 8.6. Carol Beals. Photo from the *San Francisco News,* 21 August 1941 (photographer unknown).

changed his name to Weaver). Harrison provided musical accompaniment for the troupe on piano and percussion. He also taught dance history and Labanotation at UCLA, studied composition with Schoenberg, and struck up a close association with Peter Yates and his wife Frances Mullen, founders of the Evenings on a Roof concert series.[137]

The following year Horton moved his company to New York and Harrison followed soon after. There he reestablished his association with Cage, who introduced him to his New York circle of friends—including Erdman, with whom Harrison collaborated on four more dance works in the coming years. For the next ten years (i.e., until Harrison returned to the West Coast), Cage and Harrison continued their close association, sharing both musical and philosophical ideas, although they staged no more of their West Coast-type percussion concerts. Instead Cage turned more avidly to writing for the prepared piano, and Harrison devoted his compositional efforts to works in dissonant counterpoint.

CONCLUSION

"Percussion music is revolution," wrote John Cage in 1939. In hindsight we might amend the proclamation to read: "Percussion music *began* the revolution." It was merely the first in a series of increasingly radical steps Cage took "to liberate all audible sound from the limitations of musical prejudice." While his interest in percussion ensemble music per se waned after the early 1940s, Cage never waivered in his defense of the "healthy lawlessness" it represented for him in 1939. There is a direct path from the Art of Noise to the Art of Silence.

If Cage's path was directional, Harrison's was syncretic. For him, too, percussion music was a beginning, the first of a series of stimuli that would entrance him during a long and productive career. Unlike Cage, however, when Harrison fell in love with the percussion orchestra, he could never let go. His own brand of revolution was to combine it with his other passions: Asian musics, melody, counterpoint, and even Just Intonation. In the gamelan he ultimately discovered a medium through which he could successfully link these diverse interests. From his first exposure to gamelan music in Cowell's course to his own hands-on study in the late 1970s, the sound of the Indonesian percussion orchestra pervaded Harrison's compositions: those for foraged instruments, for western instruments, and later, for Asian instruments. His compositions for standard western ensembles often embrace the heritage of the percussion ensemble as well: he uses found or newly constructed percussion instruments in his symphonies and frequently calls for percussive effects on stringed instruments or piano (e.g., playing rapid cluster passages on the keyboard with an "octave bar" or beating the strings of a double bass below the bridge with drum sticks).

For both Harrison and Cage, the attraction of the percussion ensemble was not only aural, but also social: a group of amateurs taking communal pleasure in creating a work of art. "Do you delight in this?" Cage once asked his Cornish group after an exhausting series of rehearsals.[138] The thread that bound Harrison and Cage through the years, despite their disparate directions after 1950, is this very delight: the excitement of discovery and the exhilaration of new sounds.

For both men as well, the art of composition extended beyond music to embrace poetry, dance, and painting; physics, mathematics, and politics. Their percussion music, born from interdisciplinary collaboration in music and dance, eventually achieved an independent validity drawing from both western and world music traditions. Sixty-five years after Cowell's first essay on the topic, "Towards Neo-Primitivism," the percussion ensemble has become commonplace not only on the concert stage but also in most major American college music departments. The percussionists have even established a national organization, the Percussive Arts Society, with its own journal, workshops, and annual meeting.

Cowell's groundbreaking course, "Music of the Peoples of the World," has become widespread as well: variants of it are offered at most American universities today. In one of his last papers, which he read at the East–West Music Encounter in Tokyo in 1961, Cowell offered a passionate defense of cross-cultural hybrids.[139] "The history of western music," he told the delegates, "is the opposite of an East–West Music Encounter: it is the story of an escape." As western music over the centuries developed sophisticated techniques for handling simultaneous interactions of melody, rhythm, and harmony, it necessarily left behind "the melodic and rhythmic subtlety" that were part of its "original inheritance." Cowell's plea to recapture this subtlety, which he voiced both in his music and in his classes, found a receptive audience in many younger composers, including Cage and Harrison. The rhythmic complexity of their percussion music is clearly influenced by nonwestern procedures, yet at the same time is thoroughly grounded in western practice. Cage's micro-macro system grew from his work in twelve-tone serialism. Harrison frequently linked rhythmic experimentation with traditional Western forms: his *Fugue for Percussion* (1942), for example, translates standard harmonic relationships into metric ones.[140]

"When Cage's 'prepared piano' music was broadcast to the Orient,"

Cowell remarked, "people in Indonesia wrote to say they had not known before that their music had influenced a Western composer. Actually there was no direct influence at all. . . . But the pieces do sound amazingly like a delicate gamelan." As for Harrison, "his music is permeated with . . . modes, rhythms, tone qualities and instrumental treatment (especially of percussion) that show enormous . . . influence from more than one Oriental culture."[141]

Wherever their paths led after the 1950s, both Harrison and Cage continued to be guided by Cowell's early admonitions to look beyond the traditional textures, modes, structures, and instruments of their western musical heritage. In 1940 Cage likened percussion music to "an arrow pointing to the whole unexplored field of sound." In the future, he predicted, "it will be thought of . . . as a transition from the limited music of the Nineteenth [*sic*] century to the unlimited freedom of 'electronic' music." In the former, he explained, "we are temporarily protected or transported from the noises of every-day life. In the case of percussion music, however, we find that we have mastered and subjugated noise. We become triumphant over it and our ears become sensitive to its beauties."[142]

NOTES

[1] I would like to thank Laura Kuhn from the John Cage Trust and Deborah Campana from the library at Northwestern University for graciously making archival material available to me. Thanks also to Robert Hughes, Gordon Mumma, Laura Kuhn, and David Nicholls who read this article and offered invaluable comments.

[2] Henry Cowell, "Towards New-Primitivism," *Modern Music* 10/3 (March–April 1933):153.

[3] The two works were published in Cowell's New Music Orchestra Series, the Russell fugue as No. 6 (1933) and Varèse's *Ionisation* as No. 11 (1934). The 1936 collection (No. 18) contains these works: Johanna Beyer, *IV;* Harold Davidson, *Auto Accident;* Ray Green, *Three Inventories of Casey Jones;* Doris Humphrey, *Dance Rhythms;* William Russell, *Three Dance Movements;* and Gerald Strang, *Percussion Music.*

[4] Quotations in this paragraph and the next from Cowell, "Drums along the Pacific," *Modern Music* 18/1 (November–December 1940): 46–49. Among the objectives of the futurists was the incorporation of noise (including machine sounds) into musical compositions. For a translation of their manifestos from 1910–1913, see Nicolas Slonimsky, *Music Since 1900,* 5th ed. (New York: Schirmer, 1994):1,016–1,022.

[5]For a discussion and analysis of this work, see H. Wiley Hitchcock, "Henry Cowell's *Ostinato Pianissimo," Musical Quarterly* 70/1 (Winter 1984):23–44.

[6]*Dance Observer* 1/5 (June-July 1934):52–53.

[7]Cowell does not give the title of the work, but he may have been referring to *Six Casual Developments* for clarinet and chamber orchestra, which was composed in January 1934 and performed with members of Graham's company in February of that year. See William Lichtenwanger, *The Music of Henry Cowell: A Descriptive Catalog* (New York: Institute for Studies in American Music, 1986):137 (No. 491a).

[8]"Relating Music and Concert Dance," *Dance Observer* 4/1 (January 1937):1, 7–9; "East Indian Tala Music" in the series of articles entitled "Percussion Music and its Relation to the Modern Dance," *Dance Observer* 6/10 (December 1939):296; and "New Sounds in Music for the Dance," *Dance Observer* 8/5 (May 1941):64 and 70.

[9]David Nicholls, "Cage and the Ultra-Modernists," paper presented at the 64th Annual Meeting of the American Musicological Society, Boston, MA, 30 October 1998. On the dates of Cage's studies in New York , see Michael Hicks, "John Cage's Studies with Schoenberg," *American Music* 8/2 (Summer 1990):127.

[10]John Cage, "History of Experimental Music in the United States," in *Silence* (Middletown, CT: Wesleyan University Press, 1961), 71. In addition to the composers already cited, there were other early experiments in percussion music, including George Antheil's *Ballet Mechanique* (1924) and Yuli Sergeyvitch Meitus's *Na Dneprostroye* (1929).

[11]Lou Harrison, "Asian Music and the United States," in *Third Asian Composer's League Conference/Festival Final Report* (Manila: National Music Council of the Philippines, 1976):87.

[12]Harrison, "Learning from Henry," in *The Whole World of Music: A Henry Cowell Symposium,* ed. David Nicolls (Amsterdam: Harwood Academic Publishers, 1997):161.

[13]On Scheyer, see Thomas S. Hines, " 'Then Not Yet "Cage' ": The Los Angeles Years, 1912–1938," in *John Cage: Composed in America,* ed. Marjorie Perloff and Charles Junkerman (Chicago and London: University of Chicago Press, 1994):87–89.

[14]*Conversing with Cage,* ed. Richard Kostelanetz (New York: Limelight Press, 1988):8.

[15]Cage, "A Composer's Confessions" (address at Vassar College, February 28, 1948), *Musicworks* 52 (Spring 1992):9 (reprinted in *John Cage: Writer,* ed. Richard Kostelanetz [New York: Limelight, 1993]:31). The encounter is also described in Calvin Tomkins, *The Bride and the Bachelors* (New York: Penguin Books, 1976; originally published by Viking Press, 1965):86.

[16]Cage, "Composer's Confessions":9.

[17]Ibid.

[18]Ibid.

[19]This information, culled from a variety of sources, was confirmed by Xenia Cage in a personal interview.

[20]Cage, "Composer's Confessions":9.

[21]Cage, "Forerunners of Modern Music," in *Silence* 63 (Note 2).

[22]On the background for Cage's work in percussion, see James Pritchett, *The Music of John Cage* (Cambridge: Cambridge University Press, 1993). For a list of early music for percussion ensemble, see Larry Vanlandingham, "The Percussion Ensemble 1930–1945," *Percussionist* 10/1 (Fall 1972):11–25.

[23]Cage, "Composer's Confessions":9.

[24]Tomkins, *The Bride and the Bachelors:*88.

[25]Cage, *Silence:*86.

[26]Robert Stevenson, "John Cage on his 70th Birthday: West Coast Background," *Inter-American Music Review* 5/1 (Fall 1982):8.

[27]Ibid.:9.

[28]Interview with Lou Harrison.

[29]For information on the strike, see *San Francisco: the Bay and its Cities* [compiled by Workers of the Writers' Program of the Work Projects Administration in Northern California] (New York: Hastings House, 1947); Felix Riesenberg, Jr., *Golden Gate: The Story of San Francisco Harbor* (New York: Alfred A. Knopf, 1940); and especially Mike Quin, *The Big Strike* (Olema, California: Olema Publishing Company, 1949). On Harry Bridges, see Charles P. Larrowe, *Harry Bridges: the Rise and Fall of Radical Labor in the United States* (New York: Lawrence Hill and Co., 1972).

[30]Interview with Carol Beals, 11 June 1996.

[31]A photo of this performance is reproduced in Leta E. Miller and Fredric Lieberman, *Lou Harrison: Composing a World* (New York: Oxford University Press, 1998). I have not been able to pinpoint the date of the premiere. Harrison and Beals continued to present the work on later programs, for example on a recital at the Museum of Modern Art on 15 June 1937.

[32]Interview with Carol Beals.

[33]Information from the 1936 dance festival souvenir program (University of California, Santa Cruz [UCSC], Special Collections).

[34]Ibid.

[35]Advertisement in the program for the Third Annual Dance Festival, 2 May 1937.

[36]Alfred Frankenstein, "Oakland Composer's Opera, 'Ming-Yi,' Presented Here," *San Francisco Chronicle,* 27 April 1938.

[37]Interview with Carol Beals.

[38]For example, a set of compositions listed on the 6 March 1941 program, and an incomplete piece in a notebook from 1937.

[39]The bust of Harrison in the Mills College music building gives his dates of service as 1936–1939, but these dates are apparently erroneous. The Mills College catalog from 1939–1940 lists his employment as beginning in the fall of 1937; Ruth Hunt is listed in the position of dance accompanist in the 1936–1937 catalog. Harrison remained at Mills through 1940 (not 1939 as given on the bust); he is listed on programs, as well as in the catalog from that year. Pay records from this period cannot be located.

[40]Interview with Lou Harrison, 29 December 1993.

[41]Program at the Community Playhouse, 16 November 1937. (The work is listed as "Prelude, 1937").

[42]Brief biographies are given in the Dance Council's souvenir program booklet, 17 May 1936.

[43]Margaret Lloyd, *The Borzoi Book of Modern Dance* (New York: Alfred A. Knopf, 1949), 155. The other three are Martha Graham, Doris Humphrey, and Charles Weidman.

[44]See, for example, the Mills College summer session brochure, 1936, p. 21.

[45]According to Barbara Naomi Cohen-Stratyner, *Biographical Dictionary of Dance* (New York: Schirmer, 1982), Lathrop first taught in the design department at Cornish, but was choreographing for a company there by the early 1930s. He is listed as a member of the dance faculty and a student of Lore Deja in Cornish School brochures from the mid-1930s. Lathrop left for New York in 1938, where he danced with the Graham company until he moved to San Francisco in 1945. He died in 1981.

[46]Thanks to David Bernstein, chair of the Mills College music department, for making the summer session brochures available to me.

[47]The festival, from 11–27 April, also featured a lecture and dance demonstration by Horton, billed as "a preview" of the summer session. Harrison's lecture took place on 13 April, Horton's on 20 April. From "Leaves from the College Calendar," Mills College, 6 April 1938.

[48]Karen Bell-Kanner, *Frontiers: The Life and Times of Bonnie Bird, American Modern Dancer and Dance Educator* (Amsterdam: Harwood Academic Books, 1998):102.

[49]Lloyd, *The Borzoi Book of Modern Dance:* 245; Cohen-Stratyner, *Biographical Dictionary:*336.

[50]Ibid. Articles in the *Seattle Times* and the *Seattle Post-Intelligencer* on 17 and 19 March 1940 describe Graham's satisfaction with Gilbert's work.

[51]Bell-Kanner, *Frontiers:*108 (information from Bell-Kanner's interviews with Bird). Harrison does not recall Bird offering him the Seattle position.

[52]Panel discussion at the Cornish School, January 1992. Thanks to Jarrad Powell for helping me obtain a videotape of this panel. Quotations from unpublished John Cage material used with the permission of the John Cage Trust.

[53]Ibid.

[54]Letters from Cage to Mr. and Mrs. John H. Ballinger and a "Mrs. Farwell" on 14–15 September 1939 request funds to replace this group of instruments, which were available during the 1938–1939 academic year but were sent to New York the following year. Deja, who had been an assistant to Mary Wigman in Dresden, began teaching at the Cornish School in October 1930 (information from the Cornish Summer Session brochure, 1931, and an announcement of new faculty for Fall 1930; both documents in the Cornish School scrapbooks, University of Washington archives).

[55]From a 1942 press release (John Cage Archive, Northwestern University Music Library).

[56]Horsley (1919–1981) earned a B.A. from the University of Washington in 1943 and an M.A. from Mills College in 1949. Thanks to Doris Dennison for providing me with copies of the Cornish programs. Dennison, a graduate of the Dalcroze Institute in London, joined the Cornish faculty in Fall 1938.

[57]Green (13 September 1908–16 April 1997) composed *American Document* for Martha Graham's company in 1938. See David Ewen, *American Composers: A Biographical Dictonary* (New York: G.P. Putnam's Sons, 1982):283. Various sources give conflicting information about Green's life and accomplishments (including different years of birth). The information reported herein has been confirmed by a list of "Highlights from the Life of Ray Green," sent to the author by May O'Donnell Green.

[58]Bell-Kanner, *Frontiers:*158. The work was repeated with dance on later programs, including one at the College of Puget Sound in Tacoma in January 1939.

[59]*New Grove Dictionary of Jazz,* s.v. "Russell, Bill" by Mike Hazeldine. The advertisement for the group's appearance at Mills College in 1939 states that the members of the Red Gate Players had been working together since 1932.

[60]In 1990 Russell added a fourth movement to this set, a "Tango." See review by Allan Kozinn, "A Composer Gets a Party for his 85th," *New York Times* (2 March 1990).

[61]On Cowell's arrest and his years in prison, see Michael Hicks, "The Imprisonment of Henry Cowell," *Journal of the American Musicological Society* 44 (1991):92–119.

[62]*Percussion Pieces,* New Music Orchestra Series 18 (1936).

[63]Lou Harrison, personal communication, 8 September 1997. Cowell had to send Harrison the written score by mail because prison officials, fearing the music was a type of code, forbade him from handing it over directly. For infor-

mation on *Ritual of Wonder,* see Lichtenwanger, *The Music of Henry Cowell:*154–155 (No. 539). The date of 1937 is questionable, however, since Van
Tuyl did not come to Mills until Fall 1938. An announcement for her concert of
26 October 1938 states that she "comes to Mills College this year from ten years
of teaching at the University of Chicago" and that "her program . . . will mark her
first appearance on the Pacific Coast" (Mills College, "Leaves from the College
Calendar," 9/4, 12 October 1938).

[64]Henry Cowell, "Relating Music and Concert Dance," *Dance Observer* 4/1
(January 1937):8. Cowell's work for three melody instruments and two percussionists is listed in Lichtenwanger, 148 (no. 521). The trio for oboe, clarinet, and
percussion accompanied a solo dance by Martha Graham that she titled "Immediate Tragedy (A Dance of Dedication)"; the music is called *Sarabande* (see
Lichtenwanger 153, no. 534).

[65]The violin concerto, which survives in manuscript, is not authorized for
performance.

[66]Anthony Tommasini quotes Cage's letter to Thomson in *Virgil Thomson:
Composer on the Aisle* (New York: Norton, 1997):363.

[67]Beyer (1888–1944) came to New York from Germany in 1924. For information on her life and works, see John Kennedy and Larry Polansky, "'Total
Eclipse': The Music of Johanna Magdalena Beyer: An Introduction and Preliminary Annotated Checklist," *Musical Quarterly* 80 (1996):719–779.

[68]The score is published in Leta E. Miller, ed., *Lou Harrison: Selected Keyboard and Chamber Music, 1937–1994* (Madison, WI: A-R Editions, 1998), a
volume in the series *Music in the United States of America,* and is discussed in
detail in the volume's introductory essay. In 1982 the combined movements were
given a new title: *Tributes to Charon.*

[69]Letter at UCSC Special Collections (undated, but the envelope with the
postmark has been preserved.)

[70]Interview with Xenia Cage, 30 June 1995. She was probably recalling a
review in the *Seattle Star* on 11 December 1939, following the group's third concert: "You're Wrong—Not Flat-Wheel Tram but Percussion Music."

[71]Theresa Stevens, "Talent Trails! A Column of Chatty Gossip About Your
Seattle Neighbors Who Write and Paint," *Seattle Star* (14 February 1939):9.

[72]Frankenstein, "A Program of Percussion," *San Francisco Chronicle* (28
July 1939).

[73]*Seattle Times* (1 December 1939).

[74]The title of the work subsequently became "First Construction (in Metal)."

[75]Cowell, "The New Music Society," *The Argonaut* (18 October 1930): 6.
Ritmicas I–IV are scored for wind quintet and piano; *V–VI* are for percussion en-

semble. It is not possible to determine from the review which were performed on this concert (all were composed in 1930).

[76]Cowell, "Roldan and Caturla of Cuba," *Modern Music* 18/2 (January–February 1941):98.

[77]*The Norton/Grove Dictionary of Women Composers,* s.v. "Couper, Mildred," by Catherine Parsons Smith. Thanks to Prof. Smith for supplying additional information about Couper from an interview she conducted with the composer's granddaughter in the early 1990s.

[78]Interview with Harrison's student Robert Hughes, 12 December 1994.

[79]The essay, with the erroneous date, is printed in *Silence,* 3ff. The 1937 date was taken from the program booklet for the twenty-five-year retrospective concert of Cage's music, 15 May 1958, in which the essay was first published. That date, in turn, came from Cage's memory, according to George Avakian, producer of the concert. A manuscript copy of the lecture, dated 1940, is preserved in the Cage collection at Northwestern. I have examined various clippings and programs from the Seattle Artists League which help to pinpoint a more exact date. The dating of Cage's essay is discussed further in my article "Cultural Intersections: John Cage in Seattle (1938–40)," in *John Cage: Music, Philosophy, and Intention, 1933–50,* ed. David Patterson (Garland, forthcoming). A shorter version of this article was delivered as a paper at the 64th Annual Meeting of the American Musicological Society, Boston, MA, 30 October 1998.

[80]Cage, "Goal: New Music, New Dance," *Dance Observer* 6/10 (December 1939):296–297; reprinted in *Silence:*87.

[81]David Revill, *The Roaring Silence. John Cage: A Life* (New York: Arcade, 1992), mentions the Idaho concert, but erroneously gives the year as 1939. The concerts were held on 8 January 1940, University of Idaho (Moscow); 9 January 1940, University of Montana (Missoula); and 11 January 1940, Whitman College.

[82]Quoted in a review of the University of Montana concert (John Cage Archive, Northwestern University Music Library).

[83]Doris Dennison, personal communication, 28 August 1997.

[84]*Rune* is unpublished and unauthorized for performance. For information on the other works, see Miller and Lieberman, *Lou Harrison: Composing a World,* catalog of works.

[85]The *Concerto for Violin and Percussion Orchestra* was begun as "Concerto No. 5" in 1940 or 1941. It was premiered at Carnegie Recital Hall on 19 November 1959 by Anahid Ajemian and is available on compact disk in a performance by Eudice Shapiro and the Los Angeles Percussion Ensemble (William Kraft, conductor), Crystal Records CD 853.

[86]He completed the voice parts of the entire Mass before he left San Francisco in 1942, but only finished the percussion parts for these two movements. In 1952, he revised the scoring to trumpet, harp, and strings, under the impression that the percussion accompaniment would not be permissible in the church.

[87]Quotations in this paragraph from Harrison's article in the *Dance Observer* 7/3 (March 1940):32.

[88]Bird's resignation was prompted by the dearth of talented new students at the school and by the resignation of Nellie Cornish. Bird briefly ran her own dance school in Seattle and then, discouraged by her professional prospects, explored for some years fields other than dance. For further information, see Bell-Kanner, *Frontiers:*121–123.

[89]Two copies of the list are in the John Cage Archive at Northwestern University.

[90]Ads in various Seattle papers appeared in mid-January 1940, inviting interested parties to collaborate in the establishment of the American Dance Theatre. The training program officially began on 12 February. The project is described in some detail in an article in the *Seattle Times* (28 April 1940). For further information on this project and on the rejected *Imaginary Landscape No. 2,* see Miller, "Cultural Intersections."

[91]Mills College summer session brochure. Cage's basic percussion class met M–F 11 A.M.–noon; Harrison's M–F 2:30–3:40 P.M. (Why Harrison's was ten minutes longer than Cage's is unclear.) The advanced class also met every day, from 1:30–2:30 P.M. Harrison's musical composition class met every day from 3:50–5. The summer session ran from 23 June to 3 August.

[92]*San Francisco Chronicle* (8 July 1940). This article does not appear on the standard *Chronicle* microfilm. I am most grateful to Bella Lewtizky and her husband Newell Reynolds for sending me a copy.

[93]Ewen, *American Composers:* 283; "Highlights from the Life of Ray Green" (unpublished document sent to the author by May O'Donnell Green). May O'Donnell's debut recital took place at the Veterans Auditorium, San Francisco, in February 1940; Ray Green's "So Proudly We Hail" was written for the occasion.

[94]*Time* (29 July 1940).

[95]*Report of the Chief Engineer to the Board of Directors of the Golden Gate Bridge and Highway District,* September 1937 (reprint Golden Gate Bridge Highway and Transportation District, 1987):36.

[96]Harrison, "Learning from Henry," in *The Whole World of Music:*164. Morrow was a music lover who maintained a large collection of scores. He introduced Harrison to a number of works, including the late Debussy sonatas and Falla's puppet opera *El retablo de maese Pedro,* inspiration for Harrison's own

puppet opera *Young Caesar.* He also gave Harrison a copy of *Green Mansions,* which stimulated Harrison's dance composition of the same name.

[97]Alfred Frankenstein, "A Splendid Performance Opens Red Cross Series," *San Francisco Chronicle* (19 July 1940):7. The concert referenced in the headline was not the Mills performance. Frankenstein reviewed two concerts in the same article, the "Red Cross series" concert apparently being the reason that he was only able to attend the dress rehearsal of the percussion concert.

[98]For more on Cage's three *Constructions,* see Heather Leslie Sloan, "Percussion Music is Revolution: The Treatment of Structure and Themes in John Cage's Three Constructions" (M.A. thesis, UCSC, 1992) and David Nicholls, *American Experimental Music, 1890–1940* (Cambridge: Cambridge University Press, 1990):206ff.

[99]Cowell, "Drums along the Pacific":47.

[100]Elsa Gidlow, *Elsa, I Come with my Songs* (San Francisco: Booklegger Press, 1986):296.

[101]On the question of the dating of the first prepared piano piece, see James Pritchett, *The Music of John Cage* (Cambridge: Cambridge University Press, 1993):206 (Note 15).

[102]Interview with Xenia Cage, 30 June 1995.

[103]Interview with Lou Harrison, 29 December 1993

[104]Interview with Lou Harrison, 13 January 1994.

[105]Quetzalcoatl is incorrectly spelled "Quezecoatl" on the program. Frankenstein, in his review, states that the composers of the particular works are not identified, but he was apparently confused by the program's unusual design in which a series of intersecting arrows pointed to the composer of each work.

[106]Interview with Lou Harrison, 21 October 1994.

[107]"Concert Given by Percussionists," *San Francisco News* (15 May 1941).

[108]Frankenstein, "A Varied and Rich Concert," *San Francisco Chronicle* (16 May 1941).

[109]Interview with Lou Harrison, 31 March 1994.

[110]Ibid.

[111]Ibid.

[112]*The Commonweal* (13 December 1940):204–205.

[113]Typed copy in the Cage Archive at Northwestern University.

[114]Cage told this story repeatedly. See, for example, Richard Dufallo, *Trackings* (New York: Oxford University Press 1989):225; and David Revill, *Roaring Silence:*74. The language quoted here comes from the panel discussion with Harrison and Cage at the Cornish School in 1992 (videotape by Bob Campbell courtesy of Jarrad Powell.)

[115]"The New Records in Review," *San Francisco Chronicle* (28 September 1941).

[116]Co-authored with Fredric Lieberman, Oxford University Press, 1998. A recording of the work is included on the compact disk accompanying the book. The eightieth birthday concert was held at the University of California, Santa Cruz, on 23 April 1997.

[117]"Leaves from the College Calendar," 23 July 1941.

[118]Ibid.

[119]Marcia Winn, "Front Views and Profiles," *Chicago Daily Tribune* (3 March 1942).

[120]Ibid.; Pence James, "People Call it Noise—But He Calls it Music," *Chicago Daily News* (19 March 1942); "They Break Beer Bottles Now to Make Music in Chicago," AP article (*New York World-Telegram* and *Hollywood Citizen News* [2 March 1942]); and Bob Andrews, "His Beer Bottle Music Becomes a High Art," *Chicago Daily Times* (4 March 1942). A cartoon, "Bach, Beethoven, Brahms, and Beer" also appeared in the *New York World-Telegram* on 6 March. All items are in the John Cage Archive, Northwestern University Music Library.

[121]*Life* (15 March 1943):42 and 44.

[122]For further information, see Stephen and Robin Larsen, *A Fire in the Mind: The Life of Joseph Campbell* (New York: Doubleday, 1991).

[123]The couple first stayed with Max Ernst and Peggy Guggenheim, but soon had a falling out (at which time Xenia called Campbell). See Tomkins, *The Bride and the Bachelors:*94–95. Cage tells the amusing story of contacting Max Ernst in *Silence:*12.

[124]Some documented performances are listed in Miller and Lieberman, *Lou Harrison: Composing a World,* Chapter 4 (Note 56). See also the introductory notes to Miller, *Lou Harrison: Selected Keyboard and Chamber Music, 1937–1994.*

[125]Frankenstein, "Music: A Recital on Percussion Instruments, " *San Francisco Chronicle* (8 May 1942), 13. The location is incorrectly given as the "Hollywood Playhouse."

[126]Beyer mentions Monteux and the possibility of a performance of Cowell's works in letters on 27 August and 5 September 1939 (UCSC Special Collections). On 25 March 1940 she asked Harrison for a letter of support for Cowell's parole hearing; Beyer instructs that it be sent to "Miss J. M. Beyer (agent for Henry Cowell)."

[127]*Canticle #3* is performed often and has been recorded several times at various tempos. Two recent compact disc recordings include MusicMasters 60241X (Dennis Russell Davies, conductor) and Etc KTC1071 (John Bergamo, conductor). Bergamo's tempo is decidedly slower than Davies's. Michael Tilson

Thomas's tempo in a February 1996 performance with the San Francisco Symphony was equal to or even slightly faster than that of Davies.

[128]Frankenstein, "Music: A Recital on Percussion Instruments."

[129]Lou Harrison, personal communication.

[130]The 1962 Henmar Press catalog of Cage's works not only lists the instrumentation—including the "amplified coil of wire"—but also contains the following note: "Concert Performance: Ensemble conducted by Lou Harrison, San Francisco, Calif., 1942."

[131]Thanks to Laura Kuhn for information on the 1940 *Imaginary Landscape No. 2.*

[132]Composer's autograph score (UCSC Special Collections).

[133]Dorothy Walker, "Three Girls Pool Dance Ideas to Prepare Modern Ballet Fete," *San Francisco News* (21 August 1941):10.

[134]Interview with Carol Beals, 11 June 1996.

[135]" 'Park' Ballet: The Emphasis is on the Modern Side," *San Francisco Chronicle* (25 August 1941).

[136]From the synopsis in the printed program. Though James Lyons is listed as Abel, Harrison replaced him at the last minute, according to the following day's review.

[137]For a detailed description of this series, see Dorothy Crawford, *Evenings On and Off the Roof* (Berkeley, Los Angeles, and London: University of California Press, 1995).

[138]Interview with Doris Dennison, 5 December 1995.

[139]Quotations in this paragraph are taken from Cowell, "Oriental Influence on Western Music," in *Music—East and West* (Executive Committee for the 1961 Tokyo East–West Music Encounter):71–76.

[140]The standard fugal answer at the fifth (3:2), for example, is replaced by a metric relationship of 3:2. For a discussion of the piece, see Miller and Lieberman, *Lou Harrison: Composing a World,* Chapter 1.

[141]Cowell, "Oriental Influence on Western Music."

[142]Cage's program notes to the concert at Reed College, 14 February 1940 (program in the Cage Archive at Northwestern University).

CHAPTER 9

Melville Smith
Organist, Educator, Early Music Pioneer, and American Composer

MARK DEVOTO[1]

Before American music became intercontinental, in the modern age of recording, broadcast music, and the jumbo jet, it was national, localized for the most part in major American cities and cultural centers, and for many of its most distinctive personalities this is still true today. The history of American music is marked by many excellent musicians who cultivated their own gardens; they did not rise to international prominence and are not listed in the standard musical reference works, but their activities in their own musical societies can still be reckoned objectively on a par with the best of their time anywhere, and their personal teaching and influence have remained durable for decades. One of these was Melville Smith, an organist, teacher, and all-around musician who, beginning in the 1930s, promoted the rediscovery of forgotten but treasured standards in organ building. Trained first at Harvard along German pedagogical lines like those of half a century before him, and then in France as one of the earliest of a long line of distinguished pupils of Nadia Boulanger, Smith developed as a performer and teacher who summarized the best of both traditions, at a time when the newly independent voice of American music was beginning to be recognized around the world (see Figure 9.1).

LIFE

Melville Machol Smith (he dropped the use of his middle name in his twenties) was born in Springfield, Massachusetts, on 6 July 1898, the fifth child and third son of Henry Joseph Smith and Jeannette ("Nettie") Rose Machol Smith. His paternal grandfather, Wilhelm Schmidt

Figure 9.1. Melville Smith. Used by permission of Nathaniel Smith.

(1826–1882), had changed his name to Smith upon emigrating from Cologne to Rhode Island around 1860; his mother's father, from a Jewish family in Germany, had emigrated earlier, in 1847. Including one who died in infancy, Melville Smith had seven siblings. His oldest brother, Milton Smith, was at first a teacher at the Horace Mann School in New York, and was well known in the 1930s for his work as the Director of the Brander Matthews Theater at Columbia University.[2] Another brother, Everett Smith, two and one-half years older than Melville, taught at the Shady Hill School in Cambridge, Massachusetts.

Melville Smith attended public schools in Springfield and was a choirboy at Christ Church (Episcopal), where he began lessons on the organ with the choirmaster Thomas Moxon.[3] After matriculation at Harvard College, he majored in music and played the piano for the newly-reorganized Harvard Glee Club.[4] He graduated in the Class of 1920, *magna cum laude,* and was elected to Phi Beta Kappa.

Smith's distinguished undergraduate record earned him an Elkan Naumburg Travelling Fellowship from Harvard in 1920–1921, followed by a John Knowles Paine Fellowship for the next two years. The European experience was decisive; from 1920 to 1924 he remained chiefly in Paris at the École Normale de Musique as one of the very first American students of Nadia Boulanger.[5] His studies with her included organ, piano, and composition as well as harmony and *déchiffrage* (sight reading of orchestral scores and keyboard realization of figured bass); it is fair to say that Smith's lifelong interest in the French organ repertory, both early and modern, was solidified by his work with Boulanger.

An excerpt from one of Smith's letters to Bernard DeVoto, dated 3 January 1922, reveals the delightful flavor of his days in France:

One of the young men, Jacques Bonjean, is a poet with a decided French temperament who has so fascinated and intrigued me— wrongly, I know, but *sic* (I am more and more susceptible as time goes on to uncensored impressions—and to tell the truth I invite them)— that I have been able to set some of his poetry with good effect. The enclosed program will show you that I am to make my first appearance on any stage day after tomorrow night with three of these songs. Properly speaking, the third is a product of Harvard days, which I made over this summer and dedicated to Nadia, she liked it so much. Jacques has translated it into French, and all is set for Thursday. Nadia is to play them, and Grislé is a very good contralto. Hosts of my friends are going as claques—I guess it is—so altogether it ought to be amusing. I have written so little recently that I was pleased to find that the songs came easily and not half bad. I am still plodding at counterpoint, which is the basis of the technique of composition as 5–finger exercises are to piano technique—and relearning,—rather learning for the first time— the harmony which they professed to teach me at Harvard—but didn't. Apart from that I write a little every day, as free composition in the form of a piano prelude. So I was glad to come out of my shell and write something, and still gladder to find out if it is performable or not.

Everybody so far is pleased and impressed (including the poet, which is something).

The incomparable Nadia is as incomparable as ever. One day, about a month ago, when my feelings were again at a zenith, I had the courage to profess the extent of my affection for her. Since then my feelings towards her have lost much of their sexual stimulus and retained a deep love which I hope will endure. She understood me completely—she always does—and assured me that she is extremely fond of me, but added—in a sort of maternal way (was she serious?). At any rate, my former torment is gone, and if the sure fact of having stated what I thought was a deep emotion has diminished it, far better to have done so. Between us now exists a deep friendship and comradeship which is incomparable. What a woman! Perhaps when I see her again in Gargenville next summer—where I am to spend it, as last summer— a new stage will arrive in my feelings toward her. But at present, all is calm.—It transpires—or rather I have verified what I had always heard—that the celestial Nadia has had the *grand amour* and with her characteristic decisiveness has banished it from her life for ever — from the point of view from which the word "amour" is regarded in France, *id est,*—He was Raoul Pugno, the great French pianist, who died at the beginning of the war. To say that I admire her even more since knowing this is not necessary, to you! She is dead right—and the less French—for her mode of action. "Faire l'amour" is a common French expression—but unknown, I expect, to great souls.[6]

During that same spring of 1922, Smith traveled to Rome with Aaron Copland, who had joined Boulanger's harmony class at Fontainebleau the previous summer. "Melville Smith went with me," Copland wrote later. "He knew some Italian, and it was more fun than going alone. Melville was an enthusiastic type, even though relentlessly self-effacing."[7]

It was in Rome that Smith met Howard Hanson, Director of the Eastman School of Music, who invited him to join the theory faculty there upon completion of his studies. Before beginning this appointment, Smith spent one year, 1924–1925, teaching at the David Mannes School, taking advantage of his stay in New York City to study organ with Lynwood Farnam. Smith remained at the Eastman School for five years, from 1925 to 1930, and during this time developed a comprehensive course in Fundamentals of Musicianship, "an adaptation of the Solfège system to the needs and attitudes of the American student and, as at present constituted, correlates work in harmony along with Solfège into a thorough elementary course of music."[8] Within a few years, he crystallized the principles of this course in a textbook.

During his years at Eastman, Smith kept up an active schedule of performing. As pianist with the Lobero Trio, which included Olive Woodward, violin and viola, and Wendell Hoss, horn, he performed a substantial repertory of infrequently heard works as well as the beloved Trio by Brahms. The Lobero Trio was active between 1928 and 1932 and sometimes performed with a singer as well.

In 1931, at the behest of his Harvard classmate and fellow organist Arthur Quimby, Smith moved to Cleveland, Ohio, where he was appointed Associate Professor of Music at Western Reserve University. Over the next decade he taught theory from the freshman level all the way into the graduate program, including counterpoint and fugue. During this time he was organist at the First Unitarian Church of Cleveland and, between 1935 and 1939, the organist of the Cleveland Orchestra. He gave frequent recitals in the Cleveland Museum of Art, including one series, shared with Quimby, that covered all of the major organ works of Bach.[9] In September 1936 he went back to Harvard for the Tercentenary celebrations, during which he shared a recital program in Memorial Church.

During summers from 1935 to 1940, Smith was a Lecturer in the Summer School at Northwestern University, teaching his finely honed methods of ear training to several hundred teachers who came to his workshops. In 1934 he published Volume I, and in 1937 Volume II, of his comprehensive textbook, *Fundamentals of Musicianship,* in collaboration with his Western Reserve colleague Max T. Krone. An abridged edition, for high school and junior college use, followed in 1940.

On 20 June 1937 Smith married Martha Belknap, a graduate student in art history at Western Reserve. In 1938–1939 Smith had a sabbatical year, and received a research grant from the Carnegie Foundation, which enabled the Smiths to travel to Europe. They spent a few months in Oxford, where Smith gave a recital at Hertford College, and did research on rhythm, folk song, and Morris dancing; the latter led him to Thaxted near Cambridge University, where he spent several days of Morris dancing with eighty men.[10] For a while, he studied the harpsichord with Rudolph Dolmetsch. Moving on to the continent, the Smiths first visited the Benedictine Abbey at Solesmes, where he did some work with Père Gajard, and then went on to travel in Italy, Belgium, and eastern and northern Germany. Smith was much interested in the methods of organ building as practiced during Bach's time, and many of the old instruments in Saxony had been well preserved over the years or restored without significant alteration. With the approach of war rapidly darkening the scene in Germany, Smith was lucky to examine these fine Baroque organs, including the large organ in the Thomaskirche in Leipzig where Johann Sebastian Bach had played for twenty-seven years. Smith had some lessons with the choirmaster Günther Ramin at the Thomaskirche, but he was not to see any of the great European instruments again until nearly a decade after World War II.

The war in Europe had already been raging for a year when in late 1940 Smith was sought out by the Trustees of the Longy School of Music in Cambridge, Massachusetts, who were looking for a new director. The Longy School, founded in 1915 along French conservatory models, was a small and sparingly endowed but already distinguished school with a significant base in the Cambridge community. The most renowned member of its small faculty was Nadia Boulanger, now a refugee, who had first visited Longy at the behest of her former student, the Harvard composer Walter Piston, himself a member of the Longy Board of Trustees. Melville Smith, as one of Boulanger's own who had already an impressive record of teaching music theory to talented youngsters, college majors, and graduate students, was a natural choice to promote the newest styles of theory teaching at Longy, which was already beginning to look toward setting up a graduate program of its own. But it was also obvious that America would become involved in the European war sooner rather than later, and much uncertainty hung over the immediate future of the Longy School. Smith agreed with the Trustees that the school should stay open and remain as active as possible even if it meant, during the coming war, that there would be fewer faculty and students than usual, and that men would be scarce in either rank. The Trustees offered Smith a three-year contract at an annual salary of $5,000, and he accepted on 5 February 1941.[11]

Despite the complexities of moving from Cleveland and beginning a new position with heavy and unpredictable responsibilities, Smith was happy to move back to the city of his college years where he still had many friends. For a while Smith and his wife lived on Berkeley Place, a short distance around the corner from his college friend Bernard DeVoto. In 1943 the Smiths' only child, their son Nathaniel, was born. In 1947 the family moved into a house at 3 Healey Street, a five-minute walk from the Longy School. During parts of various summers, as time allowed, they spent time at the family farm in Leverett, Massachusetts, which Smith shared with his brothers and sisters.

The proximity of the Longy School to the Music Department at Harvard also meant mutual advantages; the Music Department regularly sent its talented Harvard and Radcliffe students to Longy for practical training as a supplement to their academic coursework.

The exigencies of the war years kept Smith busy hunting for operating funds as well as for students and faculty, but he was equal to the task. He was rewarded with strong support from his active Board of Trustees, especially his Harvard teacher Archibald T. ("Doc") Davison, who was elected President of the Board in 1942. In addition to Boulanger, several other notable European musicians had joined the Longy faculty, including the Russian soprano Olga Averino and the harpsichordist Erwin Bodky; Bodky established an early music program at Longy before he became a professor at Brandeis University. After 1945, enrollments grew steadily despite Boulanger's return to full-time teaching in France.

Smith continued to be active as a performer from the beginning of his return to the Boston area, accompanying singers on the piano at Longy, playing chamber music at college campuses, serving for seven years as organist and choirmaster at the Mount Vernon Congregational Church on Beacon Hill in Boston, and from 1956 until his death at the First Church in Boston (now the First and Second Church in Boston, Unitarian-Universalist, on the corner of Berkeley and Marlborough Streets). He also became increasingly well known as a harpsichordist, often featuring the instruments of distinguished local builders such as Hubbard & Dowd and Eric Herz.

During the 1950s the Longy School continued to expand its activities in every department, and the stately Abbot mansion at 1 Follen Street became increasingly pressed for space. Saturday morning assemblies in the Preparatory Department filled the large parlor; Smith often presided over these himself, coaching children in group singing of folk songs. Because there was no auditorium or recital hall, public recitals took place in the foyer, or, during good summer weather, on the back porch facing a large yard where chairs could be set up. Large events usually were held at Sanders Theatre at Harvard; beginning in 1951 these would include an annual Spring Festival of two or three concerts to raise money for scholarships. Smith often took part in these on the harpsichord, both as concerto soloist and continuo player.

In 1955, in his thirty-fifth Reunion Report to the Class of 1920 at Harvard, Smith mentioned that in addition to his position at Longy he was Instructor in Organ at Wellesley College, a position he continued to hold until his death. With characteristic but wry modesty, he wrote, "No interests, no diversions, no publications, no charitable affiliations, no directorships—all these deficiencies make life quite simple and routine."

In 1954 Smith led the first of what became a series of annual summer visits to Europe with fellow organists, touring various locations in France, Belgium, the Netherlands, and Denmark to play old instruments in local churches and analyze techniques of Baroque organ building and restoration. What he had studied in the prewar years now became a major focus of Smith's performing activity. He took notes and made photographs, and lectured on his findings before professional groups.[12] He shared his ideas with Walter Holtkamp of the Holtkamp Organ Company of Cleveland, with whom he had served as a consultant ever since his Western Reserve years; Holtkamp built or rebuilt several important instruments in Cambridge with Smith's consultation, including the large organ in the new Kresge Auditorium at the Massachusetts Institute of Technology and the small organ in the nearby Chapel, as well as the three-manual organ at St. John's Chapel at the Episcopal Divinity School.

The expanding enrollments and diversified activities of the Longy School in the 1950s led to a renewal of a long-standing hope of the Longy Trustees, that the School should offer a program of studies leading to a degree along American lines, rather than the classical artist's diploma according to European models. When Smith came to Longy in 1941, the plans were for a specialized graduate program, such as for the Master of Music degree; but the shaky financial status of the school during the war had forced an indefinite postponement of any such expansion. When the trustees took the matter up again, a different degree-granting arrangement was considered: Longy might affiliate with a nearby liberal arts college for joint matriculations leading to the Bachelor of Music degree. In 1956, Smith wrote to Tufts College in Medford, two miles away, about the possibility of a joint degree program, but nothing came from this overture.[13]

In 1957–1958, Smith temporarily stepped down as Director of the Longy School in order to work on recording and to accept an appointment as Visiting Lecturer at Harvard, where he taught the advanced harmony class; and the next year, 1959, he took on an additional part-time appointment to teach ear training and solfège at the New England Conservatory of Music in Boston, holding this position for two years. During his absence, the Longy trustees, working with the Acting Director, Kalman Novak, concluded an agreement with Emerson College in Kenmore Square in Boston to offer a joint degree. Seven students were ac-

cepted into the program for graduation in 1960. Presented with this accomplished fact on his return to active duty at Longy, Smith could do little but try to match his vision for the school to a new arrangement that he
found essentially unsatisfactory. Whether or not the officials there knew
of Smith's lack of support for the joint affiliation, in 1958 Emerson College awarded him an honorary Litt.D. degree, of which he was proud.

During the next two years, Smith's relationship with the Longy
Trustees became increasingly strained, but he continued his busy schedule of teaching at three institutions, performing all over the Boston area,
and doing his best to run the Longy School. Yet because of the expanded
activities and mounting expenses, the day-to-day running of Longy had
developed more and more into a full-time task that suffered under
Smith's divided loyalties and outside commitments. Smith acknowledged that he was not good at estimating finances and disliked the necessary details of preparing budgets. Several frictive incidents between
Smith and other officers of the school distressed the trustees. A long internal memorandum from one of the trustees emphasized repeatedly the
enduring achievements of Smith's long service as director, as well as his
outstanding abilities as a musician and teacher, but expressed regret that
longstanding administrative problems had still not been solved, and that
his "completely negative attitude toward the joint venture with Emerson"
was a major obstacle to the further growth and progress of the Longy
School.[14]

Matters came to a head in February 1961, when the trustees voted
not to renew Smith's contract for the coming year but to request him to
accept a new status as Director Emeritus. Kalman Novak was appointed
Acting Director for one year. In June 1961, after further discussions,
Smith signed a new contract, naming him as "Director, on leave of absence 1961–62," at a reduced salary. No public announcement was made
that Smith's leave of absence was actually the termination of his directorship of the Longy School, but the musical grapevine in Cambridge
soon learned that he had been forced out, most likely because of the irreconcilable disagreement over the degree-granting issue. Smith himself
reported, in a letter to Aaron Copland dated 5 November 1961: "I am not
at Longy any more—you know me, I dont [*sic*] suffer fools gladly and
the Board of Trustees is being run by a few 'smart business men' who
want the school to be a factory, like all the others. So I am able to free
lance and am having a fine time."[15]

During this "fine time" of increased schedules of performing and
recording, Smith suddenly achieved international recognition that was

widely reported in the musical press and the Boston newspapers; his recording of the complete *Livre d'orgue* of the French Baroque composer Nicolas de Grigny, issued on three LP discs by Valois Records, was awarded the Grand Prix du Disque—a point of justifiable pride for the Longy School as well as for its director. It was a labor of love, too; he never received royalties for this banner recording, not even an artist's fee.

In June 1962, just before his nominal leave of absence would have ended, the Longy School announced that Smith would retire from the position he had held for more than twenty years. Another letter to Copland is dated 6 July [1962] from Leverett, Massachusetts:

> Dear Aaron
>
> I write you on my 64th birthday. Horrid thought! Thanks for your letter. I am glad Mme. Salabert thinks well of the Passacaglia for organ. The only thing now is that I leave for Europe on an organ tour the 15th, and I cannot see how I can get time to do it before then. I must make a *good* copy (as you have pointed out) and I want to have time to think about it. Would early September be time enough? I should judge so.
>
> Glad to hear about the Symphony. Dont forget that I am on the loose next year and if any opportunities should come up to play I should love to do so. . . .
>
> Just called Tanglewood to learn that you will not be there this summer. Probably in China or some such place! How well you have managed your life!
>
> All the best. I may see Nadia this summer en passant. I have a few days in Paris. I am enclosing a list of addresses in case you want to write me.
>
> yours ever
> Melville[16]

The plans thus outlined were not realized. A day or two before he was to leave for Europe, Melville Smith entered Mount Auburn Hospital in Cambridge with symptoms of high blood pressure. He had smoked cigarettes for most of his adult life but had given them up a few years earlier. A chest X-ray revealed an enlarged heart but a stress electrocardiogram showed no sign of danger, and his physician told him he should join the organ tour a few days late. On the morning of 16 July he was sitting up in bed in his hospital room having breakfast when he suffered a heart attack and died.

A memorial service was held at the Memorial Church in Harvard Yard on 19 July. A number of concerts and recitals later in the year were dedicated to Smith's memory at Columbia University, Wellesley College, King's Chapel in Boston, and at the Longy School, where a Harpsichord Fund was established in his name. One of the nicest tributes came on 11 December 1962 at Phillips Brooks House in Harvard Yard. The two-manual Hook & Hastings tracker organ, newly rebuilt by the Andover Organ Company, was dedicated as the Melville Smith Memorial Organ, in a recital by John Ferris, Lois Pardue, and members of the Harvard Organ Society and the University Choir.

In an editorial in the *Boston Herald,* an unidentified writer (possibly Robert Taylor) wrote: "Round-faced, bespectacled, Dr. Smith was the antithesis of flamboyance. But the clarity of his thought and the flash of his imagination belied his appearance. He was a great teacher, and quite capable of informing his students of a spring morning in his dry, crisp, even voice: 'There will be no class this afternoon in harmony. Enjoy your walk in the sun and attend Symphony. I can think of no better way to get the most out of this day.' That was the kind of man Melville was, whose life and art walked in the sun."

THE KEYBOARD ARTIST

Melville Smith's scrapbooks show that the majority of his performances on the piano occurred in his earlier professional years, especially when he was pianist with the Lobero Trio. In later years he played the piano chiefly as accompanist in vocal recitals and in chamber music. He played the piano in a number of concerts at Longy and elsewhere in Cambridge, including a Stravinsky concert when he was one of the players in the Concerto for Two Pianos Soli and the Sonata for two pianos; the Fauré Festival at Harvard in 1945; and a program of Beethoven sonatas with the Longy violinist Wolfe Wolfinsohn.

As a harpsichordist he accompanied Bach's flute sonatas and much other Baroque chamber music, and frequently appeared as a continuo player, including at Jordan Hall at the New England Conservatory and the Boston Museum of Fine Arts, and in two programs with the American Bach Society in Town Hall in New York. One of the latter, on 27 January 1953, featured François Couperin's *Apothéose de Lully* in what was billed as the "first New York performance of [the] restudied and revised version by Melville Smith." Howard Taubman's review in the *New York Times* the next day mentioned the "revised version made by Melville

Smith, busiest performer in his place at the harpsichord last night." His performing repertory of solo harpsichord pieces does not seem to have been very large (pieces by Louis and François Couperin, Rameau, Bach's Italian Concerto, etc.), but a number of performances are listed in which he was soloist with chamber orchestra: the D minor Concerto, Fifth Brandenburg Concerto, concertos for two harpsichords, and the big Concerto for three harpsichords (with Erwin Bodky and Daniel Pinkham), all by Bach; and the rarely performed Concerto by Manuel de Falla (originally written for Wanda Landowska). Once he appeared as soloist in a Concerto dedicated to him, by Nicholas Van Slyck, who later would serve the Longy School as Director from 1962 through 1976.

The list of Smith's performances on the organ is substantial, with sometimes as many as a dozen significant events yearly in addition to his Sunday preludes and postludes at churches. The repertory is wide but not comprehensive, with particular emphasis on the seventeenth and eighteenth centuries. He also performed select compositions from his own time, particularly by composers who were his personal friends, such as Copland,[17] his Cleveland colleague Arthur Shepherd, Quincy Porter, Bruce Simonds, Robert Russell Bennett, and the Danish composer Finn Viderø. From time to time names from the conservative wing of the modern German school turn up: Reger, Heinrich Kaminski, Willy Burkhard. Smith showed less interest in the Romantic composers; one or two warhorses by Liszt ("Fantasy and Fugue on B-A-C-H") appear among his scrapbooks, a few pieces by Brahms, nothing by Mendelssohn, Rheinberger, or Reubke, and only occasionally works by Widor or Vierne among the French organ symphonists. On the other hand, he showed a definite fondness for César Franck, especially the E Major Chorale and the *Prelude, Fugue, and Variation;*[18] and selections from Tournemire's *l'Orgue mystique* and pieces by the Belgian Paul de Maleingreau turn up regularly. Though not a Bach specialist, Smith certainly had a thorough knowledge of all of Bach's organ works, as we know from his series of recitals in Cleveland with his colleague Arthur Quimby and from many other programs.

Smith's absorption in the early Baroque organ repertory began early. During the Cleveland years, his programs favored the German Baroque composers, along with twentieth-century works. Some of his favorite recital pieces came from Karl Straube's popular anthologies for Peters Edition, *Alte Meister des Orgelspiels:* Sweelinck's Variations on "Mein junges Leben hat ein End'," Arnolt Schlick's chorale prelude on "Maria zart von edler Art," Georg Muffat's *Toccata Sexta,* and pieces by Girolamo Frescobaldi, Domenico Zipoli, Jean Titelouze, Johann Kaspar Kerll, Georg Böhm, and Delphin Strungk.

But the emphasis in Smith's middle career came to be increasingly focused on the French Baroque organ repertory. His ongoing involvement with the music of Nicolas de Grigny (1672–1703) can be traced as far back as a Cleveland recital of 1931, a time when this French master was still hardly known outside of France. Smith's programs included François and Louis Couperin as early as 1939, with a variety of others such as Jean-François Dandrieu, Louis-Nicolas Clérambault, Nicolas-Antoine Lebègue, Pierre du Mage, and Louis Marchand appearing soon after his return to Boston. A recital at the Mount Vernon Congregational Church in November 1941 includes de Grigny's great *Récit de Tierce en taille,* a work of melodic intensity and high drama that was a favorite of Smith's.

His last years coincided with the widespread rediscovery of older methods of organ building, especially in the revival of tracker action, in which the motion of the individual key is directly transmitted via a mechanical linkage to the valve in the windchest, without the intermediation of switches and electromagnets. Long before the development in the late nineteenth century of the modern "symphonic" organ in France and England, tracker action in organ building had been brought to a fine craft, permitting exquisitely sensitive control with the player's touch of the key. Smith was one of those who effectively restored this Baroque ideal; equally important, he argued passionately for the revival of older values in pipe construction and voicing. In a newspaper interview in 1938 or 1939 he said:

[These organs] are better than any that have been made since, and have been perfectly preserved. Germany considers these instruments national monuments and treats them as such, instead of tearing them out and replacing them as we do our old instruments. In Hamburg, North Germany, in the Jacobi Kirche I played on the Schnitger organ on which Bach played. It has been preserved just as in his time and is the finest I have ever heard.[19]

Returning to Europe in the 1950s, he found his ideal instrument for recording at the Abbey of Marmoutier, the oldest church in Alsace. This magnificent organ was built originally by Andreas Silbermann in 1710 in two divisions, including two reeds and three mixtures on the Great; in 1746 Silbermann's son Jean-André added a short *Récit* and a pedal divi-

Figure 9.2. Melville Smith at the console. Used by permission of Nathaniel Smith.

sion. A modern restoration was carried out in 1955 with no alterations, preserving the original mechanical action and voicing. Smith's first recordings on the Marmoutier organ appeared with Cambridge Records, a small company maintaining the highest technical standards of the time; the expert recording engineer was Peter Bartók, son of the composer Béla Bartók. The prize-winning de Grigny records, also made at Marmoutier, were produced in France by Valois (see Figure 9.2).

A recent article by John Fesperman, who studied with Smith during his last years, gives extensive citations from an essay by Smith that apparently was never published. Smith defended the decision of the organist E. Power Biggs to install a new three-manual tracker-action organ by the Dutch builder Flentrop in the Busch-Reisinger Museum at Harvard in 1958, replacing the two-manual, fully electrified instrument by Aeolian-Skinner on which Biggs had played his Sunday broadcast recitals for many years. Smith's essay referred approvingly to the

> foolish young Fulbrighters who, fresh from their studies in Europe, report that they like tracker action organs. . . . They are critical of the unmusicality and aridity of much that they hear [at home]. They see that European organists have been brought up in another world. . . . When they reflect further, they may decide that one of the contributory factors in their playing is the wonderful old organs upon which many students are privileged to study. . . . The Silbermanns, Schnitgers, Clic-quots, to name but a few builders of an earlier epoch, were not such blundering incompetents, after all. Their work still stands today. . . . Find me an organ with electric action which, after forty years, approximately speaking, is still fit to play. If mechanically it still holds up, tonally it is probably a total loss, unless extensively altered since its construction.[20]

For a recording of French Baroque music by Smith's disciple Frank Taylor, the organ historian Barbara Owen wrote:

> The late Melville Smith was an educator, musician, and musicologist. His name is well-remembered in some small circles, and virtually unknown in the larger ones. It's their loss. He could give an imitation of a stuffy professor that fooled a lot of people and still has some of them fooled. But he cracked the mysteries of true and inner rhythm at a time when most musicians still believed that their only salvation lay in fawning slavery to the soul-destroying metronome.
>
> And he went to France, and he had a love affair, and he won the *Grand Prix du Disque*. Now this love affair was a very personal thing between himself, the long-dead composer Nicolas de Grigny, and a very much alive classical organ in Marmoutier Abbey. These two taught him things which he brought back to America with him and taught in turn to his students.[21]

To which the organ builder Charles Fisk added:

> When Melville Smith was alive, one's chief joy in building an organ lay in the knowledge that someday one might hear him play upon it.

Whenever I personally was in process of designing or voicing, the sound of his playing—his inimitable touching of the keys—was constantly in my head. . . . And how appropriate that the music [of this record] too should be Smith's favorite, the stuff that he first brought to us for us to learn, and eventually to know, and finally to love as though it were our own.[22]

THE COMPOSER

Though it was not the primary focus of his profession, at various times in his life Melville Smith worked seriously at composition, chiefly during his college years and during his studies with Boulanger. His manuscript legacy, now at Harvard University, reveals the scope of his achievement as a composer; details will be found in Appendix I.

Smith's earliest works, on the evidence of the graphic style of manuscripts in his legacy, were songs. These include *Four Lyrics By Three Brothers,* Melville Smith's settings of three poems by Milton Smith and one by Everett. In 1979, seventeen years after Melville Smith's death, Martha Smith made a private printing of these songs from the manuscript; her conjectural date of these songs was "probably 1916," corresponding to the year that Melville entered Harvard. Very similar in graphic style, suggesting that it was composed about the same time, is another song, "In the garden of my heart," with unidentified text.

A letter (written 1935) from Bernard DeVoto to his friend Katharine Sterne mentions "the annual tone-feast of Harvard composers" at Paine Hall in the spring of 1920:

This one began with a couple of Melville Smith's songs, damned good as a matter of fact—it was before Melville's Nadia Boulanger period. . . . One, I remember, was Edward O'Brien's "Float out with me beyond yon sunset tide"—what a world it was in 1920—and the other was a lovely thing by BDeV, for, yes, dear, I wrote verse in those days.[23]

Manuscripts of both of these songs were found in the legacy.

Four songs from Smith's Paris years were called *Dits,* three with French text by Jacques Bonjean and a fourth with text by Sara Teasdale, translated into French by Bonjean. Three of these were published in 1922 by Éditions Maurice Senart.[24]

Melville Smith's largest work came from the Boulanger years: *The*

Weeping Earth for tenor solo, organ solo, chorus, and orchestra, composed in 1922 (see Figure 9.3). Of considerable power, this is a cantata in one movement, with a wide-ranging chromatic harmony seemingly influenced by such diverse sources as Debussy's *Le Martyre de Saint-Sébastien* and the later Scriabin. At the same time, *The Weeping Earth* reflects the explorations of its American contemporaries, with a feeling rather close to Charles Griffes's late works and to the youthful expressionism of Copland's *Grohg,* which was begun in the same year. The text of this cantata, by Patience Worth, is a cry of outrage in the aftermath of the Great War. It begins:

Chorus:
>What! Is the Earth sodden of anguish,
>Is she lain weeping, sobbing the fields,
>and the tears scarlet!

Tenor solo:
>White morning as thou comest,
>Art thou not afear'd,
>That thy mantle shall be stainèd,
>Oh silver-footed Eve,
>Art thou not fearful
>That thou shalt bruise the torn breast of Earth
>with thy step
>Causing her to weep anew her scarlet tears.

One of the manuscripts carries a crossed-out indication that *The Weeping Earth* was written for the Harvard Glee Club; no performance by that group has been traced. What was probably the only performance took place in Severance Hall in Cleveland in 1932; a review dated 21 July of a concert by the chorus and orchestra of the Western Reserve University Summer Session stated:

>But perhaps the biggest as well as the most exciting performance of the evening was Melville Smith's *The Weeping Earth,* for chorus, orchestra, and the fine tenor of Emanuel Rosenberg. Here is modern music, wonderfully orchestrated, contained, powerful and moving. The bitter sadness of many of its measures was perhaps the more effective in that from time to time the choral line became diffused and lost in the swelling orchestral themes.

Figure 9.3. A page from the autograph score of *The Weeping Earth*. Used by permission of Nathaniel Smith.

The Weeping Earth is also the only known work by Smith that includes the organ, his chosen instrument.

Another orchestral work, the short *Tarheel Fantasy,* dates from Smith's years at Western Reserve. It was first played by the Cleveland

Phiharmonic under the direction of F. Karl Grossman in December 1940; another performance, by the Boston Pops Orchestra at Harvard Night, 10 May 1942, was conducted by Malcolm Holmes '28. The *Tarheel Fantasy,* "based on folk songs of North Carolina," is a medley of six tunes from Cecil Sharp's *English Folk Songs from the Southern Appalachians;* the harmonizations are derived from a notebook containing Smith's piano accompaniments of fifteen of these tunes.

The *Tarheel Fantasy* is but one facet of Smith's lifelong interest in folk song. Several unpublished arrangements of square dance melodies are another, and show his interest in folk dancing as well. While in Cleveland he published a choral arrangement of a folk song from Newfoundland; and through much of his performing career French noëls, many of them traditional folk melodies, formed a regular part of his organ repertory.

Smith's *Three Songs* on texts of Carl Sandburg appear to be his last composition. With the *Dits* and the three short choral pieces of 1933, these songs, published by the Valley Music Press in 1957, are his only published compositions. A program of a performance of the songs in 1955 at Wellesley College indicates that they were composed in 1944, but this date may refer to the copyright of Sandburg's texts. The skillful, contrapuntally expressive settings reveal a complex tonal idiom, sometimes with bitonal harmony, possibly influenced by composers like Milhaud and Roussel, and probably by Copland's Western style as well (see Figure 9.4).

Smith's last letter to Copland, quoted above, mentions "the Symphony." This was Copland's Symphony for Organ and Orchestra, commissioned by Nadia Boulanger in 1924 for her to play on her American tour; the premiere in 1925, with the New York Philharmonic under Walter Damrosch, was controversial at the time, although well received by public and press. Two years later, for practical reasons, Copland reorchestrated the work without the organ, as his Symphony No. 1. The original version remained unpublished for many years, and for a long time Smith, who much preferred it to the reorchestration, was probably the only other organist to perform it; four performances have been traced, the most recent in 1952 with the Boston Philharmonic Orchestra, with the orchestral parts lent for the occasion by the Fleisher Collection of Philadelphia.

At the time of his death in 1962, Smith had completed correcting proofs for his own organ-piano score of the Copland Symphony, which carries the copyright date of 1962 by Boosey & Hawkes (B. &. H.

LOST

Figure 9.4. Melville Smith, "Lost," from *Three Sandburg Songs* (1957). Used by permission of Nathaniel Smith.

18914). Smith's prefatory note reads, in part: "The orchestra score is reduced for piano in such a way that it may be played in general by one pianist. In several places, the top stave must be played by the page turner,
and in the Fugato at [52] in the third movement, the *lowest* stave must be
played by the page turner." The orchestral score, originally copyright

1931 by the Cos Cob Press, was not published until 1980 (B. & H. 19029; Hawkes Pocket Score HPS 745); the first recording was by the New York Philharmonic under Leonard Bernstein, with E. Power Biggs as soloist.

THE TEACHER AND *FUNDAMENTALS OF MUSICIANSHIP*

Fundamentals of Musicianship, in two volumes of nearly two hundred pages each, is Melville Smith's most important publication in music pedagogy. Developed partly in Smith's teaching at Eastman and partly in collaboration with his colleague Max T. Krone, who headed the division of music education at Western Reserve, the book was published by Witmark Educational Publications, but has been out of print for many years. Yet much of the book makes good reading even today for its practical approach and its wide-ranging examples from masterworks of all periods and from many areas of folk song.

"The development of a serviceable feeling for time and rhythm is particularly stressed," the authors write in the Introduction. "While in the presentation of tonal problems the approach is first through the ear, in rhythmic training it is primarily through physical response and not through a mere understanding and writing of rhythmic notation. The system of rhythmic symbols and of rhythmic reading proposed in this work provides an easy transition from the former to the latter." The rhythmic symbols mentioned are in the form of continuous loops in a line, grouped according to beats in a measure and somewhat analogous to beat patterns in conducting; these are correlated to a precise system of counted metric syllables matching the beats.

Of no lesser importance from first to last is the perception of tonal functions:

> The development of sight singing outlined in this work is based upon harmonic feeling rather than upon mere mechanical learning of intervals and scales. Good sight singing is musical interpretation. The reader must grasp at a glance the underlying musical significance of the passage to be performed. The sequence of tonal development here presented is directed towards a vivid appreciation of the harmonic structure underlying a melody as a means to its proper interpretation. . . . The presentation of chords before scales are studied, of intervals as part of chords, of melody tones as part of the harmonic background, and of rhythmic response before the traditional notation of rhythm is learned will all seem strange, to say the least.

Solmization syllables are not used, but the suggestion is made that letter names may be helpful. The authors recognize that the Movable Do system is popular in the public schools because it is easy to learn, but they stress that it is only a beginning, insufficient for advanced musicianship. Sight singing from the book is to be supplemented with the classic solfège series by Lavignac and Gédalge, and, most important, Volume 4 of E. C. Schirmer's Concord Series (the "Green Book"). Later, the sight singing book of choice for elementary use would be *Music-Reading,* compiled by Minna Franziska Holl, Smith's predecessor as Director of the Longy School; Holl's assistance is acknowledged in the Introduction to *Fundamentals of Musicianship.*[25]

An abbreviated Table of Contents of *Fundamentals of Musicianship* is given in Appendix II.

In his curriculum vitae for publicity purposes in 1941, Smith mentioned that he was currently "working on a harmony book, which will incorporate a new idea of teaching this subject." No part of this project seems to have survived. It is possible, though regrettable, that the appearance that same year of the first edition of *Harmony* by his friend Walter Piston may have suggested to Smith that his own book might not be needed yet.[26]

In the end, the remembered vitality of Melville Smith's teaching has outlasted his published influence as a pedagogue. As the composer and harpsichordist Daniel Pinkham wrote later:

> He was a man of great integrity, and so encouraging to me when I was starting out. Melville and Martha Smith took me into their house like a member of their family. There was enough pepper in his disposition that he could not be silent in the face of disagreement. In his own right perhaps he never rose to the level of his potential, but as an influence he was one of the bright lights for an enormous number of people.[27]

NOTES

[1]Author's Note: This essay is written in tribute to the memory of a fine musician and a family friend.

When my father, Bernard DeVoto (1897–1955), returned to Harvard College after a two-year stint in the Army during World War I, he roomed for one year with Melville Smith. DeVoto did not attend his own graduation with the Class of 1920, but went back to his native Utah to get a job; nevertheless (or so the family story goes), Smith nominated him for Phi Beta Kappa and made sure that he was elected. They kept up an occasional but lively correspondence during the subsequent years but did not see much of each other again until 1941, when Smith moved back to Cambridge to take up the directorship of the Longy School of Music. My own acquaintance with Melville Smith essentially began in 1946 with my childhood musical studies at Longy. Beginning in my teen years I had a few organ lessons from him, and I began to recognize him for the superlative musician and teacher that he was. I heard him play in a number of concerts as well as at my father's memorial service, and I remember that he presided over my entrance exam to the freshman harmony class at Harvard in 1957. Shortly after that, he began to make the recordings that consolidated, for a brief period before his early death, his growing international reputation as a Baroque keyboard performer.

I am grateful to John Howard and Virginia Danielson of the Eda Kuhn Loeb Music Library at Harvard University and Michael Rogan of the Bakalar Library at the Longy School of Music for valuable assistance in preparing this essay. I also wish to thank Elizabeth Roberts, David Fuller, and especially Nathaniel Smith and Lynette McGrath for personal recollections and information. I wish also to thank Wayne Shirley of the Music Division of the Library of Congress, and Tom House and Roland Goodbody of the Dimond Library of the University of New Hampshire, for their assistance in locating documents.

[2]See Anthony Tommasini, *Virgil Thomson: Composer on the Aisle* (New York, W. W. Norton & Company):378. Apparently Tommasini did not realize that Melville Smith and Milton Smith were brothers.

[3]The original organ of Christ Church (the church itself was reconsecrated in 1929 as Christ Church Cathedral, the seat of the Western Massachusetts Episcopal Diocese) was built in 1841 by E. and G. G. Hook of Boston. In 1885, a three-manual tracker organ was built by J. W. Steere & Son, a Springfield firm; in 1911, working from Moxon's specifications, Steere enlarged the instrument to four manuals with electropneumatic action and approximately forty-eight ranks, Opus 639. This would have been the organ on which Melville Smith received his first training. The firm of J. W. Steere & Son was later bought out by Aeolian-Skinner of Boston. I am very grateful to Peter Beardsley of Christ Church Cathedral for this detailed information.

[4]See Walter Raymond Spalding, *Music at Harvard: A Historical Review of Men and Events* (New York: Coward-McCann, Inc., 1935); and Elliot Forbes, *A History of Music at Harvard* (Cambridge, MA: Harvard University Press, 1988).

[5]For a thorough chronicle of Nadia Boulanger's circle in the 1920s, see Léonie Rosenstiel, *Nadia Boulanger: A Life in Music* (New York: W. W. Norton, 1982). A photograph taken in 1923 of Nadia Boulanger with her students, including Melville Smith, is printed in Aaron Copland and Vivian Perlis, *Copland:*

1900 through 1942 (New York: St. Martin's/Marek, 1984):66. Another student in this photograph, identified as "Armand Marquint," is probably the composer Armand Marquiset; a volume of songs by Marquiset, inscribed to Smith "pour sa jolie voix," was found in Smith's legacy (see Appendix I). Aaron Copland also describes Boulanger's teaching in a conversation with Edward T. Cone, published in *Perspectives of New Music* 6/2 (Spring–Summer 1968):57–72, in which he mentions that Virgil Thomson came to Boulanger on Smith's recommendation.

⁶Unpublished letter in the Bernard DeVoto Archive, Special Collections, Stanford University. Gargenville, a village north of Paris, was the site of the Boulanger family estate; according to Rosenstiel, only Boulanger's best pupils were invited to study with her there during the summer. The song with English text would seem to be Smith's setting of "The Broken Field," by Sara Teasdale, which was translated by Bonjean as *Le Dit de celui qui connut la douleur*. It was not included in the published *Trois Dits* (see Appendix I).

⁷Copland and Perlis, *Copland: 1900 through 1942*:81.

⁸From Smith's curriculum vitae, prepared for the Longy School for use in news releases.

⁹The McMyler Memorial Organ in the Cleveland Museum of Art was built by Aeolian-Skinner. A much admired Rückpositiv division, playable from the Choir manual, was added later by Votteler-Holtkamp-Sparling Organ Company of Cleveland; Smith and Walter Holtkamp collaborated on the design of the rebuilt instrument. Smith continued as a consultant for the Holtkamp Organ Company until his death.

A report on the Bach programs appears in *The American Organist* 16/11 (November 1933): 555–556. A detailed article about the McMyler Memorial Recitals appeared a few months later [*The American Organist* 17/3 (March 1934):118–120], listing the specifications of the organ, with a photograph of Smith. The organ is further discussed in Smith's own article "Playing the Rückpositiv," and Holtkamp's "Building the Rückpositiv" [*The American Organist* 17/3 (March 1934):121–124]. Lee Garrett, in "American Organ Reform in Retrospect" [*The American Organist* 31/6 (June 1997):58–65], cites Smith's importance as a pioneering leader: "This was a singular event in American organ reform, marking the first direct collaboration between performer and builder in planning an organ for a specific repertoire."

¹⁰Smith's interest in folk dancing was lifelong and intersected frequently with his study of folk music. Some of the materials resulting from his dance studies are part of the Archives of the Country Dance and Song Society of America, now housed in Special Collections at the Dimond Library at the University of New Hampshire. These include a scrapbook with newspaper clippings, programs

(often annotated by Smith), and photographs, mostly from the years 1926–1928. Several folk dance events at the Eastman School of Music and in New York City are reported; there are also flyers and announcements from the English Folk Dance Society of London and affiliated chapters in New York and Rochester, and programs of events in Cleveland and at the Massachusetts Agricultural College in Amherst. Melville Smith's brother Milton is listed as Director of the New York Branch; Melville himself was on the Executive Committee and held various offices in the Rochester chapter. The several dozen carefully made photographs show various kinds of stick dances and sword dances, several with dancers in costume, including Melville Smith. One large clipping from an unidentified British newspaper, dated 4 June 1938, includes eight half-tone illustrations devoted to the "Morris men of Thaxted, Essex."

One musical manuscript was found in the collection, an orchestration (2–2–2–2, 2–2–0–0, timpani, tambourine, strings) of a dance in 6/8 meter, siciliana rhythm, entitled *Lumps of Plum Pudding.* 4 pp. 12–stave paper, medium folio, in pencil.

[11]Some of this information derives directly from the Archives of the Longy School of Music. See also Jean McBee Knox, *Longy School of Music: The First 75 Years* (Watertown, MA: Windflower Press, 1991).

[12]I vividly remember Melville Smith's illustrated lecture, following an overlong business meeting, to the Boston chapter of the American Guild of Organists in the fall of 1958, sprinkled with pungent remarks. "A number of these instruments are very old; but I feel that all of them have aged considerably since the beginning of the meeting."

[13]Copy of letter in the Longy School Archives.

[14]Unsigned and undated document in the Longy Archives.

[15]Unpublished letter, Aaron Copland Collection, The Library of Congress.

[16]Unpublished letter, Aaron Copland Collection, The Library of Congress. Smith was not able, before his death, to make a new fair copy of his arrangement of Copland's *Passacaglia,* but he did leave two working manuscript copies.

[17]Smith arranged Copland's piano *Passacaglia* for organ with the composer's blessing (see the letter to Aaron Copland of 6 July 1962, above) and performed it many times.

[18]I remember my father's fondness for Franck's *Prélude, Choral et Fugue,* which he told me he first knew from Melville Smith's playing.

[19]From an unidentified clipping in Smith's scrapbook.

[20]Quoted from John Fesperman, "A Twentieth-Century Perspective: Melville Smith," *The Diapason* (September 1996):16.

[21]Liner notes for Frank Taylor's recording of works by du Mage and Dandrieu, Elysée Editions (Wellesley College) SD 1001.

[22]Ibid.

[23]Unpublished letter, Bernard DeVoto to Katharine Sterne, 5 March 1935, Bernard DeVoto Archive, Special Collections, Stanford University.

[24]A typewritten contract in French, dated 24 March 1922, for publication of *Trois Dits,* was found in the legacy. At just this same time, Aaron Copland signed a contract with Senart for publication of his *Passacaglia* and a song; see the facsimile of Copland's letter of 21 March 1922 to his parents, in Copland and Perlis, *Copland: 1900 through 1942:*79. This would have been only a few days before Smith and Copland traveled to Italy.

[25]Holl's *Music-Reading,* with 346 examples in all the major and minor keys and church modes, was privately printed in 1942. During Smith's tenure, the Longy School, unlike nearly all others, remained resolutely a Fixed Do institution.

[26]Piston's text is by now a classic exposition of the subject. The first edition of 1941 was followed by a second (1947), third (1962), fourth (1978), and fifth (1987), the last two edited and revised by the present author.

[27]Quoted in Knox, *Longy School of Music:*69.

APPENDIX 1

Catalogue of Manuscript and Printed Works of Melville Smith. From the collection at the Eda Kuhn Loeb Music Library, Harvard University; gift of Nathaniel B. Smith

All manuscripts in ink unless otherwise stated.

Song, *In the Garden of My Heart,* one double sheet, ten–stave large octavo. "It was before I met you that my life was drab and drear, / I know not how I let you make it bright and crystal clear." thirty-two mm., four pp. Text unidentified. An additional double sheet, marked "In the Garden of my heart / 2nd verse." "Your words are gratifying / But they have been used before." Sixteen mm., three pp. Graphic style immature, probably earlier than 1920.

Song, *Whither away,* half of a double sheet, twelve–stave small octavo. "Whither away? Whither away? Love in the heart, shall hate come in?" Twenty-three mm., one p. Unsigned and undated.

Song, *Gregorian Ode,* one double sheet of fourteen–stave paper, small folio. Text by Edward J. O'Brien: "Ebb on with me across the sunset tide / And float beyond the waters of the world." Signed at top; dated "1918" in pencil. Thirty-one mm., three pp. Inside the folded sheet: the same song on three sheets of vellum, fair copy by a copyist. Another copy of this song, title *Ebb on with me—*, thirty-one mm. On pp. 2–3. "To J. F. L."

Song, *The Dead,* three single sheets of twelve–stave paper, folio. Autograph, but probably not in MS's hand. Text by David Morton: "Think you the dead are lonely in that place?" Ninety-six mm., four pp.

Song, untitled: "The wind is hushed / The leaves are still." Text not indicated (by Bernard DeVoto). One double sheet of fourteen–stave paper, small folio, in pencil, signed at the top: "M M Smith." Forty-four mm., four pp. 1920 or earlier.

Song, untitled: "A garden is a lovely thing, / Where spring sweet grasses cool and green." One double sheet of twelve–stave paper, folio. Thirty-five mm., three pp. Text unidentified. The refrain of this setting is pretty much identical, with some rearrangement of text, with that of "In the garden of my heart," above.

Song, untitled: "I sometimes wonder why dark clouds are in the sky, / I sometimes wonder when bright days will come again;" One and one-half double sheets of ten–stave paper, folio, in red ink. Sixty-six mm., six pp. Text unidentified.

Song, *Le dit de celui qui se résigne,* forty-two measures on pp. 1–3 of a double sheet of fifteen–stave paper (five systems per page). Signed at end, similarly to above, "le 12 Dec. [*sic*] 1921."

Song, *Le dit de celui qu'on attend,* sixty-eight mm. on pp. 1–3. "le 13 Dec, 1921." p. 1: "à mon ami Maurice Gievre."

Song, *Le dit de celui qui doit partir,* twenty-five mm. on pp. 2–3. Signed at the end: "Poésie de Jacques Bonjean. Melville M. Smith 1922." The last digit of the year, 1, is overwritten 2.

Song, *Le dit de celui qui connut la douleur / The Broken Field.* Twenty-one mm. On pp. 1–3. at end: "Words by Sara Teasdale. / Paroles traduites de l'anglais par Jacques Bonjean." Signed but not dated; probably composed at Harvard but revised December 1921 (see MS's letter to DeVoto, 3 January 1922). This song was not included in the published *Trois Dits,* below.

A copy of the published score of *Trois Dits,* copyright 1922 by Éditions Maurice Senart, E. M. S. 4832, was acquired in 1963 by the Eda Kuhn Loeb Library at Harvard. This score shows many small differences from the foregoing autographs, mostly in terms of added expression marks and articulations. The first song, *Le dit de celui qui se résigne,* is dedicated "à Mademoiselle Nadia Boulanger." The second song, which in the autograph carries the title *Le dit de celui qu'on attend,* here has the title *Le dit de l'indifférent.* (A program in the legacy shows a performance of the *Trois Dits* at the Brookline Public Library, Massachusetts, 7 March 1961.)

Songs, *Four Lyrics / by / Three Brothers /* Milton, Everett, and Melville Smith [pencilled title on paper cover]. Blackline copies; twelve–stave folio paper. Incomplete copy (pp. 7–14 missing). These four blackline prints with individual paper covers; in envelope marked "Original MS," together with the foregoing incomplete copy. The four songs are:

1. *Rovers* (Milton M. Smith), twenty-four mm. on three pp. "My lover he came like a bee to a clover / In black and yellow, all gallant and gay;"

2. *A New Carol* (Milton M. Smith), fifty-eight mm. on six pp. For voice and organ. Typewritten text, with typewritten organ registrations. "With the return of Christmastide / Men dream of angel choirs above,"

3. *An Olden Love Song* (Milton M. Smith), twenty-eight measures on four pp. "Show me the jeweler who cunningly carveth / A necklace to circle the throat of a queen,"

4. *A Song of Old Japan* (Everett H. Smith), eighty-eight mm. on five pp. "By the stream lay Yoki Kami / 'Neath her willow tree. / Sitting all alone and playing / Tunes of old Japan and saying, / 'Tell me, drooping willow tree, / Is my lover true to me?' ".

Envelope, approximately 11" x 14", marked [ink] "Negatives for Four Lyrics [pencil:] and paste up." Includes eight yellow makeup sheets for negatives (two per sheet), plus another for a negative cover sheet. The cover sheet is typeset: "FOUR LYRICS BY THREE BROTHERS / Milton, Everett, and Melville Smith / Privately printed, 1979 / from Manuscript ca. 1916."

Published score, *Three Songs,* Valley Music Press, signed, with corrections and additions: end of m. 11 (p. 2, third measure) "senza rit" at end; "*mp*" circled but "*mf*" added in voice in next measure, and "*p*" two measures later ("Hunt-") etc. fingerings, conjectural rebarrings of voice part in Song 2. Included: two sheets three–hole 8–1/2" x 11" notebook staff paper with ink ms. of No. 1, *Lost,* few markings included.

Tarheel Fantasy, full score, twenty-six pp. in various inks, marked up in red and blue pencil with conducting indications. 2(+picc.)-2-(+ Eng.hn.)-2-2, 4-2-3-1, timpani, triangle, xylophone, cymbals, bass drum, harp, piano, strings (9–7–6–5–5, pencilled in). Spiral wire bound, twenty-four stave-paper, heavy blue paper covers. With typewritten note on folksong origins, plus a collette of staff paper listing the six folksongs and texts:

1. The Green Bed
2. Rain and Snow
3. Sweet William
4. George Reilly
5. Pretty Nancy of Yarmouth
6. The Warfare is Raging

"The tunes were all collected by Cecil Sharp, and are published in *English Folk Songs from the Southern Appalachians,* Oxford Press." Title page: "To Karl Grossman and the Cleveland Philharmonic Orchestra." Some pages have revised passages, glued or taped in over the original. Last page indicates a durata of six minutes. All the harmonizations in this orchestral piece are based on the folk song arrangements enumerated below. With the full score is an apparently complete set of orchestra parts, handcopied except for strings, which are photocopies or blacklines of manuscript copies.

Folk song arrangements, in a folder in boards with loose double sheets, twelve–stave folio, ms. in ink. Thirteen of these are for piano solo. Pasted to each of these is a small separate sheet containing the original melody and text.

I. *Putnam's Hill.* "Sung by Mrs. Rosie Hughes at Woodbridge, Va." "When I went over Putnam's Hill, / There I sat and cried my fill." Signed in pencil at the top; at the bottom: "Melville Smith / Western Reserve University / Cleveland, Ohio." Marginal marking next to pasted melody: "pentatonic." Sixteen mm.

II. *The Wagoner's Lad.* "Sung by Miss Zilpha Robinson at Clay Co. Ky." "I am a poor girl and my fortune's been bad, / So ofttimes I've been courted by a wagoner's lad." Twenty-six mm.

III. *Rain and Snow.* "Sung by Mrs. Tom Rice at Big Laurel, N.C." "Lord! I married me a wife, / She gave me trouble all my life." Twelve mm.

IV. *The Tree in the Woods.* "Sung by Mrs. Jane Gentry at Hot Springs, N.C." "There was a tree all in the woods, / Very nice and a handsome tree." Nineteen mm.

V. *The Trooper and the Maid.* "Sung by Mrs. Tom Rice at Big Laurel, N.C." "Feed your horse we're able, / Here's oats and corn for you, young man." Nineteen mm.

VI. *The Cruel Ship's Carpenter.* "Sung by Mr. Hilliard Smith at [?]Hardman, Ky." "O where is pretty Polly? / O yonder she stands." Twenty-four mm.

VII. *Sweet William.* "Sung by Mrs. Rosie Hensley at Carmen, N.C." "She run her boat against the main, / She spied three ships a-sailing from Spain." With other penciled notes: "* sometimes sharpened" [referring to one note in the melody]." "M. B. acc. uses B♮, B♯." Seventeen mm.

VIII. *Good Morning, My Pretty Little Miss.* "Sung by Mrs. Hester House at Hot Springs, N.C." "Good morning, good morning, my pretty little Miss, / The beginning of my song." Thirteen mm.

IX. *The Warfare is Raging.* "Sung by Mr. T. Jeff Stockton at Flag Pond, Tenn." "The warfare is raging / And Johnny you must fight." With second verse added in pencil. Eighteen mm.

X. *The Daemon Lover.* "Sung by Mrs. Bishop at Clay Co., Ky." "Well met, well met, / my own true love." Thirty mm.

XI. Unidentified (pasted-in melody missing), except for pencilled note: "Pretty Nancy of Yarmouth 184." Another note: "bridge for No. 3." Fifteen mm.

XII. Unidentified (pasted-in melody missing.) With a collette, two measures added to beginning. Total twenty-six mm. Entire song crossed out (?) with one diagonal line in pencil.

XIII. *Awake! Awake!* "Sung by Mrs. [?]Anelize Chandler, Allegheny, N.C." "Awake! awake! You drowsy sleeper, / Awake! awake! it's almost day." Twenty-nine mm.

XIV. *George Reilly.* "Sung by Mrs. Sarah Buckner, Black Mountain, N.C." "As I walked out one cool summer morning / To take the cool and pleasant air." Arrangement for piano four hands. Thirty-eight mm.

XV. *The Green Bed.* "Sung by Mrs. Jane Gentry at Hot Springs, N.C." "O come you home, dear Johnny, / O come you home from sea? / Last night my daughter Polly was dreaming of thee." For piano four hands, forty-six mm. Part of last sheet cut away, probably for pasting into something else. On back of double sheet: apparently sketches for harmonizations in *Tarheel Fantasy,* in pencil.

In the same folder: three double sheets of eighteen–stave paper with piano arrangements [in ink] of folk songs, simpler than the foregoing and without texts but identified by title:

[?]*Glosses Over*
Hullabaloo [crossed out in pencil]
Goin' to Boston
Duke of York [marked "Repeat until the last couple is coming through the arch." "D.C. as many times as there are couples."]
   Goin' to Boston (revised) [crossed out in pencil]
   O, Belinda (with two measures pencil sketch at bottom, text "Promenade around / O Belinda")
   Weevily Wheat (mostly in eight-measure phrases marked with various segni and repeats, "A1," "A2," etc. through "A6" followed by "B (last time)."
   Hullabaloo (more extensive than the one above)

Chorale and Fugue for mixed voices, two double sheets of twelve–stave paper, folio, with another double sheet as wrapper identifying composer as "James McCall" (pseudonym), and "Francis Boott Prize Competition, April 1920." Text: "Inclina, Deus, aurem tuam." 120 mm., seven pp. Chorale, eighteen mm., followed by *Fuga cromatica:* "Adspice Domine de sede tua."

Published choral score, *Lully, lullay,* Christmas carol, SSAA a cappella, Witmark Choral Library No. 2722, copyright 1933. Forty-three mm., five pp. Signed copy, with rubber-stamped "Longy School of Music." Text: same as the well-known Coventry Carol.

Published choral score, *Shepherds' Song (Terli, Terlow),* SATB a cappella with oboe solo. Witmark Choral Library No. 2711, copyright 1933. Sixty-nine mm., seven pp. with oboe part on separate sheet. Text: "As I rode out this enderes night." Two copies, with Longy School rubber-stamp. Dedication: To the 1933 University Singers of Western Reserve University, Cleveland, Ohio.

Published choral score, *Noël,* SSAATTBB a cappella, Witmark Choral Library No. 2685, copyright 1933. Forty-nine mm., eleven pp. Text: "Noel, Noel, Tidings good I think to tell, / The boar's head that we bring here." Dedication: To Mr. Jacob Evanson and the Western Reserve University Choirs.

Published choral score, *She's Like a Swallow,* Newfoundland folk song, arranged by MS, SATB a cappella with baritone solo. Witmark Choral Library 5–W2937, copyright 1938. Text: "She's like a swallow that flies so high, / She's like the river that never runs dry." Forty-six mm., seven pp. Dedication: for Mack Evans and The Midway Singers.

(No manuscripts of these choral works were found.)

Esquisse for flute, oboe, clarinet, and bassoon. Score, three double sheets of twelve–stave paper, small folio, in pencil. Sixty-seven mm., nine pp. With four instrumental parts, ms. in purple ink on four half-sheets of sixteen–stave paper torn in half. These parts are only for the first twelve measures of this piece; but they also include a "Scherzoso" movement of twenty-three measures that do *not* appear in the score, followed by a thirty-nine–measure third movement mostly identical with the last forty-three measures of the score.

Fugue, subject by Onslow. Two and one-half double sheets of fourteen–stave paper, folio. 144 mm., four pp., with an extra half-sheet showing alternative ending of twenty-eight mm. for the last eighteen mm. (or vice versa!), plus four further alternative bars in pencil; various corrections and erasures. G minor, $\frac{3}{2}$ meter, written in a severe *fugue d'école* style, probably for Boulanger.

The Weeping Earth, for chorus SAATBB, tenor solo, organ and orchestra. Poem by Patience Worth. 2–1–2–1, 3–2–1–0, timpani, cymbals, tamtam. Full score, photopositive, thirty-eight pp., sixteen– and twenty–stave paper, partially marked by a conductor. Another score, seventeen pp. of sixteen–stave paper, piano-organ-vocal reduction, partly in a copyist's hand (purple ink; apparently the same as the *Esquisse* parts, above), signed "Melville M. Smith, Gargenville 1922." This score has many corrections in pencil, black ink, etc., with collettes. With a set of orchestra parts, the strings separately handcopied. Additionally: a single chorus part without accompaniment; a solo organ part; an arrangement "pour choeur mixte et deux pianos," Piano II's copy only; one chorus part, two blackline sheets folded in two, one-sided (four pp. total), ms. by a copyist; a negative photostat of a part for Violin I; and other miscellaneous pages.

APPENDIX II

Writings

A proper bibliography of Melville Smith's published writings is a task for the future. It would include occasional articles in *The American Organist* and a few other periodicals, liner notes and program notes for concerts, and contributions to newsletters. His most important publication is *Fundamentals of Musicianship,* of which an abbreviated Table of Contents is given here:

BOOK I (first published 1934)

Chapter 1: The Tone and Time Elements in Music
Lesson 1   Section A: The Tone Element in Music
            Section B: The Time Element in Music
Lesson 2   Section A: The Organization and Grouping of Tones
            Section B: The Organization and Grouping of Time Units,
            and of Tones Within the Time Unit

Chapter 2: Pitch and Time Notation
Lesson 3   Section A: The Notation of Pitch
            Section B: The Notation of Duration

Chapter 3: Major Chord Function and Spelling
Lesson 4   Section A: The Harmonic Basis of Music. Major Chord
            Feeling
            Section B: Alterations. Major Chord Spelling
Lesson 5   Section A: Third Feeling
            Section B: The Major Triad in All Positions

Chapter 4: Meter
Lesson 6   Section A: The Metrical Grouping of Time Units
            Section B: Irregular Groups Within the Time Unit

Chapter 5: Intervals
Lesson 7   Section A: Intervals Based on Fundamental and Fifth
            Feeling
            Section B: Intervals Based on Third Feeling

Chapter 6: Tonality and Scales
Lesson 8   Section A: The Tonal Grouping of Chords
            Section B: Harmonic Movement and Cadence Feeling
Lesson 9   Section A: Major Scale Feeling
            Section B: Scale Spelling and Key Signatures

Chapter 7: The Inharmonic and Chromatic Elements in Music
Lesson 10   Section A: Inharmonic [*sic*] Tones. The Chromatic Scale
            Section B: Inharmonic Tones in Melody. Dissonant Inter-
            vals

BOOK II (1937)

Chapter 1: Minor Chords and the Minor Mode
Lesson 1   Section A: Minor Chord Feeling and Spelling Minor
            Chord Forms
            Section B: Minor Key Construction. Cadences in the
            Minor Mode
Lesson 2   Section A: Minor Scale Feeling

Section B: Minor Scale Spelling and Key Signatures
Supplementary Lesson: Modal Scales and Melody
Chapter 2: The Rhythmic Organization of Music
Lesson 3   Section A: Extended Groups
Section B: Durational Accent, Ligature, and Syncopation
Chapter 3: Dissonant Triads and the Substitute Function of Secondary
Chords
Lesson 4   Section A: Diminished and Augmented Chord Feeling
and Spelling
Supplementary Lesson: Non-tonal Use of the Augmented
Triad
Section B: Secondary Triads in the Major and Minor
Modes
Chapter 4: Chords of the Dominant Seventh and Ninth
Lesson 5   Section A: The Chord of the Dominant Seventh
Section B: Chords of the Dominant Ninth

APPENDIX III

Discography

Precise dates for Melville Smith's commercial recordings have not been
completely determined, but all of them were presumably made after 1956.

French Noels of the Seventeenth and Eighteenth Centuries. Cambridge Records
CRS 505, monaural only.

A Treasury of Early French Organ Music. Two discs, Cambridge Records, CRS
506 and 507.

Songs by Francis Hopkinson and Poems and Ballads by Robert Burns. Thomas
Hayward, tenor; Melville Smith, harpsichord. Cambridge Records, CRS
711 monaural, CRS 1711 stereo. A note on the jacket mentions that Smith
died just as the record was about to be released.

Heinrich von Biber: Fifteen Biblical Sonatas for violin and continuo. Sonya
Monosoff, violin; Melville Smith, organ and harpsichord; Janos Scholz,
viola da gamba; John Miller, bassoon. Cambridge Records, CRS 811
monaural, CRS 1811 stereo. This recording was issued after Smith's death.

J. S. Bach: Complete Sonatas for flute and harpsichord. Philip Kaplan, flute;
Melville Smith, harpsichord. Two discs, Boston Records, B 408 and 409.

Nicolas de Grigny: *Le Livre d'orgue.* Three discs, Disques Valois (Paris) MB
425, 426, 427 monaural; MB 925, 926, 927 stereo. Recorded 1960; Grand
Prix du Disque, 1961. Smith's personal copy was numbered three hundred
of a priority edition.

CHAPTER 10

Toscanini and the NBC Symphony Orchestra
High, Middle, and Low Culture, 1937–1954

DONALD C. MEYER

The NBC Symphony was unique among great American orchestras for several reasons. Unlike most orchestras of this time, the NBC Symphony only lasted for seventeen years, from 1937 to 1954. In part because of this fact, this orchestra, more than others, also was associated with a single music director, the famous Maestro Arturo Toscanini, who was the main conductor for most of the orchestra's history. But the most unique aspect of this orchestra is embedded in its name: this ensemble was owned and operated by a single corporate entity, the National Broadcasting Company (NBC). Granted, there were precedents for this, most notably the BBC (or British Broadcasting Company) Symphony, founded in 1930. The BBC, however, was and continues to be funded mostly by the British government. In the NBC Symphony we find a uniquely American phenomenon: a commercial network dabbling in fine orchestral music, struggling with its conflicting urges between public service and profit, high culture and entertainment.

The very existence of the orchestra is owed to just such a conflict. Although visionary leaders at the network such as David Sarnoff—the chairman of NBC's parent corporation Radio Corporation of America (RCA)—had a genuine fondness for classical music, there were also practical considerations that compelled the network to assemble these musicians in 1937. First among these were the demands of the powerful musicians' union. In the previous year the union had ordered that the networks increase their quotas of musicians. As Russell and Marcia Davenport wrote in *Fortune* magazine at the time, "in giving Toscanini

301

ninety-two men, NBC was not giving him any more than it was going to have to hire anyway."[1] In a memo to NBC president Lenox Lohr in December 1937, vice president John Royal cited the union demands in his explanation of the increasing costs of the orchestra department. "The orchestra figures have been increased because we have had little control over this. It is largely a Union matter."[2]

By supporting the NBC Symphony, the network also was satisfying important political demands. In the 1930s, there was still some disagreement over how the American system of broadcasting should operate. Some people advocated the British system, where a tax on receiver sets paid for programming. Educators saw radio as a perfect tool for learning, and pleaded with Congress to set aside at least fifteen percent of the frequency band for nonprofit broadcasters.[3] Congress had already stipulated in the Radio Act of 1927 that all broadcasts must in some way serve the "public interest, convenience or necessity," and were looking at ways to control the growing advertising on commercial radio. The major radio networks of the time—Columbia Broadcasting System (CBS) and NBC, joined by the Mutual system in the early 1930s—were beginning to make tremendous profits from advertising, and were steadily decreasing programming in their schedules. Eventually the Federal Communications Commission (FCC) held hearings to determine whether the power of the networks should be curbed for the sake of public service.

The networks then launched a dazzling public-relations campaign to demonstrate that the profits from advertising were used to fund high-quality "sustaining" programs—shows paid for by the network. These shows were designed to be associated with high culture: Shakespeare plays, poetry readings, university lectures and—notably—fine music produced by fine orchestras. It was at this moment that the decision to create this fabulous new orchestra was made. CBS immediately responded to the NBC Symphony announcement by launching a new Shakespeare series, in what today seems a bizarre contest to be the "prestige" network. NBC's John Royal quickly wrote to David Sarnoff, "I don't think it's possible for any Shakespearean program Columbia does to compare in any way with Toscanini."[4] Even as late as 1946, according to music critic B. H. Haggin, network announcers

> kept informing listeners to the NBC Symphony broadcasts that their cost was being borne by the network itself out of revenue from commercially sponsored programs, and that they were thus part of "a balanced service of the world's finest programs" which, "sponsored

directly or not," were "all dependent on the sound American plan of fi-
nancing radio by advertising revenue."[5]

The NBC Symphony was created, in part, to demonstrate the network's
willingness to serve the public.

The close relationship between broadcast networks and recording
companies provided NBC with yet another reason to sponsor the radio
orchestra. Toscanini had been leading concerts with the New York Philharmonic—concerts that were broadcast over CBS, owner of the Columbia record label. If Toscanini signed with NBC, he also signed with RCA
Victor, NBC's sister company in the RCA family. Broadcasts would presumably help sell records, and record sales would increase listenership.

Finally, by sponsoring the NBC Symphony, the network also was
able to develop a core of much-needed musicians. In the 1990s listeners
commonly hear CDs broadcast over the air, but in the 1930s the sound
quality was much better when a station broadcast a live performer rather
than a 78–r.p.m. record. To play a record over the air with its scratchy,
thin sound was only considered an option at small local stations that
could not afford live talent. At this time it also was considered somehow
dishonest to play a recording over the air, a kind of hoax on the listener
who assumed all broadcasts were live.[6] Radio stations also tried to differentiate their broadcasts from recordings because a part of their public
service mandate was to present material not available in any other
medium. The networks' biggest threat came from syndicators, who distributed recorded programs via the mail; so there was yet another reason
why, as historian Michele Hilmes writes, "it behooved the networks to
promote the superior value of live over recorded programming."[7] The
networks therefore tended to avoid broadcasting recordings, and thus relied on live programs. The NBC Symphony helped fill this need.

This meant that the NBC Symphony was simultaneously the great
Toscanini Orchestra and a house band for other programs that the network funded. Musicians would finish a grueling rehearsal with the Maestro, then rush to another studio in Rockefeller Center to play on less
prestigious shows such as the *Variety Musicale* featuring "The Lullaby
Lady." Quartets drawn from the NBC Symphony's ranks presented Sunday morning chamber concerts. On Friday afternoons, most of the players could be found demonstrating their instruments or classical music
forms on the *NBC Music Appreciation Hour,* which was broadcast to
schools and colleges. On any particular day these players would spend a
morning rehearsing great symphonic literature with the world's most

celebrated conductor, then after lunch move to another studio and play "mood music" for some drama with the most celebrated radio stars of the day. And so we find an important aspect of the orchestra's character, embodying in one organization the awkward conglomeration of high and low art that has often characterized American culture. Some of the NBC Symphony players didn't even consider themselves orchestral players in the traditional sense. "I was a staff musician," NBC cellist Alan Shulman told me. "Part of our duties was to play in the symphony programs."[8]

Some programs were very concert-like, featuring a full complement of players. One of these was a progressive series called *Our New American Music,* which aired on Tuesdays from 10:30 to 11:00 P.M. during World War II. Among the unusual works that the program presented were the *Aria and Hymn* by David Diamond, Meredith Willson's Second Symphony ("Missions of California"), as well as pieces by South American composers and even some composed by NBC Symphony players. After the war, on Thursdays from 11:30 P.M. to 12 midnight, there was another program called *Concert of Nations,* intended to "explore the music of the fifty-one countries that constitute the United Nations organization, with special emphasis on the work of living composers."[9] Yet another symphonic show was *The Story of Music,* which began airing in 1942. This was one of four "classes" of *The NBC University of the Air,* the others being *Your United Nations; Our Foreign Policy; The World's Greatest Novels;* and *Home Is What You Make It*—this last a show "to keep the American homemaker in touch with developments in her community, in national and international circles, as well as under her own roof."[10] The programs, narrated by NBC's resident music critic Samuel Chotzinoff with scripts written by staff musicologist Gilbert Chase, were usually oriented around a particular theme, that is, the scherzo, regional dances in orchestral music, anthems in orchestral music, humor in classical music.

For certain programs, such as the NBC String Symphony, the orchestra was divided into smaller units. Milton Katims, who was both a violist and a house conductor at NBC, told me that this

> was what the NBC Symphony was used for. It was broken up into smaller segments. . . . For instance, I did one program that was called *Serenade to America,* which was on every day of the week from 6:15 to 6:40 P.M., a twenty-five minute program. We went from one piece to the next with harp connection—or piano, or xylophone, or some-

thing—to improvise between things. So it was straight music for twenty-five minutes.

Another program that I did, that [NBC producer] Don Gillis and I put together, was called *Vest Pocket Varieties.* It was a fifteen-minute program every morning. We would do whatever insane thing came into our heads. . . .

Then, for ten or more years I conducted a script program every Sunday morning, which was sponsored by the Jewish Theological Seminary and NBC, called *The Eternal Light.* When I would travel with chamber music [groups] that I would be playing with throughout the country, I would be known as the conductor of that rather than the NBC Symphony.[11]

This points to another function of the NBC Symphony: Its players were also useful to the network for commercial programs, those put on by some sponsoring company. These companies usually provided their own musicians, but an NBC player could expect to obtain overtime work as a substitute, especially if he or she were friendly with NBC's union contractor. One of these was the *Bell Telephone Hour,* which used the Donald Voorhees Orchestra. In this case the players were used during their regular NBC hours; Bell Telephone reimbursed NBC for the players who substituted on the program, reducing the salary the network had to pay that week. NBC bass player David Walter explained to me:

Don had almost all his own players, but . . . I did the *Telephone Hour* a few times, if one of the people Don wanted was not available and he had nobody else. Especially in our group, he would say, "It's probably okay if you get somebody from the Symphony." So everybody would benefit: he would get a good bass player, [and] NBC would get paid, so to speak, for this man's salary. Because if you worked, it was on your weekly schedule.[12]

Other commercial orchestral programs heard at NBC included the *Voice of Firestone,* the *Cities Service Variety Hour,* and the *International Harvest of Stars.* NBC's desire to get the most out of its expensive orchestra was restricted by union rules, however. During the first season, Royal lamented to Chotzinoff, "When you realize that we are only entitled to twenty-five hours a week and between fifteen and twenty are taken up by the symphony, it leaves a very small amount of time for other purposes."[13]

There also were ensembles drawn from the ranks of the orchestra that bridged the gap between high and low culture. In 1938 Alan Shulman, along with his brother Sylvan who played violin in the orchestra, started an in-house jazz ensemble they called "New Friends of Rhythm" (this is a play on the name of the New York chamber music society "New Friends of Music"). The core of the ensemble was the brothers' string quartet, and guitar, bass, and harp were added to complete the group. The New Friends of Rhythm reworked famous classical tunes into jazz pieces: the overture to *The Marriage of Figaro* became "The Barber's Hitch"; ballet music from Schubert's *Rosamunde* became "Shoot the Schubert to Me, Hubert"; and so on. In a feature article on the New Friends of Rhythm in *Time* magazine in 1940, the group was nicknamed "Toscanini's Hep Cats."[14] The New Friends of Rhythm recorded on RCA Victor and sold more than twenty thousand records in their first three years.[15]

Shulman also was a composer of orchestral music, and in his works we once again find a blending of high and low culture. His compositions include the beautiful, serious *Variations on an Original Theme for Viola and Orchestra,* which Toscanini himself praised, as well as light occasional pieces such as *Oodles of Noodles*—and both works were featured on NBC programs. When we uncover the true history of this orchestra we find that light classical music was an important ingredient in its musical gumbo. Toscanini himself was fond of programming light works such as Ferde Grofé's *Grand Canyon Suite,* especially in the summer. Alan Shulman was just one of several player-composers in the orchestra—among the others were violist Carleton Cooley and cellist Frank Miller. Producer Don Gillis also composed on the side, and Toscanini himself presented the world premiere of Gillis's silly *Symphony No. 5½* in 1947.

This popular work of the NBC Symphony has now largely been forgotten, in part because virtually the only evidence of the ensemble that is audible today is the recorded legacy conducted by Toscanini, long on such fixtures of high culture as Beethoven and Brahms. Toscanini, in fact, was a major figure in the sacralization of high culture. As music director of La Scala, starting in 1898, he made profound changes to the operatic world that would shape the art form in the next century. He rebuilt the orchestra with better musicians. He insisted that operas be heard in their entirety, removing the standard cuts. He battled with egocentric opera singers to limit their vocal acrobatics for the sake of the music and drama. He demanded that women on the ground floor not wear hats, and that there be darkness in the house. If he felt dissatisfied with the way a production was going, he would cancel the performance, even on the night of the dress rehearsal. Perhaps most scandalous of all, he began to refuse the audience its right to demand an encore in the middle of an opera, more than once electing to stop the performance altogether rather than accede to their demands.

Toscanini, who was severely myopic, memorized every score he conducted and knew it note for note. Even as a student, he was able to memorize a piece of music after playing it only once. Biographer David Ewen tells a story of when one of his teachers tested his memory by presenting him with the full orchestral score of Wagner's *Tannhäuser,* then relatively unknown in Italy. "Toscanini read through the overture, then, pushing the score aside, he sat down to a nearby table and wrote out for Carini all the orchestral parts."[16] Along with his amazing photographic memory came an equally remarkable ear. There are countless stories of Toscanini's uncanny ability to balance a chord by minute adjustments to instrumental dynamics, and of his being able to detect subtle imperfections of one instrument in a complex chord—all without consulting a score. NBC Symphony first cellist Frank Miller recalls:

> Nature gave him weak eyes, but the most accurate and sensitive musical ears we have ever known, which enabled him to hear in a big orchestral tutti the wrong note of the third bassoon or a string-player in the back of a section. With his infallible ear for intonation and balance he would have the winds repeat a chord until he had balanced it perfectly.[17]

When something missed his standard of perfection, Toscanini's rage was legendary. According to Ewen:

> He would kick his music stand in fury, smash his baton, trample his watch, sometimes even take off his alpaca coat and tear it to shreds. . . . His tongue was vitriolic as he subjected the musicians to withering abuse that was often downright insulting. "Pigs," he would shriek at the top of his voice, "you are all pigs!" . . .
>
> It was taxing to work with him, taxing every single moment of the rehearsal. But the musicians knew if he was hard with them, he was even harder with himself; they could therefore accept his abuse tolerantly. Often when a rehearsal failed to achieve the ideal he had in mind, he would blame no one but himself. *"Stupido, stupido,"* he would yell, banging his fists at his temples. "Toscanini—*stupido!"* Or he would

leave the platform and sit in a distant corner of the stage and whine to
himself.[18]

The result of his exacting work was that he brought greater attention
to the music, drawing it away from performers who had dominated the
music scene throughout the nineteenth century. For Toscanini, the intentions of the composer were paramount. William Carboni, violist in the
NBC Symphony, recalled:

> He gave no interviews, accepted no honors: he felt he was merely
> doing his job of serving the composer. . . . He did nothing for show,
> nothing for himself; and that was why we worked. *He* was working
> like crazy for the composer; so *we* worked like crazy with him.
>
> I remember when we did the *Grand Canyon Suite* he kept asking
> [the composer Ferde] Grofé if the tempo was right and so on; after all,
> Grofé was the composer, and the Old Man always felt the composer
> was much more important than the conductor.[19]

It was perhaps inevitable that someone with Toscanini's temperament should end up conducting on radio. John Sullivan Dwight, who
shared Toscanini's dedication to the composer over the performer, wrote
in the 1870s that "it would be better if the performer were invisible."[20]
This dream could only be realized fifty years later with the advent of
"mechanical" music, phonographs and radios, when disembodied musicians could enter every living room.

This sanctification of culture in the late nineteenth and early twentieth centuries was accompanied by a strong democratic vision that it was
within reach of any person. Especially after World War I, there was a
growing movement toward cultural egalitarianism, manifesting itself not
only in a sharp increase in high school and college enrollments, but also
in the Book-of-the-Month Club, founded in 1926, advocating such cul-
ture-disseminating tomes as H. G. Wells's *Outline of History* and Will
Durant's *Story of Philosophy*.[21] This also was the birth of the music appreciation movement, which had a father figure in Walter Damrosch, director of NBC's *Music Appreciation Hour,* mentioned above. It was also
Damrosch who co-edited the Universal School Music Series, which attempted to aid the memorization of famous symphonic tunes by the addition of banal lyrics.[22] When radio exploded on the scene in the early
1920s, there was great hope in its potential to be a missionary for cultural
populism. The aging composer Daniel Gregory Mason expressed this

optimism in his book *Tune In, America,* written in the early 1930s, predicting that the radio audience, accumulating experience with classical music, would naturally turn away from the evils of jazz:

> Now it is interesting to those of us who have high hopes for the future of radio to find that while jazz is still probably the preference of the majority of the vast radio audience, there is already a distinct tendency to that taste to refine itself, automatically, by accumulating experience. A newspaper note that farmers are asking that less jazz be broadcast is highly suggestive. So is the correlative fact that as audiences have progressed in experience more and more good music has been recorded and broadcast.[23]

Hazel Kinscella in 1934 noted the rise in appreciation in opera due to radio's beneficial influence. "Many [Americans] will never see [an opera], but now, thanks to the magic of radio, and to the meticulous care given to operatic broadcasts by the great broadcasting companies, all may now *hear* it frequently, sung by the finest artists in the world."[24] Russell and Marcia Davenport, in their article on the hiring of Toscanini by NBC, outlined the history of arts patronage from the Esterházys to the great American broadcasting companies, which would "complete the democratization of symphonic music."[25] The hiring of Toscanini was seen by many as a milestone in our nation's "musical development."[26]

Toscanini ironically had little interest in proselytizing to the masses. With his singleminded focus on musical perfection, he had trouble understanding why his audience would applaud what he would consider mediocre performances. "Anything you do is good enough for them," he despaired.[27] But others were excited about the potential of this radio orchestra for the spread of "good music." When NBC first hired Toscanini, Orrin Dunlap of the *New York Times* exulted that "Radio, as a winged missionary of a new art, has spread the gospel of good music; it has taught multitudes music appreciation. . . . [And] in the words of a proud broadcaster, 'Toscanini now belongs to the radio'."[28] David Sarnoff declared when he hired Toscanini that his "incomparable genius . . . will further stimulate and enrich musical appreciation in our country."[29] When Sarnoff renewed Toscanini's contract in 1938, a *New York Times* editorial ascribed quasireligious qualities to Sarnoff:

> Mr. David Sarnoff, who began his life in America as a messenger boy, has again glorified his office. Last Saturday night, when the closing

concert of the transcendent Toscanini symphony air series was nearing its end, came Mr. Sarnoff with the news that plans had been perfected for a like series next year, with prospect of still others in years to come. . . .

It was sung of Saul and David to the accompaniment of "timbrals" and "instruments of music," that Saul had slain his thousands and David his ten thousands. But our David, employing a "sounding alchemy," has become a messenger of "the greatest good that mortals know" . . . and that can now be reached and enjoyed by the ten millions. We pick out of the air harmonies that were unheard by the masses of the people a generation ago. Not only is there a mighty musical thoroughfare, leading from coast to coast and traversed with the speed of light, but Wagner, Beethoven, Bach, Sibelius, Brahms are made manifest in many a remote farmhouse and in many a plain home. So, while we hear the grating discords of the world's terror and confusion, we hear also its symphonies—the strings and brasses singing together, the woodwinds bearing them unquarrelsome company, and no dissenting note: man at his best.[30]

Bruno Walter, at the time of his 1939 NBC guest appearances, declared of the NBC Symphony, "This radio machine is building up a new kind of community. The people are being united in the spirit of Beethoven and Brahms by listening in. A new harmony is brought into the world, not so harmonious otherwise."[31] The NBC Symphony was thus an agent of both peace and progress.

In their day, Toscanini and the NBC Symphony were unquestionable representatives of high culture, but this status has been challenged recently. During his NBC Symphony years, the argument goes, Toscanini increasingly programmed nineteenth-century music at the expense of modern music and especially American music. In the subsequent generation of conductors and orchestral programmers, continue Toscanini's critics, this led to an ossification of the repertory that produced to a horrible malaise in the classical scene, all due to Toscanini's willful disdain for modern music and NBC's relentless marketing urge. Although this idea had some currency in Toscanini's time, it was with Joseph Horowitz's seminal revisionist biography *Understanding Toscanini* that it became the accepted version of the history of this conductor and his orchestra. It was Horowitz who most effectively argued that Toscanini's stilted repertory and the "cult of personality" surrounding him have had the effect of "dragging high culture downward."[32]

Since *Understanding Toscanini* appeared in 1987, this attitude has seeped into popular consensus. In an interview with John Adams in 1991 in the *San Francisco Examiner Image Magazine,* for example, the composer points to Toscanini (and indirectly, NBC) as the source of our current problems. "Orchestra programs just aren't very interesting. . . . The orchestra goes on automatic pilot, it gets a standing ovation, and that's culture. As it was in the 1930s, when Toscanini was elevated into a totem, culture still speaks with a foreign accent."[33] William Graebner's history of the 1940s, *The Age of Doubt,* follows the same line:

> Many of the issues surrounding mass culture came together in the 1940s around the figure of Arturo Toscanini, the Italian-born musician who as conductor of the NBC Symphony after 1937 achieved the status of media idol and cultural celebrity. By midcentury, his popularity cresting with television, Toscanini had taken on godlike proportions and was deemed capable, or so it seemed, of bringing the gospel of high culture to the masses of Americans.[34]

Looking first at the repertory issue, there is no doubt that Toscanini's most progressive phase ended long before he came to America. As the music director of La Scala, he presented several important new works, including *La Bohème* and *Turandot,* but by the time he assumed command of the NBC Symphony at the age of seventy, most of his adventurous programming was behind him. Even so, he gave premieres of several new works at NBC, including *Adagio for Strings* by Samuel Barber in 1938. And Toscanini's conservatism is in a way compensated by the more adventurous programming of his guests, since Toscanini only directed, on average, twelve to sixteen concerts of a full fifty-two–week season. Looking at the NBC guest conductors' repertory, sixty percent of their concerts contained music with at least one piece by a living composer on the program; if we include composers who had died within the previous ten years, the number goes up to sixty-five percent. Music by American composers, living and dead, was less frequent, appearing on thirty-eight percent of their programs.[35] These were certainly not uniformly significant works, especially in the summer. On 24 July 1949, for example, the only American work presented by Canadian conductor Wilfred Pelletier was George Kleinsinger's *Tubby the Tuba.* Common on summer programs were medleys of popular hits by musical composers such as Richard Rodgers and Irving Berlin. On the other hand, there were several more serious all-American programs, especially during the war. On 26 May 1946, for example, Leonard Bernstein dedicated the entire program to a performance of Marc Blitzstein's *Airborne Symphony,* complete with soloists and narrator, which had been premiered in March of that year.

Another forgotten point about the NBC Symphony is the fact that Leopold Stokowski took over as general director of the NBC Symphony in 1941, almost immediately after he shook hands with Mickey Mouse in *Fantasia,* and stayed for three seasons. Stokowski certainly programmed more modern works than Toscanini did, confirming his high-culture credentials with such critics as Virgil Thomson of the *Herald-Tribune.* But he also dabbled in mass culture with equal enthusiasm. With Stokowski at the helm, one never knew whether to expect one of his populist Bach transcriptions or the world premiere of Schoenberg's Piano Concerto (which occurred at NBC on 6 February 1944). Under Stokowski NBC ran composition contests, and the conductor was fond of lecturing his audience from the podium. If ever there was a conductor who traversed the realms of high and low culture, Stokowski was he; but when he conducted modern works—which was on almost every concert he presented at NBC—he was a firm advocate of the musical avant-garde.

NBC was at best ambivalent about the programming of modern music. Stokowski claimed that it was his modernist tendencies that prompted NBC to dismiss him in 1944. He wrote in a letter to a friend:

> If I am an acceptable American conductor who enjoys bringing music of American composers to the American public, it would seem fair that I should have the same consideration as a conductor who has not made himself an American citizen and who very seldom plays American music and who ignores the inventions and new methods of broadcasting, which have mainly developed in the United States. In one sentence, it is the *old* trying to stop the *new*—Europe trying to dominate America. There is a great principle involved in all this. The people of the United States have the right to hear the music being composed by young talented Americans as well as the great music of all countries composed by great masters. The radio stations are permitted by the Government to use certain wave lengths. This gives the radio stations *privileges* and also demands of them to fulfill their *responsibilities* to the American people. No one is saying that I do not know how to conduct—they are only saying that I use methods different from the old European tradition formed in pre-radio days.[36]

Although there is no evidence that NBC ever interfered with a conductor's programming—"I wouldn't have taken it if they had!"[37] declared NBC conductor Milton Katims—it also is clear that the network preferred less controversial repertory. In a letter written by Chotzinoff to Bruno Walter's manager in the late 1930s, he urged the conductor to steer clear of contemporary works:

> As to programs, NBC hopes that its conductors will make selections with a view to the needs of a radio audience which numbers many millions. This audience differs somewhat from the audiences at regular symphony concerts. A great many listeners are coming in contact with serious music for the first time in their lives, and it is essential for them to encounter the tried and true classics of the symphonic repertoire. In time this audience will manifest a curiosity about the less popular items of the concert hall. Mr. Toscanini himself appreciates this condition, and willingly cooperates in NBC's desire to interest the greatest number of people in the best music.[38]

Yet there also are signs that NBC welcomed adventurous programming. During World War II the network put on a weekly program of contemporary American music—and like most classical music shows the network paid for the program entirely without sponsorship. Even in the late 1940s when classical music on the air was being programmed less and less frequently on the networks, an NBC executive put forth an adventurous idea for programming contemporary music in the following memo:

> This [show] is a revival, on a broader scale, of an orchestral series called "New American Music," given over NBC some years ago (1941), with Frank Black conducting and Samuel Chotzinoff as commentator. The "gimmick" that made this series click was the device of inviting listeners to write letters expressing their opinions of the music, and having Chotzinoff read excerpts from the letters on the air.
>
> Since most people do not like new music, their comments are usually caustic, or downright abusive. When a new work by a great contemporary composer like Schoenberg is performed, there are always some people who will write to the papers saying that the perpetrator of such atrocious stuff is crazy and should by confined in a straightjacket. This kind of thing would be grist to our mill. People who agree with the writer will be delighted. People who disagree will be angry.

People who don't care one way or the other will probably be amused. The total result is that nobody will be indifferent.

This approach takes the bull by the horns. In other words, it makes the most of a controversial subject. It performs the important public service, of giving new music a hearing, it invites audience participation, it gives a lively and humorous slant to what might otherwise be strictly high-brow, and it is guaranteed to attract attention.

Prominent composers of all countries would be invited to submit new works for this series. The conductor of the series would then select the compositions judged most suitable for performance, on the basis of intrinsic musical value plus controversial possibilities. After all, we have to remember that the music of Mozart, Beethoven and Wagner was considered "controversial" and received plenty of abuse in its day![39]

As usual, the network's motives are somewhat suspect, but there is no denying that an underlying commitment to new music permeates this memo. At another time, a listener named Walter G. Mitchell wrote to NBC to complain about the new music on one guest's concerts: "No doubt, some people like the modern composers, but I doubt if the majority of music lovers do. . . . Your programs would be better if the majority of it is music composed by the old masters."[40] Chotzinoff replied that he happened to share those views, but, interestingly, considered it "the duty of a radio network to broadcast a portion of modern music."[41] The network, like the country at large, seems to have had widely mixed feelings about contemporary music.

If we focus on Toscanini's repertory alone, however, Horowitz is perfectly justified in calling it conservative. It is in the conclusion that Horowitz draws from this observation that his logic falters, that Toscanini's repertory became the model of classical music taste for America. As Horowitz himself notes, America's fondness for Beethoven and Brahms predates Toscanini's arrival at NBC by at least two generations. There is no doubt that Toscanini's programming helped make him popular with the American public, but this is because it happened to coincide with what Americans already liked to listen to—those Americans, that is, who actively listened to classical music, which even in those days was a minority. If Toscanini's influence was so pervasive, where is Martucci, an obscure nineteenth-century Italian composer whose symphonic works Toscanini liked to conduct, on today's programs? Where is Toscanini's old friend Catalani? If Toscanini had presented more

Schoenberg, would *Pierrot Lunaire* be playing on every Walkman? Or even on more of them? I doubt it.

Horowitz's arguments are more plausible when he criticizes the cult of personality surrounding Toscanini. Fame is not particularly healthy for any kind of music, popular or classical, and certainly has nothing to do with quality—just one of a multitude of examples from popular music might be the immensely popular New Kids on the Block, who garnered extraordinary unwarranted fame in the early 1990s, then disappeared from the scene as rapidly as they had appeared. Toscanini's fame was indeed excessive, laughable to read about from a contemporary perspective. Still, Toscanini himself shunned publicity, never granting interviews and avoiding photographers. The cult of personality that surrounded him certainly did not develop by his design—conductors such as Leopold Stokowski and, later, Leonard Bernstein, are more vulnerable to the criticism that they cultivated the limelight. And it seems to me the American publicity machine is much broader than that represented by the Toscanini phenomenon, something embedded into our national means of receiving entertainment (which, again, Horowitz demonstrates through his history of P. T. Barnum, who cashed in on this national predilection as early as the 1840s). We have always blown up our cultural figures into larger-than-life mythic emblems. Serious listeners simply ignore the hyperbole surrounding musicians and concentrate on their music.

The question is inevitable: Why does Horowitz care so much about Toscanini? One possible answer can be found through a close reading of an article Horowitz refers to frequently: postwar social critic Dwight Macdonald's famous "Masscult and Midcult." This term "Midcult," which Macdonald coined in the article, refers to the attempt to popularize high culture, exemplified by music appreciation courses and book clubs that deliver abridged versions of classic literature. Although Macdonald clearly disdained mass culture, like Horowitz he believed "Midcult" is far worse, resulting from high culture's "unnatural intercourse" with mass culture. "In Masscult the trick is plain—to please the crowd by any means," Macdonald wrote. "But Midcult has it both ways: it pretends to respect the standards of High Culture while in fact it waters them down and vulgarizes them."[42] The same image appears in Horowitz's biography when he claims that music appreciation makes for "watered-down" high culture.[43] Theodor Adorno, an early critic of Toscanini's and another hero of Horowitz's, wrote that one of the symptoms of the decline of culture was "the fact that the distinction between autonomous 'high' and commercial 'light' art," is not "even noticed any more."[44]

Toscanini and the NBC Symphony are dangerous to Horowitz because people might think such a popular phenomenon could represent high culture.

The fact that Horowitz seems to be so worried about what people think constitutes high culture is revealing. What does it matter if a group of people enjoy the Public Broadcasting System's *Great Performances* (a program he also criticizes) and then fancy themselves as a part of the cultural elite? If Horowitz believes that people enjoyed Toscanini and the NBC Symphony primarily because it conferred cultural status, the obvious solution is to attempt to remove the status-bearing property from musical life. No serious music listener can claim there is no inherent interest in the standard repertory—so why not encourage people to enjoy what they want to for musical reasons alone? San Francisco Symphony conductor Michael Tilson Thomas, among many others, has suggested this. "There has been altogether too much separation of different types of music," he said in 1976. "There's no reason why a person can't be ardently into rhythm-and-blues and chamber music as well—they're so different, yet beautiful human realities."[45] But Horowitz is not advocating this. Throughout the book he reveals disdain for popular taste, combined with a pervasive desire to "rescue" high culture, a high culture that apparently includes much more American music and contemporary music than appeared on Toscanini's NBC programs. Horowitz likes the heirarchization of culture; he just wants to be the one to establish what constitutes "real" high culture.

Ironically, Horowitz participates in the long tradition of cultural heirarchization he criticizes in his Toscanini biography. Lawrence Levine charts the history of this process in his 1988 book *Highbrow/ Lowbrow: The Emergence of Cultural Hierarchy in America.* This hierarchical view of culture in America seems to have emerged only after the Civil War. Levine points to the advent of chromolithography in the middle nineteenth century as one turning point. Cultural critics worried that lithography—and later photography—with the capability of reproducing paintings, would give people "the false confidence of being 'cultured'." Eventually these were reclassified from fine arts to "industrial" arts.[46] This kind of classification turned to music with the appearance of such late nineteenth-century cultural leaders as Boston music critic John Sullivan Dwight; benefactor John Lee Higgenson, who singlehandedly created the Boston Symphony Orchestra (BSO) and funded it for forty years; and conductor Theodor Thomas, founder of the Chicago Symphony Orchestra. Prior to this time, according to Levine, American musical culture involved a freewheeling exchange between classical and popular idioms; Italian operas would appear in translation, often in truncated or grossly altered form; orchestra and band programs would mingle symphonies with arrangements of minstrel songs.[47] After the Civil War, classical music gradually became a sacred cultural artifact; one critic complained about an 1867 performance of Beethoven's Violin Concerto in which the soloist had the temerity to insert his own cadenza. "Who is worthy to append a bit of his own writing to a composition of Beethoven's?" he asked, apparently forgetting the historical improvisational function of cadenzas.[48]

When Horowitz speaks of the "midcult menace"[49] that Toscanini represents, he follows in this tradition of cultural critics attempting to protect high culture from its biggest threat: popularity. This is the same process that leads some fans to abandon the "cult" filmmaker, author, or artist when he or she receives wider recognition. Sociologist Herbert Gans observed in 1974 that "when a culture of lower status borrows the content of a higher one, the latter usually drops the item from its cultural repertoire."[50] Pierre Bourdieu makes a thorough study of this "cultural disownership" in France in his *Distinctions,* stating categorically that "legitimate culture . . . ceases to be what it is as soon as [the middle-class man] appropriates it."[51] This process helps explain the rise of the musical avant-garde in the first half of the twentieth century, with some composers deliberately emphasizing dissonance in order to carve out a high-culture niche. "I can't get over the idea that if a thing is popular it can't be good," wrote Aaron Copland during his first progressive phase in the 1920s.[52] And this is precisely the process going on in Horowitz's *Understanding Toscanini:* Toscanini is at fault simply because he was popular, and because to many he was a representative of high culture. As anything the common man embraces cannot be a part of the high culture, Toscanini must be expelled from the pantheon.

Thus the history of "Toscanini Reception" takes a number of ironic twists and turns. Toscanini, the son of simple Italian artisans, contributes to the association of operatic and symphonic music with a dying aristocracy. NBC then appropriates Toscanini's cultural clout in part to enable it to sell commercial programs several rungs down on the cultural hierarchy. And then, after his death, Toscanini's popularity is reevaluated and considered a betrayal of high culture, and Toscanini is exiled as a "midcult phenomenon." All this would seem exceedingly pointless if there were not something important at stake: Toscanini's legacy. With this inane juggling of cultural status we can easily forget to recall the music he made. And when we listen to his recordings, reissued over the last decade by BMG on CD, we find music of fire, intensity, passion and, most important, of *unique interpretation* so often missing in today's routine performances of the standard repertory. Each time he conducted a piece, even if he had performed it dozens of times before, he restudied the score and came up with a new interpretive solution. His performances may not always be "right," but they are almost always interesting. Most of his players remarked on his ability, as Milton Katims puts it,

> To make us feel—and this, for me, was the greatest facet of his conducting—that no matter how many times we had performed the music at hand (be it the Schubert *Unfinished,* the Dvořák *New World,* or the Beethoven Fifth) that *this* was really the first performance, *this* was the first time we were really playing it—the first time we were really *hearing* it. There was always the freshness, the spontaneity of a first performance. That's how he approached every score he conducted.[53]

Horowitz tries desperately to find some intrinsic quality of Toscanini's conducting that can illustrate how he never really belonged in the high-culture camp, but ultimately concedes that, "beyond his unquestioned extramusical attributes, Toscanini was an unquestionably great conductor."[54] If what we are concerned with is musical interpretation—and when speaking of a conductor, what else is more important?—then this should be what we remember of the man.

But the greatest significance of the NBC Symphony might lie outside Toscanini. Lawrence Levine implies that by the middle of the twentieth century, the walls between high and popular culture were in place:

> Certainly, what I have called a shared public culture did not disappear with the nineteenth century. Twentieth-century Americans, especially in the palaces they built to the movies and in their sporting arenas, continued to share public space and public culture. But with a difference. Cultural space became more sharply defined, more circumscribed, and less flexible than it had been.[55]

In the work of the NBC Symphony Orchestra during the 1930s, 1940s, and early 1950s, however, we see this mixture of different strata of musical culture in one ensemble on a day-to-day basis. Not only did the orchestra perform music all across the spectrum from high to low, but in all cases its music reached out to the broadest possible audience. The orchestra could be the exception that proves the rule; it could be that there were indeed greater divisions between high and low cultures by this time. But it also could be that this democratic interchange between popular and high cultures is a wonderful, maddening and wholly permanent characteristic of American musical life.[56]

NOTES

[1]Russell and Marcia Davenport, "Toscanini On The Air," *Fortune* (January 1938):116.

[2]John Royal, memo to NBC President Lenox Lohr, 2 December 1937, National Broadcasting Company Corporate Archives, State Historical Society of Wisconsin, Box 108, Folder 17.

[3]Robert McChesney, "The Battle for America's Ears and Minds: The Debate Over the Control and Structure of American Radio Broadcasting, 1930–1935" (Dissertation, University of Washington, 1989):73–75.

[4]John Royal, memo to David Sarnoff, 7 June 1937, National Broadcasting Company Corporate Archives, State Historical Society of Wisconsin, Box 102, Folder 12.

[5]Bernard H. Haggin, *The Toscanini Musicians Knew.* Reprinted in Haggin, *Arturo Toscanini: Contemporary Recollections of the Maestro,* ed. Thomas Hathaway (New York: Da Capo Press, 1989):271.

[6]Laurence Bergreen, *Look Now, Pay Later: The Rise of Network Broadcasting* (Garden City, New York: Doubleday, 1980):78–79.

[7]Michele Hilmes, *Hollywood and Broadcasting: From Radio to Cable* (Urbana: University of Illinois Press, 1990):143.

[8]Alan Shulman, interview with Donald C. Meyer, Mt. Tremper, New York, 22 July 1993.

[9]"Five Broadcast Series Will Be Presented As Part of the NBC United Nations Project," *This Is The National Broadcasting Company,* April 1946, National Broadcasting Company Corporate Archives, State Historical Society of Wisconsin, Box 220, Folder 42.

[10]*The NBC University of the Air,* publicity material, National Broadcasting Company Corporate Archives, State Historical Society of Wisconsin, Box 373, Folder 1, p. 4.

[11]Milton Katims, interview with Donald C. Meyer, Seattle, Washington, 8 March 1997.

[12]David Walter, interview with Donald C. Meyer, Princeton, New Jersey, 28 July 1993.

[13]John Royal, memo to Samuel Chotzinoff, 17 June 1938, National Broadcasting Company Corporate Archives, State Historical Society of Wisconsin, Box 108, Folder 22.

[14]"Rhythm's New Friends," *Time* (10 June 1940):45–46.

[15]Ensembles at CBS were experimenting with similar approaches; the zany compositions of the mercurial pianist Raymond Scott and his Quintette achieved great popularity on radio and, later, in Warner Brothers cartoons.

[16]David Ewen, *The Story of Arturo Toscanini,* rev. ed. (New York: Holt, 1969):12–13

[17] Quoted in Haggin, *Arturo Toscanini:*206.

[18]Ewen, *The Story of Arturo Toscanini:*74–75.

[19]Quoted in Haggin, *Arturo Toscanini:*57–58.

[20]Quoted in Lawrence Levine, *Highbrow, Lowbrow: The Emergence of Cultural Hierarchy in America* (Cambridge: Harvard University Press, 1988):121.

[21]For a history of this movement, see Joan Shelley Rubin, *The Making of Middlebrow Culture* (Chapel Hill: The University of North Carolina Press, 1992):1–33.

[22]Joseph Horowitz, *Understanding Toscanini: How He Became an American Culture-God and Helped Create a New Audience for Old Music* (New York: Knopf, 1987):193–204.

[23]Daniel Gregory Mason, *Tune In America: A Study of Our Coming Musical Independence* (New York: Knopf, 1931):87.

[24]Hazel Gertrude Kinscella, *Music on the Air* (New York: Viking Press, 1934):40.

[25]Russell and Marcia Davenport, "Toscanini On The Air," *Fortune* (January 1938):67.

[26]Olin Downes, "Return of Toscanini," *New York Times* (14 February 1937): sec. 10, p. 7, col. 1.

[27]William Carboni; quoted in Haggin, *Arturo Toscanini,* 56.

[28]Orrin Dunlap, "Radio Invades Strongholds of the Musical World: Broadcasters in Signing Toscanini Stir Discussion of Radio's Effect on Old Art," *New York Times* (7 March 1937): sec. 11, p. 12, col. 1.

[29]Eugene Lyons, *David Sarnoff* (New York: Harper & Rowe, 1966):198.

[30]Unsigned editorial, "The Messenger Boy," *New York Times* (6 March 1938): p. 16, col. 2.

[31]Quoted in Orrin Dunlap, "Bruno Walter Discusses Broadcasting's Effect on Music and the Masses," *New York Times* (26 March 1939): sec. 10, p. 12, col. 1.

[32]Horowitz, *Understanding Toscanini:*7.

[33]Allan Ulrich, "Getting the Most Out of Minimalism: With his Inventive, Unclassifiable Creations, Berkeley Composer John Adams Proves that Art Music

Doesn't Have to Be Painful," *San Francisco Examiner Image* Magazine (1 September 1991):15.

[34]William S. Graebner, *The Age of Doubt: American Thought and Culture in the 1940s* (Boston: Twayne Publishers, 1991):140.

[35]There were 576 concerts given by conductors other than Toscanini for which I have programs; these statistics presume there were no last-minute substitutions not printed in the *New York Times*. For more information on the NBC Symphony's programming, see this author's "The NBC Symphony Orchestra" (Dissertation: University of California, Davis, 1994).

[36]Charles O'Connell, *The Other Side of the Record* (New York: Knopf, 1948):305.

[37]Milton Katims, interview with Donald C. Meyer, Seattle, Washington, 8 March 1997.

[38]Samuel Chotzinoff, memo to Bruno Zirato re Bruno Walter, 7 November 1938. National Broadcasting Company Corporate Archives, State Historical Society of Wisconsin, Box 73, Folder 42.

[39]Author unknown, "Recommendations for Sustaining Musical Programs, NBC Network, 1948," National Broadcasting Company Corporate Archives, State Historical Society of Wisconsin, box 372, folder 6.

[40]Walter G. Mitchell, memo to Samuel Chotzinoff, no date, National Broadcasting Company Corporate Archives, State Historical Society of Wisconsin, Box 371, Folder 14.

[41]Samuel Chotzinoff, memo to Walter G. Mitchell, 13 February 1950, National Broadcasting Company Corporate Archives, State Historical Society of Wisconsin, Box 371, Folder 14.

[42]Dwight Macdonald, "Masscult and Midcult," *Partisan Review* (Spring 1960). Reprinted in *Against the American Grain* (New York: Random House, 1962):37.

[43]Horowitz, *Understanding Toscanini:*431.

[44]Theodor Adorno, "Perennial Fashion–Jazz." Reprinted in *Prisms,* trans. Samuel and Shierry Weber (London: Neville Spearman, 1967):127.

[45]Quoted in Levine, *Highbrow, Lowbrow:*243–244.

[46]Ibid.:160–163.

[47]Ibid.:85–168.

[48]Ibid.:138.

[49]Horowitz, *Understanding Toscanini:*435.

[50]Herbert J. Gans, *Popular Culture and High Culture: An Analysis and Evaluation of Taste* (New York: Basic Books, 1974):115.

[51]Pierre Bourdieu, *Distinction: A Social Critique of the Judgment of Taste,* trans. Richard Nice (Cambridge, Massachusetts: Harvard University Press, 1984):327.

[52]Quoted in Nicholas E. Tawa, *American Composers and Their Public: A Critical Look* (Metuchen, N.J.: Scarecrow Press, 1995):41.

[53]Quoted in Haggin, *Arturo Toscanini:*225.

[54]Horowitz, *Understanding Toscanini:*323.

[55]Levine, *Highbrow, Lowbrow:*233–234.

[56]This article is an expanded version of the paper *The Intersections of High and Low Art in the Work of the NBC Symphony Orchestra,* delivered at the Annual Meeting of the Sonneck Society for American Music, Seattle, Washington, 9 March 1997.

CHAPTER 11

Cinema Music of Distinction
Virgil Thomson, Aaron Copland, and Gail Kubik

ALFRED W. COCHRAN

Three American composers exerted a profound influence on film music from the mid-1930s through the early-1960s. Although their individual styles differ from one another, they shared many similarities: each won the Pulitzer Prize in music, studied with Nadia Boulanger, made his career primarily away from Hollywood, and considered the concert hall his compositional focus. None was interested in writing for the cinema full time, and the total number of film scores composed by these individuals is relatively few. Yet their impact upon cinema music was significant. Fundamentally, all three shared a similar philosophy about film music— that one should respect the medium and not write down to it. Individually and collectively, they raised the standards of film scoring and helped to establish bench marks of excellence for their colleagues, beginning when the cinema with synchronous sound was less than a decade old. Most of their important contributions were made prior to 1950. They were Virgil Thomson (1896–1989), Aaron Copland (1900–1990), and Gail Kubik (1914–1984). Thomson was the first of the group to compose film music and his work encouraged Copland, who emerged as the most influential member of the triumvirate. Their success in the idiom—first in New York, then in Hollywood—inspired the youngest of the group, Kubik, whose earlier functional music experience was in radio.

The past decade has witnessed a tremendous growth in the scholarly study of film music.[1] This interest is welcome, for the genre is a worthy one and contains quality music that is compelling. Sadly, scholars ignored the topic for decades, despite the insightful observations of Frederick Sternfeld, Lawrence Morton, and others whose early work led the way.[2] Fortunately, leading composers were interested in the cinema, virtually from its inception.

The so-called silent cinema was never really silent and was rarely referred to as so prior to 1926. Music paired with film dates from at least 1895, when the Lumière family presented their films to the Parisian public.[3] Soon thereafter, filmmakers demanded music written specifically for their pictures and composers responded eagerly. In 1908, Camille Saint-Saëns scored *L'Assassinat du Duc de Guise,* setting a precedent that other concert-hall composers followed quickly. From then until 1927, when *The Jazz Singer* inaugurated the age of "talkies," a number of well-known, classically oriented composers wrote music for the cinema; most were European.[4] In the next decade, the list grew to include many of the finest composers from France, England, Germany, Mexico, and the Soviet Union, yet few American concert-hall composers were represented.[5] Some felt that writing cinema music was beneath them; others wanted to follow the lead of their European colleagues but found it difficult to do so.

With the advent of "talkies," Hollywood studio profits soared as producers took advantage of the public fascination with synchronous-sound pictures. This prosperity lured a number of Broadway composers to Hollywood, including Alfred Newman and Max Steiner, where they were welcomed. Together with Erich Wolfgang Korngold, Franz Waxman, Dimitri Tiomkin, Victor Young, and others during the 1930s, Newman and Steiner were influential in creating what came to be called "The Hollywood Sound." Many of the composers who contributed to this "sound" were European-born and they shared a similar compositional aesthetic. Their work prompted well-deserved praise and criticism. Irwin Bazelon, speaking from the latter perspective, said:

> Their music reflected the lush, impassioned romanticism of mid-Europe in the late nineteenth century. For the most part it was pure schmaltz. While the violins throbbed and the woodwinds and brasses sighed and pulsated, the entire orchestra drenched itself in a lachrymal sentimentality.[6]

Copland saw inherent limitations in their approach:

> Most scores, as everybody knows, are written in the late nineteenth-century symphonic style, a style now so generally accepted as to be considered inevitable. But why, oh why, the nineteenth century? . . .

What screen music badly needs is more differentiation, more feeling for the exact quality of each picture.[7]

One of the first concert-hall composers to be successful in Hollywood was George Antheil, who scored over twenty films between 1935 and 1957. Upon arriving in California, Antheil began a regular column about film music in the periodical *Modern Music*. His first article asserted:

> The truth of movie-music is becoming apparent; slowly and with infinite patience music is going forward with our new shadow pictures and their miraculous sound effects.
>
> This is especially true of European picture productions of recent date. The credit titles of contemporary movies feature the names of contemporary musicians with increasing frequency. Shostakovich, Auric, Milhaud, Honegger, are among the many who are not too proud to try their hand in the service of a so-far rather despised art. Picture music—a new art form—is coming into its own.[8]

In a later column, Antheil tweaked his peers again:

> American composers may regard the sound track of the motion picture as a crass medium for the propagation of their musical thoughts. Nevertheless they should remember—especially in this day when the hue and cry is for new audiences—that 90,000,000 persons a week hear movie music in America alone, and over 500,000,000 persons a week hear various Hollywood scores throughout the world. . . . No one interested in wider publics, the education of the people, or the general emotional vibrations of the times, can leave motion pictures out of his calculations.[9]

For composers everywhere, the 1930s brought a new artistic approach and philosophy, while political turmoil, military conflict, and worldwide economic depression enveloped the globe. Many younger composers of concert-hall music wanted less complex contemporary music and, consequently, made their compositions more accessible to the public. Copland wrote:

> How could the ordinary music lover, comparatively unaware of the separate steps that brought on the gradual changes in musical methods

and ideals, be expected to understand music that sounded as if it came from some other planet? Composers, by the end of the twenties, began to have an uneasy feeling that a larger gap was separating them from their listeners. They would have been dull indeed not to have realized that this lack of contact with any real audience was placing them in a critical situation. Moreover, the additional fact that new music was beginning to "normalize" itself made it seem more than ever desirable and even necessary that an effort be made to regain the active interest in contemporary music of the entire music-listening public. . . . As a result, two steps were taken: first, many composers tried to simplify their musical language as much as possible, and second, they attempted not only to make contact with audiences in the concert hall, but to seek out music listeners and performers wherever they are to be found—in the public schools and colleges, the teaching studios, the movie house, over the air waves, through recordings—anywhere, in fact, where music is made or heard.[10]

Copland's interest in cinema music is evident as early as 1931, when he scheduled "A Program of Music and Films" for the Copland-Sessions concerts. This event featured film scores by three of his friends: Marc Blitzstein, Colin McPhee, and Darius Milhaud. Later, Copland was encouraged by Antheil's success in Hollywood and by Thomson's highly-acclaimed documentary scores *The Plow That Broke the Plains* (1936), *The River* (1937), and *Spanish Earth* (1937).

The films Virgil Thomson scored deal with compelling social issues and share a philosophy that human suffering can, and should, be relieved through government action.

Pare Lorenz's *The Plow That Broke the Plains* is a remarkable documentary film that chronicles the devastation of the Great Plains through overzealous farming practices and land mismanagement. Recognizing the tremendous suffering this engendered, the U.S. government took unprecedented steps to underpin farmers whose operations were salvageable and relocated others more desperate.

Thomson's sensitive music joins with the images and sparse narration to form a uniquely compelling film. He recalled, "*The Plow That Broke the Plains* was powerful storytelling; documentaries so dramatic had not been made before."[11] Its success was helped greatly by Thomson's evocative score. He continued:

> The music of *The Plow* had poured forth easily. I knew the Great Plains landscape in Kansas, Oklahoma, New Mexico, Texas; and during the War I lived in a tent with ten-below-zero dust storms. I had come to the theme nostalgic and ready to work. . . . The subject, moreover, was highly photogenic—broad grasslands and cattle, mass harvesting, erosion by wind, deserted farms.[12]

Thomson's music is especially noteworthy, as movies with synchronous sound were but seven years old. He showed, convincingly, that a quality musical score could greatly enhance a motion picture. Filling almost every moment of the film, Thomson's music consists mostly of a series of vignettes tied one to another. Its style ranges from the cerebral and austere to the quaint—it even includes some Ellington-inspired blues—but is always sensitive and carefully wrought. Thomson uses thematic transformation successfully and includes effective uses of irony. At one point, for example, the "Doxology," played on organ, blends with desolate images onscreen. As the abandoned homes, ruined soil, and barren landscape are seen, the hymn's words are subtly invoked—"Praise God from whom all blessings flow"—highlighting the incongruity and emphasizing the ecological tragedy that has occurred. Critics noted Thomson's contribution immediately and Edwin Denby wrote:

> Mr. Lorenz . . . is also to be thanked for having chosen one of our most gifted composers to do the music. To listen to interesting music during a movie is an unexpected pleasure. This was Thomson's first movie job, and he did it well. The music is pleasant, with more distinction than any Hollywood music, and better suited to the microphone, that's a little too awkward for heavy sonorities. . . . All our young composers ought to get such a chance.[13]

The careful attention Thomson gave the score for *The Plow that Broke the Plains* stands in marked contrast to what was then often done in Hollywood. There, the studios cranked out film scores as quickly as possible. Many were written by several composers working simultaneously according to formulas, or assembled *in pasticcio* from previously composed works.[14] David Raksin recalls, with amusement and vexation, that this was done to "cope with the insane pressure imposed by the people in charge of seeing that schedules made no concessions to the limits of human endurance."[15] Scores like these were often of uneven quality and many deserved the harsh criticism they received. They were parodies of what film music can, and should, be and reflected the front office's sensibility, which was primarily financial.

As 1937 began, Thomson accepted Lorenz's offer to score a new government documentary, *The River*. The film told the story of the mighty Mississippi and how it brought both prosperity and misery to a large part of the country. It explained how the government acted to control horrific flooding that occurred regularly along its course, and how the Tennessee Valley Authority, and other government initiatives, enhanced people's lives.

Thomson found it more challenging than *The Plow That Broke the Plains*:

> [The] theme [of *The River*] was soil erosion by water, not by wind. Its landscape of streams and forests was pastoral, static. Its historical narrative covered a century, its geographical perspective half the continent. And floods, though murderous to land and houses, are not at all dramatic to observe. A film explaining how they come about and how they can be controlled by dams demands a far more complex composition, if one wants to make it powerful, than the blowing away of our dry high-lying West.[16]

Thomson responded by using indigenous music as the basis of his score. This included a number of White spirituals, folk tunes, and songs from *Southern Harmony* and *The Sacred Harp*. His music provides a touching and fitting accompaniment to Lorenz's sometimes trenchant images and compelling story, without being maudlin or overblown. While some of Thomson's score invokes the past, other parts are fully contemporary in their language and use. His dissonant music in scenes of steel being made, for example, is particularly effective and influenced Copland when the latter set similar images to music in *The City*. Because narration is more prominent in *The River* than *The Plow That Broke the Plains*, Thomson's scores function somewhat differently in each case, but both are derived from the same creative wellspring. Thomson was pleased with the film and reflected that "*The River* seems now, seemed then indeed, to have achieved a higher integration of filmed narrative with spoken poetry and with music than had existed since the sound track's coming into use some eight years earlier."[17]

Later in 1937, Thomson and Marc Blitzstein assembled a score of recorded music to accompany Joris Ivens' wartime documentary *The*

Spanish Earth. The film praises the Republican defenders of Madrid who fought Axis-supported rebels in the Spanish Civil War; Ernest Hemingway wrote the narration, which was read by Orson Welles. Thomson and Blitzstein chose indigenous music with a strong Spanish flavor, replete with Moorish influences, which enhances the "authenticity" of the film and adds musical interest. Although the score was an afterthought, Thomson and Blitzstein did a commendable job assembling it and adapting the music to their purpose.

In June 1937, Aaron Copland went to Hollywood hoping to land a film-scoring assignment. He stayed a month but was unsuccessful. Somewhat frustrated, he confided, "Antheil was right about needing a film credit in order to snag a contract in Hollywood. But how was one to go about that?"[18] Other New York composers also made the trip to California and returned empty-handed. Antheil remarked:

> Meanwhile many excellent composers have come out to Hollywood and returned East again. Scarcely any of them have gotten jobs. While on the other hand, the routine Hollywood composers who have been here many years, have grown alarmed at the influx of new men, and have used their influence to sew up every future score available. In other words Hollywood music is, at the present writing, a closed corporation.[19]

If Hollywood movies were inaccessible to these composers, documentary and independent films were not, as Thomson had shown. Copland's break came in 1939, when Ralph Steiner and Willard Van Dyke hired him for their documentary entitled *The City*—a work commissioned by the American City Planning Institute for screening at the 1939 New York World's Fair. Both Steiner and Van Dyke had worked with Lorenz and knew the power of well-made films to sway people's thinking. Indeed, it was clear to many that documentary films could initiate social change. Richard Griffith has spoken to this very point:

> The nation-wide success of Lorenz's two government films [i.e., *The Plow that Broke the Plains* and *The River*] has put documentary on the map with a flourish. Never before have pictures dealing with social problems captured the attention of an audience which includes all levels of American opinion. And this popularity, as widespread as it is unprecedented, has raised high hopes among those who have for years

wanted to enlist the films as an instrument for social education. Educators and publicists everywhere are hailing documentary as a vivid, ur-
gent method for developing the social attitudes of masses of people,
for reconditioning their civic thinking.[20]

Steiner and Van Dyke wanted a quality film and sought talented
people to assist them. Van Dyke recalled that others were less concerned:

> A supervisor [was provided] by the Institute who did nothing of con-
> structive value. . . . I remember him as a man who didn't have much to
> offer. One time he suggested that we hire a German brass band and film
> them in Central Park so that we could use their music as the score for
> the film. I politely thanked him and never told Ralph, whose temper
> was on a shorter leash than mine. We have joked about the "supervi-
> sor" many times.[21]

Steiner explained how he came to ask Copland to compose the score:

> [I f]irst met Aaron around 1926–7–8 when I, feeling I should know
> about music a bit, took [a] course at [the] New School on 23rd
> Street. . . . Walked him to [the] subway one day and . . . invited him to
> dinner with his room mate, Harold Clurman. . . . Then when we
> needed music for *The City,* my former wife, who was a great friend of
> Aaron's, suggested Aaron to do it. I said, "Too damned modern." She
> collected some UN-modern of his things, and I was won over.[22]

For *The City* Copland produced an extraordinary score of power, intelligence, wit, and sensitivity, which helped the film claim its distinction
as one of the best documentaries ever made. Critics from coast to coast
praised the music, as did Steiner and Van Dyke. Recognizing what Copland had done, Steiner explained that,

> [w]hen I heard for [the] first time the music (recorded) with the film I
> saw that the shots were held together more by the music than by film
> cement. I was bowled over not only by what Aaron had done but also
> by what Willard and I had done—it was an unbelievable amount more
> exciting—Pittsburgh and the automobile sequence—well, all the se-
> quences. . . . *The City,* a documentary, was composed of hundreds of
> various shots. It could have been jumpy and lacked flow. Aaron tied all
> the miscellaneous shots together and made the climaxes climactic.[23]

Van Dyke concurred:

> [Copland] did the score by watching the picture, play a little bit on the
> piano, and when there was a wedding between the image and the
> sound, he wrote the appropriate notes on paper. . . . We all thought
> the score was exactly right, there were no requests for him to change
> anything. Once or twice he asked us to shorten or lengthen a sequence
> by a small amount. . . . Although subsequently I had film scores by
> Marc Blitzstein, William Schumann, Morton Gould, Mel Powell, and
> others less famous, I have always liked the score Aaron did the best.[24]

Later, several versions of the film were circulated; these vary in
length from ten to forty-three minutes (the latter being the length of the
original film). While working at the Museum of Modern Art, Van Dyke
reconstructed the film to its original specifications; this reconstructed
"original" is now available for rental through the museum.

Copland's score takes thirty-one minutes of *The City* and is cast in
four sections. The music eschews thematic repetition from part to part,
but is logical and coherent enough to make thematic repetition unneces-
sary.[25] The entire score emanates from germinal material presented in the
first moments of the film; motives derived from this are used consistently
throughout the score. There follows a five-minute section without narration, which Copland uses to establish the proper feeling of time, place,
and mood. The music is carefully crafted, with a distinctive harmonic
language imbued with quartal elements and modality, a lean and transparent style of orchestration and, in places, prominent dissonance. Most
important, the music captures the spirit of the film, which is alternately
pastoral, light-hearted, shocking, and disturbing. Copland's score for
The City is compelling music of great distinction. It continued Thomson's work in setting the standard for what American film music could be
and provided the film credit Copland needed for Hollywood.

Just as Steiner was reluctant to entrust *The City* to Copland, fearing
a style too modern and acerbic, Hollywood film makers also were hesi-
tant to hire him. But their skepticism was laid to rest with the stunning
success of *The City,* which was hailed universally as a superb film score.
Within months, Copland was offered the first of two Hollywood films he
was to score within a year's time: Lewis Milestone's *Of Mice and Men*
(1939). This adaptation of John Steinbeck's celebrated play pleased Copland, who recalled: "I viewed *Of Mice and Men* twice, but once was
enough to know how fortunate I was to have this film offered for my first

major movie score. . . . Here was an American theme, by a great American writer, demanding appropriate music."[26] He added:

> In composing the score of *Of Mice and Men,* however I succeeded, the primary purpose was to write music which somehow suggested the background of the film—daily life on a California ranch. To do this, I occasionally employed music of a folk song character, though using no direct quotations; simple tunes that might have been whistled by George and Lennie. The temper of the music varied, of course, with every scene, but always I tried to keep away from the over-lush harmonies that are so common on the screen and usually defeat their own purpose by over-emphasis. As a matter of fact what you do not do is often as important as what you do in scoring a motion picture.
>
> On the whole though, the score, as any score, is designed to strengthen and underline the emotional content of the entire picture.[27]

Copland's first Hollywood score was a success and earned him an Academy Award nomination. The music succeeds on several levels and demonstrates his uncanny ability to establish a feeling of time and place and to perceive the film's deeper meanings and associations. He showed great skill in using music to link dramatically related, noncontiguous parts of the film and in portraying the psychological mood and underpinning of the scenes.

As in *The City,* the first part of the music for *Of Mice and Men* is uninterrupted by dialogue or narration and functions like an overture in that it contains seminal material from which the rest of the score is built. Harmonically, the scores for both films are much alike, replete with quartal elements, pandiatonicism, modality, and prominent dissonance. They also share a certain leanness; there are no extra notes or chord doublings, and careful attention is paid to the orchestration. In every way, the scores bear Copland's unmistakable musical imprint. Unlike *The City,* however, thematic repetition is important to the music for *Of Mice and Men* and is used to strengthen the dramatic impact of the film. For example, the final music, which accompanies scenes of great emotional intensity when George kills Lennie, consists almost entirely of recapitulated passages. These recollections remind the viewer of the dramatic events they first accompanied and form a tightly knit musical fabric that pulls the film together in a powerful conclusion.

One of the film's most poignant and important scenes is the "Death of Candy's Dog," which mirrors the message of the story and presages

Figure 11.1. "Death of Candy's Dog" from Aaron Copland's score for *Of Mice and Men*.

Lennie's death. One critic found the music for this scene objectionable: "We noted but one flaw in Mr. Milestone's direction: his refusal to hush the off-screen musicians when Candy's old dog was being taken outside to be shot. A metronome, anything would have been better than modified "Hearts and Flowers."[28] Other critics, however, considered Copland's music stunningly effective.

Compositionally, the "Death of Candy's Dog" scene poses the difficult problem of how to intensify emotion without calling undue attention to the music (see Figure 11.1). Copland's solution is noteworthy. First, it employs a binary scheme of thirty-seven measures, with one repetition. There are frequent meter changes throughout these measures, and the outer voices assume special importance as a two-voice framework. No one meter is used for longer than four measures and often meters change even more quickly. The converging direction of each part of the outer two-voice framework is distinctive: the melodic line is built primarily of statements of concise motives—most often seconds and thirds—with periodic interruptions rather than traditional melody. All this allows the polarity of the outside voices and the harmony to assume greater importance without becoming distracting. It is a subtle touch that avoids the overt sentimentality of a single, drawn-out melody. Copland was pleased with the music for this, his first Hollywood movie:

My overall experience with *Of Mice and Men* was a good one. I was satisfied that the score enhanced the movie, making it more intense and more meaningful. To some in Hollywood my music was strange, lean, and dissonant; to others it spoke with a new incisiveness and clarity. I was an outsider to Hollywood, but I did not condescend to compose film music; I worked hard at it. Perhaps this is why I was accepted. And I genuinely liked some things about the film industry, particularly that music was made to be used on a daily basis, and that composers were actually needed there. Also, the accent was entirely on the "living" composer.[29]

Copland's next Hollywood project followed quickly: the music for *Our Town*. In the spring of 1940, he arrived to do Sol Lesser's production of Thornton Wilder's Pulitzer Prize-winning play. Once more Copland was offered a first-rate story by an imaginative author, yet one quite different from *Of Mice and Men*. Copland knew at once that it called for a different kind of score than he had written thus far for the cinema: "I was irritated that film music had become so pat, so conventionalized, when the medium was still so young. . . . Here was my chance to show that a composer, within a short period of time, could write different-sounding scores, each appropriate to the film it accompanied."[30] The composer was as good as his word, and his music surprised almost everyone.

Those who admired Copland's music saw it as a sensitive accompaniment to Wilder's portrayal of everyday life. Others considered both play and film suspiciously arty, and Copland's music inconsequential. This criticism is unworthy of Copland's elegant, understated score where restraint and simplicity rule. Neither does it acknowledge the compositional sophistication that Copland brought to this music. For example, a harmonic analysis of the score shows a long-range plan of tonal organization derived from ideas introduced early in the film in the "Story of *Our Town*" scene.[31] In a score where thematic repetition is prominent, the music for this scene is repeated most often (see Figure 11.2).

As in *Of Mice and Men,* Copland uses thematic repetition in *Our Town* to intensify the dramatic unity of the film, linking characters and situations. Of the score's eighteen sections, all but six employ musical ideas introduced earlier. There are also subtle examples of craft and humor present, as when Copland transforms the hymn "Blest Be the Tie that Binds"—played by a drunken organist during choir practice—into a bizarre caricature of itself as the organist staggers home after rehearsal.

Figure 11.2. "Story of Our Town" from Aaron Copland's score for *Our Town*.

Another example is Copland's choice of music for the scene in which George and Emily are married—viz., his own arrangement of the hymn "Art Thou Weary?" (a title that imparts a bit of humor and may reflect a thirty-nine-year-old bachelor's jest at matrimony). Still another example is Copland's use of a musical saw to impart an other-worldly quality to the music for "Emily's Dream," which occurs at the end of the film just prior to the birth of her child. Copland's score for *Our Town* is wonderful music and deserved its Academy Award nomination. Julia Smith, Copland's biographer, aptly describes it as "of infinite sweetness and gentleness."[32]

Copland's first three film scores established him as a major voice in American cinema music. Although each deals with a different subject, all three scores are stylistically much alike, which made it easy for him to refashion them into *Music for Movies* some years later.

Gail Kubik was fourteen years younger than Copland and eighteen years younger than Thomson. He admired his older colleagues and was well aware of their successful film scores; not surprisingly, he wanted to compose one too. Given a chance, Kubik quickly established himself as the premiere composer of wartime documentaries and made important contributions to Hollywood scoring practices through his music for animated films and dramas.

Kubik was precocious. When he was approached in 1940 to score George Gercke's documentary film, *Men and Ships,* Kubik was a staff composer and musical program advisor for NBC radio. The twenty-six-year-old Kansan had recently left the faculty of Teachers College, Columbia University, having taught at two other colleges and universities prior to that. He also had the distinction of being the youngest student admitted into Harvard University's doctoral program in music.

Men and Ships was produced by the U.S. Maritime Commission and was of comparable quality to the documentaries of Pare Lorenz, with whom Gercke had served as an assistant. Kubik worked virtually non-stop to meet Lorenz's deadline, composing and orchestrating the music in less than three weeks. Kubik produced an outstanding score that was recorded by members of the New York Philharmonic and conducted by Alexander Smallens. Its impact was pronounced and immediate; Kubik's music spoke with a voice that was contemporary and distinctive. He recalled, "One of the [New York] theaters played it and had my name out in big letters—MUSIC BY GAIL KUBIK."[33] This boosted his ego but he enjoyed the more important accolade of conducting the NBC Symphony Orchestra, Toscanini's group, in a concert performance of the score over the network—an unusual honor, and one that reflected the esteem afforded his score.

America was soon at war with the Axis powers. The Office of War Information (OWI) quickly put together a documentary film called *The World at War.* Kubik remembered how it happened:

> [The film] was made out of documentary clips, beautifully written. And so, there arose the moment when the film needed a score. Because I had attracted so much attention with *Men and Ships,* I was engaged to do the score for *The World at War.* I was paid a thousand dollars, a fantastic amount of money it seemed to me in those days. I wrote about a forty-minute score. In some respects, some of those sequences are the best functional music I've ever written. So I did the score, we recorded it, and it came off well.[34]

The World at War won universal praise and Kubik's score garnered unprecedented acclaim. Indeed, before its release, he was offered the position of music head for the OWI's Bureau of Motion Pictures, which he accepted. Critics were unanimous in their praise for his music, which came as a fresh wind to those interested in the cinema. Henry Simon wrote:

The success of Mr. Kubik's score is all the more remarkable in that it is uncompromisingly modern, in places violently cacophonous. The subject of war naturally lends itself to this treatment. Sweet music certainly would be inappropriate; and when he ironically used the Brahms *Lullaby* to accompany German soldiers asleep between acts of violence, he presents the familiar tune in ugly, distorted form. He uses other familiar material, like *Deutschland über alles,* similarly distorted, this particular one as a march in 5–4 time, giving the effect of monstrous men going along in files on three legs apiece.

Most of the score, however, is based on entirely original material and invariably succeeds in adding some comment, deepening the meaning of the picture.[35]

Even the usually prosaic UPI news service reported that "Kubik . . . built his ideas with musical logic in symphonic form."[36]

Kubik held his influential OWI post until he entered the military in 1943. During that time, he scored several OWI films and was responsible for persuading respected composers—including Virgil Thomson, Morton Gould, and Paul Creston—to score others.[37] After joining the Army Air Corps, Kubik went to work in Culver City, California, with the First Motion Picture Unit. His duty station was unlike any in the military and occupied the prewar Hal Roach studios. Euphemistically referred to as "Fort Roach," the army post included among its ranks such Hollywood luminaries as Arthur Kennedy, Clark Gable, George Montgomery, and Ronald Reagan. While stationed at "Fort Roach," Kubik scored several films,[38] one of which emerged as perhaps the best wartime documentary ever made: William Wyler's *The Memphis Belle.* Kubik's music for this outstanding film cemented his reputation in Hollywood as the foremost composer of wartime documentaries. Composer David Raksin orchestrated part of the score for Kubik:

They were, as usual, in a jam; you know, "We need it right away!" So Gail needed help with the orchestration. He was a fine orchestrator, but when the heat is on, it saves time to compose a "sketch," from which somebody else takes the individual parts and puts them into a full score. That's what I did for Gail on Memphis Belle, about half of the music, I think. . . .

I admired his music and we became friends. It isn't always that orchestrators come away admiring the music of composers; too often, you see the seamy side of a composer's work.[39]

Once again, critical reaction to the film and its score was enthusiastic; furthermore, because *The Memphis Belle* was distributed by Paramount Pictures, it reached millions of people around the world. The score reveals Kubik's innate dramatic sense and ability to transform mundane parts of the film into something special that holds our attention, pulling us deeper into the film's story.

While Kubik was composing these scores, Copland was writing music both for Lillian Hellman's *The North Star* (1943), and for an OWI documentary entitled *The Cummington Story* (1945). Both are little known today. *The North Star* was produced by Samuel Goldwyn at great expense but it received a lukewarm reception. Moreover, the movie became a political embarrassment for Copland because it was unabashedly pro-Soviet. When it was made, the Soviet Union was America's ally in the fight against German hegemony in Europe. With the advent of the Cold War, McCarthyism, and the escalation of tension between the two superpowers, such films became unpopular and were rarely seen. (In recent years *The North Star* has reemerged.) Because of the movie's variegated nature—part propaganda vehicle, part melodrama, and part tribute to Soviet peasant life—Copland faced a difficult job composing a suitable score, one that incorporated background music as well as dance sequences, solo songs, and choruses (some of the latter with lyrics by Ira Gershwin). In one scene, Walter Brennan sings a Russian folk song in English, demonstrating that his acting skills outweighed his vocal ability! Indeed, much of the score for *The North Star* has a strong Russian folk song flavor and it is unlike anything else in Copland's cinema oeuvre. Yet it earned him a third Oscar nomination.

The Cummington Story (1945) is a well-made documentary that, unfortunately, few people have seen, as it was intended for distribution only to American servicemen and countries abroad. The score for this film provides a deft accompaniment to the story of European war refugees temporarily relocated in Cummington, Massachusetts. *The Cummington Story* makes a plea for tolerance and understanding as it chronicles the difficulties faced by the refugees and their hosts in accepting one another. The music for most of the twenty-minute film is lyrical and restrained, calling to mind the pastoral music in *The City*. It is an elegant score, finely crafted, that uses thematic repetition effectively to reinforce its message, as well as a Polish lullaby to add poignant realism. One of the score's highlights is a jaunty and ebullient sequence that accompanies scenes of a county fair. Copland's exuberant music provides just the right touch to make this part of the film particularly memorable. In 1962, he refashioned the film's main theme into a short piano piece, "In Evening Air."

Early in 1948 Copland returned to Hollywood to score a film of John Steinbeck's *The Red Pony.* The movie was not a box office hit, although it featured Robert Mitchum, Joseph Cotten, and Myrna Loy, but Copland's score is a masterpiece. Had he composed no other music for the cinema, the score of *The Red Pony* would command attention and respect. It profoundly influenced people's notions of what appropriate music for the American West should be. The film was directed by Lewis Milestone, with whom Copland had worked on *Of Mice and Men* and *The North Star,* and was made with sensitivity and skill.

The score for *The Red Pony* is particularly effective, with themes and melodies that are captivating and tuneful. Indeed, the music is crafted with such skill that one can easily overlook the depth and sophistication that Copland brought to bear in creating the illusion of apparent simplicity. Infusing the score as a whole is a carefully conceived harmonic idiom from which its melodic elements are derived. Also noteworthy is the composer's penchant for maintaining a harmonic fabric that permits and suggests a degree of tonal ambiguity and flexibility. Copland accomplished this in various ways, including quartal and pentatonic aspects. The score unfolds naturally from the most meager of initial materials into a highly unified entity. Portions are quite dissonant; Copland uses dissonance as an effective expressive tool to heighten emotion and emphasize affect. The score has an unmistakable clarity and directness of expression that gives it power and authority. Furthermore, Copland's masterful reiteration of thematic material pulls the film's story together convincingly. An example is the music for the third musical cue, "Walk to the Bunkhouse," which is often repeated in the film. In this scene, Tom and Billy's spirits are high and it is clear that they share a bond of friendship and trust; the music reflects this (see Figure 11.3).

Later, Copland returns to this music but with a different message. The pony has grown ill and Tom must leave for school. The carefree nature of the music is mitigated by new thematic material that alerts the audience that trouble approaches. The "Walk to the Bunkhouse" music in this more ominous setting conveys Tom's growing skepticism about Billy's reliability and veracity. Earlier, Tom had viewed him as all-knowing.

Other cues are also extraordinary. Among these are the two dream sequences, which provide fitting music for the fantasy-laden imagination

Figure 11.3. "Walk to the Bunkhouse" from Aaron Copland's score for *The Red Pony.*

of the young boy ("March Dream," "Circus Dream"). So, too, the score's hushed beauty when Tom is given the pony is nothing short of magical ("The Gift"), and its exuberance as Tom trains the pony is quintessentially right for the scene ("Morning Training"). One of the most moving passages is heard as Tom accepts the pony's death and anticipates the birth of Billy's colt ("Tom Readjusted"). It is music of pronounced lyricism and quiet beauty; its gentleness and unadorned simplicity make it one of the most memorable cues in a score that is a masterpiece of the cinematic art.

The year 1948 saw Virgil Thomson at work on Robert Flaherty's *The Louisiana Story*. The film is rather odd, being part pro-oil industry documentary, part paean to Louisiana bayou life, and part melodrama. According to Thomson, the Standard Oil Company of New Jersey, which sponsored the film, grew parsimonious before its score could be commissioned; this kept the project in limbo for two years. Eventually Standard Oil relented and Thomson was hired to compose the score. As he was wont to do, Thomson studied the indigenous music of the Louisiana bayou country and used that material in his score.

Flaherty's film was his last before his death in 1951. It is exceptional because of the limited narration and dialogue and the extraordinary role that the score is allowed to assume. In this regard, the music for *The Louisiana Story* is much like Thomson's first film score, *The Plow that Broke the Plains,* though more sophisticated. The *Louisiana Story* score is equal to Flaherty's visual images and storyline; it is rarely absent from the film and, when it is, the pace of the movie slows down markedly. The score emerges as an eloquent, sensitive, and powerful force in the film, whose varied moods are alternately majestic, pastoral, dance-like, and evocative. The score was recorded by the Philadelphia Orchestra under Eugene Ormandy and earned Thomson an Academy Award nomination and a Pulitzer Prize, the only film score to have received such an accolade. Subsequently, Thomson drew two orchestral suites from the score, which he said, "have been played more, I think, than any other of my orchestral works."[40]

In November and December 1948, Copland returned to Hollywood to score William Wyler's *The Heiress,* an adaptation of Ruth and Augustus Goetz' play, which was based on Henry James's novel *Washington Square. The Heiress* was a period piece of the mid-nineteenth century, seemingly not well-suited to Copland's experience in the cinema or compositional predilection. Yet the film's psychological aspects and implications interested him; so did its inherent quality. Copland and Wyler reached agreement about what kind of music should be written, and the composer looked forward to his fourth Hollywood assignment.

Although superficially different from his earlier film scores, Copland's music for *The Heiress* had an affinity to his previous work:

> I saw certain similarities in *The Heiress* to what I had encountered when composing the score for *Our Town,* where it was necessary to recreate the feeling of life in a typical New Hampshire town around 1900. My method then had been to make use of every resource in order to suggest the essence of a particular time and place. I hoped to do the same for *The Heiress.*[41]

Not surprisingly, the film contains a considerable amount of period music—dance pieces, primarily, arranged by Copland or his orchestrator, Nathan Van Cleve. Moreover, an eighteenth-century song by Giovanni Martini, "Plaisirs d'amour," receives special attention when Catherine Sloper's suitor, Morris Townsend, sings it while trying to win her affections. Wyler liked the tune and encouraged Copland to use it in other places in the film, which he agreed to do.

Copland worked hard at the score but found it difficult because of its specific requirements, being so different from his previous film work. Nevertheless, he persevered, even when confronted with demands for rewrites when his music prompted audiences in test screenings to laugh at the jilted Catherline Sloper, rather than sympathize with her plight. Copland's second try at this scene produced the desired results and both he and Wyler were relieved. Overall, Copland gave the score the same restraint and attention to detail that he afforded his previous cinema scores, and the music for *The Heiress* emerged as a superlative effort that won him the Academy Award. His feelings about the film and its director were marred, however, when the title music he composed was altered after he left Hollywood. His repudiation of the altered passage was published in the *New York Times*. Later, Copland recalled that he

> had not objected to using the song "Plaisirs d'Amour" in the film, and I even adapted it in my own style after it was heard in its original form. I balked, however, when I was asked to ditch my title music and make an arrangement of the tune instead. I had the right to refuse, but it seems that the producers had the right to ask someone else to arrange the title music. After the score had been completely finished and recorded and I had returned to New York, I learned that "Plaisirs d'Amour" had been inserted into my title music![42]

In fact, Copland himself altered the score of *The Heiress* at Wyler's request, before leaving Hollywood, as the manuscript score clearly shows.[43] On the other hand. Copland's alteration isn't part of the film's sound track. The version of "Plaisirs d'amour" used in the film has the distinctive "Hollywood Sound" that Copland disliked so much. It does not require a refined ear to note the stylistic difference between this music and Copland's own. Unfortunately, Wyler did not possess such discrimination; his hearing had been damaged during the war while filming *The Memphis Belle* and he was notoriously insecure about musical decisions in his films. Despite what Copland said in print, however, his primary disagreement with Wyler probably stemmed from this issue rather than whether the song should be included in the "Main Title" cue music; Copland had already acquiesced to that.

Although Copland said that he used conventional Hollywood recording "tricks" to alter the sound of the score for *The Heiress,* the music is fundamentally akin to his previous cinema work—it is never intrusive and always serves the dramatic action. Special attention is given to create specific sonorities in the musical fabric, and the orchestration is customarily lean and transparent. Most important, Copland demonstrates in this score that he knew how and when to use music to best effect. While the film's strengths would have not been diminished by a traditional Hollywood score, Copland's sensitive accompaniment lends the movie charm and grace that are quite special.

Soon after Copland finished scoring *The Heiress,* Kubik was approached by Joseph Lerner of Laurel Films in New York City to write music for a taut and brutal drama *C-Man* (1949). Lerner's film was shot in New York City and starred Dean Jagger and John Carradine. *C-Man* is a standard cops-and-robbers picture, but was rather violent for its time. Kubik's music reflected this violence effectively and generated positive critical attention. A review in *Variety* exemplified this:

> One of the . . . standout features [in *C-Man*] is the musical score directed and composed by Gail Kubik. Dominating the soundtrack even more than the dialog, the background music has a nervous, pounding, pulse-quickening quality which, combined to the headlong action, results in a powerfully stirring total effect.[44]

C-Man's score also caught the attention of musicologist Frederick Sternfeld, who was intrigued with the music and its innovative effects. Sternfeld contacted the composer, asked to look at the score, and he and Kubik soon became friends. Later Sternfeld published articles in the *Hollywood Quarterly* and *Musical Quarterly* that praised the music's originality and Kubik's ability. Surprisingly, the score for *C-Man* was written for only thirteen players—a group Kubik utilized effectively and ingeniously. Indirectly, the music won Kubik his Pulitzer Prize, for it was the basis of a subsequent concert work, the *Symphony Concertante* (1951).

Just as *The City* gave Copland his entry into Hollywood, so *C-Man* enabled Kubik to land a job there. Early in 1950, he traveled to Hollywood seeking a film assignment. He came close to getting one on several occasions but grew discouraged and was ready to return to New York; then he met John Hubley of United Productions of America (UPA) at a cocktail party. UPA was Columbia Pictures' innovative cartoon unit and was respected for its forward-looking approach to the medium. Kubik and Hubley discovered an artistic common ground and they hit it off well. In their conversations the composer spoke of his difficulty in landing a job and, in short order, Hubley asked Kubik to score two cartoons: *Gerald McBoing Boing* and *The Miner's Daughter*.

McBoing Boing is a story by Dr. Seuss "about a little boy who didn't say words but went boing boing instead," while *The Miner's Daughter* tells the story of Clementine and John Harvard and how she won her man by cooking his favorite food, Boston baked beans. Both cartoons are clever but *McBoing Boing* is extraordinary. Kubik accepted Hubley's offer and produced two wonderfully apt scores. Kubik's score for *McBoing Boing,* especially, is a masterpiece of cinema music and helped the cartoon win its Academy Award. The score also served as the progenitor for Kubik's concert piece *Gerald McBoing Boing: A Children's Tale,* while *The Miner's Daughter* was transformed into *Boston Baked Beans: An Opera Piccola.*

Kubik's score for *Gerald McBoing Boing* is sophisticated music— ebullient and witty, full of asymmetrical rhythms, frequent meter changes, and jazz-inflected harmonies. It is a tightly knit score that gives the film unity and coherence, while capturing the humor and mock pathos of the cartoon effectively; and it, too, received immediate critical acclaim. Sternfeld's article in *Film Music Notes* gave the score a big league stamp of approval:

> In re-hearing and re-studying the score one is impressed with the composer's ability to capture the essence of the dramatic problem in the first few bars and to mirror the hero's trials, dejection and final victory so poignantly in the music. By the time the listener returns to the themes of the beginning the intervening stages have been so intense and convincing that one hardly realizes how little time they have taken. But the ten minutes or so that separate the first statement from the final peroration are packed with music of both dramatic and stylistic integrity.[45]

Copland, Thomson, and Kubik all returned to film scoring in later years, but their post-1950s scores fall outside the time limits of the present volume. One such score should be mentioned, however, because it is of particular interest: Kubik's dissonant music for William Wyler's *The*

Desperate Hours (1955). Like *C-Man,* Wyler's film is a psychological thriller, and Kubik's music for it was crafted with great skill and enhances the tension-laden drama.

At the test screening of *The Desperate Hours,* the score received special praise from many individuals; unfortunately, it also aroused the ire of Paramount's head Don Hartman. Hartman was offended by Kubik's angular, strident music and forced Wyler to remove most of it from the soundtrack, effectively eviscerating this last Humphrey Bogart film. As composer David Raksin put it, "The people at the studio didn't understand what the hell Gail was doing. His style was much more acerbic than was usually accepted. When he did the score, all hell broke loose."[46] Some years later, Paramount made the unheard of gesture of returning the music rights to Kubik and publishing, at their expense, a suite he drew from the score, *Scenario for Orchestra.* His experience with *The Desperate Hours,* however, soured Kubik on Hollywood, and he wrote no more film scores there (although he accepted offers elsewhere). Interestingly, Kubik's bad experience in films, like Copland's, occurred while working with director William Wyler.

Had Thomson, Copland, and Kubik never written film music, the American cinema could still boast extraordinary scores of power and sensitivity written by other 1930s and 1940s composers. Yet the decision by these three men to do so changed the course and direction of film music profoundly. Their collective cinematic oeuvre raised the standards in an industry where hack work was often the rule and imitation frequently took the place of originality. Copland, Thomson, and Kubik proved that quality music could enhance the meaning and power of a film, and equally important, that good film music could be interesting and stimulating music in its own right. Their work from the mid-1930s until the early 1950s challenged younger composers to follow their lead in composing music worthy of the medium. It is fitting that two of the three—Thomson and Kubik—earned their Pulitzer Prizes for work that originated in the cinema. We owe a debt of gratitude to these three American composers for ennobling a theretofore rather scorned art form and for bequeathing to us a music of distinction.

NOTES

[1]See, for example: Gilliam Anderson, *Music for Silent Films, 1894–1929* (Washington, D.C.: Library of Congress, 1988). Royal S. Brown, *Overtones and Undertones: Reading Film Music* (Berkeley: University of California Press,

1994); George Burt, *The Art of Film Music* (Boston: Northeastern University Press, 1994); Alfred Cochran, "The Spear of Cephalus: Observations on Film Music Analysis," *Indiana Theory Review* 11 (Spring and Fall 1990):65–80; William Darby and Jack DuBois, *American Film Music: Major Composers, Techniques, Trends, 1915–1990* (Jefferson, N.C.: McFarland, 1990); Caryl Flinn, *Strains of Utopia: Gender, Nostalgia, and Hollywood Film Music* (Princeton, N.J.: Princeton University Press, 1992); Claudia Gorbman, *Unheard Melodies: Narrative Film Music* (Bloomington: Indiana University Press, 1987); Kathryn Kalinak, *Settling the Score: Music and the Classical Hollywood Film* (Madison, WI: University of Wisconsin Press, 1992); Fred Karlin, *Listening to Movies: The Film Lover's Guide to Film Music* (New York: Schirmer Books, 1994), and *On the Track: A Guide to Contemporary Film Scoring* (New York: Schirmer Books, 1990); Randall D. Larson, *Musique fantastique: A Survey of Film Music in the Fantastic Cinema* (Metuchen, N.J.: Scarecrow Press, 1985); Gary Marmostein, *Hollywood Rhapsody: Movie Music and Its Makers* (New York: Schirmer Books, 1997); David Neumeyer, "Source Music, Background Music, Fantasy, and Reality in Early Sound Film," *College Music Symposium* 37 (1997):13–20, and "Melodrama as a Compositional Resource in Early Hollywood Sound Cinema," *Current Musicology* (1995):61–94; Christopher Palmer, *The Composer in Hollywood* (London and New York: Marion Boyars, 1990); Roy M. Prendergast, *Film Music: A Neglected Art: A Critical Study of Music in Films*, 2nd ed. (New York: W. W. Norton, 1992); Steven C. Smith, *A Heart at Fire's Center: The Life and Music of Bernard Herrmann* (Berkeley: University of California Press, 1991); and Steven Westcott, *Comprehensive Bibliography of Music for Film and Television* (Detroit: Information Coordinators, 1985).

[2]They include Hans Eisler, Kurt London, John Huntley, and Roger Manvell.

[3]See Roy M. Prendergast, *Film Music: A Neglected Art,* 2nd ed. (New York and London: W. W. Norton, 1992):5.

[4]The group included Georges Hue, Pietro Mascagni, Darius Milhaud, Arthur Honegger, Frederick Sheperd Converse, Eric Satie, Edmund Meisel, Paul Hindemith, and Jacques Ibert.

[5]These included Hans Eisler, Maurice Jaubert, Dmitri Shostakovich, Georges Auric, Gustav Holst, Alexandre Tansman, Eugene Goosens, Serge Prokofiev, Arthur Benjamin, Arthur Bliss, Benjamin Britten, Aram Khachaturian, Cyril Mockridge, Karol Rathus, Silvestre Revueltas, Ernst Toch, William Walton, William Alwyn, Werner Janssen, and Dmitri Kabalevsky.

[6]Irwin Bazelon, *Knowing the Score: Notes on Film Music* (New York: Van Nostrand Reinhold Company, 1975):23.

[7]Aaron Copland, "Second Thoughts on Hollywood," *Modern Music* 17/3 (March–April 1940):141–143.

[8]George Antheil, "On the Hollywood Front," *Modern Music* 14/1 (November–December 1936):46.

[9]Antheil, "On the Hollywood Front," *Modern Music* 15/3 (March–April 1938):188.

[10]Copland, *Our New Music* (New York: Whittlesey House, McGraw-Hill, 1941):117–118.

[11]Virgil Thomson, *Virgil Thomson* (New York: Alfred A. Knopf, 1966):260.

[12]Ibid.:270.

[13]Edwin Denby, "Thomson Scores a New Deal Film," *Modern Music* 13/4 (May–June 1936):47.

[14]Described in Antheil, "Breaking Into the Movies," *Modern Music* (January 1937):82–86; Lawrence Morton in *Clifford McCarty's Film Composers in America:*xii–xiii; and David Raksin, quoted in Prendergast, *Film Music:*30–31.

[15]David Raksin, quoted in Prendergast, *Film Music:*30.

[16]Ibid.:270.

[17]Ibid.:274.

[18]Copland and Vivian Perlis, *Copland: 1900–1942* (New York: St. Martin's/Marek, 1984):271.

[19]Antheil, "On the Hollywood Front," *Modern Music* 15/1 (November–December 1937):48.

[20]Richard Griffith, "The Film Faces Facts," *Survey Graphic* 27 (December, 1938):595. Quoted in Howard Gillette, Jr., "Film as Artifact, *The City* (1939)," [Journal of] *American Studies* (Fall 1977):72.

[21]Correspondence with the author, 21 July 1983.

[22]Ralph Steiner, correspondence with the author, posted 19 July 1983.

[23]Ibid.

[24]Willard Van Dyke, correspondence with the author, 8 July 1983.

[25]Thematic repetition between parts one and two is evident, but results from editing. It is not present in the actual score.

[26]Copland and Perlis, *Copland: 1900–1942:*297.

[27]Copland, "The Aims of Music for Films," *New York Times* (10 March 1940), sec. 11, p. 7.

[28]Frank S. Nugent, "The Screen," *New York Times* (17 February 1940), sec. L+, p. 8.

[29]Copland and Perlis, *Copland: 1900–1924:*300.

[30]Ibid.:302.

[31]This is more than coincidence for, with many other film composers, the idea of harmonic unity and planning in a film score is not operable. In Copland's hands such unity and planning serve as a way of providing internal unity and cohesion. Examination shows that the background tonal organization of the score is

an amplification of the harmonic movement that begins the "Story of Our Town" music (see Figure 11.2 on page 335).

[32]Julia Smith, "Aaron Copland, His Work and Contribution to American Music" (Ph.D. dissertation, New York University, 1952):458.

[33]Gail Kubik, interview with Ralph Titus, Manhattan, Kansas, 1979.

[34]Ibid.

[35]Henry Simon, "Themes and Variations (The OWI and Music)," *PM,* 15 September 1942.

[36]"Today's Profile," *United Press International* (October–November 1942).

[37]Jack Schaindlin, Morris Mamorsky, Arthur Kreutzer, and Gene Forrell also scored OWI films during this time.

[38]*Earthquakers, The Memphis Belle, Air Pattern Pacific,* and *Thunderbolt.*

[39]David Raksin, interview with the author, Los Angeles, California, 16 June 1989.

[40]Thomson, *Virgil Thomson:*393.

[41]Copland and Perlis, *Copland Since 1942:*98.

[42]Ibid.:106.

[43]This score is owned by the Library of Congress and shows the additional material in Copland's hand, along with where it was to be inserted in the original "Main Title" music.

[44]Signed Herm, "Film Reviews," *Variety* (20 April 1949).

[45]Frederick W. Sternfeld, "Kubik's *McBoing Boing* Score," *Film Music Notes* 10/11 (November–December FILL).

[46]David Raksin, interview with the author, 16 June 1989.

CHAPTER 12

The New Tin Pan Alley
1940s Hollywood Looks at American Popular Songwriters

JOHN C. TIBBETTS

When George M. Cohan got an advance peek at the Warner Bros. movie about his life, *Yankee Doodle Dandy* (1942), he exclaimed, "My God, what an act to follow!" As if daunted by the very notion, he died two months later, on 29 May 1942. His astonishment at what Hollywood had wrought was disingenuous. He had conspired with the filmmakers to unleash upon the viewing public not his life, but the life that could have been, or should have been—the kind of life, as his daughter Georgette declared, "Daddy would like to have lived!"[1]

Yankee Doodle Dandy is but one of dozens of Hollywood biopics purporting to tell the story of the great American popular songwriters, from Stephen Foster to the tunesmiths of Tin Pan Alley and the Broadway musical show (see the Appendix to this chapter for a selective listing of classical and popular biopics, 1930–1950). These pictures came in a flood, from roughly the 1930s to the late 1950s, from the major studios like MGM, Columbia, Paramount, Warner Bros., and Twentieth Century-Fox, produced by heavyweights like Arthur Freed, Hal Wallis, and Darryl F. Zanuck. They boasted big budgets, glossy production values, and major stars.

If occasionally they flirted with the truth, more often they careened wildly off into fantasy worlds of their own. For example, *Yankee Doodle Dandy* perpetuated the legend that George M. Cohan was born on the Fourth of July; *Swanee River* (1939) claimed that Stephen Foster (Don Ameche) introduced and sang "My Old Kentucky Home" with E. P. Christy's minstrels; *Stars and Stripes Forever,* that John Philip Sousa (Clifton Webb) wrote "Stars and Stripes Forever" for the Spanish-American

War effort; *Till the Clouds Roll By* (1946), that Jerome Kern (Robert Walker) learned everything he knew from a student of Johannes Brahms; *Words and Music* (1948), that lyricist Lorenz Hart (Mickey Rooney) sang duets with real-life Judy Garland; *Night and Day,* that a battle-scarred Cole Porter (Cary Grant) wrote the title song while convalescing in a World War I hospital; and *Alexander's Ragtime Band* (a thinly disguised biopic of Irving Berlin), that ragtime was introduced and first popularized in 1915 by a White, classically trained violinist.[2] Moreover, in the films there was no trace of Jewish ethnicity in the lives of Gershwin, Kern, and Berlin; no direct references to Cole Porter's homosexuality; and little evidence anywhere that African Americans made any contributions to the shaping of ragtime and jazz.[3]

Ironically, considering the plethora of films touching on the subject, audiences learned little about the workings of Tin Pan Alley. According to the aptly titled *Tin Pan Alley* (1940), which chronicled the career of the fictitious songwriting team of "Harrigan and Calhoun" (John Payne and Jack Oakie), all the song writers were White, Protestant, and in search of beautiful singers to "put over" their tunes.[4] The serious grind of writing, plugging, and publishing songs along the Alley is reduced to the following scrap of dialogue:

QUESTION: What's happening on Tin Pan Alley?
ANSWER: The same old grind: Irving Berlin is still ringing the bell with
    every number.
QUESTION: Is Anna Held still packing them in at the Casino?
ANSWER: Yes, dear; and the Statue of Liberty is still packing them in at
    Bedloe's Island!

As for the nuts and bolts of songwriting, the process apparently consisted merely of the composer accidentally stumbling upon a few musical notes that, in a furious montage of images, he instantly transforms into a full-fledged show number, replete with sumptuous strings, blaring brass, and high-stepping chorines. Success was simply a matter of determination and grit: "When you have something and you know you have it, nothing can keep you down," explains Harrigan.

Apart from an occasional word of praise about the staging and performance of the musical numbers, most critics were appalled. A sampling of contemporary critical responses indicates the nature of their displeasure: *The New Yorker* complained about the "exasperating cliches" and the "foolish attempts to inject synthetic melodrama" into

the life of Jerome Kern.[5] *Time* lamented *Swanee River*'s superficial treatment of the creative urge: "In pictures about composers a vacant look,
head noddings and rhythmic hand flourishes denote musical inspiration."[6] And in the *New York Times* Bosley Crowther's complaints about
Rhapsody in Blue sum up the whole sad business: "There is never any
true clarification of what makes [Gershwin] run, no interior grasp of his
nature, no dramatic continuity to his life. The whole thing unfolds in
fleeting episodes, with characters viewing the genius with anxiety or
awe, and the progression is not helped by many obvious and telescoping
cuts."[7]

Audiences generally took a different, perhaps more enlightened
view, as it were. Even if they knew better, they seem to have willingly
subscribed to these reconstituted versions of history and biography.
Critic Philip T. Hartung was speaking on their behalf in his review of
Rhapsody in Blue: "In spirit the film succeeds in its purpose although the
facts are selected and readjusted for dramatic unity, and characters are
even invented to further the story and action."[8] Of course, film producers
knew just how much they could get away with: They were well aware
that unless the distortions and errors were particularly outrageous, or unless the history in question too recent to be tampered with, most viewers
would accept the Hollywood version of history, even when they knew
better.[9]

If these films had been badly made, if their aggregation of half-
truths, distortions, and outright fabrications had been solely the result of
ignorance on the part of the filmmakers, and if they had told us nothing
of the cultural conditions that produced them, they could be dismissed
outright. Indeed, they—and their more prestige-oriented brothers, the
classical composer biopics—are conspicuously absent from current
books about history and biography on screen.[10] Yet, there are important
reasons for giving them a closer look.

In the first place, it is significant that they were made at the precise
time that the Hollywood studio system was at its height, from approximately 1930 to 1960. Most film historians, notably Thomas Schatz and
David Bordwell, refer to this as the "classical" period, when powerful
producers and supervisors oversaw a "mature-oligopoly," that is, a system where a group of companies co-operated to control the market.
MGM, Paramount, Warner Bros., RKO, Universal, Twentieth Century-
Fox, and Columbia maintained through four decades "a consistent system of production and consumption, a set of formalized creative
practices and constraints, and thus a body of work with a uniform style—

a standard way of telling stories, from camera work and cutting to plot structure and thematics."[11]

Although a minor genre, far fewer in number than other genres, like westerns and horror films, biopics were shaped by the same pressures— the established agendas of producers and writers, the exigencies of the star system, the restrictions of the censorship codes of the Breen Office (reinforced after 1934 by proddings from the Catholic Legion of Decency), and the dictates of marketing research and audience demographics. At the same time, however, biopics stood somewhat apart from the herd in that they deliberately sought to exploit the prestige allure of the "great lives" of statesmen, scientists, entertainers, and artists. In other words, they pretended to be high art while they catered to the lure of popular acceptance. What resulted were sidelong glances, as it were, at history and biography; chronicles not so much of individual realities but of a collective American fantasy of consumer culture, what cultural historian Robert Sklar has refered to as "The Golden Age of Order."[12] Fantasy or not, contends George Custen in his pioneering study of the biopic, it insisted on its own reality: "The Hollywood biography is to history what Caesar's Palace is to architectural history, an enormous, engaging distortion, which after a time convinces us of its own kind of authenticity."[13]

In other words, these biopics may be seen today as not individual biographies so much as contributions toward an American cultural autobiography. As such, they are relevant to an ongoing discussion regarding what has been dubbed "meta-history," or "The New History." Heretofore, a founding presupposition of western historiography has been the opposition of fact and fiction, and the presumed ability of the consumer to differentiate the two. As historian Hayden White has noted, however, we have seen in our time the abolishment of "the taboo against mixing fact with fiction." New genres, in both written and visual form, have appeared, bearing tags like "para-historical representation," "faction," "infotainment," "transgressive history," and "historical metafiction." Movies and biopics like *JFK* (1991), *Schindler's List* (1993), and, most recently at this writing, *Amistad* (1997)—and, of course, all the biopics under consideration here—"fictionalize" to a greater or lesser degree the historical events and characters that serve as their referents in history. In abeyance—as outraged critics and commentators claim—is our ability to distinguish between the real and the imaginary. Everything is presented, explains White, "as if it were of the same ontological order, both real and imaginary—realistically imaginary or imaginarily real."[14]

At the heart of this postmodernist discussion is the rejection of naive assumptions about the "knowability" of the past and the "reliability" of the supposedly objective scholar and historian. All claims to knowledge about past lives and events are inevitably provisional, or partial. Was there ever a time when the facts of an event or a life were presumed to be the meaning of that event or life? Rather, if facts have value at all, they can only deployed in the search for meanings. "What is at issue here," continues White, "is not the facts of the matter regarding such events but the different possible meanings that such facts can be construed as bearing." The best we can do is consider a wide variety of interpretations of "what was really going on" in a given subject.[15] Thus, postmodernist historians are not interested only in history and biography written by professional historians, but also in the more popular conceptions and reconstructions of the past—like the Hollywood biopic. As Robert A. Rosenstone has written in *Revisioning History,* the historical and biographical film "must be taken on its own terms as a portrait of the past that has less to do with fact than with intensity and insight, perception and feeling, with showing how events affect individual lives, past and present. To express the meaning of the past, film creates proximate, appropriate characters, situations, images, and metaphors."[16]

I propose, then, to do just that—to consider these popular composer biopics on their own terms—not to dismiss them as foolish fabrications, but to accept them as fascinating (and, admittedly, frequently hilarious) speculations on the unexpected intersections of biography, media, and culture.

At the outset, I must again insist that these "speculative histories" are the results of willful calculation at every level of the filmmaking process. In the first place, living composers like Irving Berlin, George M. Cohan, Jerome Kern, and Cole Porter, actively participated in the fictionalizing of their lives. Berlin, whom Darryl F. Zanuck regarded as "show business incarnate, his life story the history of popular entertainment," first came to Twentieth Century-Fox in 1936 to write the music for an Alice Faye vehicle *On the Avenue.*[17] It was not a happy experience for him, but it did lead to his being invited to write the scenario for his own life story, *Alexander's Ragtime Band.*

Convinced his life held no real dramatic value, and disinclined to refer to his Jewish background and early experiences at Nigger Mike's on New York's Lower East Side, Berlin fabricated a surrogate personna, "Alexander," a classically trained, WASP clarinetist who scores with the title song in a New Orleans honky-tonk in 1915, makes his way to Broadway, enlists in the Army at the outbreak of World War I, goes to

Camp Upton (where he meets a songwriter named Irving Berlin), and ultimately winds up at Carnegie Hall, where he conducts a symphonic arrangement of "Alexander's Ragtime Band."[18] Fox's production chief, Darryl F. Zanuck, rejected the script, complaining of its lack of a romantic interest (Berlin had omitted references to his two marriages). Discouraged, Berlin withdrew from the writing process, allowing scenarists Kathryn Scola and Lamar Trotti to take over. The story that emerged retained some of Berlin's plot points, but transferred the story's opening to San Francisco's Barbary Coast, cast Tyrone Power as "Alexander," and brought in Alice Faye as the honky-tonk songstress who can't make up her mind between Alexander and his songwriting friend, Charlie Dwyer (Don Ameche). Ironically, Irving Berlin's name, which appears above the title, is referred to only once in the film, when it is seen on the sheet music cover of the title song. The resulting film, directed by Henry King, featured thirty Berlin songs—ranging from the early songs, like the title number, patriotic World War I ditties like "It's Your Country and My Country," 1920s hits like "A Pretty Girl Is Like a Melody," and the 1938 present with new Berlin songs, like "Walking Stick" and "Now It Can Be Told" (composed especially for Alice Faye)—cost $2 million, and received six Academy Award nominations. *Alexander's Ragtime Band* was the closest Berlin ever got to a biopic of his own.[19]

George M. Cohan also had no hesitation in altering his own life story. By 1941 Cohan, who had not written a musical play on Broadway since 1928, and who had been unsuccessful in his foray into early talkies, was hungry for a comeback.[20] But he still had enough clout that when he signed a contract with Warner Bros. for a musical biography, he stipulated that he retain script approval and that James Cagney play his part. Like Berlin, Cohan wished to avoid anything too close to his private life and personal obsessions—in this case, his rabid anti-unionism (his bitter opposition to the Actors Equity Strike of 1919), his two marriages (to Ethel Levey and Agnes Nolan), bitter battles with critics, and so on. He rejected a preliminary script by Robert Buckner, who, after many hours of interviews and conversations, thought he had wrought a fairly credible storyline. Cohan insisted instead on fabricating everything. He sat down and wrote a two hundred–page screenplay of his own, which removed most of the domestic details and created a fictional girl friend, "Agnes," whom he meets after his retirement from the stage. Now it was Cagney and producer Hal Wallis's turn to be dissatisfied at what they felt to be a humorless script with no real love interest. A letter was immediately dispatched to Cohan. Dated 21 April 1941, it affords a revealing glimpse into the machinations behind the crafting of a Hollywood biopic:

> We do not wish to make your domestic life the main theme of the picture, but it is such an important and essential part of a man's life that its complete exclusion is very likely to result in an unbalanced story.
>
> We are willing to follow any questions which you may have on this problem, either to ignore it completely or else to represent it as you wish. We could eliminate any reference to your first wife and depict only your present wife. If possible, we would like to include the children. . . . As I said, we are completely willing and anxious to fit our story to your own personal wishes, and if you should disapprove of any representation of your family life, we will forget it at once.[21]

Eventually, a compromise story was hammered out, in which were added a composite sweetheart-wife named "Mary" (Joan Leslie), a moving death scene for Jerry Cohan (Walter Huston), and some anecdotal details (such as a meeting with Eddie Foy, portrayed by Eddie Foy, Jr.). Counterpointing these fictions were the authentic recreations by Cagney and vaudevillians William Collier and Johnny Boyle of the staging of the classic *Peck's Bad Boy* and routines from *Little Johnny Jones,* including "Give My Regards to Broadway." The framing device of a meeting with President Roosevelt—like the flag-waving patriotism of the "Grand Old Flag" number—was directly calculated to bolster the morale of audiences still recovering from the shock of Pearl Harbor (see Figure 12.1).[22]

When Jerome Kern was approached by MGM, he balked. He had guarded his private life from the public too long to readily consent to such an idea. Besides, he quipped, his relatively dull life would not be an interesting subject. "If you tell the truth," he said, "it'll be the dullest picture in the world."[23] When the studio executives persisted, Kern finally granted permission, but with the stipulation that his story be largely fictitious, confining itself to a few well-known anecdotes. Writers Guy Bolton and George Wells took him at his word.[24]

In his negotiations for the scripting of *Night and Day,* Cole Porter willingly signed away his rights to a factually accurate account. Encouraged by his wife and mother, Porter agreed to a contract that stipulated that "it is understood that Producers in the development of the story . . . upon which the photoplay shall be based shall be free to dramatize, fictionalize, or emphasize any or all incidents in the life of the Seller, or

Figure 12.1. *Yankee Doodle Dandy* (Warner Bros. 1941) starred Jimmy Cagney as George M. Cohan. In this scene, Cagney recreates a number from Cohan's show *Little Johnny Jones*.

interpolate such incidents as Producers may deem necessary in order to obtain a treatment of continuity of commercial value."[25]

He had his reasons. This not only cleared the way for a strapping Cary Grant and a youthful, elegant Alexis Smith to play the diminutive, balding Porter and his older wife, Linda, but it provided Porter the opportunity to construct a movie "life" that could confirm the public image he so avidly sought. After all, he never had been averse to fictionalizing his own life; and he had already expended considerable energy in embellishing and embroidering it. "Considering the numerous fibs about himself that Cole had foisted on an unsuspecting public for decades," writes biographer Charles Schwartz, "one could hardly expect a Hollywood film biography to come any closer to the truth."[26]

Problematic as far as Hollywood was concerned, for example, were inconvenient realities such as the substantial inheritance that allowed Porter a life of relative ease, his many extramarital affairs, his indulgence in the New York-Paris-Beverly Hills cafe society, and career successes that had come to him easily. Accordingly, producer Wallis ordered that the script depict scenes suggesting Porter's solid work ethic, sturdy individuality, and romantic attachment to Linda. This "new" Porter now bravely rejects his grandfather's support, declaring, "I can't come back here and live on your money and all the time wonder what would've happened if I'd gone out on my own." Later, adrift in Tin Pan Alley and on Broadway, Porter lives hand to mouth while struggling to get his shows produced. Then, after the outbreak of World War I interrupts the run of his show, *See America First* ("I guess it was just one of those things," the disappointed Porter muses meaningfully as he emerges from the darkened theater), he enlists in the French Army and is wounded during an enemy artillery barrage. Coming to his rescue is his wife-to-be, Linda, who just so happens to be serving as a nurse in the hospital, and who immediately assists him in writing "Night and Day."

The subsequent rifts in the marriage with Linda are to be explained away not by Cole's lusts for other partners but by his all-consuming obsession with his musical shows. "You shouldn't have gotten married in the first place," scolds Porter's friend, Monte Woolley (played by himself). "In the second place, as long as you did, act like a husband instead of a guy who shouldn't have gotten married in the first place!" As for the riding accident in 1937 that disabled Porter for the rest of his life, even Hollywood couldn't have devised anything more appropriate to its purposes. Here was the ideal opportunity to confirm his nobility and strength of character. In all the foregoing ways, insisted Wallis, Porter and his work could be seen as "springing from the heart of a normal American homelife."[27]

But the biggest problem still had to be addressed: Porter's sexuality. Specifically, Porter was gay in an era when "coming out of the closet" was tantamount to professional suicide. He had carried on the pretense of an active heterosexual public life while maintaining an actively gay private life. Moreover, his marriage to Linda was probably a marriage of mutual convenience, as she purportedly carried on lesbian affairs on her own.[28] The subject of homosexuality, if not exactly forbidden by the Motion Picture Production Code, was certainly discouraged.[29] Thus, it was in Porter's best interests to support Wallis' determination to "normalize" his sexuality. If Porter were forbidden by the script to look at another woman, now he was also abjured not to look at another man. As the script tap dances around these issues, the effect is occasionally rather comic, intended or otherwise. Witness this exchange between Porter and a singer in a sheet music store:

GIRL: I work with lots of piano players. They make propositions. They're always trying. You haven't made a single pass. You treat me as if I were a lady. Frankly, Mr. Porter, I resent it!

PORTER: I never realized. Here, have a sandwich.

GIRL: I know I've got natural attributes. I'll be frank, Mr. Porter, you've got natural attributes, too. Seems a shame we can't "attribute" with each other.

PORTER. You're extremely attractive, Carol. But you're not eating your sandwich.

Just as the composers themselves could not be counted upon to safe-guard the historical accuracy of their lives, their friends, admirers, and associates were no more trustworthy. Their admiration for their subjects amounted to reverence, and it derailed any possibility of a factually responsible account. The opening title card of *Till the Clouds Roll By* pretty well sums up the process as well as the attitude:

> This story of Jerome Kern is best told in the bars and measures, the quarter and grace notes of his music—that music that sings so eloquently his love of people, love of country, love of life. We who have sung it and will sing it to our children can only be grateful that he gave his life to music—and gave that music to us."

The scenarist of *Rhapsody in Blue* was Sonya Levien, who had worked with Gershwin in Hollywood and had been a good friend during his last days.[30] Co-starring in the cast was Oscar Levant, who portrayed himself and who provided the keyboard support on the soundtrack.[31] The producer of *Till the Clouds Roll By,* Arthur Freed, and the writer, Guy Bolton, were both longtime admirers and associates of Kern. Bolton had been a friend and collaborator with Kern since 1915, when they began their run of the legendary Princess Theatre shows. Freed was a Tin Pan Alley graduate himself, an accomplished lyricist who had been with MGM since 1929, writing such memorable hits as "Singin' in the Rain" and "You Are My Lucky Star." Freed had known Kern since 1917, when they met during the run of *Oh, Boy!* It was Freed who first approached Kern about the possibility of bringing his life to the screen. Later, after Kern's death, Freed assured his widow, Eva, "Jerry Kern was always an ideal of perfection to me, as an artist, as a showman and as a friend."[32] Freed and Bolton also collaborated on *Words and Music*. Their contract with Richard Rodgers and the estate of the late Lorenz Hart granted them script approval.[33]

Quite apart from the censorial restrictions of the Motion Picture Production Code and the donning by composers and their acolytes of self-
protective camouflage, these biopics also were the direct results of the
very structure and purpose of the aforementioned Hollywood studio system as it existed in the years 1925–1960.

In many respects Hollywood and Tin Pan Alley were joined at the
hip. Since the beginning of the nineteenth century, both had been partici-
pating in the fashioning of an indigenous, nationally homogenous culture—"reinventing America," as today's parlance would have it. Both, in
their beginnings, were centered in New York City. Both were shaped and
dominated by foreign-born and first-generation Jews in a hurry to assimilate themselves into the American mainstream.[34] And both developed
efficient systems for the mass production and distribution of their prod-
ucts—powerful publishing houses established and guided by the likes of
Jerome Remick, Max Dreyfus, and Isidore Witmark; and monolithic
movie studios—vertically integrated structures controlling movies' production, distribution, and exhibition—organized by men like Adolph
Zukor, Louis B. Mayer, and William Fox.

These entrepreneurs shared in common an understanding of public
taste, an expertise in merchandising and marketing stemming from their
backgrounds in sales and retail, and, as the 1930s wore on, a willingness
to promote a "mainstream" American fantasy that had little to do with
the contemporary realities and controversies of labor unrest, Depression
woes, women's issues, sex and violence, and racial and/or ethnic problems. Even if these entrepreneurs themselves were barred from the "real
corridors of gentility and status in an America still fraught with anti-
Semitism," as cultural historian Neal Gabler states in his *An Empire of
Their Own: How the Jews Invented Hollywood,* they could fashion in
their songs and in their films "a new country—an empire of their own, so
to speak. . . . They would create its values and myths, its traditions and
archetypes."[35] A cultural language was evolving that became common
currency all across the nation, the result of the "commingling" of disparate and ethnic influences that Dvořák had predicted in 1893—of high
and low culture, Old World classicism and New World multiculturalism.[36] It appropriated them all but remained bound to none.[37]

The biopic genre played its own part in this process. Almost three
hundred biopics were released by the eight major Hollywood studios—
MGM, Paramount, RKO, Warner Bros., Twentieth Century-Fox, Columbia, United Artists, Universal—during the classical Hollywood period,
roughly 1930 to 1960. Warners and Fox were the leading producers.
One-sixth of that total are biographies of either classical or popular

composers (as well as a good number of concert and stage enter-tainers).[38]

Although popular composers hardly offered movie producers the kind of "prestige" value afforded by their classical brethren, they did possess something just as important—and perhaps comparable—to audiences in the 1930s and 1940s, the aura of money and success. The year after he published "Alexander's Ragtime Band," for example, Berlin's royalties amounted to more than $100,000; and a decade later he was worth $4 million dollars. In their peak years during the 1930s, Porter and Rodgers and Hart each earned more than $500,000 annually from their songs alone. Kern was wealthy enough to pursue his passion for rare book collecting, amassing libraries worth millions. Gershwin enjoyed a lifestyle that rivaled that of the movie stars whose company he cultivated.

Furthermore, according to Edward Pessen in his recent study of Tin Pan Alley songs, about eighty-five percent of them were about love. Hollywood, always preoccupied with romance, took notice. These were songs of a smarter, at times more worldly cast than the earlier sentimental effusions of songwriters like Victor Herbert and Reginald De Koven. While the tunes and lyrics thus paid a certain lip service to the realities of Depression and wartime America, they also offered the solace of a carefree optimism and occasional loving, backward glance at a simpler, rural past.[39]

Yet, significantly, beyond their high profiles, the Tin Pan Alley composers were, as far as the general public was concerned, vague figures hidden in the shadow of their music, who led lives more fraught with hard work than dramatic incident. As far as Hollywood was concerned, this was as it should be.[40] Filmmakers could recast them into any desired shape, creating a contrapuntal weave of fact and fiction, frequently sacrificing biographical detail to the music itself.

The films themselves reveal striking similarities. Most of them are set between the years 1865 and 1920. The composers are a fresh-faced lot, young, handsome, and dreadfully in earnest—indeed, they seem to be distantly related members of the same family. They are either born in humble circumstances and yearn for the big city, or they come from an urban environment and long for a simpler, rural life. Though gifted with the knack of popular songwriting, they restlessly yearn for classical training and legitimacy. Just to get established, they opt for the former. Once established, however, career setbacks (quirks of fate, a weakness to drink, an ill-starred romance, or just plain overwork) trigger a sentimental backward glance at their classical ideals. Somewhere in all this, there is a Great Love, a girl of exceptional qualities, who is left behind in the composers' desire to work themselves to death. It is only when they reject the siren song of High Art, accept their status as spokespersons for the masses, and reunite with their Great Love, that they realize the true value of their genius and their manhood.

Swanee River, the first in chronological order of production, establishes the essential paradigm.[41] Stephen Foster (Don Ameche) is a struggling composer torn between the inspiration of the chants of the black stevedores working on the docks of Louisville, Kentucky—"It's—it's music from the heart, from the heart of a simple people . . . by jingo! the only real American contribution to music"—and the desire, supported by his old music teacher, Professor Kleber (Felix Brassart), to write classical music. Against his parent's wishes, he leaves his desk job and pursues a career in music (see Figure 12.2).

But while his "Negro songs" find favor with minstrel man E. P. Christy (Al Jolson) and popular audiences, his Suite for chamber ensemble is a crashing failure. Foster and Kleber both learn a lesson. "Stephen can write American folk songs," opines Kleber, "but classical composi-

Figure 12.2. Stephen Foster (Don Ameche) teams up with E. P. Christy (Al Jolson) in *Swanee River* (Fox 1939).

tion needs another kind of training. I don't want to see a first-class Stephen Foster turned into a tenth-rate Beethoven." Now estranged from his wife, Jeanie, Foster relocates to New York, where more rejections and loneliness lead him to indulge his "weakness" (the film's euphemism for his alcoholism). He dies, but not before he fulfills his true genius by returning to the wellsprings of his art and writing "Old Black Joe" for a dying black servant (and not before he reunites for a few last moments with the beloved Jeanie). We are left with the assurance that his musical legacy is secure when a performance of "Old Folks at Home" brings tears to the eyes of a concert audience.

Of course, most of this is nonsense. Despite the efforts of the Fox research department, writers John Tainter Foote and Philip Dunne ended up rewriting everything.[42] The film reveals the lengths producer Darryl F. Zanuck and his ilk would go to rework the clay of a particular genius into a shape recognizable to their mass audiences. Yes, genius must be normalized and chastened if it pursues elitest tendencies, ignores the needs of the common folk, and rejects romance for the sake of career ambitions. And yes, the distressing realities of the African American slave experience must be replaced with a more cozy and comforting series of outrageously patronizing and (perhaps unintended) racist stereotypes. In the meantime, the whole thing is bound together and summed up by a "theme song," a *Leitmotif,* as it were—in this case, the song that Foster wrote in tribute to his wife, "Jeanie with the Light Brown Hair."[43]

Like Foster, the other composers represented here also are portrayed as being bedeviled by ill-advised elitest ambitions that jeopardize their true populist calling. You can almost sense a Hollywood scenarist off in the wings, shaking his finger reprovingly at such temerity: What'll the folks in the audience say?

Thus, when Cohan in *Yankee Doodle Dandy* fails in his ambitious attempt to write a dramatic, nonmusical play, he becomes the laughing-stock of Broadway; and only when he publicly denounces his own show does he regain his artistic balance. In *Alexander's Ragtime Band* Alexander's High Art pretensions are rebuked by the saloon singer, Stella (Alice Faye): "Maybe I don't know the tripe they play up Snob Hill, but I know what they like down here; and that's more than you'll ever know." (See Figure 12.3.) Subsequently, a dutifully chastened Alexander reunites with Stella after shrewdly blending the best of both worlds by dressing up ragtime in symphonic clothes for a Carnegie Hall concert. In the first attempt by Gershwin (Robert Alda) to write a "Negro Opera," "Blue Monday Blues," for a George White's Scandals revue, it is soundly rejected as audience members leave in boredom and confusion. Publisher

Figure 12.3. In *Alexander's Ragtime Band* (Fox 1938), Alice Fay is Stella Kirby, the love interest for "Alexander" (Tyrone Power), a thinly disguised version of Irving Berlin.

Max Dreyfus (Charles Coburn) grumbles, "Gershwin must have lost his mind." Even the more sympathetic Paul Whiteman (played by himself) advises, "George, it's great, but it doesn't belong in this kind of a show." Elsewhere in the film, none other than Maurice Ravel is on hand to remind Gershwin of the real genius of his populist, vernacular gifts. His words are an echo of Kleber's in *Swanee River*: "Gershwin, if you study with me, you'll only write second-rate Ravel instead of first-rate Gershwin. . . . Tell me, how did you get your inspiration for your rhythm?"[44]

In *Words and Music* the usually effervescent Larry Hart (Mickey Rooney) goes into a funk whenever he falls in love and tries to write serious romantic lyrics. When asked by partner Richard Rodgers (Tom Drake) about his problem, Hart replies: "No more love songs, that's all, Just those fast, bright things from here on in." Later, Hart confesses sardonically, "I'm just a guy that writes lyrics, runs away, hides, has a few laughs, comes back and writes . . . lyrics." In *Stars and Stripes Forever* John Philip Sousa abandons writing art songs when he finds out that one particularly mournful effusion, "My Love Is a Weeping Willow," comes off better when quickened into march tempo and retitled "Semper Fidelis." Later, a newly enlightened Sousa proclaims, "Our job, our only job will be to put on a good show. Which means that if our audiences prefer 'Turkey in the Straw' to 'Parsifal,' we'll play 'Turkey in the Straw'."

In *Till the Clouds Roll By,* Kern (Robert Walker) is congratulated by none other than Victor Herbert (Paul Maxey) for his populist musical achievement: "You've got a song to sing. Look down at that city, Jerry. It's made up of millions of people. And music has played a part in all their lives. Lullabies, love songs, hymns, anthems." A misty-eyed Kern replies, "It makes me feel grateful, and very humble." (Even the cab driver, to whom Kern tells his life story, pronounces his admiration for *Show Boat:* "That was a swell show!") (See Figure 12.4.) The worst comeuppance, of course, is reserved for the snootiest songwriter of them all, Cole Porter in *Night and Day*: When Porter disdains the "people's music"—"I'm fed up with the riverboats, honky-tonks, and music counters"—his wife deserts him, his friends disappear, and he suffers a terrible riding accident. Later, suffering brings him enlightenment, and, after writing "Don't Fence Me In" for Roy Rogers, he returns to hearth, home, and songwriting.[45]

Sharing in the songwriters' comeuppance are their Old-World mentors. We've already met the model of this character, Stephen Foster's teacher, Professor Kleber.[46] In *Alexander's Ragtime Band* the wholly fictitious Professor Heinrich (Jean Hersholt) monitors the performances of his classically trained violinist pupil "Alexander" with this stern advice: "You did very well, my boy, but your pizzicato, we still have to work on it." Later, however, when Alexander gives a ragtime concert in Carnegie Hall—the newspaper headline reads, "POPULAR MUSIC OUT TO WIN HIGHBROW RECOGNITIONS"—an enlightened Heinrich occupies a box seat and nods his approval. In *Rhapsody in Blue* it's Professor

Figure 12.4. Jerome Kern was the subject of MGM's *Till The Clouds Roll By* (1946). From left: Robert Walker as Kern, Judy Garland as Marilyn Miller, and Paul Langston as Oscar Hammerstein II.

Otto Franck, a former pupil of Johannes Brahms, who potters among the busts and paintings of Schubert and Beethoven and disapproves of young Gershwin's attempts to "improve on the classics" with jazzy riffs. Eventually he gives way to the grudging acceptance of his pupil's true calling: "I have such hope for you, my boy," he confesses finally. "America is a growing country, a mixture of things that are very old with more that is new. Your nature has the same contradictions, ideals and material ambition. If you can make them both serve, you will give America a voice." On his death bed, Professor Franck listens to the radio broadcast of George's *Rhapsody in Blue,* after which he dutifully expires.[47]

In *Till the Clouds Roll By* an academically trained composer and arranger named "James Hessler" (Van Heflin) takes one look at his new pupil, Jerome Kern, and declares: "The trouble with you songwriters is that all you ever think about is making money. You never think about doing anything big or worthwhile. . . . No, all you fellows want to do is write sugary little tunes and make a lot of money." He changes his tune, so to speak, in the face of Kern's genius, and, after abandoning his Symphony, collaborates with him on his musical shows. Finally, on his death bed, Hessler confesses to Kern: "You were writing the real music, the folk music of America. Thanks, Jerry, for letting me stick around." Gasping his last, Hessler whispers, "It looks like a time for strings"; and the film's soundtrack obediently wells up in a funereal burst of string music.[48]

Even if other biopics don't feature a mentor figure like Heinrich, Kleber, Franck, and Hessler, there is always the implication of one. For example, in *Night and Day* Monte Woolley (who plays a Yale professor inexplicably named "Monte Woolley") fits the professorial model; and in *Stars and Stripes Forever* a bearded, monocled Clifton Webb (who looks for all the world like he strayed in from the latest "Mr. Belvedere" picture) does double duty, alternately functioning as a March King and a High Art Counselor.

Issues of gender, racial and ethnic identity were problematic in the Tin Pan Alley biopic. The peak studio years in Hollywood, as we have seen, contributed to a collective fantasy on screen wherein they were conspicuously absent. For example, as we have seen, Foster's Jeanie, Porter's Linda, "Alexander's" Stella, and Kern's Eva, and so on, were women who were present mostly to perform the songs and/or provide their men with inspiration and support (except when they were chiding them for neglecting domestic duties for professional goals). They were never professional composers in their own right.[49]

If Hispanics, Jews, Native Americans, African Americans, and other minorities and people of color appeared, they were, with few exceptions, secondary characters (like servants, maids, and other "faithful family retainers")—caricatures that served as the targets of stereotyped humor. This was not just true of the songwriters' biopics, but of Hollywood movies in general during these years. One looks in vain for a trace of Jewish heritage evident in the portraits of Berlin, Kern, Hart, and Gershwin.

The situation with African American characters and culture was particularly problematic. With the exception of *St. Louis Blues* (1958), a biopic about W. C. Handy, these biopics give no indication that there were any Black publishers or composers on the Alley, or that White composers benefited from connections and/or affiliations with them.[50] "Hollywood during the depression provided few new opportunities for blacks," writes Thomas Cripps in *Slow Fade to Black: The Negro in American Film*. "[They] were represented only by memorable bits in films not really dealing with their needs or problems."[51] During these years, for example, there were only twelve biopics made about nonwhite

Americans, and only one was about a Black composer, *St. Louis Blues* (1958).

On those rare occasions when African Americans do appear, they merely serve as a kind of obbligato to the main action, as in *Swanee River*, when they provide musical cues for Foster's writing of "Oh! Susanna" and "Old Black Joe"; and in *Stars and Stripes Forever*, when they dutifully obey Sousa's injunction to accompany him in a performance of "Battle Hymn of the Republic."[52] This sort of appropriation of Black culture by a White consumer class is spelled out in no uncertain terms in *Till the Clouds Roll By*: In the Prologue, a Black performer, Caleb Peterson, sings "Ol' Man River" with a simple, and moving dignity. But in the Finale a white-garbed Frank Sinatra takes over the song: Standing atop a white pillar, surrounded by a vast pink-and-white art deco set and a bevy of leggy chorines, young Frankie belts out the song in his smoothest crooner's manner (endowing the words "*jest* keeps rolling along" with a little too much emphasis). Critic James Agee was appalled by this White Apotheosis, objecting to its "misplaced reverence," as if it were a musical translation of the Emancipation Proclamation: "This I realize is called feeling for music; for that kind of feeling I prefer W. C. Fields' cadenza on the zither."[53]

More difficult to classify are those occasions when the viewer can't precisely determine a performer's racial identity. There was nothing accidental about this feat of Hollywood sleight-of-hand. The staging of the "Blue Monday Blues" number in *Rhapsody in Blue,* utilizes a whole complement of dancers and singers who are dressed and made up in a manner carefully calculated to keep viewers guessing about their racial identity.[54] And in *Stormy Weather,* an all-Black musical revue purporting to chronicle the career of legendary Black tap dancer Bill "Bojangles" Robinson, skin color seems to be relatively irrelevant to the plot. At first glance this twenty-five-year survey of African American music might seem to be the Black alternative to *Alexander's Ragtime Band*. On closer inspection, however, the two films display not only a resemblance, but a similarity that borders on exact identity. As film historian Gerald Mast has pointed out, with the exception of Fats Waller's gutsy rendition of "Ain't Misbehavin,' "black life and entertainment look no different from white life and entertainment in the Fox films that survey the same turf with the same plot."[55] Most of the music numbers "take the high white road," in Mast's words, like those featuring Cab Calloway in his trademark white tails, the Nicholas Brothers in their impeccable tuxedos, the Katherine Dunham Dancers in their stylish ballet, and a light-skinned Lena Horne in her "I Can't Give You Anything But Love" number.[56]

Creative processes, too, had to be presented in a manner consistent with the biopic paradigm—that is, they had to be normalized and rendered understandable to the average viewer. The long hours of training in composition, harmony, and instrumentation seemed to play little part in the process. A favorite Hollywood ploy was to place the composer in a setting whose sights and sounds could be counted upon to stimulate a creative response, provoking in the inspired artist a sort of musical "automatic writing." "Every time I pick up a law book," explains Cole Porter to his mother, "I hear a tune. Every contract I read turns into a lyric. I don't know how it happens or where it comes from. But there it is." After listening to the chants of Black slaves unloading a merchant ship, Stephen Foster rushes into a saloon to bang out "Oh! Susanna" on the piano.[57]

When Cohan hears a trumpet call at a World War I rally, "Over There!" is instantly born. In a burst of imaginative reconstruction, Jerome Kern's scenarists depict him writing "Ol' Man River" while in Memphis, his interior monologue accompanying his nocturnal walk along the banks of the Mississippi River:

> "I walked along the river that night, with the river wind in my face and the taste of it on my lips. And I stood there, listening. The sudden excitement was thrilling to me, listening to the song of a river that makes its way right through the heart of America. and the voice of that river was the laughter, the tears, the joys, the sorrows, the hopes of all Americans."[58]

And, in a similar situation, John Philip Sousa strides the deck of a ship under foggy night skies, musing to himself:

> Suddenly, as I paced the deck, I began to sense the rhythmic beat of a band playing in my head, ceaselessly, echoing and re-echoing the most distinct melody. Though I did not know it then, my brain band was composing my most popular march—not one note of which, once I had transferred it to paper, would ever be changed.[59]

In *Tin Pan Alley* Jack Oakie spends most of his screen time trying to fashion lyrics to a catchy tune. Determined that the words should refer to a geographical place name, he tries a variety of two- and three-syllable options, including "Dixie," "Hawaii," "Ireland," "Australia," and "Bermuda" ("Bermuda, lovely Bermuda, where the onions and the lilies scent the air"). It's not until near the end of the film, when our frustrated lyricist stumbles over the name of his pal's girl friend, "Katie," that the song achieves its final, familiar form: "K-K-K-Katie."[60] Lest we dismiss this example of fortuitous biassociation as just another Hollywood hallucination, we should remember that more than one song standard has evolved under similar circumstances.[61] (See Figure 12.5.)

By far the most elaborate and (in this writer's opinion, at least) beautifully crafted creative "reconstruction" in these films—at least in a cinematic sense—are two set pieces in *Night and Day* and *Rhapsody in Blue*. In the first, Porter is convalescing from wartime wounds in a French hospital (as explained earlier, a wholly fictitious scene). A high-angle shot reveals him in his dressing gown sitting at the piano, his cane resting against the bench, a clock ticking audibly in the stillness. Absently, he strikes a note on the keyboard. He repeats it. When the clock interrupts and strikes the hour, he imitates the sound in the bass register. As if in a trance, he speaks: "Like the tick-tick-tock of the stately clock as it stands against the wall." A pause. Rain spatters against the window. Porter

Figure 12.5. Any resemblance Fox's *Tin Pan Alley* (1940), starring John Payne and Alice Faye, had to the real Tin Pan Alley was purely coincidental. All photos courtesy Wade Williams Productions.

touches the keys again, intoning, "Like the drip-drip-drop of the rain-drops when the summer shower is through. So a voice within me keeps repeating—you, you, you!" His hands sweep across the keyboard. At that moment his wife-to-be, Linda, enters the room and turns out the lights. Seating herself beside him, she joins in and declaims: "Night and day—." He instantly finishes the phrase: "—You are the one." Another pause. He murmurs to her, "It's giving me much trouble." They chat a few moments as he fiddles with the tune. Impulsively he kisses her. He unexpectedly modulates the phrase and exclaims, "Wait a minute! I think I've got it!" The music swells up on the background music track, fully in-strumented, as the camera retreats up and away from the scene.[62]

Gershwin's creation of his famous *American in Paris* transpires thus: It's a bright morning and the composer is seated in his Paris apartment, listening through the open window to the street sounds below. A car horn blares. Gershwin goes to the piano and taps out the three-note phrase. Without a pause, he leans forward and inscribes the title, *An American in Paris,* on the music paper. As the now fully instrumented music wells up on the soundtrack, the scene dissolves to a train station. A montage of shots, seen from the subjective point of view, follows the arrival of a trav-eler, the transfer of his bags (labeled "G. G.") to a waiting taxi, and a drive through the streets and boulevards. Cut to Gershwin's studio (the time is later in the day). The composer gestures with his hands, as if conducting the soundtrack orchestra. Dissolve to a view of Notre Dame as the music's mood grows more stately. Again, from the subjective point of view, our traveler alights from the cab and enters a hotel lobby, where he signs the register "George Gershwin." Cut to a street scene as the trumpet wails its memorably bluesy melody while we amble past an outdoor cafe. Cut to a ballet performance as the trumpet theme shifts to the strings (Gershwin's shadow is thrown against the wall of his box seat). Cut back to Gershwin's studio again: It's twilight now, and the composer has left the piano to stand at the window. Cut to Paris again, the Folies Bergère as the raucous brass theme accompanies a line of high-kicking dancers. Cut to streams of water flowing along a brick pavement. Cut back to Gershwin's studio as he signs his name to the music. Cut to a concert hall where Walter Damrosch conducts the finale. The sequence, which roughly follows the programatic notes that Deems Taylor and Gershwin wrote for the work's premiere, is a masterly example of image and sound editing and prefig-ures the music videos of today.[63]

In conclusion, I said at the outset that as these biopics partake of what today is called a "metahistorical" speculation about the elusive meanings of biography and historical events, so, too, do they engage the knowing viewer in an amusing game of "peek-a-boo" with fact and fiction. It's a game most of us willingly subscribe to. An amusing example in *Words and Music* demonstrates the point. Larry Hart (Mickey Rooney) throws a lavish party in his Hollywood estate ("Who built this place, Metro-Goldwyn-Mayer?" he quips). Among the attendees is Judy Garland, appearing as herself. Immediately, she and Hart launch into a song-and-dance rendition of "I Wish I Were in Love Again." Think about it. It's not so much that Hart and Garland probably never danced together (that's a justifiable quibble, but hardly an important consideration). Rather, remember that this 1948 film has situated this particular scene in the mid-1930s. Judy Garland would have been a child of thirteen, up past her bedtime. But we accept the scene because we know she's not dancing with Larry Hart but with Mickey Rooney. This is a "reality" that overrides the fictive "reality," because we've seen them perform so many times together in previous films (made for MGM, of course). The moment even acquires a special poignancy when we realize it was to be the last time they were to appear together on screen.

What is it to be: The lives that late these songwriters have led (to paraphrase a Cole Porter song); or, as we saw at the outset with George M. Cohan, the lives they would wish to have lived? When these worlds collide, we're hard put to identify the results.

It's always a tough choice. My best advice is to follow the immortal Yogi Berra's advice, "When you come to a fork in the road, take it!"

NOTES

[1]Quoted in Fred Andersen, "My God, What an Act to Follow!" *American Heritage* (July–August 1997):74.

[2]For the record—*Yankee Doodle Dandy:* Despite Cohan's persistent assertions to the contrary, his birth certificate states that he was born on 3 July 1878.

Swanee River: It is doubtful that Foster ever met Christy. Moreover, while actor Don Ameche might sing beautifully in public, composer Foster's almost terminal shyness prohibited him from such displays. See Ken Emerson, *Doo-Dah! Stephen Foster and the Rise of American Popular Culture* (New York: Simon and Schuster, 1997):102.

Stars and Stripes Forever: The title song was written in 1896, before the outbreak of the Spanish-American War. Sousa himself claimed he wrote it after receiving the news of the death of his manager. See Paul E. Bierley, *The Works of John Philip Sousa* (Columbus, OH: Integrity Press, 1984):85.

Till the Clouds Roll By: Kern's teacher, one "James Hessler," has no basis in fact. The *New Yorker* critic at the time dismissed this fiction sarcastically: "Maybe Guy Bolton, who cooked up the story on which the film is based, confused Hessler with Marie Dressler, for whom Kern was once accompanist, but it doesn't seem likely." See "Well, the Songs Are Good," *The New Yorker* 22 (14 December 1946):88.

Words and Music: As this paper later demonstrates, Judy Garland would have been only thirteen at the time of the alleged incident with Larry Hart.

Night and Day: Biographer Charles Schwarz asserts that while little is known about Porter's wartime activities in France, it is probable that he never served in the American Army or the French Foreign Legion, as he alleged, nor did he sustain any war-related injuries. See Charles Schwartz, *Cole Porter* (New York: Da Capo Press, 1979):45–48.

Alexander's Ragtime Band: Ragtime had peaked and waned as a national craze long before 1915. As for its introduction to the general public, Edward A. Berlin reports in his biography of Scott Joplin that ragtime "surfaced from its incipient stages in black communities and became known to the wider American public" during the World's Columbian Exposition in Chicago in 1893. See Edward A. Berlin, *King of Ragtime: Scott Joplin and His Era* (New York: Oxford University Press, 1994):11–12.

[3]Unavailable for screening, unfortunately, is an exception to this, a biopic about W. C. Handy, *St. Louis Blues* (Paramount, 1958), starring Nat King Cole. It is the only songwriting biopic from the studio era about a Black composer. Since I have not seen it, and since little information is available about it, I am forced to refer to it in only general terms.

[4]Songs attributed to the fictitious "Harrigan and Calhoun" include "K-K-K-Katie," composed by Geoffrey O'Hara in 1918; "America I Love You," by Edgar Leslie and Archie Gottler in 1915; and "Good-Bye Broadway, Hello France!" by Francis Reisner and Billy Baskette in 1917.

[5]"Well, the Songs Are Good," *The New Yorker* 22 (14 December 1946):88.

[6]"*Swanee River,*" *Time* (15 January 1940):62.

[7]Bosley Crowther, "*Rhapsody in Blue,*" *New York Times* (28 June 1945):22.

[8]Philip T. Hartung, "Fascinating Rhythms," *Commonweal* 42 (6 July 1945):286.

[9]Darryl F. Zanuck allegedly remarked: "No one, in my opinion, will ever pin us down to dates except the later dates in the past two or three years which are clearly remembered." Quoted in George Custen, *The Bio/Pic: How Hollywood Constructed Public History* (New Brunswick, New Jersey: Rutgers University Press, 1992):37–38.

[10]For an overview of classical music biopics, see my "The Lyre of Light," *Film Comment* 28/1 (January–February 1992):66–73. A useful overview of the biopics of Ken Russell, a preeminent figure in the field, is Robert Phillip Kolker, "Ken Russell's Biopics," *Film Comment* 9/3 (May 1973):42–45. As far as popular composer biopics are concerned, it is indeed strange that, aside from several references to the subject in the aforementioned *Bio/Pic* by Custen, none of the many book-length volumes that have appeared in the last twenty years investigating issues of history and biography on film has devoted any attention to the subject.

[11]The quotation is from pp. 8–9 from Thomas Schatz, *The Genius of the System* (New York: Pantheon Books, 1988). See also David Bordwell, Janet Staiger, and Kristin Thompson, *The Classical Hollywood Cinema: Film Style & Mode of Production to 1960* (New York: Columbia University Press, 1985).

[12]For one of the finest and most lucid examinations of this period, see Robert Sklar, *Movie-Made America: How the Movies Changed American Life* (New York: Random House, 1975):175–214.

[13]Custen, *Bio/Pics:*7.

[14]Hayden White, "The Modernist Event," in *The Persistence of History: Cinema, Television, and the Modern Event,* ed. Vivian Sobchack (New York: Routledge, 1996):18–24.

[15]White, "the Modernist Event":21.

[16]*Revisioning History: Film and the Construction of a New Past,* ed. Robert Rosenstone (Princeton, New Jersey: Princeton University Press, 1995):7. A pioneering collection of articles pertinent to these issues by writers Robert Brent Toplin, John E. O'Connor, Robert A. Rosenstone, and Hayden White appeared in *The American Historical Review* 93/5 (December 1988). Among several recent books on the subject, the following are particularly recommended: *American History/American Film,* ed. John E. O'Conner and Martin A. Jackson (New York: Frederick Ungar, 1979); *Hollywood As Historian.* ed. Peter C. Rollins (University Press of Kentucky, 1983); Susan Porter Benson, Stephen Brier, and Roy Rosenzweig, *Presenting the Past* (Philadelphia: Temple University Press, 1986); John A. Walker, *Art & Artists on Screen* (Manchester and New York: Manchester University Press, 1993; Leger Grindon, *Shadows on the Past: Studies in the Historical Fiction Film* (Philadelphia: Temple University Press, 1994); *Revisioning History: Film and the Construction of a New Past,* ed. Robert A. Rosenstone (Princeton University Press, 1995); *Past Imperfect: History According to the Movies,* ed. Mark C. Carnes (New York: Henry Holt and Company, 1995); Robert Brent Toplin, *History by Hollywood: The Use and Abuse of the American Past* (Urbana and Chicago: University of Illinois Press, 1996); and *The Persistence of History* (cited above).

[17]Laurence Bergreen, *As Thousands Cheer: The Life of Irving Berlin* (New York: Viking, 1990):359.

[18]In his detailed history of the writing and performance of Berlin's "Alexander's Ragtime Band," Charles Hamm contends that, contrary to myth, "It was a hit with audiences from the moment of its first performances" by Emma Carus at the American Music Hall in Chicago, 17 April 1911. It was not his first song to attract international attention, however, nor was it his bestselling song ("White Christmas" enjoys that distinction). See Hamm, "Alexander and His Band," *American Music* 14/1 (Spring 1996):65–101. For background on the Fox film, see W. Franklyn Moshier, *The Alice Faye Movie Book* (Harrisburg, PA: Stackpole Books, 1974):101–103.

[19]Despite the fact that several later films were virtual cavalcades of Berlin's music—including *You're in the Army Now* (1941) and *There's No Business Like Show Business* (1954)—no "official" biopic on Berlin's life was ever made. Producer Arthur Freed attempted the task in the early 1960s in the never-completed *Say It with Music* (the title derived from a song Berlin had written in 1921). Although Berlin's biographer Bergreen notes in *As Thousands Cheer,* "The durable legend of Berlin's career—the rise from busker to Tin Pan Alley and Broadway, the death of his first wife, the famous courtship of Elin Mackay—offered splendid material for another exercise in cinematic hagiography" (Bergreen:549). Berlin, as usual, demurred. It was decided to drop the biographical angle and develop an original script that would showcase Berlin tunes. Within a year's time, however, the project was dropped. The portrait that emerges of *Alexander,* by the way, is now so vaguely conceived that it also could fit several other figures in American music, notably Paul Whiteman, whose career in popularizing ragtime and jazz took him from San Francisco to the concert halls of New York and Europe.

[20]Cohan had attempted a Broadway comeback in 1940 with an original drama, *The Return of the Vagabond,* but the show failed after just seven performances. Cohan's film career is far more extensive than is generally acknowledged. While his biographers duly note that he made his talkie debut in *The Phantom President* (1932) for Paramount, they tell us little about his extensive career in silent films. In 1916 he signed with Artcraft Pictures, a producing entity for Paramount, and during the next two years appeared in movie versions of *Broadway Jones, Seven Keys to Baldpate,* and *Hit-the-Trail Holliday.* Subsequently, throughout the 1920s, he also wrote and/or produced other adaptations of *Forty-Five Minutes to Broadway, A Prince There Was, Little Johnny Jones,* and other plays. Near the end of his life he bitterly summed up his experiences in Hollywood: "If you want the truth . . . I can only say that my Hollywood experience was the most miserable I have ever had in my life. . . . On the level . . .

Hollywood to me represents the most amazing exhibition of incompetence and ego that you can find anywhere in the civilized world." The irony is that, in the assessment of historian Audrey Kupferberg, "*Yankee Doodle Dandy* has done more to keep the memory of George M. Cohan alive than any of his plays or films, any history book or statue." The only detailed information to be found on this subject is in Audrey Kupferberg, "The Film Career of George M. Cohan," *American Classic Screen* 4/1 (Fall 1979):43–52. The quotations are from pages 51–52.

[21]Letter to George M. Cohan, dated 21 April 1941. Although the copy in the Warner Bros. Museum in Burbank, California is unsigned, it was probably written by Finlay McDermitt, Chief of the Warner Story Department.

[22]The speech written for Cagney/Cohan regarding America's entry into World War I was really tailored to refer to the recent Pearl Harbor attack: "Seems it always happens—whenever we get too high hat and too sophisticated for flag waving, some thug nation decides we're a pushover, all ready to be black-jacked. And it isn't long before we're looking up mighty anxiously to make sure the flag is still waving over us."

[23]Quoted in Hugh Fordin, *The World of Entertainment: Hollywood's Greatest Musicals* (New York: Doubleday and Company, Inc., 1975):175.

[24]Gerald Bordman, *Jerome Kern: His Life and Music* (New York: Oxford University Press, 1980):404.

[25]Quoted in Custen, *Bio/Pics:*119.

[26]Schwartz, *Cole Porter:*223.

[27]Custen, "*Night and Day*: Cole Porter, Warner Bros., and the Re-Creation of a Life," *Cineaste* 19/2–3 (1992):44.

[28]See Schwartz, *Cole Porter:*102; and Bergreen, *As Thousands Cheer:*417.

[29]Under the heading, "Particular Applications," Section II ("Sex"), Subsection 4 of the Motion Picture Production Code, March 1930, appears this prohibition: "Sex perversion or any inference of it is forbidden." (This was amended in 1961 to permit "sex aberration" when treated with "care, discretion, and restraint.") Correspondence from Code executives warned producers to eliminate "pansy action," which was the code word for gay or lesbian behavior (although this did not preclude the ridiculing of same). For a complete text of the 1930 Code, see Jack Vizzard, *See No Evil* (New York: Simon and Schuster, 1970): 366–380.

[30]Levien scripted *Delicious* for Fox in 1931, which featured many Gershwin tunes. She was also present with Gershwin in the hours before his final collapse.

[31]Levant and Whiteman were longtime friends and associates of Gershwin's. Among the many anecdotes Levant added to the film's script are George's lines to Levant regarding why he, and not Levant would occupy the upper berth

of a passenger train: "Upper berth, lower berth—that's the difference between talent and genius." Whiteman's band, with Gershwin as soloist, introduced the *Rhapsody in Blue* at Aeolian Hall in New York, 12 February 1924. Whiteman himself was the subject of an extravagant biopic, *King of Jazz* (1930), a wildly fictionalized account of his jazz career, which featured an elaborate staging of the *Rhapsody in Blue*.

[32]Kern died of a stroke before the picture was completed. As a result the original opening, which depicted a birthday party in Kern's Beverly Hills home, was changed, and a new ending was written. Quoted in Fordin, *The World of Entertainment:*181.

[33]It is therefore odd that in later years Rodgers would voice his dissatisfaction with the film: "The most terrible lies have been all those Hollywood musicals which purport to be the life story of people like Gershwin, or Porter, or Kern. They give no insight whatsoever into the working patterns of the men they're supposedly about. They did it to Larry and me. The only good thing about that picture was that they had Janet Leigh play my wife. And I found that highly acceptable." Interview quoted in Max Wilk, *They're Playing Our Song* (New York: Atheneum, 1973):66. Rodgers fails to mention the film in his autobiography *Musical Stages* (New York: Random House, 1975).

[34]Recent waves of immigration from Eastern Europe had brought a majority of the Jewish emigrants to New York City. It has been estimated that at this time only thirty-six percent of the city's population was native born, while Blacks accounted for sixty thousand and Jews approximately one million. See Hamm, *Music in the New World* (New York: W.W. Norton and Company, 1983):340–41.

[35]Neal Gabler, *An Empire of Their Own: How the Jews Invented Hollywood* (New York: Crown Publishers Inc., 1988):5–6.

[36]Since around 1865 American composers had sought academic respectability and public recognition by studying and imitating the classical European traditions, particularly in Germany. In American classrooms, pioneering musical educators like John Knowles Paine of Harvard and Horatio Parker of Yale had emphasized conservative musical studies. Well into the twentieth century, Parker continued to use as his text Waldo Pratt's *History of Music* (1907), which emphasized the history of Austro-German music and paid relatively little attention to the moderns.

As the result of many factors, however, including the popularity of the minstrel shows before mid-century, the achievement of Stephen Foster and Louis Moreau Gottschalk in the Civil War Era, the preachments of Antonin Dvořák during his three-year sojourn in America in 1892–1895, the emergence of Black-inspired ragtime near the turn of the century, the pioneering work of proto-ethnomusicologists like Arthur Farwell, and the increased dissemination of music by means of the growing sheet music industry, player piano rolls, the nickelodeon, and the phonograph, American music was rapidly finding a more indigenous voice—or constellation of voices, so to speak. See Alan Howard Levy, "The Search for Identity in American Music, 1890–1920," *American Music* 2/2 (Summer 1984):70–81.

Similarly, while several of the pioneering motion picture studios, like Famous Players, produced so-called photoplays that drew upon the classical models and personnel of the legitimate theatrical establishment, other film studios, like Biograph, Keystone, and Ince, were drawing heavily upon "lower" forms of entertainment, like vaudeville skits, slapstick chase comedies, and open-air western melodramas. See the present author's *The American Theatrical Film* (Bowling Green, Ohio: The Popular Press, 1985).

[37]In a remarkably prescient written statement published during his New York sojourn, Dvořák defined what he called "the music of the people" as deriving from "all the races that are commingled in this great country"—that is, "the Negro melodies, the songs of the creoles, the red man's chant, the plaintive ditties of the German or Norwegian . . . the melodies of whistling boys, street singers and blind organ grinders." To our modern ears, he seems to have anticipated the rise of the ragtime song and the work of the Tin Pan Alley songwriters. See Antonin Dvořák [assisted by Edwin E. Emerson, Jr.], "Music in America," *Harper's New Monthly Magazine* 90/537 (February 1895):433. For the full text of this and his other newspaper articles, see my *Dvořák in America* (Portland, Oregon: Amadeus Press, 1993):355–384. For a discussion of Dvořák's pronouncements, see my "Conference Report: The New Orleans Dvořák Sesquicentennial," *The Sonneck Society Bulletin* 17/3 (Fall 1991):100–102.

[38]The undisputed king of the Hollywood biopics was Darryl F. Zanuck who, during his years as production chief at Warner Bros. and Twentieth Century-Fox, oversaw dozens of screen biographies of statesmen, inventors, entertainers, and composers. As far as the latter category is concerned, Zanuck left the classical composers to Columbia and MGM while he doted on the popular songwriters, like Stephen Foster (*Swanee River,* 1939), Irving Berlin (*Alexander's Ragtime Band,* 1938), Paul Dresser (*My Gal Sal,* 1942), Ernest R. Ball (*Irish Eyes Are Smiling,* 1944), Joseph E. Howard (*I Wonder who's Kissing Her Now,* 1947), Fred Fisher (*Oh, You Beautiful Doll,* 1949), John Philip Sousa (*Stars and Stripes Forever,* 1952), and the team of B. G. DeSylva, Lew Brown, and Ray Henderson (*The Best Things in Life Are Free,* 1956). Many of these were produced in conjunction with former vaudevillian George Jessel. A particularly pertinent discussion of Zanuck and his work can be found in Custen, *Twentieth Century's Fox: Darryl F. Zanuck and the Culture of Hollywood* (New York: Basic Books, 1997).

[39]Edward Pessen, "The Great Songwriters of Tin Pan Alley's Golden Age: A Social, Occupational, and Aesthetic Inquiry," *American Music* 3/2 (Summer 1985):193–195.

[40]*Words and Music* begins with Richard Rodgers (Tom Drake) addressing the camera with the following apology: "This is the Metro-Goldwyn-Mayer sound stage No. 1. I am Richard Rodgers. If in telling you about Larry, I talk quite a bit about myself, it's because there hasn't been a day in my life that didn't have something to do with Larry Hart. I'm almost sorry to say there were none of the standard trials and tribulations you would ordinarily expect. In fact, we were just two lucky fellows who had success very young. From the dramatic standpoint, we didn't even have the advantage of being very poor. We weren't very rich, either."

Leo Braudy defines the phenomenon this way: "Such people are vehicles of cultural memory and cohesion. The ability to reinterpret them fills them with constantly renewed meaning, even though that meaning might be very different from what they meant a hundred . . . years before. . . . they allow us to identify what's present with what's past." See Braudy, *The Frenzy of Renown: Fame and Its History* (New York: Oxford University Press, 1986):15.

[41]Two other biopics have been made about Stephen Foster: *Harmony Lane* (Mascot, 1934), starring Douglass Montgomery as Foster; and *I Dream of Jeanie* (Republic, 1951), featuring Ray Middleton. Both are unavailable for screening at this writing.

[42]In an interview with this writer, Deane Root of the Stephen Foster Memorial recounted a visit by Twentieth Century-Fox researchers to the Memorial in the late 1930s. "All people know about Stephen Foster is what they've seen in the movie *Swanee River*," noted Root. "the people at Fox came here to research the picture, then threw everything out and rewrote his life!" See my "In Search of Stephen Foster," *The World and I* (July 1991):253–259.

Ironically, Fox's scenarists ended up following the usual "line" handed down by Foster's brother, Morrison, in his 1896 biography. That remarkable document established what today—and for the movies—remains the core myths about Foster: that he was an untutored genius, that he longed for the past and the Old South (and thus was a glorifier of slavery), and that he was inept at the practicalities of life. Regarding Stephen's relationship with his wife, Jane, whose family's sympathies with antislavery causes ran counter to those of the Foster family's politics, there was little account. According to Root, Morrison "altered and perhaps destroyed documents that might have given us countering versions." See Root, *Family, Myth, and the Historical Sources: Why We Don't Know the Truth about Stephen Foster,* a paper delivered at the American Music at Illinois Conference in Urbana, Illinois; 29 September, 1990.

[43]Oddly, although "Jeanie with the Light Brown Hair" is heard on the background score, it is never sung or performed in a full-scale rendition. There has been some dispute as to whether or not "Jeanie," written in 1854, was a tribute to Foster's wife, Jane Denny McDowell (nicknamed "Jennie"). For a discussion of the issue, see William W. Austin, *Susanna, Jeanie, and the Old Folks at Home: The Songs of Stephen C. Foster from His Time to Ours* (New York: Macmillan Publishing Co., Inc., 1975):89–99. The selection of a particular tune as a leitmotif throughout a film is, of course, standard practice in the biopic. Just a few more examples include "My Funny Valentine" in *Words and Music* and the eponymous tunes in *Till the Clouds Roll By* and *Night and Day*.

[44]There are several versions of this anecdote. The most famous is that George visited Ravel in Paris in 1928, at which time Ravel declared, "Why should you be a second-rate Ravel when you can be a first-rate Gershwin?" Charles Schwartz concludes that because Gershwin himself spread this and other variants of the story, none of them may be regarded as definitive. See Schwartz, *George Gershwin: His Life and Music:*125–126. Biographer Joan Peyser notes that it is probable that Gershwin first met Ravel in New York City in 1928 at a party given by Eva Gauthier for the French composer. Gershwin responded by taking Ravel with him for a visit to the Harlem nightclubs. Later that year, while Gershwin was in Paris, Ravel told an audience in Houston that he hoped the American school of music would "embody a great deal of the rich and diverting rhythm of your jazz and a great deal of sentiment and spirit characteristic of your popular melodies" (Peyser, *The Memory of All That: The Life of George Gershwin* [New York: Simon and Schuster, 1993]:159).

[45]There is no question that most of these composers harbored what might be best described as "classical" ambitions. For example, Sousa yearned to write an American opera, but it never materialized. He did write, however, hundreds of "art" songs and several influential comic operas, like *The Queen of Hearts* (1885) and *El Capitan* (1895), which, as Paul Bierley writes, "rivaled the works of more prominent composers in the field." As the movie implies, Sousa was hurt that these works were not as popular as his marches (see Bierley, *The Works of John Philip Sousa:*5).

Berlin frequently inserted classical references into his rags, including quotations from Bizet's Carmen in "That Opera Rag," from Gaetano Donizetti's *Lucia di Lammermoor* in "Opera Burlesque"; and from Mendelssohn's "Spring Song" in "That Mesmerizing Mendelssohn Tune." Like Joplin before him, he often spoke of writing "an opera completely in ragtime," which would be set in the South. "A grand opera in syncopation may sound like a joke now," he said, "—but someday it's going to be a fact—even if I have to write one" (quoted in Bergreen, *As Thousands Cheer:*78).

Although Kern rarely dabbled in ragtime or jazz stylings, he struggled to revolutionize the revue-oriented musical theater with a more integrated form of show, as in the epoch-marking series of "Princess Theatre" productions and, of course, *Show Boat.* He idolized Gershwin who, in his words, was "the first composer who made me conscious that popular music was of inferior quality, and that musical-comedy music was made of better material" (quoted in Wilk, *They're Playing Our Song:*12).

Gershwin most successfully fused the classical and popular worlds in works like the *Concerto in F* and *Porgy and Bess.* "Throughout his career," writes Charles Hamm, "even during the periods of his greatest success as a writer of popular songs, he insisted that there need not be an irreconcilable gap between popular and serious music, and attempted to write music that would reach listeners of both persuasions." See Hamm, *Yesterdays* (New York: W.W. Norton & Company, 1979):349.

[46]There really was a Professor Kleber, a German immigrant who had come to Pittsburgh in 1832. He was a man of many parts in the community, a composer, church organist, teacher, and music store manager. Emerson says he was very eclectic in his musical tastes and "epitomized the genteel tradition and exploited it to the fullest with entrepreneurial energy." See Emerson, *Doo-Dah! Stephen Foster and the Rise of American Popular Culture:*100–101.

[47]"Otto Franck" is probably based on Gershwin's piano teacher, Charles Hambitzer, who did indeed teach the music of Beethoven, Bach, Chopin, and Ravel. While generally sympathetic to Gershwin's interests in popular music, he insisted on traditional training first. Gershwin concluded his lessons with Hambitzer at age sixteen. Hambitzer died in 1918, bitter over what he regarded as George's "defection" from the classical world. Gershwin's later teachers included Wallingford Riegger, Henry Cowell, and Rubin Goldmark (a former associate of Dvořák's at the National Conservatory). By all accounts, Gershwin's evenly divided interests in popular and classical music was genuine. For more information about Hambitzer, see Schwarz, *Gershwin: His Life and Music:*16–18.

[48]Hessler might be modeled after the two music arrangers who played a prominent part in Kern's life, Frank Saddler, who orchestrated the Princess shows, and Robert Russell Bennett, the arranger who worked with him in Hollywood. In either case, the professional relationship likely had nothing whatever to do with classical music. Indeed, Bennett recalls that Kern once derided the music of Beethoven and Brahms. See Wilk, *They're Playing Our Song:*20.

[49]Even in the MGM classical composer biopic about Robert and Clara Schumann, *Song of Love* (1947), the compositions of Clara are neither mentioned nor performed. She is portrayed solely as a performer, not as a composer.

Acknowledgement of her gifts had to wait for the 1985 biopic, *Spring Symphony,* starring Nastassja Kinski as Clara.

[50]*St. Louis Blues* ignores issues of race to concentrate instead on the complications Handy (Nat King Cole) faces in romance and in the oppositions to his career of his Bible-loving, show business-hating father. Handy's achievements as one of the first Black music publishers on the Alley are mostly omitted.

Among the many composers who avidly cultivated the acquaintance of Black composers and performers and acknowledged their influences were Berlin and Gershwin. The lyrics of a number of Berlin's early songs have Black musicians as protagonists, like the personna "Mose" that appears in "He's a Rag Picker" and "That Humming Rag." As Hamm notes, "[Berlin] did develop an honest and deep appreciation for black musicians and their music." Even the sheet music cover of "Alexander's Ragtime Band" reveals a racially integrated ensemble. See Hamm, "Alexander and His Band":73–74. Gershwin's absorption in the Black experience was intense, and he maintained contacts with Black artists like James P. Johnson and Luckey Roberts. His research into the African American culture for his opera, *Porgy and Bess,* would alone demand an entire volume. See Schwartz, *Gershwin:*243–271. "There was something in the music of black Americans that struck a responsive chord somewhere deep in Gershwin, something about their music that he grasped in an instinctive way. In turn, this same indefinable quality found its way into many of his songs, to which black Americans responded in a similarly instinctive way." See Hamm, *Yesterdays:*352.

[51]Cripps, *Slow Fade to Black:*268. Although the appearance of Bill "Bojangles" Robinson as Shirley Temple's dancing partner might seem an important exception, it should be noted that he was rarely permitted to touch his diminutive partner. See Custen, *Twentieth Century's Fox:*210–211.

[52]The Hall Johnson Choir performs "Old Black Joe" in *Swanee River,* and the Stone Mountain Choir sings "Battle Hymn of the Republic" in *Stars and Stripes Forever.*

[53]James Agee, "Till the Clouds Roll By," *The Nation* 163 (28 December 1946):766. George Sidney directed this concluding sequence, which is a veritable movie within a movie. "All the gaudy and indulgent vulgarity [MGM] had suppressed throughout the picture is slopped all over the screen, as if MGM simply could not hold it in any longer." Moreover, "the spectacle of this scrawny kid [Sinatra] in his bulky white suit singing 'You and me, we sweat and strain' brought audible titters from audiences and a few well-deserved swipes from the press." See Miles Kreuger, *Show Boat: The Story of a Classic American Musical* (New York: Oxford University Press, 1977):172.

[54]When the number first appeared in the *George White Scandals* of 1922, White actors in blackface appeared in the leading roles.

[55]Gerald Mast, *Can't Help Singin': The American Musical on Stage and Screen* (New York: The Overlook Press, 1987):231.

[56]The celebrated Black composer, William Grant Still, withdrew as the film's music supervisor because the film "degraded colored people." But in Hollywood everything is relative, so to speak, and the fact that Zanuck and Fox would produce an all-Black revue at this time merits some admiration. Zanuck himself at this time hosted a Hollywood luncheon in which the NAACP was given a forum to plead for a more enlightened treatment of Blacks in motion pictures. He publicly urged that "the program of casting colored persons in more normal roles be put into effect at an early date." Still and Loeb are quoted in Daniel J. Leab, *From Sambo to Superspade: The Black Experience in Motion Pictures* (Boston: Houghton Mifflin, 1975):124–130.

[57]"Oh! Susanna" was actually introduced at a gala concert at the Eagle Ice Cream Saloon in Pittsburgh, 11 September 1847. Ken Emerson, in *Doo-Dah!*, notes its mixture of sources—such as the use of Black vernacular in the words and of musical allusions to the European troubadour (the banjo on the singer's knee) and English balladry. The name "Susannah" probably refers to Foster's late sister, Charlotte, whose middle name was Susannah. The song marks "the birth of pop music as we still recognize it today. No popular song is more deeply rooted in American consciousness than 'Oh! Susanna'" (Emerson, *Doo-Dah!*:127–130).

[58]Contrary to the movie's suggestion, it was Kern, not Hammerstein, who first came up with the idea of writing a musical based on Edna Ferber's novel *Show Boat*. Through the agencies of Alexander Woollcott, Kern got an introduction to Ferber and received permission to proceed. It was only thereafter that Kern brought the thirty-one-year-old Hammerstein in to the project. See Kreuger, *Show Boat:*18.

[59]See Note 2 for the circumstances of the song's composition.

[60]See Note 3.

[61]The most notorious example of this sort of lyric switching is Irving Berlin's "Easter Parade." It began life as an unsuccessful song called "Smile and Show Your Dimple." In 1933 Berlin exhumed the song for a musical, *As Thousands Cheer,* and substituted the lyrics best known today. See Bergreen, *As Thousands Cheer:*317.

[62]Porter's own accounts of the writing of "Night and Day" vary. In one interview he claimed that he had been inspired by hearing the monotonous wail of Moroccan music. But Charles Schwarz contends that it was written for Fred Astaire in 1932 for *The Gay Divorce*. See Schwarz, *Cole Porter:*142–143.

[63]Although Gershwin initially downplayed the programatic aspects of the work—describing it as "programmatic [*sic*] only in a general impressionistic way"—he prepared more detailed notes with the assistance of Deems Taylor for the work's premiere. The stimulus for *An American in Paris* did indeed derive from two trips to Paris in April 1923 and March 1928. The taxi-horn inspiration is authentic, and Gershwin brought four French taxi horns back to America with him. Walter Damrosch, who had come to the New York Philharmonic during the 1928–1929 season, premiered the work at Carnegie Hall on 13 December 1928. See Schwarz, *George Gershwin:*153–170.

APPENDIX

A Select List of Classical and Popular Composer Biopics, 1930–1950

King of Jazz (Universal, 1930)—with Paul Whiteman as himself. Directed by John Murray Anderson.

Harmony Lane (Mascot, 1934)—with Douglass Montgomery as Stephen Foster. Directed by Joseph Santley.

Waltzes from Vienna (Gaumont-British, 1934)—with Esmond Knight as Johann Strauss II (released in the U.S. as *Strauss' Great Waltz*). Directed by Alfred Hitchcock.

Un Grande Amour de Beethoven (Generales Productions, 1938)—with Harry Bauer as Ludwig van Beethoven. Directed by Abel Gance.

The Great Waltz (MGM, 1938)—with Fernand Gravet as Johann Strauss II. Directed by Julien Duvivier.

Alexander's Ragtime Band (Twentieth Century-Fox, 1938)—with Tyrone Power as a highly fictionalized Irving Berlin. Directed by Henry King.

The Great Victor Herbert (Paramount, 1939)—with Walter Connolly as Victor Herbert. Directed by Andrew Stone.

The Starmaker (Paramount, 1939)—with Bing Crosby as Gus Edwards. Directed by Roy del Ruth.

Swanee River (Twentieth Century-Fox, 1939)—with Don Ameche as Foster. (Fox's first musical biopic filmed in Technicolor.) Directed by Sidney Lanfield.

My Gal Sal (Twentieth Century-Fox, 1942)—with Victor Mature as Paul Dresser. Directed by Irving Cummings.

Yankee Doodle Dandy (Warner Bros., 1942)—with James Cagney as George M. Cohan. Directed by Michael Curtiz.

Symphonie Fantastique (L'Atelier Francais, 1942)—with Jean-Louis Barrault as Hector Berlioz. Directed by Christian-Jaque.

The Great Mr. Handel (J. Arthur Rank, 1942)—with Wilfrid Lawson as Georg
Friedrich Handel. Directed by Norman Walker.

Irish Eyes Are Smiling (Twentieth Century-Fox, 1944)—with Dick Haymes as
Ernest R. Ball. Directed by Gregory Ratoff.

Shine On, Harvest Moon (Warner Bros., 1944)—with Ann Sheridan and Dennis
Morgan as vaudeville performer/composers Nora Bayes and Jack Nor-
worth. Directed by David Butler.

A Song to Remember (Columbia, 1945)—with Cornel Wilde as Chopin and Merle
Oberon as George Sand. Directed by Charles Vidor.

Rhapsody in Blue (Warner Bros., 1945)—with Robert Alda as George Gershwin
(piano performances by Oscar Levant). Directed by Irving Rapper.

Night and Day (Warner Bros., 1946)—with Cary Grant as Cole Porter. Directed
by Michael Curtiz.

Till the Clouds Roll By (MGM, 1946)—with Robert Walker as Jerome Kern. Directed by Richard Whorf.

The Magic Bow (GFD/Gainsborough, 1946)—with Stewart Granger as Nicolo
Paganini (violin solos by Yehudi Menuhin). Directed by Bernard Knowles.

I Wonder Who's Kissing Her Now? (Twentieth Century-Fox, 1947)—with Mark
Stevens as Joseph E. Howard. Directed by Lloyd Bacon.

Song of Love (MGM, 1947)—with Katharine Hepburn and Paul Henreid as Clara
and Robert Schumann (piano solos by Artur Rubinstein). Directed by
Clarence Brown.

My Wild Irish Rose (Warner Bros., 1947)—with Dennis Morgan as Chauncey Ol-
cott. Directed by David Butler.

Song of Scheherazade (Universal, 1947)—with Jean-Pierre Aumont as Rimsky-
Korsakov. Directed by Walter Reisch.

Words and Music (MGM, 1948)—with Tom Drake and Mickey Rooney as
Rodgers and Hart. Directed by Norman Taurog.

Oh, You Beautiful Doll (Twentieth Century-Fox, 1949)—with "Cuddles" Sakall
as Fred Fisher. Directed by John Stahl.

Three Little Words (MGM, 1950)—with Fred Astaire and Red Skelton as Bert
Kalmar and Harry Ruby. Directed by Richard Thorpe.

Contributors

Jean A. Boyd earned a Ph.D. in musicology from the University of Texas, Austin, in 1985. She has taught at the Baylor University School of Music in Waco, Texas, since 1972, and currently holds a position as Associate Professor of music history and American music studies. Professor Boyd's book *The Jazz of the Southwest: An Oral History of Western Swing* was published in 1998.

Alfred W. Cochran is Professor of Music at Kansas State University, where he has taught since 1979. He earned a Ph.D. in musicology at The Catholic University of America, Washington, D.C., with a dissertation on the early film scores of Aaron Copland. Cochran has lectured on film music at the Museum of Modern Art (New York City), the Eisenhower Library, New York University, and Oxford University. His articles have appeared in the *Indiana Theory Review, The Cue Sheet,* the *Kansas Music Review,* and *The New Grove Dictionary of Music and Musicians.*

Raymond E. Dessy is Emeritus Professor of Chemistry at Virginia Polytechnic Institute and State University, Blacksburg. His publications include more than two hundred papers in the areas of organometallic chemistry, computer applications in science, microbiosensors, and historical musical instruments. Professor Dessy's articles on instruments have appeared in *The Woodwind Quarterly, American Recorder,* and *Early Music America,* and he has presented papers at the Boston Early Music Festival and the Berklee College of Music. He also trains dressage horses to the Grand Prix level.

Mark DeVoto, Professor of Music at Tufts University, is a composer and musicologist. The primary focus of his research is musical analysis, particularly of the early twentieth century. Professor DeVoto is the editor and co-author of the revised fourth and fifth editions of Walter Piston's *Harmony* (1978, 1987).

Kent Holliday is Professor of Music at Virginia Tech. A composer and performer, he earned his M.A. and Ph.D. degrees at the University of Minnesota and has held National Endowment for the Arts and IREX grants and fellowships. Among his prize-winning works for acoustic and electronic instruments are a series of sonatas for wind soloists and piano, and compositions for computer and keyboard instruments. Holliday has published a book on reproducing pianos and articles on that and several other musical subjects. His "Four Evocations" for piano solo won the Virginia Music Teachers Composition Competition in 1998.

Timothy M. Kalil is an Instructor of Music at Kent State University's Ashtabula campus, where he also founded and organizes a concert series. He earned a Ph.D. in musicology and ethnomusicology from Kent State in 1993, with a dissertation on Black gospel piano music. Among his publications is a contribution to the *International Dictionary of Black Composers*. An accomplished pianist, Dr. Kalil holds an M.M. degree in piano from the Cleveland Institute of Music and on M.A. in ethnomusicology from Kent State in 1989. He is also a former Ashtabula County tennis champion.

Ellen Knight, a freelance writer and historian, specializes in the art world of the Boston area at the turn of the twentieth century. She is the author of *Charles Martin Loeffler* (1983), the editor of a collection of Loeffler's songs, and the author of articles and other studies. Dr. Knight worked for many years in and around Boston as a concert producer.

Donald C. Meyer is Assistant Professor of Music at Lake Forest College on the north shore of Chicago. He received his Ph.D. in musicology from the University of California at Davis in 1994, with a dissertation entitled *The NBC Symphony Orchestra*. He also has written articles on medieval notation and rock music, and is a composer of electronic music.

Leta E. Miller, Professor of Music at the University of California, Santa Cruz, is the co-author (with Fredric Lieberman) of *Lou Harrison: Composing a World* (1998) and the author of a new critical edition of Harrison's music in the series *Music in the United States of America.* Her previous musicological work has included books, articles, and critical editions on the sixteenth-century chanson and madrigal, music and science in the baroque, and the flute music of C. P. E. Bach. She also is an active flutist, with thirteen solo recordings, including three recordings of music by Lou Harrison.

Karen Rege received her Master of Arts degree in historical musicology at the University of Michigan in 1990, and her Master of Science degree in Library and Information Science from Drexel University in 1995. Her scholarship has appeared in *The Sonneck Society Bulletin* and *American National Biography.* In addition to her work as director of the library at the Delaware College of Art and Design, Ms. Rege recently served as the World Wide Web editor for the Society for American Music.

Marc Rice recently completed his Ph.D. at the University of Kentucky, with a dissertation on the Bennie Moten Orchestra and its African American audience in Kansas City, Missouri. Professor Rice currently teaches music history at the University of Louisville.

Michael Saffle took his Ph.D. in Music and Humanities at Stanford University. A professor in Virginia Tech's Center for Interdisciplinary Studies, he has written two books about Franz Liszt and edited several series of volumes for Garland Publishing and Pendragon Press of Stuyvesant, New York. A contributor to the new *Die Musik in Geschichte und Gegenwart,* as well as its editor for American biographical entries, he has also published articles in the *International Dictionary of Black Composers.* Recently the Fulbright Foundation awarded Professor Saffle the Bicentennial Chair of American Studies at the Renvall Institute of Historical Research, University of Helsinki, Finland, for the 2000–2001 academic year.

John C. Tibbetts is an author, educator, and broadcaster as well as a pianist and visual artist. He holds a Ph.D. degree from the University of Kansas in multidisciplinary studies, has hosted his own television show in Kansas City, Missouri, worked as a news reporter and commentator for CBS Television, and has written and illustrated four books, several short stories, and more than two hundred articles. Professor Tibbetts's *Dvořák in America* was published in 1993, and his *Encyclopedia of Novels into Film* in 1998. He teaches at the University of Kansas.

Index

Photographs and music examples are indicated by *italic* page numbers.